METAPHYSICS

SUNY Series in Philosophy
George R. Lucas Jr., Editor

METAPHYSICS

Josiah Royce

His Philosophy 9 Course of 1915–1916
as stenographically recorded by
Ralph W. Brown
and complemented by notes from
Bryon F. Underwood

William Ernest Hocking, Initial Editor

Co-edited by Richard Hocking and Frank Oppenheim

State University of New York Press

Published by
State University of New York Press, Albany

Printed in the United States of America

Frontispiece with permission of Richard Hocking.

For information, address State University of New York Press, State University Plaza, Albany, N.Y., 12246

Production by Diane Ganeles
Marketing by Fran Keneston

Library of Congress Cataloging-in-Publication Data

Royce, Josiah, 1855–1916.
Metaphysics / Josiah Royce ; William Ernest Hocking, initial editor ; co-edited by Richard Hocking and Frank Oppenheim.
p. cm. — (SUNY series in philosophy)
"His Philosophy 9 course of 1915–1916 as stenographically recorded by Ralph W. Brown and complemented by notes from Bryon F. Underwood."
Includes bibliographical references and index.
ISBN 0-7914-3865-1 (alk. paper). — ISBN 0-7914-3866-X (pbk. : alk. paper)
1. Metaphysics. I. Hocking, William Ernest, 1873–1966. II. Hocking, Richard, 1906– . III. Oppenheim, Frank M., 1925– . IV. Title. V. Series.
B945.R63M48 1998
110—dc21

97-47449
CIP

"That elvish figure with the unconventional dress and slouching step, that face which blended the infant and the sage, that total personality, as amused, amusing, and intent on righteousness as Socrates himself—happy the University that had for a long time so vitalizing a presence!"

So spoke George Herbert Palmer of Josiah Royce in 1916.

Contents

Foreword

The nine chapters of this book bring us into the classroom of Josiah Royce during the period 1915–1916, the last year of his life and teaching. Some thirty years earlier, Royce had completed the journey from his native California to the Harvard Philosophy Department to become its third member, along with George Herbert Palmer and William James of "the Great Department." From 1894 to 1916, the course on metaphysics, Philosophy 9, had become essentially Professor Royce's course.

From 1915–1916, the First World War was in its second dreadful year. It intruded at times into Royce's classroom with tragic intensity. Belgium's neutrality had been violated. The torpedoed *Lusitania* had carried four Harvard graduates to their graves. For Royce, the trauma was personally heightened by reason of his grateful debt to Germany's literature and philosophy and to its great university tradition.

During this year, as it happened, Royce offered his course in metaphysics for the last time. He was carefully perfecting his position, as it had already been given shape in his major works, *The World and the Individual* and *The Problem of Christianity*. Thus, he here provided a definitive rethinking of these works and their most authentic interpretation. Furthermore, he was engaged in coming to terms with his major contemporaries, be they realists who fell short or pragmatists who fell short. Many were still active—Perry, Russell, and Santayana—but two, James and Peirce, had recently died. Although Royce revered James, he finds that James confused truth with probability and certainty. He treasures the clear precision of his student Santayana but finds the latter's distinction between essence and existence too sharply drawn. He has no doubts about Whitehead's brilliance as physicist and mathematician but cautions that cosmology is not the whole of metaphysics. His regard for Dewey is supplemented by the insistence that ontological judgments about unique individuals are central.

Among all of his contemporaries, Royce finds himself increasingly indebted to Charles Sanders Peirce as a logician and pragmatist. Peirce, in turn, comprehends and appreciates Royce's distinctive, dialectical, and logically rigorous type of idealism and even points to him as alone worthy of the name "pragmatist."[1] It is the mature Royce's deepening insight into Peirce's philosophy of signs and interpretation that leads him to his own social approach to metaphysics. Royce is instrumental in saving for Harvard Peirce's published and unpublished papers. He begins the assaying of the "nuggets of gold" in that mother lode, discerning the spirit and key ideas in Peirce's thought and disclosing the architectonic in his numerous drafts.

In this context, then, our hopes of finding new and renewed ideas coming to the fore during these lectures from the period 1915–1916 are warranted. At least seven of these call for special attention.

1. Royce's doctrine of the social nature of reality is based on the unending process of interpretive social action that brings contrasting parts of truth into growing coherence. His new social approach to metaphysics lets him emphasize more than formerly that reality, knowledge, and truth, if abstracted from a progressively realized community of interpretation, dwindle into incoherence.

2. Royce establishes a relational form of the ontological argument, a new view that, unlike Anselm's primarily theological version, is both cosmological and existentially focused on individual uniqueness. He finds, ironically, that even nominalists presuppose of necessity this relational form of the ontological argument.

3. Royce gives us a thoroughly inductive and experiential metaphysics. A widened meaning of experience comprises, for him, the lived achievements of all kinds of human communities, the paradoxes of commerce, the pressures of wars, the imaginative disclosures of poetry and the arts, the givens of his own dramatic intellectual biography, the mixture of evil with good—literally everything that invites interpretation.

4. One student recalls, after many years, that "something arresting had occurred in the Metaphysics [course]." Whereas *The World and the Individual* "proposed an idealistic Absolute, a *totum simul*, *The Problem of Christianity* expanded on the time–process, if I remember the phrase. That was the arrest."[2] The time–process of interpretaton all but displaced an Absolute. Thus Royce silently brushes aside his critics' stereotype about an "absolute block universe."

5. Royce enlarges on the ancient theme of individuation by turning to judgments of individual identity, employing that aspect of inductive logic which yields conclusions about the unique individual (<u>this</u> person, <u>this</u> atom). The

world as a whole is a self-individuating process in which judgments of identity and individuality are achieving a steadily increasing coherence.

6. Royce reaffirms his earlier respect for mysticism in its philosophical, poetical, and musical expressions, before leading his students, by means of the critical rationalist interpretation of being, to his own concluding idealistic interpretation.

7. Last, in a surprising irony, Royce claims a fuller realism than that of his realist critics. By the logic of interpretation, he requires, as a start, the rejection of the realist's utter independence of being and thought. Then, by the same logic of interpretation, he establishes the reality of the wholly teleological other. Our "whole intention is to be as realistic as we can."[3] In this process we approach conformity with the being of the world of a higher and prior interpreter. Such a metaphysical realism, as Royce points out, is in essential harmony with the tradition of Judaism and Christianity.

History has fortunately saved this lively classroom record of Royce caught in the act of teaching. The aim of the editors, in the present text, has been guided by the question, "What would Royce have done in preparing his lectures for publication, had he lived?" Hence, the grouping of the year's lectures into the nine chapters of this book.

Richard Hocking
Emeritus Professor of Philosophy
Emory University

Frank Oppenheim, S.J.
Professor of Philosophy
Xavier University

Symbols and Abbreviations

—	underscoring, an emphasis transferred from Typescript B
( )	an expression in parenthesis found in Typescript B, the selected basic documentary text*
[ ]	an insertion made by Ralph W. Brown {RWB} or by Byron E. Underwood {BEU}
{ }	an insertion made by the present editors
#	This signal, in superscript, denotes a place where RWB interjected into his stenographic notes a personal response, reproduced later after the Critical Apparatus, pp. 329–330.
*	designates a footnote
1,2,3, . . . n,	in superscript, designates an endnote (e.g., endnote 1 on p. 7 starts at p. 303)
BEU	Bryon E. Underwood Jr., note taker during Ralph W. Brown's occasional absences

*The present editors simply reproduce these parenthetical expressions as such in the present edition. They cannot distinguish between the various possible sources of these parenthetical remarks, whether made by Josiah Royce through the tone of his voice or by RWB (or BEU), WEH, or one of the typists employed by R. C. Cabot or WEH. Furthermore, if the parenthetical remark came from the stenographer RWB, we cannot determine whether it originated during his stenographic note taking in the classroom or during his translation of these notes into Typescript A, their first typewritten form.

CA This signal, in superscript, e.g.,: . . . psychology[CA], designates a note in the Critical Apparatus, (starting on p. 321)

CPP *Collected Papers of Charles Sanders Peirce*, edited by C. Hartshorne, P. Weiss (vols. 1–6), and A. Burks (vols. 7–8), (Cambridge: Harvard University Press, 1931–1958), followed by volume and paragraph numbers

RWB Ralph Wolcott Brown, stenographer of Royce's last lectures on metaphysics (1915–1916)

U This signal, in superscript after the lecture date, indicates that the present report was made by Bryon E. Underwood, Jr.

WEH William Ernest Hocking, who around 1930 initially edited Royce's last lectures on metaphysics into Typescript B

Published Works of Royce Frequently Cited in This Volume

CG[2] *The Conception of God*, 2d edition (New York: Macmillan, 1897)

HGC *The Hope of the Great Community* (New York: Macmillan, 1916)

PC *The Problem of Christianity*, 2 vols. (New York: Macmillan, 1913)*

RAP *The Religious Aspect of Philosophy* (Boston: Houghton Mifflin, 1885)

SGE *Studies in Good and Evil* (New York: D. Appleton and Co., 1898)

SMP *The Spirit of Modern Philosophy* (Boston: Houghton Mifflin, 1892)

War *War and Insurance* (New York: Macmillan, 1914)

WI *The World and the Individual*, 2 vols. (New York: Macmillan, 1899, 1901)

**PC* references in footnotes and endnotes, however, are to the one-volume re-edition of *The Problem of Christianity* (University of Chicago Press, 1968), with a new introduction by John E. Smith, because it is more available.

High points in Josiah Royce's Intellectual Development

Frank Oppenheim

1855–1875: Born in 1855 in Grass Valley, California, Josiah finds that his mother and sisters become his first "teachers of philosophy." Voraciously he reads the Bible, science, history, mathematics, literature, and philosophy. As a college undergraduate, he is deeply stirred by the evolutionist Joseph LeConte and the poet Edward Rowland Sill.

1875–1883: "determined my philosophical thinking." Reading J. S. Mill made Royce a "decidedly skeptical critical empiricist" but his study of German Romantics and philosophers soon supplied a counterbalance. His Johns Hopkins' thesis, Berkeley research, and earliest Harvard teaching led him gradually toward the breakthrough that would thereafter steadily orient his philosophy.

January 11–12, 1883: Royce's "Religious Insight" concerning an All-knowing Judge, his **first maximal insight**; later published in *RAP* (1885).

1891: From Ernst Schroeder's *Algebra der Logik*, vol. 1, Royce gains a major insight that only an infinite self-reflective series fits the inner logic of the idea of Reality (*WI* 1: 553, n. 1).

1896: **Second maximal insight**, his "'American' definition of the Individual," defined pragmatically as an "object of exclusive interest," or of love; soon published in *CG*².

1898: Royce finds C. S. Peirce's Cambridge Conferences "epoch-marking." "They started me on such new tracks" (*Letters*, 422), as shown in his Gifford Lectures, published as *WI*. Hereafter, and often in dialogue with Peirce, Royce deepens his logical studies of idea, continuity, and system until his death.

1906–1908: Royce's renewed focus on ethics flowers in his most popular *The Philosophy of Loyalty.* This work expresses another major insight: "loyalty to universal loyalty," which is loyalty in its "'reflective' form as an essentially self-sustaining process, that . . . becomes truly universal and truly individual" (*Letters* 533).

1910: He writes his *Principles of Logic*, featuring "System Sigma" with its "modes of action."

1912: **Third maximal insight** into Peirce's theories of Signs, Interpretation and the three Categories. This insight governs Royce's *PC*, *War, HGC*, his later articles in Hastings' *Encyclopedia of Religion and Ethics,* and his 1915–1916 metaphysics course. It also leads him to his "social approach" to metaphysics, which undergirds his "logical approach."

1913–1916: The ideas of Community and Spirit are "working daily in my mind," along with that of Process, and increasingly taking on a new vitality and deeper significance (*Letters*, 645).

September 14, 1916: Royce dies.

Analytical Table of Chapters

Richard Hocking

gressive self-correction. Peirce, unlike other major pragmatists, sees that this inductive process yields only a variable probability of truth, never immutable truth itself. Since the world has given rise to its own interpreter, the metaphysical thesis of idealism is suggested through the contrast between "*the* world as a community" and either "*a* world as a self" or "the Absolute viewed as *an* ego."

Just as probability is not truth, so certainty is not truth, despite some pragmatists' acceptance of variable truth. Holding a correspondence theory of truth, realists save its immutability but miss the social role of intention in judgments of truth. To confirm the truth or error of a belief requires an interpreter able to compare a believer's intention and its intended object in a single moment—a comparison which is impossible if only finite mortals in the flux of time are involved. The endless social process of interpretation merely moves toward such a truth-limit. The immutability of truth is related to the irrevocability, and hence constancy, of past time and its contents. This is a *logocentric* predicament which reaffirms itself if one tries to deny it. Induction is endlessly self-correcting. "The character of winning an end everywhere belongs to the world." This developmental social view is an essentially Christian principle.

Essence is the "what" of a thing; existence is its "that." Curious questions arise concerning the "whatness of the that" and the "thatness of the what." In exploring four meanings of "is," Santayana widens the gap between essence and existence. For the realist, a changing existent embodies in space and time a changing selection of unchanging essences. In contrast to Santayana's realistic "sharp distinction" between essence and existence, idealism finds intimate relations between essence and existence within the progressive and temporal realization of purposes.

Does the existence of anything make any difference to its essence? Does the essence of anything make any difference to its existence? To both questions, the realist says "No" and the idealist says "Yes." For instance, every judgment of existing individual identity requires a unique essence, not only a present experience; hence, "one concludes an existence from an essence." Time is a relational essence of past to present to future, which has to exist if there is to be a world at all. The existing uniqueness of each individual (this person, this atom) inheres in the necessary existence of time's relational essence. Everyone unavoidably employs the relational form of the ontological argument when making judgments about individual persons, time, causal relations, essences, the existent world, and natural objects. Nominalists assert that the world's basic realities essentially are nothing but individuals. By this assertion, nominalists become the principal users of the relational form of the ontological argument.

Nominalists agree that the "distinction between essence and existence is a conceptual difference." If so, then the essence of an individual must be such that the essence of the world requires that individuality characterize Being. Whether one thinks of identity either in persons or in essences or in natural objects, identity always involves difference. Even in the obvious proposition, "A is A," the left A is different from the right A. Examples of personal identity: on his return to Ithaca, Odysseus presented to its inhabitants a problem of identification; so, too, does the signer of a traveler's check, whose identification depends, not on experience and evidence alone, but also on the truth of the statistical probability that "nobody but the original signer could sign so similarly." Example of identity of essences: Spinoza's identification of blessedness and virtue. Example of identity of natural objects: a rainbow in a fleeting shower. "How long do I see the same rainbow?" Identification of any of these types requires, beyond experience, the coherence of a plan of action. This requirement indicates the need for a "Fourth Interpretation of Being." Identification is a process of interpretation, the activity of progressive reconciliation of contrasts within the Heraclitean flux of time. The static, timeless eternity of Santayana's realm of essences fails to support identity and identification.

Philosophically, the mystic is concerned with the immediate as real. Only the immediate <u>that</u> of a thing gives us its <u>what</u>. Ironically, mystics, though "ineffective as thinkers", show great moral vigor. Tennyson's *In Memoriam* captured the mystical experience when he "came on that which is and caught the deep pulsations of the world." The fourteenth-century Meister Eckhart calls God both an unnamed nothingness and an unbecome beingness. Typically, the dialectic of the mystic reaches the immediate by negations. Eckhart, having none of the Hindu quietism of the *Bhagavadgita*, keeps the negative and the positive in balance. In the art of music, two giant composers, Wagner and Bach, express the mystical experience in very different ways.

By the reflective method, we see that to say "This is" is to say "It is true that this is." This reflexivity is prominent in Extreme Realism and the several New Realisms. Realists share the reflective method with the mystics. For instance, Santayana is drawn to Spinoza, and Russell's scientific bent does not exclude a mystical attitude toward the human mind's freedom in comprehending the infinite.

Extreme Realism asserts both that the world is totally independent of knowing, and that this is true. If true, then the world is rational; hence, not totally independent of rational knowing. Knowing independence becomes a degree of dependence when one claims truth. The Sânkhya philosophy rejects this difficulty by interpreting independence between knower and know as total and symmetrical, thus offering a balm of salvation from all entanglements. Herbart foreshadows New Realism in exploring more carefully the relation of independence. May not independence be a one-sided relation—A dependent on B; B independent of A? Consider various distinctions among relations: internal–external; symmetrical–asymmetrical; effective–ineffective; mutual and transitive. Hegel's master-slave relation illustrates mutuality without symmetry. Paradoxically, in a world of total mutual independence, things could not have qualities in common, that is, no internal relations. However, there are internal relations. Maybe there are no external relations.

Contrast the New Realists: Santayana and Russell. For Santayana, essences are reals that do not exist. He has no explanation of how an essence is transformed into an existent. The later Russell defines the real as the object of a possible true experience. Possibles constitute the real in terms of the true, though without a coherent whole view.

What is possibility? Example: Socrates's possible escape from prison. Every person is part capabilities (possibilities) and part living up to them (facts). Reflectively, the attempt to exclude possibility reinstates it. Other examples of possibility include Mill's consideration of matter as "a permanent possibility of sensation," Kant's critical account of the world of physics as the world of possible experience, and Vaihinger's "as if."

Perception cannot give us Being in a present moment. Conception cannot give us Being solely through essences. Being is the object of a quest through time, sought by the process of interpretation, requiring the whole of life. For the complete meaning of fact, the Fourth Conception of Being adds individuality to essence, which the Third Conception of Being fails to do. "The problem of Being is the problem of truth. . . . The progressive process of interpretation is the reality of the world." Thus we are being "as realistic as we can."

Perry tries to refute an overly personal idealism by calling an accidentally personal predicament essential. Mill's world of the permanent possibility of sensations is as impersonal as Santayana's world of essences. Idealism is at least as impersonal, since it requires the logic of the relational form of the ontological argument. Since the Fourth Conception of Being is a universal teleology, the philosophical problem of evil is unavoidabale. James and Perry discount it as such. In Santayana's materialism, this philosophical problem cannot even arise. For idealism, the central issue is how to atone for failures in the past which, as past, is essentially irrevocable.

PHIL. 9, METAPHYSICS, 1915–1916

Notes of Lectures Delivered by

JOSIAH ROYCE

First half-year: September 30, 1915, to January 24, 1916

Second half-year: February 15, 1916, to May 27, 1916

{Stenographer's Prefatory Remarks}

"The notes of the first half-year were meant only for my father and myself. They were not shown to the lecturer, and it was not expected that they would be seen by other people.

"The second half-year's records are of a different character, and were designed for presentation to Professor Royce as well as for my own benefit. The volume which I placed in his hands at the end of the course contains only this portion of the work. He expressed his pleasure with it, but did not revise it in any way."

Ralph W. Brown
710 Barristers Hall, Boston

{Catalogue Statement}

"9. Metaphysics.—The Fundamental Problems of Theoretical Philosophy. The Concepts of Truth and Reality.—Realism, Modern Pragmatism, and Idealism in their Relations. - Lectures and theses. Tu., Th., Sat. at 11.

Professor Royce

"Course 9 is open to students who have passed in Course 1 or 2, or in any full course in philosophy, or philosophy and psychology."* CA

* {Stenographer R. W. Brown copied this description of Royce's course on metaphysics from the *Harvard University Catalogue 1915–1916*, p. 469.}

Part I

The "Social Approach" to Metaphysics

Chapter 1

Introduction: The "Social Approach" to Metaphysics

Metaphysical Problems and Contrasts[1]

Substances and insubstantial facts*

First Meeting Sept. 30, 1915

Entities and their characters

The what and the that

Mental and non-mental

Actual and possible

Present, past, future

Real and apparent

This is a general course on metaphysics.** I have given something equivalent since the year 1894. The course has changed its shape a good deal since that time. Various changes have been made as to textbooks and some in the views maintained, more perhaps in the mode of presentation. This year I shall follow in the presentation the lines which I developed last year in this course.[2] The courses in this department used to be rather more in the history of philosophy. The department agreed that certain topics, psychology, logic, ethics,

* [On the Board]

**{Referring to his records for the first half-year, R. W. Brown warns, "These notes are greatly condensed."}

metaphysics—ought to be prominent in our work. At present, our historical courses no longer receive quite as much attention as I think they ought to receive. Mr. Bradley's *Appearance and Reality* at the time it appeared was almost alone as a deliberate careful treatment of certain problems of metaphysics. I don't know that in the early days when I used Bradley's book the reputation for difficulty of this course was fully warranted, for the possibility of writing theses without knowing why one said a thing was present. I think the recent changes in philosophical discussion make that possibility less feasible, and on the whole I suppose that since 1900* the course has been more difficult than it was before.

Arthur James Balfour in his *Defence of Philosophic Doubt* (1879), tried to make a sharp distinction between a man's ethics and his morals: you can differ with a man ethically without necessarily taking potshots from behind a hedge. In metaphysics, questions arise which involve problems about this or that object said to be real. Someone may hold opinions of the materialistic sort. One ought to criticize those opinions altogether with respect to whether or not they follow from certain principles, or with respect to what they mean. We may condemn a man's metaphysics both as to what he holds in general and as to what follows from it in particular, without leaving the field of theoretical metaphysics.

From another side, the issues of metaphysics are practical. As in ethics, the questions will inevitably bear upon practical consequences somehow, and if a man deals with metaphysical questions, his opinions involve matters of deeply practical interest somewhat and will have results that will bear upon them. Thus our metaphysical differences are practical differences, but when we study metaphysics we don't intend them to be. If I take up the question, "Is there a God or not?" assuming a definition of God, I should make the inquiry without regard to the practical issue. It would not be our question as students of metaphysics, "What are you going to do about it?" The issue isn't intended to be practical. The question, "Is there a God?" is directly raised by a good many positively disposed theologians who are not talking about something expressly and explicitly practical. St. Thomas Aquinas[CA] raises this question very early in his compendium; he first considers what you mean by God, what, and then he definitely raises the question, "Is there a God?" and he treats the question with characteristic calmness as a philosopher. He didn't mean there should be any concern. Metaphysical topics are peculiarly free from that character.

The questions of logic also have an indirect relation to conduct. The pragmatists say we think in order to act. But the questions of logic are not ques-

*{Approximate publication date of Royce's *The World and the Individual*}

tions in which the interests are passionate interests. We shall see where the connection between theory and practice come in.

The atmosphere ought to be one of decided freedom, and authority ought to count for nothing in metaphysics. We shall approach the problems of metaphysics from two intimately related but distinct sides.

(1) Social approach to metaphysics. Royce's *The Problem of Christianity.* First half-year.

(2) The logical approach to metaphysics. Royce's *The World and the Individual.* Second half-year.

The philosophy of Bergson has been much affected by his interest in the biological sciences, and the philosophy of Bertrand Russell has been largely determined by the fact that he is a mathematician and logician; his interests in nature have been much affected by his studies in physical science. He said to me, "I think that the influence of the biological sciences upon philosophy has been altogether evil." Russell expresses the concepts of philosophy so far as possible in terms drawn from the physical sciences. Metaphysics can be approached also from the side of Aristotle; a scholastic philosopher has an interest in certain problems above others and a tendency to certain views. Any religious views would decidedly affect at least one's approach to metaphysics. Some come to the subject from the study of economics or from some interest in the so-called sociological studies.[3] *Oct. 2*

If the teaching in this course succeeds, and if the reports are written with sufficient care, one ought to anticipate as a result the growth in his own interest in some of the large issues in human life. There is, no doubt, an outlook naturally connected with a course in metaphysics which ought to be of value to a student sufficiently interested in the course to approach it. Metaphysics is a sort of astronomy of life. Here are ethical issues, the problem of the good and the bases of human destiny. There ought to result a greater clarity about certain large problems.

There is in metaphysics an interest which may have survived since childhood. Herbert Spencer, in his *Autobiography,* reports something which his father told him about one of his earlier sayings.[4] Children often say such things, he comments. There is a good deal of naive metaphysics in childhood. From that side, one interest in this course would be the generality of many of the topics; you would be led closer to a connection with your own childhood.[#] Wordsworth was an instance of a metaphysically disposed child. That influenced him later, and although he was never a technical metaphysician, he tried to express life experience. He was something of a mystic, and that was important for his whole work as a poet.

Spencer's story as told to him by his father: When he was sitting on the floor playing with his toys, he seemed to be very meditative, and his father asked him what he was thinking of. "I am thinking," said he, "how it would be if there hadn't been anybody or anything in the world but myself."

One day on a train on Cape Cod returning towards Boston, I heard by chance two little boys talking behind me, mere voices in my memory. The little one was appealing to the elder, "What is the sky?" The elder was somewhat materialistic, "There ain't no sky." He had been taught that the sky was appearance and not reality, an optical illusion; there is no solid object there as children often think. He had reached the stage where he knew the vanity of this illusion. But the younger was the deeper thinker of the two, and asked a further question which was technically metaphysical: "What is it that ain't?" This implied that where there is appearance there has to be a basis and that basis has to be real; there must be a some what that lies at the basis of this appearance. The apparent sky being a fact of experience, he asked about the what of this. That insistent question of the boy, "What is it that ain't?" mentions the problem of metaphysics in as good shape as you could give it at first trial.

Oct. 5 The word "idea" and the meaning that I give to that word will be the subject of both halves of this course, the "social approach" and the "logical approach" to metaphysics. I don't mean that the approach in the first half-year will be illogical, but the stress will be laid on certain considerations which will not be prominent in the second half-year's work, problems namely about our social knowledge and the things that we know in our social world, and certain aspects of the nature of knowledge. On the whole, the schools of metaphysical discussion have made quite an inadequate use of our social experiences and problems.

We have today a very strong interest in a number of social problems which are also metaphysical problems. The most passionate interests of the current war are defined by some people in terms of a contest between a certain kind of individualism and a certain kind of collectivism; and these people are thinking of metaphysical matters, realities that belong to the ultimately real. From a now familiar point of view, the present war involves a conflict between nations and civilizations, one of which lays special stress on the rights of individuals, while the other side is committed to the dignity, authority, importance, welfare, and consequently to the reality of the State. The war has been defined as a conflict between people who believe in individuals and people who believe in States as real beings. I don't believe it is altogether right to identify the over-individual with the State. In my book *The Problem of Christianity* you will see that this is a metaphysical issue and also an intensely practical issue. There are conditions under which it would be my solemn duty to oppose my State insofar as it is a political entity, so that the State hasn't any such authority over me as has been maintained by some. There is another overindividual entity that I regard as much more important than the State, the type characteristic of the Christian religion, the ideal Church, the community of mankind. Thus metaphysical discussions can be about intensely practical matters.

Aristotle defined the function of what we now call metaphysics: to consider Being in so far as it is Being.[5] It is to define the meaning of reality, what it is to be real. I just gave you some illustrations of what is involved in the question of the meaning of the word "real." "The sky is not real," "There ain't no sky," and the child raised the question, "What is it that ain't?" So one may well raise related questions: What do you mean by being real? In what sense isn't it real? Explain to me the appearance that I have taken to be real. What do you mean by calling that object real or unreal? What is the difference insofar as that difference is generally definable? How real is it? Is it quite real or only partially real? Such questions make the topic of metaphysics.

Having thus given a perfectly elementary approach to the subject, it is well to become a little better acquainted with such questions by giving a few illustrations.

The one that my story was intended to bring before you may well serve to define an important metaphysical problem, the distinction between what is sometimes called the phenomenon or that which appears, and the noumenal or fundamentally real object. This question is suggested by a familiar distinction: we frequently call a thing real and later illusory.

Further, I may know what I mean by a certain kind of object without knowing whether anything of that kind is real or not. The question, "What do you mean by that?" can be answered by a definition involving various mentions of what you mean by reality. At any rate, the definition involves what you are talking about. But suppose you assert that this is, that it is real. There is then a distinction between what you are talking about and the reality or unreality of what you are talking about. That is the difference between the what and the that. The difference is often called the difference between essence and existence. You will find this difference discussed in the ontological vocabulary in *The World and the Individual*.[6] The difference between the essence or nature of a thing and the existence or reality of that thing is a very important difference. A case in question is about God. It is one thing to know what you mean by God; it is another thing to decide whether God is or not. Is that which this idea defines also a reality? This is the difference between the what and the that.

This is a very fundamental metaphysical difference. You can gather how deep it is from the fact that there have been theologians and philosophers who have endeavored to prove the existence of God by declaring that his existence followed necessarily from his essence. He is such a being, if you understand the definition, that he must be real. This ontological proof has been questioned. The fact that the question has played a part in philosophical thought shows the importance of the difference in question. People say the State is an important reality and can determine my duties to a certain extent. These people are open to the question, "What is the State?" and their assertion that the State is real is a different matter. Or if a man says, "The only real things in the world are individual men," he would have to tell what are individual men.

The difference is not at all stupidly abstract. You can define beforehand the what of an enterprise, some success you hope for. You hope to "pass" in a certain college course. It is another thing to know the that I am to do so.

Another question of metaphysics—actual and possible. This distinction struck the mind of Aristotle. So far as his early training went, he was something of a naturalist; he was the son of a physician, and his enemies are fond of calling him an apothecary. He was a student of living things and loved the living sorts of beings with the fascination of a naturalist. One of the most characteristic things about a living being is that you can't tell about it very fully without making a distinction between what it is and what it is capable of, what it might be. There is a difference between the wakefulness of the man actually awake and the possibility of awakening which belongs to the normal sleeper. A builder by trade is a possible maker of houses; if this house is made, he is the actual builder of it. Aristotle says you can't get on in the world without recognizing the difference between the actual and the possible. Shut your eyes and you are a possible perceiver: can you see? Yes, if I open my eyes. This distinction becomes harder from another point of view. The possible extends further than the actual. You conceived of tentative events such that if they had occurred, events which now occur would not be actual. Some slight change of events would have prevented you from meeting this man with whom you are now associated. Thus you see your actual life surrounded by a vast range of possible lives that might have been yours. Haven't the possibilities some sort of quasi-reality? A possibility may come so near to your actual life that you think of it as a very important affair. It is an issue as to what reality possibilities possess. Aristotle found that they have a great deal of reality about them. A student of life can't very well get on without distinguishing between what an organism is at a given moment and what it might be under different circumstances.

Again, the world has certain kinds of real beings in it, material and nonmaterial, mental and nonmental. These are not altogether identical differences.

Aristotle further noted that when you speak of any object to which you ascribe reality or being, and which you may therefore call an entity, you make a distinction between the object and its characters, its connections, its relations. Aristotle loved to say, "Being is a word of many meanings," and one way in which its meanings may be diversified is according to the categories. In grammar, the divisions into subjects and predicates, relations, qualities, places, times, and such things are categories. Aristotle closely connected with the categories the difference between substances and attributes.

When we put problems of that kind together, they suggest the feasibility of a philosophical study devoted to clearing up these distinctions and their accompanying problems. Metaphysics is concerned with what you mean by the term reality, or what it is to be real.

The Scope and Purpose of a Social Approach to Metaphysics

The social approach is emphasized in my *Problem of Christianity,* especially in the second volume, and you will be likely to associate it with problems in the field of the Christian religion; but I have so much else in mind in that connection that I do not wish you to confine yourselves to that. The social approach will be guided and represented especially by these two problems: *Oct. 7*

1. *Ego* and *alter*; the self and the *socius*

2. Individual and group

Ego and *alter*

This reminds you of a certain persistent illusion which we all have: every man seems to himself to be rather at the center of the world. In the field of vision, the sky is a great globe such that I am about at the middle. This world of the ego presents problems from the side of a realistic metaphysics: Professor Perry has made prominent the problem of the "egocentric predicament." But however egocentric a man is, everyone is disposed to contrast himself and the other fellow.[7] Max Stirner, a schoolmaster who lived a quiet life, put out a book on ethics under a pseudonym entitled *Der Einzige und Sein Eigenthum* (1845), which means "the only one and what belongs to him," a doctrine of the most nearly complete and conscious selfishness that is possible: a man's business is to look out for himself as opposed to society, neighbors, friends, and enemies; it is his right to have his own way in his own world so far as he can; it is an art and a difficult one. The question of this dual structure of the world is important for our view of what it is to be real, and it appears that the whole metaphysical study of reality, as well as of ethics, could be approached in this fashion.

Individual and Group

Any portion of the world which possesses any kind of unity consists of individual men in a group somehow distinguished from the rest of the world.

Most social questions are describable in terms of the relation between any individual and his group. Is the individual so related to his group that there are no groups except collections, like pebbles on the beach? What sort of reality and what sort of unity belongs to a social group? In what sense is this class a collective unit, and in what sense is it simply a collection of the individuals that belong to the class? If one looks at the class list, the names give you some account of all that belong to the class. Does the being of the class consist in the several members of the class, or is there something else that makes it a class?

Aikins' little textbook in logic[8] reiterates that the world consists wholly of individual things, including persons, every one of which has certain qualities and characters, and stands in certain relations to certain other things, so that all you know, when you know facts, consists of individual things, their relations, qualities, and characters, and there is nothing else there to know. With that in mind, Aikins condemns people who talk misleadingly about the world as if other things than individuals were real. The expressions that such people use, says Aikins, are sometimes metaphorical: they commonly forget that by the State you mean just all of us; when you say the State does this and that, you mean we the individuals do it; everyone of us does his part in the activity, with the result that such and such things get done. "This nation fights" means that such and such members do the fighting. Since one's part resembles the part that other people take, you can shorten the matter by saying that the group shoots, the army shoots, the nation is at war. —I don't think that that account of the matter covers all the facts. The issue is metaphysical.

(Other Minds)

A third matter to which we may point as indicating how important the social approach to metaphysics may be: What is the evidence that I have for the existence of my neighbor as a conscious being with a mind of his own? What knowledge have I of the mind of my neighbor? How do you know that there is anybody in the world but yourself? What being or reality belongs to my neighbor, and how do I know that it belongs to him? That is connected with the question, "What do you mean by the other man?" Certain experiences lead to a certain answer to that question, an answer to which I have decidedly lively objections. It is said, "It's all a matter of analogy: I notice that I move thus and thus when I want to do something, and the analogy between your movements and mine is the main basis of evidence that I have of your existence." I don't accept that as the account of the evidence; I think that if we were confined to that, our evidence would be very poor; but on the whole it is the predominant tradition among philosophical writers.

Whether we are talking about beings or physical facts, there is a relation between what we assert and believe we know about them, and what we take our social order to be. However it is that we come to believe in the existence of the other man, we use the hypothesis that the very nature of things is that they can be known or experienced by many individuals. The physical world is a world that we can have in common—in some respects at least. People don't always notice that this affects the sense in which the world is real. Heraclitus said when we are asleep every man lives in his own world, but if we are awake then we all see the same world. A man can have a dreamworld pretty vividly and persistent before him, as in delirium. We have a test as to that world: it isn't real because nobody else can get it. We all hold that the real physical world has a character that makes it more or less common to many people. If we look at the blackboard and touch it, we have experiences very much in common. It couldn't be a reality if it appeared consistently to one of us only.

The social problems about things have to do with our very definition of reality.

The Nature of Ideas

In beginning this section, I want to expand on *The World and the Individual*, vol. I, Lecture 1, especially pages 19–37.[9] *Oct. 9*

In what sense have you reality? Either "knowledge of acquaintance" or "knowledge about" is very baffling. I don't know much about myself that I should like to know.

Bergson, in his essay on the right method of metaphysics, defines a method of intuition.[10] You must get into a position in which you are somehow in the interior of the object itself and know it as from the interior. He mentions the self as the being such that if we know it at all we know it by intuition, by direct acquaintance.

Bertrand Russell, a natural and profound opponent of Bergson's type of method, said in his Lowell Institute lectures, somewhat sardonically, "Most men, for example, have in their nature meannesses, vanities, and envies of which they are quite unconscious, though even their best friends can perceive them without any difficulty."[11]

What sort of knowledge have I of myself that I have of nobody else and that nobody else has of me? What is the nature of the evidence whereby we may prove to ourselves that we are not alone in the world? What is the evidence against the view of solipsism? What is the evidence for the existence of a social order of even two people?

James says the reason for belief in other minds is psychological; the best logical argument is that from analogy.[12] But I say you can see plainly that this would not lead readily to a belief in the reality of a group, for the movements of a group are decidedly unlike those of myself. I don't believe that the argument from analogy plays any great part in our belief in the existence of our fellowmen. My uncanny double who did precisely what I did would not impress me as showing great evidence of another mind.

Contrasts are the interesting and fascinating proof of intelligence. I am quite ready to believe that a social group, which is not very analogous to a person in many ways, is real by virtue of its very contrast with the individual.

The real argument is something of this kind: Suppose you look at an advertisement which arouses in you an idea. What I mean by an idea you can best find out by reading the pages I have just mentioned.[13] You don't reason either tacitly or explicitly that whenever you wanted to advertise your wares, you'd take such means of doing it as are present in that advertisement, so that it must have been written by an intelligent being. No; the idea intrudes upon you and strikes you. What strikes you is the contrast. The experience isn't, "Perhaps there is an idea there," but, "Obviously, this idea isn't mine. I didn't write this advertisement: that isn't myself; here is an idea not my own."

If such ideas hang together well enough, they constitute another mind. Another mind is a system of ideas which is intelligible in itself but which certainly isn't mine.[14]

{If someone shouts "Fire!"}[CA] I didn't know that news. I am not crying fire; but it is an expression of an idea and it isn't my idea. The signs of another mind are peculiarly direct in this way. Any idea that isn't my own is *ipso facto* an expression of a self not my own.

A company of selves satisfies that notion of a self just as well as an individual self. I can't see nearly so well the evidence that there is an individual here as that there is somebody here not myself. The writer of a newspaper article isn't an individual man—I don't know who it was—but a locus where certain ideas have germinated. There is no reason why the individual should have the priority. In beginning the acquaintance of a neighbor, you deal with ideas that have a certain amount of coherence; you don't begin with an individual. I regard the idea of a group as a primary thing.

In his *Principles of the History of Language*,[15] page xxxvi, {Hermann} Paul says that the reality of individuals must be insisted upon as the primary fact of social life. Minds don't influence minds except through bodies. Therefore, we must never speak of a group as if a group of minds could work as a unit.

{Wilhelm} Wundt, a German psychologist, maintains that a social group has a mind of its own. On page 27 of his *Ethics: Principles of Morality* {sic},[16] is a passage on the individual will and the social will, in which he maintains that the social group has a consciousness and a will of its own which is in some respects prior to that of the individual.[17]

Oct. 14 [U] If you raise the question, "Is the State a reality?" or "Is there such a being as Harvard University?" you find there are two answers.[CA] One would say that a supposed reality—an institution, or a corporation—has no reality except as an abstract or legal fiction. The State, or any given railway corporation, or the Church, exists only as a group. The law has many fictions, such as the corporation treated as a person. Thus some would say that social groups are real, first as abstractions, second as legal fictions. They are treated as though they were real. This constitutes one of the views.

On the other hand, there is this view. To me, a social group may be a reality, an entity, which is just as real as an individual human being can be. Or, if you are going to make a difference in grades of reality—upon which I should not insist—there are corporations which are more real than any individual.

A group of individuals standing on the street corner is not a social group to which I should ascribe any reality as a group. The State, on the other hand, has that character; but it is by no means the most interesting or important social group. I shall defend the thesis that there are social groups as real as any individual can be.

There is a familiar technical expression used by those who deny this—"hypostatizing an abstraction." Over against this kind of discussion about social groups you will find a well-known discussion as to the human individual. Those who say that a social group has no reality, say that there exist only individual men. Notice the book of Professor Sumner of Yale, *What Social Classes Owe One Another.*[18] By the State, we mean, said Sumner, simply "all of us." If anybody should say that the State should have institutions to look out for the defective, for example, that would mean that some of us ought to cooperate in looking out for the rest of us. The result was that when Sumner treated social classes, he claimed that there were no such things as "capital" or "labor." What are the rights of labor? That means, what are the rights of certain laborers? This we call "nominalism."

The nominalist declares that social groups are nothing but collections. If the world consists of individual men, then the metaphysical student who undertakes to study this will be led to ask, "What is a human individual?" Most of the nominalists treat this as self-evident. An individual is regarded as an axiom.

How do you know that the world of human beings consists of individuals? What is an individual? You cannot define this obvious entity, the individual, merely in terms of relationships. We cannot define things merely in terms of relations.

I have often used this illustration of the difficulty of defining facts in terms merely of their relations. Lotze used to say that the being of things is the standing in relations. This illustration takes the form of a story of a faithful servant maid who took care of an aged man. She was asked as to his condition and replied, "Sometimes he be's one way, sometimes t'other; but most of the while he be's the same way."

If you answer that question as to what an individual human being is, you have answered all the questions in metaphysics. The matter of knowing that you are the same self is involved here. If your assertion that this is true is called into question, what proof are you to offer? If a man's identity is once questioned, it forms one of the most baffling problems.

Many years ago the {Roger} Tichborne case in England attracted much attention.[19] It was to the effect that a man of the laboring class from Australia claimed to be the long lost heir. While he could give some evidence which would seem hardly to be in the possession of any one who was not the heir, it was objected that he had gained this knowledge from the true heir who had died in Australia; and it was on these grounds that his claim was finally rejected.[20] Notice the identification in cashing a check. You don't prove you are the right man by a signature. Notice {Oliver Wendell} Holmes' poem on Dorothy Q., where he speculates as to what a difference it would have made in him, had she answered "No" instead of "Yes." Questions of this sort show us how little it is self-evident as to what a person is. How abstract a being the ordinary human being is will be shown shortly.

Oct. 16 I have just presented to you some problems that ought to make you pause a little when you say it is perfectly obvious that this "community" is simply a collection of individual men. Why is one so sure that only individual men exist? If you say it is just plain common sense that a social group is just a collection of individual men, you presuppose that it is obvious to you that an individual man is a reality and that the human world consists of such realities; but neither in your own case nor in the case of your neighbor is it easy to define <u>what you mean by this individual self</u>.

I desire to show you that you yourself have some of the characters that may be said to belong to a group of men. I am going to maintain the thesis that we cannot say what an individual man is without some of the characters of a social group. On the other hand, a group under certain circumstances can get the characters of an individual man.

<u>I am not merely my physical organism</u>. If you try to get at what an individual is, you cannot define an individual man merely in terms of an organism, for the organism can be very slightly changed and yet the individual man be very decidedly out of our ken. A slight change in the state of my organism sets me, for example, dreaming, and when I wake up I say there was something about the dreaming self which is foreign to me. The difference between your <u>self</u> and your organism comes out further in the variations which come from excitement, ether intoxication and the like. Patients partially etherized notice that the self is considerably changed; the question who I am is somewhat confused by the intervention of an ether intoxication.[21] The etherized organism differs from the unetherized organism in a different way from that in which the etherized self differs from the unetherized self.

James says that a good deal of what we call <u>self</u> sometimes is our own view of our organic sensations.[22] James analyzes the varieties of selfhood which appear as we grow and meet various influences. Since a man undertakes a good many things, he normally tends to have as many selves as there are such ideals. The choice may be said to take the form of suppressing one possible self and trying to live up to another, the different selves being different plans of life. James said he would be a saint and a lady killer and many other things {at the same time}, but this is not possible. My life depends on my choosing amongst rival selves. In saying, "Evidently all social activities are carried on by individuals," one forgets that if you look for the individual, you will find a crowd, a collection.

James was disposed to limit the varieties of selfhood. In the normal man these "selves" are not so distinct from each other as "different men" are. Conflicts within the individual self are not so great as the rivalry and contrasts between selves in the community. James was unwilling to accept the view that the abnormal divisions of a self are extreme cases of these normal contrasts. James was interested in cases of more or less permanent double and treble personality, as when a man declares that he is somebody who he cannot be. In cases of head injuries, men sometimes show a loss of their old personality. Those cases suggest to me that the normal variations of selves are minor instances of the same thing, multiple personality. We are all of us made up of a variety of personalities. I as a lecturer am not the same self as a person who last evening was lecturing in a University Extension course. The self of Phil. 9 is distinct from the self of an elementary ethics course. The lecturer in one course questions the lecturer in the other as to how they agree or differ. The abnormal cases are an extension of that. James would never admit it.

The so-called individual man is in certain respects a social group. He consists of various selves. Anybody is more or less a multiple personality. This belongs to the normal plasticity and fecundity of social life. In abnormal cases, because of loss of memory, the transition from one self to the other is not easy.

However unified I am, you notice this. I must live some sort of a life in order to be conscious. The self isn't given, it is expressed in a life. You must be conscious of some enterprise, work, interest, concern. You are yourself by virtue of the fact that you are engaged in doing something. The coherence involves memory and expectation; you remember a past life and expect a future life. If your memories and all your expectations dropped out, you wouldn't be the same self that you are now. You must remember a past life, you must look forward to a future life. Such and such things have happened to me, and I expect such and such things to happen to me. In vain you look for the self of this instant; you find only a fragment of self; you have certain throat sensations perhaps, or somebody calls your name, but such experiences don't give you yourself. You are obliged to think of your past self and your future self.

In consequence, every man has a life past and future as an essential part of him. The relations of the self at any moment to its past and future are relations to whose analysis we shall devote considerable attention. The situation is this: I am the doer of so and so, the lecturer in Phil. 9, and in view of this in which I am engaged, these and these things have been done by me; I remember these deeds and I propose to go on to something more. The life of the self is always this: at present it is doing something which it connects with a past set of deeds and also with future deeds. It is the connection of these deeds that constitutes the connection of self. In view of what I have so far done and undertaken and of the present situation, hereupon I proceed to the next, to adjust myself to the future. That is a stereotyped form of autobiography. It is every man's life. The self is a being who just now connects its past with its future. At present I act because my past demands of me this act with reference to my future. I must get on with this enterprise one step more. Only the self can expect to judge the connection, the coherence, though he never likes to judge it wholly alone. The dreaming self has a certain difficulty in finding the coherence: What have I been doing? What did all this mean? In any case, the self consists at any moment, if it is active, of an attempt to bring its past into a coherent connection with its future. If I wholly forget what I have done so far in this lecture, then the self fails and I am confused. For that reason I should say to you that every acting self consists from its own point of view of what at every instant may be called three different personalities: the past self, the present self, the future self.

The past self in certain moods may loom up with importance as by far the most significant of these three. The future self, when we are eager, is sometimes the most important self. The present self has a different function. It knows that beyond the value of contributing its share to the development of this triple personality it has no value except its current pleasures and pains.[CA] The present self may feel as if it were the most important part, as in the case of the doctor with a broken leg who cried out under ether that he alone knew how to set bones; but as soon as a man gets a little clearer about the situation, it appears to him that the present self isn't such an important personality. The present self is deliberately subordinated to the past or future self.

This community of three selves is always changing as life goes on. The past self is the self up to the present moment; it is growing all the time. The future self we seem to be chasing or creating it. The present self changes while you watch it, so you can never say, "This I am now." These three are needed in order that there should be a self at all. I am that threefold self. You can't get your unity of personality without having this endlessly fluent variety of these three.

I call the self a social group for excellent reasons. These three selves are constantly communicating with each other. The present self remembers the past self. The future self is expected by the present self, and the expectations of it affect one's present self. The relations are well represented by the ordinary memorandum book where one has noted something in the past and now consults it. Every man is a society of at least three selves, and on occasion of many more. Therefore, a self is a community. I shall soon show you how a community can be a self.

If we start from the literal social order, we shall find all sorts of unity there which determine our loyalties and the significance of our family and political ties. We find certain communities characterized by extremely practical features; these communities occur in business life and are not the product of mystical thinking at all. Such communities consist of at least three individuals who are joined by a linkage which I regard as peculiarly apt to illustrate to you what I mean by three different individuals forming one united self. I call them communities of interpretation. Wherever these communities exist at all, they have powers which no individual man can possess unless he borrows or learns them from some such community. In my little book, called *War and Insurance*, there is a passage, pages 44–64, which gives several instances of this kind of community, which we should all regard as consisting of individual human beings who are characterized by their function in that community, so that you would speak of them by speaking of their functions.[CA] They have familiar names: *Oct. 19*

1. The judicial community, {consisting of}
   A. plaintiff
   B. defendant
   C. judge
2. The banker's community, consisting of
   A. borrower
   B. lender or depositor
   C. banker
3. The agent's community, consisting of
   A. agent
   B. principal
   C. client
4. The insurance community, consisting of
   A. insurer, usually a corporation
   B. an "adventurer"
   C. beneficiary

By chance any two of these persons may be identified in the same individual. In the case of the insurance community, for instance, a man may identify in himself the owner of the property and the beneficiary; but the beneficiary is in general the future man. He who is insuring against accident is obviously a different man from the future man who may get hurt. The whole business depends upon the fact that there are three here. In case two of them are one, then you have the difference of past, present, and future keeping them apart. In the case of an endowment policy, the man twenty-five years hence is another man, for the reason that this present man may be dead long before the endowment accrues.

The community in question is essentially triadic. If I insure my own house and it burns, it is my future self who gets the money. Again, to save money for oneself is wholly social. You meet with this triadic structure in vast numbers of socially significant business transactions. The threefold man divides up into three socially different men. Our selves have a structure which literally breaks up, on notable occasions, into the life of three different people, held together by the same sort of bond that makes the self.

The contemporaneous people in a borrowing transaction are also temporal people: the man who lends is a present man, but the man who is going to receive the return of the loan (an important element) is a future man; and so also of the borrower.

In the case of individual men there is no particular psychological continuity between the past, present, and future selves; and some of these triadic communities, like country banks, hold together better than almost any individual man. I insist upon the stable character of the ethical relations between a man and his past self, but even there a change occurs.

The general formula for identity is coherence of life plan. I am unable to define the unity of a man in any other terms that are satisfactory to me. Of course we make all the use we can of the permanence of a man's body; but when we examine the sense in which a part of the material world exists, we shall find it a very puzzling metaphysical problem.

The self I define as a life lived in accordance with a plan, or to use the word idea, as a life with a coherent idea. A man hopes to keep a good deal of his coherence within him, but he is always failing to keep as ideally coherent as he ought to be.

I am trying to arouse in you a doubt of the proposition that it is perfectly obvious that a man is an individual, because here he is, you can shake hands with him and he will be the same man when you come back!

In response to your questions, I say that these triadic communities have a sense of selfdirection as communities.[CA] There is a general unity of feeling. When you say, "It was I that felt in my individual self that feeling," you are out of the crowd; but there are moments in life when you can't express the thing otherwise than by saying "we."[#] In chorus singing I don't say to myself, "I am singing with them." For the moment I don't exist apart from the chorus. You don't say, "I agree with you in feeling this," when you are excited; you say, "We feel this," and the other people say "We." There are feelings that are expressed only by the first person plural. In case you object that some organism must thrill with them, that is a psychological comment; but that isn't the important fact that you express when you say "We."

It was my older view that the individual man is more or less the product of civilization and specialization; but I am now impressed by the fact that along with these individualizing tendencies there are highly unifying tendencies. There are so many things which we do together that I think it belongs to a highly developed community to do these things together.

When Thackeray was asked about the marriage with which *Henry Esmond* closes, he said, "They did it themselves; I didn't do it." That word "they" expressed a fact; not he did it or she did it, but they did it. Aren't there some things that we do?

A crossing policeman told me that he too is chased by the automobiles *Oct. 21*
when he takes off his uniform and puts on citizen's clothing. Here he was making these metaphysical distinctions between past and present self, and between the self of the uniform and the private self.

Duns Scotus had his name for the abstract quality, the thisness of the this, that makes an individual such: he called it *haecaeitas*, meaning that which makes this this.

How would I answer a question about the distinction between the present self and the past and future selves? A deed is a perfectly natural discontinuity of life. Suppose I sign a contract: the moment of signing my name to that paper stands out from both my past and future life. This act is against all that preceded it, and before all that followed it; the deed was never done before and it will never be done again.

A naughty boy, to entice a younger playmate to go to town with him said, "I will show you something that nobody ever saw before and nobody will ever see again." In the Sunday school book, this proved to be the kernel of a nut, which the elder immediately swallowed. There is the present moment for you. You will look vainly for the Bergsonian fluidity there. Our deeds are breaks in the time process. The character of the present is well expressed in the saying, "I shall come this way no more." Nietzsche, before he reached the abyss of madness, amused himself with the idea of recurrence, the doctrine that everything happens again and again: we have been here in this room an infinite number of times before, exactly as today. Nietzsche had experiences, somewhat pathological, which made this very interesting to him. It led him to poetical metaphors: the process of the world is spoken of as a ring. But this raises the question: this particular recurrence, this time when we are together, has never occurred before; the *haecaeitas* of this particular lecture is distinct, and would remain so even in Nietzsche's fancied world of recurrence.

The passage in my book, *War and Insurance*, pages 44–64, is in connection with an inquiry into the motives that lead to war. The relations of individual men and individual men are especially provocative of strife, and the same is true of communities in their relations one to another. When two are together, there are constant causes of friction.

But as a matter of fact, our social relations are not limited to pairs of individuals. Some communities consist of three people, or three groups of people, where B is the agent of A in approaching C. The agent represents the principal in approaching the client. This is a community of interpretation, consisting of A, B, and C, one of whom, B, is in the position of the interpreter of A to C. The interpreter is the agent, banker, insuring corporation, or other intermediary. Page 51 is most important: "This cooperation . . . will bring A and C into some kind of social unity, such as will make them act in a certain respect, as if they were one man." The main function of B is to keep A and C together. The agent desires not to do A's will alone, or C's will alone, but his whole business is to create, keep conscious, and carry out their united will. Since B has this united will of A and C, he must be what I call loyal, the thoroughgoing servant of the cause of uniting the will of A to the will of C, and the will of C to the will of A. If he succeeds, all of them act as one man, though no two of them do the same thing.

The community is essentially one man if the self means the coherence of a life. That is the community acting as one man.

The Triadic Community of Interpretation

Oct. 23 As set forth in *War and Insurance*, pages 44–64, a community of interpretation consists of three persons or groups of persons, A, B, and C. These may tend to vast size, greater than any now existing nation. If the individuals are atoms, the atoms are grouped in a molecule such that each atom has two different affinities. The community in itself is a peaceful group and often a highly active affair. The most potent and reasonable factor in the modern world consists in such communities.

A, B and C then are individuals whose relations in the community I have described.[23] Although this is not a complete picture, and there is more to consider than this, the point at present is that A has a relation which looks toward B; B has a relation which looks towards C: $\overparen{A \rightarrow B \rightarrow C}$. There is some tie which ties two pairs which have a member in common. If you merely mention pairs, if you try to limit yourself to dyadic terms, you have to mention what is really essential to triads. They work together upon a task which is in its social aspects at once businesslike and ideal. The task is this: A and C have their own individual business and desires such as they are; every man has business and desires such as they are. The remaining member, B, has as his peculiar business in this community the task of addressing C. He appeals to C, or makes use of his social relations to C, and explains or interprets to C what A's business or desire is, in order that C may be brought into relation with A.

The cooperation of A and C will bring them into some sort of social unity which may make them think and feel and will as if they were one man. There is the same sort of unity which constitutes the life of an individual man. An individual man is not an individual because he has an individual organism, for a self is a self by virtue of the fact that he is doing something that constitutes a plan having a unity or coherence, which you can't tell by watching an organism but by telling what a man means, what he is up to, what he is after.

In communities of interpretation, the time-order plays a somewhat various part. In consequence of the intermediation brought about by B, A, B, and C act as if they were one man. To bring about this solidarity is B's main business. The interpreter is the one who addresses C on behalf of A; he is the agent in an ordinary agency transaction.

A self is a self by virtue of some coherence of a plan. So far as one's selfhood is the selfhood of the interpreter of a community, that is his main business, and to do it in one direction, that of addressing C on behalf of A. B is a self who desires to carry out a plan which furthers not A's will alone, or C's will alone, but to create and to make conscious and to carry out their united will, insofar as they are both to remain members of the community in which he remains as interpreter. Therefore, B must be loyal, the willing and thoroughgoing servant of the cause and plan of C and A.

B is always the most important member of the community in question. He both defines and expresses its united purpose; he more or less invents its united purpose. He brings C into touch with A, A into touch with C. His essential aim as interpreter is that the will of the three shall be done. He loses his position as interpreter unless he is engaged in that business. If he is there as A's or C's servant, then he is not the interpreter of the community; or if he is there for his own good. It is his will that A and C should act as one man. If he doesn't bring this to pass, he doesn't succeed. I mean just precisely as one of us acts as one man.

The combined will of A and C has constantly to be created. In bringing A and C together, B usually discovers or creates their common will; hence, B is above all the most obviously and explicitly loyal member of the community. In his will, when he finds it and expresses it, is the peace both of A and of C. To this end he comes into this community. He furthers and enlightens its aims insofar as he furthers his aims as interpreter.

There is no ideal activity of man which is too lofty to be interpreted by a community of interpretation. The unity and cooperation of men cannot be stable, secure, and enlightened unless there is added a third man whose business and desire it is to keep these two in touch with each other. He has the function of transforming the essentially dangerous pair into the consistently and consciously harmonious triad. I call him the "spirit of the community."

One very notable community might be called the "community of scientific investigation." It consists of the (1) collectors or observers of nature or some group of natural facts; (2) the more speculative theorists; (3) a group or individual whose business it is to test the theories. A very large group of naturalists had collected the facts upon which Darwin depended; he advanced the theory of natural selection as the origin of species. Darwin was the interpreter: he summed up the results of the past, he addressed the future. He stood in the same place in which in an individual life a man stands to his past and future. Darwin was appealing for his authority to the collectors of facts, and he was appealing for the conflrmation of his theory to future investigation. This is the "inductive community." There are also similar instances in the case of the deductive sciences.[#]

Our present civilization depends for all its peaceful activities upon judges, bankers', insurers', agents' communities. If you removed all these from our social order, it would deteriorate into the dangerous pair type. The judicial community consists of a pair of contending individuals or groups; the judge interprets to the defendant the will or rights of the plaintiff.

President Lowell, in his recent book on party politics,[24] talks about this as the age of brokers. Solon had to deal with the hostility between borrowers and lenders. Polonius tells his son to be neither a borrower nor a lender. The most dramatic appearance in modern civilization has been that of the banker community of interpretation. The banker's interest is that both parties should be content; his interest is their interest.

The interpreter is engaged in a business that goes beyond his individual power to invent. He meets constantly the borrower's appeal and the lender's willingness. But in bringing them together he has to be constantly inventive.

I don't see how you can define an individual as a life according to a plan, without saying that a community of interpretation, insofar as it is successful, is a self. The unity found in any one of the members is of the same nature as the unity of the larger entity. Any man is such a community of interpretation insofar as his present is interpreting his past to his future. You can have a triad of functions where there are only two persons.

It is a curious fact that while human language always involves the effort of a man to make himself clear to another man, it is still a fact that languages which have never yet been written and which are spoken by a people without "cultivation," express a wisdom and ingenuity which has never become conscious in any individual persons who spoke that language. No Greek of the Homeric period knew the difference between a noun and a verb—the language was so much wiser than the individual Greek. It became so because a peaceful conversation involves an endless process of interpretation. The roles constantly change. A language which always passes through groups with a tendency for the interpretation to become predominant tends to become wiser than any of the people who speak it.

C. S. Peirce's Stages of Scientific Process:[25] *Oct. 26*

Retroduction
Deduction
Induction proper.

The Scientific Community:

1. The collector
2. The theorizer
3. The verifier.

These examples in *War and Insurance* which we have been discussing are my favorite instances of communities that tend to act as one man: agents', bankers', and insurers' communities. In each of these there are three persons or groups of persons, and one of them interprets one of them to the other. He is always a mediator, and mediation is an unsymmetrical function in all these cases.

There are other communities of that sort. One such community exists on a purely natural basis without the conscious intent of anybody that it should become a community at the outset: the family. The family consists of the father, mother, and child. There the mediation relations commonly vary in the successful case with the age and outward circumstances of all those concerned. The child may well mediate between mother and father, leading to their closer unity; in this case the child acts as a tie, a holder together of the group. Then under other circumstances the mother very frequently mediates between father and son when they become what I have called the dangerous pair; and the father may also be the unifier between child and mother.

There are other more or less voluntary communities of the triadic sort. The process of constructing such communities goes on all the time. Scientific investigation involves three functions which may be united in one individual, giving to the man in that case the kind of unity of life that an individual tries to get into his life in uniting his past and future. To Peirce is due that threefold division of the scientific process.[26] CA A concrete science depends upon collecting facts, whether or not systematically, and forming some impressions from these facts.

1. The process of making a trial generalization on the basis of a collection of facts is what Peirce calls a retroduction. It is present at the stage when a science has the form of a classification. In medical science at the end of the eighteenth and the beginning of the nineteenth century, great stress was laid upon classifying diseases, sometimes by external marks. Every classification is of

the nature of a retroduction. This process hasn't acquired any classical name. Peirce sometimes preferred to call it abduction. It is taking a mass of facts and leading them up to some kind of a trial generalization.[27]

2. The next stage in the science is when the reasoning used becomes deductive. On the basis of a retroduction, one is led to a hypothesis. If the facts are complicated, you can't collect your facts and see what they point to. Generally you have to make hypotheses by which the facts can be marshalled and comprehended. The hypothesis when first presented must contain much more than the retroductions already made make manifest.

3. The next procedure is induction proper, the process of testing the hypothesis by seeing whether a consequence of the hypothesis is true. The whole school of pragmatists have laid most stress on this stage.

You may speak of the scientific community as consisting of three persons, by naming[CA] their functions:

1. The collector or primary generalizer (retroductive methods)
2. The theorizer (deductive methods)
3. The verifier (inductive methods).

Without these three functions the work of the scientific community could not be done. In case these communities are successful as such, they tend to work as one man. This is not true of all communities, but it is true of certain triadic communities whose reality I want you to consider.

In Wundt's *Völkerpsychologie,*[28] he develops his theories on the basis of what he calls the *Gesamtbewusstsein*, a total consciousness which is by Wundt empirically illustrated. He insists that there are three principal regions—custom, language, religion—where you get illustrations of this total consciousness. In later volumes he added art.

He states his theory of the reality of these communities as empirically as possible, and has illustrated it with a great wealth of empirical material. The mental processes that go on in the world are partly to be referred to the minds of individual men, but there are processes that go on in groups. These processes are marked by products like language, whose development is not due to processes that go on in individuals. It takes a more or less well combined collection of men to produce a language. Custom is not due to individual action, nor can any number of individual men acting as individuals account for it. They must act in respect to the custom as one.

The inventors of a Volapuk or Esperanto get the content of their language simply by copying. They don't invent a real language, but take from existing languages bits of form and type and simplify the situation. Such a language, if successful, would get into the hands of the collective consciousness and would change.

It is exactly so with religion. There are cases of men who would be called founders of religion, but no man has ever invented religion itself, and the "founders" have built on ages of development by the collective consciousness. Wundt makes the State one special development of custom. If a collection of people do what cannot be reduced to the deeds of individuals and the collection of the deeds of individuals, then you have a mental process which is due to a community. What has mind is real. A community behaving as one man, accomplishing what an individual can't accomplish, must be real.

I once heard a business man refer to Le Bon's *Psychology of the Crowd.* This writer calls the crowd a kind of collective unit, a bad unit, much stupider than any of the better individuals in it and no better than the worst one in it. It is guilty of social and political stupidities. But those Boards that I am a member of, he commented, are much wiser than any of the members; and he mentioned the Metropolitan Water Commission. It was at that time that I was first attracted to the psychology of those groups which Wundt describes. The triadic community is highly teleological, but no member in it proposes to do the group's deed.[CA]

Wundt has made out a very decided case for the distinction between a *Oct. 28*
collection viewed merely as a collection, and these social wholes. Since communities behave like individuals in the sense of producing what has the general coherence of the life which you attribute to an individual man, the communities have a life of their own.[29]

If we generalize, accepting the general thesis of Wundt, we can say that *Oct 28*[U]
the social group actually does produce something which no individual can. Wundt regards language, custom, and religion to be the three functions which you cannot deal with adequately from individual psychology. If 100 men each do 100 things, each being determined by his own individual consciousness, you would not have a social product.

The psychology of religion he founded in an ingenious way. He regarded it as a product of the collective imagination of a group of people. Later on, he had art. I see no reason for limiting the functions of a community to these four, but for these he has made out a good case. Thus the community accomplishes as a whole what no individual human being could accomplish. Wundt had made out a good case in the fact that so far as communities behave like a single individual, they are then truly acting.

We saw that in a triadic relation there is one member which is the most important, but he would never be able to do what he does were it not for the constant cooperation of the others. Lectures I and II of *The Problem of Chris-*

tianity deal with this. Read Lectures II, IV, of the first volume, then Lectures V, VI, and VII.

The Christian Church: a Community of Interpretation

The thesis would be the idea that the Christian Church has somehow a unity; the idea is essentially a metaphysical idea. It has a historical beginning and has a character that the Church is regarded as one, in much the same way as Wundt regarded the social organism. The thesis of my first volume is one that would arouse considerable opposition from the followers of the different forms of the Christian religion. When you grasp the metaphysical doctrine, it is substantially in agreement with that set forth in *The World and the Individual. The Problem of Christianity* is founded on a deliberately maintained agnosticism with regard to the origins of Christianity. The various accounts, including Harnack's, seem uncertain. Neither a natural nor a supernatural account would appear to be sufficiently assured to give us an understanding as to the nature of Christianity. We shall never find out as to what really happened. With the documents that we have, too many highly critical minds have been at work on them to give us hopes of finding out anything definite in the future. I have no hypothesis as to the origin of Christianity save that so far as the early Christian Church is concerned, the writer of the Epistles stands in the presence of a certain definite religious community. Paul's part in Christianity was a very brief part. Compare the part the Buddha played in Buddhism.

The peculiarity of this religion was that the founder became what he was by his spirit being translated into the language of the community as the inspirer and unifier of the early Christian community. It is in the concern for the character of an individual man, in the effort to treat one another as individuals, that the Christianity which Paul described is characterized.[CA] Notice such a phrase as "Are one in the spirit." What the Church soon regarded as essential—to have a record of the sayings of its Lord—had not yet come about. The essence of the religious experience was not the experience of the "mind alone with the divine," as James says, but of minds together with the divine. A good many of the more enthusiastic sects had life of that kind for a while—the life of a social religious experience, often very highly mystical in character. If this religious experience was formulated, then you had a new variety of Christianity; but most of these were very ephemeral—unlike, for instance, the Quakers.[CA]

Very frequently a sect has degenerated. On the other hand, there have been men who had something of the spirit of which Paul speaks. The essence is to have a community religious experience, and it is this experience which has found in the Pauline documents an actual record.[30] The Pauline charity of the thirteenth chapter of 1 Corinthians is not identical with the Christian love which explicitly appears in the writings about Christ's teachings. In the Gospels you nowhere get explicitly that perfect expression of the Christian spirit which Paul gives in the thirteenth chapter of I Corinthians.

Paul's thesis is that the community is real. This life doesn't belong to any one member alone; it is characterized by what Paul called the "unity of the spirit," with "many members." That life upon which Paul layed stress was one which could become extremely practical. This union of mysticism and shrewdness shows us the combination of Paul's personality. Thus Christianity can best be called a religion of loyalty. The {two versions of the} Sermon on the Mount[31] do not give us the whole of Christianity but rather the thirteenth chapter of I Corinthians {does}.

The Stoics gave a social character to the World Reason which expresses itself in all nature and especially in the social life of man insofar as that life is rational. The world is the expression of the divine reason. The individual sage never meets the Stoic ideal; that is best expressed in human nature, and human nature is best expressed in its political unities which tend to constitute a kind of State or City of the Divine Reason. The community of mankind, though still ideal, is that which if we could reach it would be a reality and would express a metaphysical reality that already belongs in a way invisible to us human beings inherent in the order of the world. *Oct. 30*

The religion of Israel is a fine example of Loyalty, which means practical devotion to the work or united life of some Community. I think the name Community is in many ways better than the name Cause. The loyal person has found a community which sufficiently realizes or expresses the cause. The nation of Israel was regarded as a united whole, much more valuable than any individual Israelite. They regarded their history as the history of their community. Israel was treated as a being by the God who had chosen it. Metaphors were used—the faithless wife who has forsaken her true husband, the divine being; the people as a whole have been unfaithful; or again, the future of the redeemed Zion is pictured as the future of a being that is at once a society and an individual; its reality was at once superindividual and having the life of an individual.

By a process which is very obscure there came in a conception of a being which was all mankind, a community which expressed the will of God.[32] CA If my salvation occurs at all, it occurs in connection with the salvation of the community. Northern Buddhists had some such idea. Professor Anesaki has written an account of the teaching of Nichiren, a thirteenth century Buddhist sage.[33] Analogies {arise} with George Fox.[34]

At the outset of Chapter 7 of Romans, Paul sketches certain characteristics which he finds both in the civilization of the Jews and of the Gentiles. In both those branches civilization is profoundly base. He tells us why the Graeco-Roman world is corrupt and why Judaism shares this corruption. This *Nov. 2* is set against a dark view of human nature; man is essentially a corrupt being in his present condition. There is however a way out of this natural desolation of our present human nature. Not by the practices of the Jewish legal tradition can a way be found. The way is opened by the new life presented in Christianity. Through the influence which humanly was initiated by the Founder of that faith, the way of salvation has been opened.

The way of salvation involves some sort of transformation which Paul undoubtedly regarded as miraculous. Something of that sort must happen to every believer who is to get the good of the new faith. The salvation which Paul expects comes to the individual solely because he gets a new union with a community which Paul conceives as divine in its origin. It is that community which saves.

But look in the other direction. Man is lost. This pessimistic view of our evil human nature has a meaning apart from the Pauline religion in the sense in which it came to him as a tradition. Paul thinks he is telling you in this chapter a thing that is universal in its significance. A man becomes conscious of the inborn sin of Romans 7 by reason of a process which develops out of human nature the very baseness which he describes. This is quite apart from any Pauline setting. The communities in which we grow up bring us to self-consciousness by a process that involves mutual criticism and hostility. We reach our highest levels of civilization and of loyalty through a process that involves a high degree of conflict. Man the social animal gives us the picture that Paul sums up in this chapter.

Hence, for a summary of the "social approach" to metaphysics, see chapters 3 through 7 of *The Problem of Christianity*. {Now that this approach has been introduced, the need arises to apply it to the social nature of knowledge and to form an adequate theory of this inescapable dimension of knowledge.}

Chapter 2

The Social Nature of Knowledge: The Theory of Interpretation

There are three forms and sorts of knowledge: *Nov. 4*

> Perception, which shows us data of sense and reveals their reality.
>
> Conception, which shows us meanings.
>
> Interpretation, which shows us other sorts of realities.

Both the self and the community are objects of interpretation. What sort of experience convinces us of the reality of communities? An interpretation of human life.

The theory of knowledge has been dominated in the past by the notion that perception and conception are the two sorts of knowledge. These are a rather dangerous pair, and consequently many of the various problems of epistemology have arisen. I follow Charles Peirce in proposing a third mode of knowledge, interpretation, which has the character of a triadic form of knowledge and requires distinctly a social relation to make it such. Wherever there is an interpretation, there is a community of interpretation. It may all occur within the psychic life of an individual: how do you know that you had a past? It is a knowledge very like the knowledge that you have of the community. The past is dead, inaccessible, yet how profoundly significant! It is as easy to call it the living past as the dead past. The future isn't there yet, and tomorrow is a day that never came yet; but how real the future from a certain point of view! You interpret your life so that the interpretation depends upon the recognition of the past and the expectation of the future.[1]

Plato had the notion that we can know in a way by our senses, which give *Nov. 6* us mere illusions, but the use of reason brings us into contact with realities. We learn through the reason what justice is in itself apart from conditions, as a general object; we learn the universal nature of justice. Plato's epistemology is a doctrine to the effect that we are guided by our reason. This involves a metaphysical theory that the only genuine realities are of the type of justice, equality, man, etc., as they are in their essence, while the world of mere opinions are fleeting things. This theory depends upon a contrast between two kinds of knowledge: the kind you get through the senses and your passing emotions; and the right sort which the reason gives, the knowledge of universals. You know what justice or equality or man is, and in such cases you know a universal object, and the kind of knowledge you have is the knowledge of reason.

This classic dual contrast between knowledge of sense and knowledge through the reason, or knowledge of particulars and knowledge of universals, has persisted; and the theory of knowledge has been dominated by the view that there are two kinds of knowledge. In general, the philosophers have regarded one of these two as better than the other, leaving the other as the wrong kind of knowledge. Or in case both kinds are recognized as present, there is still some difference in their rank.

William James, in his *Introduction to Philosophy,*[2] has stated this contrast. It runs all through the *Pluralistic Universe*. We have two sorts of knowledge, perceptual and conceptual. Their objects are particulars and universals. In his *Psychology,* James used another set of names: perceptual knowledge is called knowledge of acquaintance, and the conceptual kind is called knowledge about. You have a knowledge about the numbers when you know that 2 and 2 are 4. On the other hand, when you know the difference between red and blue, or between tone and color, you know something that you have learned through knowledge of acquaintance. James always emphasized this contrast. It got a special significance for him during the period of his pragmatism, and he was accustomed to say that he had contributed something definite to the solution of the problem of the relative value of the two kinds of knowledge: both kinds of knowledge are equally necessary, each in its own place is as valuable as the other; but the knowledge of acquaintance is the kind for the sake of which knowledge about is employed or tolerated or valuable. What we are seeking is always knowledge of acquaintance; but owing to the narrowness of our powers of perception and our incapacity to take in so much, we have constantly to substitute for our knowledge of acquaintance words, symbols, and all the devices of science. This knowledge about we use when we are engaged in computations or scientific investigations; but what we want is knowledge of acquaintance. It is because the knowledge about under certain circumstances can be turned into knowledge of acquaintance that the knowledge about is practically valuable.

Bergson makes this prominent. Knowledge about is compared to credit values; knowledge of acquaintance is compared to cash values. Since we are unable at a given time to get into contact with more than a limited amount of wealth, we have to be content with representatives of value; but promises to pay have their value in the fact that they can be turned upon occasion into cash. So we need abstract ideas to put experiences into order, to record them, instead of merely staring at them all the time. Percepts are the form in which all the valuable knowledge appears, while concepts are guides to experience, devices for a purpose, and have a character which notes and bonds represent in the commercial world. That is Bergson's story of knowledge.

By "social knowledge" one means knowledge of social facts, such as other selves. It is a question of the theory of knowledge.[3] *Nov. 9*

In any statement, "X is real," the predicate "real" is the ontological predicate. If knowledge is valid, its object is reality. By a "real" you mean a fact that is a possible object of knowledge. A real fact is that which can be a proper object of a successful knowledge. By "knowledge" you mean a function characterized by the fact that its proper object is a kind of fact. We define knowledge in terms of reality and reality in terms of knowledge, a circular process. #

Perception and conception give you two kinds of knowledge: perceptual and conceptual facts. This is to define the nature of knowledge by the nature of facts, and the nature of facts by the nature of knowledge.

One sort of knowledge is exemplified by sensation, feeling; by this kind of knowledge you know colors, pains, pleasures, love, hate, etc. Over against this you have the sort of knowledge exemplified by the nature of man, the nature of a triangle, of equality—the logical objects of a universal thought.

The whole theory of knowledge has been dominated by the notion that those two kinds are exhaustive of the divisions of thought.

According to James and the pragmatists generally, we never have pure percepts in our actual live efforts to get knowledge. We are always partly conceptual and partly perceptual.

The necessity of defining our live knowledge as some kind of union of perception and conception became prominent in the 18th century. In the *Critique of Pure Reason*, Kant points out that pure concepts would not give us what we call complete knowledge, and neither would pure perception.[4] Percepts without concepts are blind; concepts without percepts are empty. Thus

(1) If you attempt to get a concept, such as <u>number</u> or <u>triangle</u>, in such wise pure that you leave out the perceptual elements which the concept contains, and try to consider what is left, you find that the thus eviscerated or washed-out concept is empty, it has no content; and if you want to give it a content, you have to turn to something that has its origin in perception. Purely pure concepts would be empty. #

(2) On the other hand, if you consider what you know through pure perception, if you merely see without thinking, you can't tell what you perceive; you wouldn't have any genuine content for your knowledge.

Bergson lays stress upon the view that perceptions and conceptions differ in their value for the purposes of one who is trying to know. Perception, says Bergson, will have the value for the human knower that if he could at pleasure get all that heart could desire in the way of data, he would have no use for concepts. Concepts look to percepts for that which gives them their value; they lead the way to perceptions; they have their use not in themselves but in their relation to possible perceptions. (Recall the banknote analogy.)[CA] Thus the dual contrast is still emphasized, but the relation between the two is brought out. Kant himself laid some emphasis upon the synthesis between perceptions and conceptions.

To these two kinds of knowledge we must add a third cognitive process. The object of perception is the datum of sensation; the objects of conceptual knowledge are the universals. So also this third kind of knowledge has its proper kind of object: social phenomena. Whether the object be yourself or the community in which you belong or any social order of any type, it is by this third sort of knowledge that you know it. To this essentially distinct cognitive process I give the name "interpretation." This theory in its explicit form came to me altogether from Charles Peirce. Volume 2 of *The Problem of Christianity* is devoted to this form of knowledge.

If one says, as the empiricists said, that the ideal sort of knowledge is that of immediate contact with the facts; or on the other hand, if one says with the conceptualists like Plato that the typical sort of knowledge is that of relations, types, general characters and essences, then the demand may be made upon either of these persons: Then what sort of knowledge have you of your neighbor's mind or of your fellow man? Is your fellow man or any mind that you have any acquaintance with an object of perception? Do you see or feel your fellow's feelings or perceptions? Do you feel your own past pains or sorrows merely as a matter of sense? As to physical pains, we have a poor memory somewhat in conceptual terms; but even if it is a question of the significance of past sorrow and grief, nothing past is an object of sense; and yet you know about the past. And on the other hand, the past, or other people's minds, are not the object of conceptual knowledge. Not thereby do you know that it was past. Such knowledge as we have of the past is not adequately expressed in terms of either concepts or percepts.

Kant said that our knowledge of time is not an object of conception. His own solution was that time is neither concept nor percept, but one of the forms which our conceptions have.

Bergson endeavors to meet this difficulty by his highly original theory of immediate memory. He supposes us to have an immediate acquaintance with the past, which is of the nature of a perception.

To my mind, the most essential feature of the past, that it is irrevocable, is not to be understood in terms of either perception or conception. The snowball of the past is endlessly and ceaselessly freezing into unchangeable adamant.

If you have any social knowledge at all, your fellow man is certainly no object of your perception or conception insofar as you limit yourself to these forms of knowledge. His nature as you attribute it to him is inadequately expressible in terms of any concepts. What makes him this man and no other, the principle of individuation, is a problem which you can't solve in conceptual terms. Our social knowledge, if it is knowledge at all, is not adequately expressible in conceptual or perceptual terms.[5]

As for James's compounding of consciousness, he speaks of some kind of consciousness which may be regarded as perceiving what various minds perceive.[6] The difference between James's view and mine comes out in this way: To my mind the community is both for our knowledge and metaphysically speaking an object of interpretation. It is a result of interpretation if we ask what sustains it.

You may say with Bergson that the value of a concept is that it tends to *Nov. 11*
show us the way towards a perception. If we undertake to verify a general description, we look at specific data. The kind of knowledge which we have when we form a judgment is validated by the act of finding the perception that corresponds to the requirements of the judgment as asserted. Or the process of finding the perception may be compared to the process of cashing a draft.

The resulting view of knowledge agrees with Kant in thinking that our knowledge is a synthesis of perception and conception. When we put them together as well as we can, we get as a result what James called repeatedly an idea. My definition of idea in the first lecture of *The World and the Individual* is based on that view. It was due in my own mind to lectures on knowledge and its character which I heard from James when I was a student at Johns Hopkins University in 1878.[CA] James himself had derived some of the aspects of that view from Charles Peirce, though certainly the pragmatism of James's later philosophy was never the pragmatism of Charles Peirce, and Peirce's own doctrine was in fairly conscious opposition to James's view.

What Are Ideas?

James's psychological views about knowledge preceded his later pragmatism. Almost the first words that I ever heard him utter about the problem of knowledge were the opening words which he spoke as a visiting lecturer at Johns Hopkins University:

> I call your attention to the fact that our minds are never engaged in merely copying objects; we are always reacting, responding, making over our world; it is our response to the world about us that constitutes our consciousness of it; and if you define the mind in terms of the responses in question, you will understand it better.[7]

As a naturalist and as a student and teacher of philosophy, James was offended by the tendency in the traditional English empiricism to view our knowledge as copying and holding firm the impressions which the environment makes upon us. Locke expresses that view in the beginning of his book *On the Human Understanding*. Ideas for Locke are in the main results of impressions which have been made on us. Our knowledge is a collection, retention, and rearrangement of such impressions. In judging we are comparing our ideas and seeing whether they correspond or not; the guiding thread of the problem of knowledge is, How comes the mind to be furnished with its store of ideas? Locke's answer is, "It's experience."

Locke is not responsible for the view that our ideas are necessarily like the things which they represent. Some of them are, some of them are not. Our ideas of the primary qualities of things repeat in our minds the primary characters of the environment. There our ideas simply represent the things. But in the case of the secondary properties of matter (smell, taste, hearing), what happens within us is in sharp contrast with the physical source. The order and connection of sounds or odors or tastes, so far as they follow one another in time, would be determined by the order in which certain physical experiences take place in an organism. Thus according to Locke, we copy the structure of the world as to its primary qualities, and the connection of our ideas copies more or less the arrangement of the things that thus impress us. Such is the Lockean theory of knowledge, a theory that laid the basis of the later critical studies of Hume.

There is a difference between our experiences at the moment when they come to us, and our ideas proper, which are the results, the outcomes, of our former experiences. Experience leaves traces in the memory, and our knowledge in our natural state depends upon what has happened to us as well as what is now happening. The connection makes the idea or image more or less a copy of what has happened before in our experience.

Hume says our knowledge consists of impressions and ideas proper. Impressions are momentary, ideas are the copies. Conceptual knowledge belongs to the world of the results of our experiences, the residues. Impressions are the results of our momentary contact with the world.

James was offended by that as a psychologist. He was very much struck by the fact that the organism isn't simply engaged in taking copies or keeping copies of its environment. It is constantly engaged in remaking its environment, changing its own relations to its world. It is highly selective. It is prepared to make responses, instinctive in their origin, depending on the reflex mechanism of the organism. Just as, if you want to understand the activities of an organism, you must consider the nature of the tendencies to action with which it comes to experience, so, if you want to consider knowledge, you must consider it in connection with activities. We learn not from our environment merely insofar as our environment impresses us, but insofar as our environment sets us doing things. For James, knowledge is always a making over of our world.

In consequence, for James an idea is not what it was for Locke or for Hume. It is neither the direct result of an impression which the world makes, nor a copy of it. It is not, like Locke's primary ideas, a copy of the external world, and it is not a copy in the memory of past contact with the world. It is always a changing of things, a making over of the relation of the knower to the world. You never know what the world is apart from your manner of taking it, a manner which is constantly subject to alterations as you go, but always it is your own way. Hence, knowledge is no copy merely; it is always, if a copy, along with a response, with a changing.

James would declare that all our knowledge is an interpreting of the world, though not in the technical sense in which I employ the term. So far, our development of the theory of interpretation would presuppose the background of James's pragmatism. By ideas you mean mental conditions which are always connected with modes of response, with dispositions to certain forms of activity and their results.

The later doctrine of knowledge in James's pragmatism depends upon a further consideration. By your ideas you mean your mental states which are related to the environment in the sense that they express your way of reacting to the environment, thus forming views of what you are further prepared to expect from the environment in virtue of your actions. Locke said we get all the wealth of ideas with which the mind is so richly furnished from experience. Yes, that is true, James agreed; but Locke was wrong in thinking that the environment stamped its imprint upon us. For James, the copying principle of the knowledge process is in the background. Here you get the essence of the view that James developed later in pragmatism. Our ideas are significant in view of what they lead to. They mean to lead back again to experience. The aim of our empirical knowledge is guidance to ways of taking our world which shall prove valuable ways upon being tested. The complete situation of one who acts is that he gets a result that he wouldn't get if he didn't react to the experience in the way in which he does. The ideas which you get from your world are always of the nature of idealized motor tendencies to action. These again are the source of new experiences. The only sort of revelation about the world which you can hope for is about the results that will come from further experience of contact with the world. You get it in the form of tendencies to reaction, expectation of the result, and then verification of those expectations. You know the world in the form of a sort of guidance due to sense–impressions and to the training of your centers. Then you test the resulting knowledge by its success in guiding your further action, and this process goes on indefinitely:

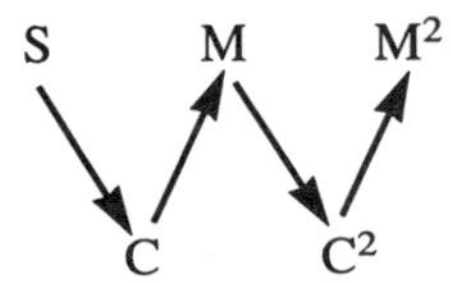

S—Sensory

C—Center (conscious)

M—Motor

James was later led to the generalization: ideas are true so far as they work, so far as they successfully guide to the sort of experience that the possessor of the ideas has been led by previous experience to expect. Knowledge consists in possessing the ideas that are successful, in getting the guidance that leads to what meets the ends of that percipient.

The metaphysics that results from that theory of knowledge was incomplete in James's opinion. Our knowledge of the world takes the form of active tendencies established through contact with the environment, active tendencies whose value comes not from copying but from guiding and leading. An idea therefore is especially defined by James as a leading.

A good instance is that of your knowledge about Memorial Hall. Do you retain a picture of it? That isn't the most important feature of your knowledge. You can form ideas of it that are true when you are not there. The ideas which you form are valuable if they lead you to form expectations which you can verify. The idea takes the form of an ideal leading, a motor tendency or activity which can be verified: "This is what I was looking for."

The whole process of knowledge consists in ideal leadings and their verification. From that which sense presents, from the cash of experience, you go through processes which stir your centers to new movements; and these movements themselves create new situations which give rise to new ideas. What gives your ideas their value is their relation to successful activities. I have used that definition of an idea in the first lecture of *The World and the Individual*.[8]

What has always remained to me permanently significant about this view of James about ideas is this: it isn't their function to portray so much as to constitute an expression of a certain active interest in things. Knowing things is not in its most important aspect the portraying of things. Our ideas are copies in virtue of our interest in certain things, as guides to our activities. An idea can better be expressed as a plan of action. There is no such thing as a purely intellectual process. Our ideas are in a way always expressions of purpose. An idea is always much more perfectly represented by any form of action by which you get what you want, than by a process which consists in the acceptance of something that is impressed upon you. Therefore I use the term "idea" with stress laid on this active sense. The getting of a man's ideas is taking up the same attitude toward things that he takes. Hence, in the first lecture of *The World and the Individual,* I have defined an idea as "the present conscious fulfillment of a purpose."

Interpretation and Time

The theory which dwells upon a third sort of knowledge distinct from both perception or conception involves a new feature not present in James's pragmatism. I don't think James ever appreciated the views of Charles Peirce.[9] What seems to me to have constituted Peirce's discovery is this: There is a familiar process involving intellectual modes of action which can't be defined either in terms of perception or of conception. It is not the process of getting acquainted with objects or of representing them. It is the process which you may call the process of comparing ideas. It involves a genuine third kind of knowledge.

Suppose you have two ideas and you need to know about these ideas not merely by repeating them nor yet by merely responding to them. Suppose you want to compare two ideas with reference to what can be found out by comparison. The comparison is not identical with either of the ideas compared. A genuine third is present. This mode of knowledge, which depends upon perception and conception, which involves having those two kinds of ideas and putting them together by contrast and comparison, is that mode of knowledge which Peirce called knowledge of interpretation.

The comparison in question is what may be called a directive comparison. Take one of the most familiar instances: often a man has at a moment a tendency to do something, and at that moment he thinks of something in his own past which bears on the matter, and thereupon he reconsiders the situation. [Here Royce described at length the meeting a friend who asks you to accompany him.] You recall a previous appointment, and you decline the new proposal or cancel or postpone the previous engagement. Three elements are involved:

1. the interloping idea.

2. the memory idea.

3. the resulting decision or interpretation.

Nov. 16 The triadic process of interpretation, whatever its value, is an elementary type of knowledge, distinct from either perception or conception and actually entering into our relations with one another and to the world.[10]

If you ask what is the kind of validity and certainty that ought to attach to these forms of knowledge, the question as to what we know by one of these modes of knowledge is not at all decided by merely mentioning instances of that type of knowledge and comparing them with instances of the other types. Each type of course wants to bring you into contact with something real. Nobody can look over human knowledge without recognizing that whatever form of knowledge you make use of, you can use erroneously. The question of finding out how to use one of these types of knowledge so as to guide you to a genuine acquaintance of the real, brings before you metaphysical questions.

If you <u>conceive</u> objects, if you take them in the conceptual way, you are led to the question of the problem of <u>deductive inference</u>: What can follow from certain premises? Can you by deductive reasoning discover matters of fact in the physical world? Or what is it that you learn when you carry out a process of deductive inference and draw certain conclusions from certain premises? Questions of that sort lead you over into questions of metaphysics. Even, what conception is, you can best learn only from examples that you get from deductive processes.

Again, to speak of the process of <u>perception</u> is by no means to mention a process that is by itself infallibly connected with fact. Of course we can be deceived by our perceptions. One who makes as prominent as Bergson does the process of perceptual knowledge would be sure to look out for some instance of perception that does give us access to reality; but he thinks we do not usually clear our perceptual knowledge of conceptual inference. To perceive and to perceive rightly, according to him, demands that we should get into a peculiar contact with life, which you can best conceive when you retire into the interior of your own self-consciousness; you have to enter into the interior of the object that you are discussing. On the deceitfulness of perception, a conceptualist like Plato lays a good deal of stress; the facts of perception shift and we are thus in contact with flux.

The doctrine of pragmatism gives us a union of perception and conception. In his Lowell Institute lectures on pragmatism, James raises the question by what means we get knowledge of truth. He finds that an idea is a union of perceptual and conceptual elements, a leading towards a selection of percepts determined by the past or the tendency indicated by the concepts you have.

When your concepts take the form of leading towards the kind of percepts which they emphasize, then you are seeking for truth. The truth of your idea consists in its perceptual validation. The truth of a proposition consists in the fact that the idea which the proposition declares to be true works. The true is the expedient in our conceptual leadings, just as the good or the right is the expedient in the realm of our actions.

You have then an idea; it has a conceptual aspect precisely so far as it involves a consciousness of relations or universal types, the sort of consciousness that Plato hoped to have quite pure as the consciousness of an ideal truth. But in your live assertions {and} beliefs, you are not dealing with the purely conceptual element: you have on your hands a leading such that thereby you expect to succeed.

To summarize:

1. Perception may be illusory. For a perceiver, that which he perceives may turn out to be an illusion. Images are present in dreamlife, but the perceptions may be in that case dream-objects.

2. Conceptions may be subject to logical defects, or if their combinations are in question as in mathematics, the propositions in question may be false; the inferences may be incorrect inferences.

3. In the union of perception and conception with which you are constantly dealing according to the pragmatists, your search for truth may at any time fail.

Precisely similar considerations may arise in the account of knowledge by interpretation. Our metaphysical view about the sorts of facts does indeed reflect our view about the sorts of knowledge. The real is that which would be the proper object of a certain sort of knowledge, which in turn would be defined by its appropriate facts. There is no royal road to the correct interpretation. The process of finding out whether our interpretations are true interpretations may be as extended as the process of science or art or philosophy.[11]

Interpretation is not a type of knowledge so superior to perception and conception that your interpreted knowledge will infallibly be true. Every proposition has to stand on its merits. The assertion of the reality of the community depends upon using the process of knowledge called interpretation: a community is an object which must be known, if at all, through interpretation. That is true; but the question whether the community is or is not, is not settled by that fact. You can interpret your fellow falsely, and we are constantly engaged in correcting misinterpretations in all our social intercourse. There is no royal road to correct interpretations. Everything which is said to be known through interpretation must be tested.

But something is gained if you don't look for knowledge in the form of immediate intuition in the form in which Bergson looked for it. Something is gained by not saying, "If I know facts, then I perceive them." Something is gained if you don't set up axioms conceptually defined but supposed to be immediately apparent.

The process of interpretation can never give you in any finite time a complete knowledge of anything. Its very essence is deliberate incompleteness. One who seeks for finality in his views of life or of his fellowmen will not be satisfied so long as he is living in time. Whoever is looking for finality looks for it in vain in the form of perception, because the perceptions in terms of which he seeks for the finality are inadequate to know reality, and they change with the changing and shifting of his state of mind. So the mystic and so Bergson never get a view of reality that can be said to be of final value. As for conceptual knowledge, Bergson, in criticizing the attitude which he attributes to conceptualists, points out that another philosopher can always come along and advance another set of concepts which he says are sufficient to give us the real. The process so far as it is supposed to be final is an endless failure.

The difference between the failure of mystics like Bergson and of conceptualists like Plato and Spinoza on the one side, and the failure which goes with the work of the interpretationalist, would consist in this: The mystic who changes his mind gives up in a way a kind of infallibility of perception on which he had been resting his case. Again, if the conceptual philosopher changes his group of conceptions, he seems to have admitted a failure in the process to which he had intrusted himself. But you may say that from the very nature of the process of interpretation, the process is a process that never could reach a goal and a finality so long as it was a process carried out by a being who is living in time. "Up to date this interpretation is thus far revealed." It is as impossible to get a final interpretation as it is impossible to do a final good deed. [#]

Kant said that a moral individual can never possibly get his work done. If you try for lesser goals, you can know that you have won or lost. The ethical individual accepts this imperfection as constituting the dignity of his task. This on the ethical side is the "glory of the imperfect" of which Professor Palmer writes. Therefore Kant demands immortality as the opportunity to continue the moral task.

So the kind of knowledge that you get through interpretation insofar as it is attained at all is attained up to a certain date with a problematic degree of completeness, but it doesn't involve finality.[#] Whether the result is your acceptance of some form of absolutism or something else, it is not the assertion that a final form of philosophy has been reached. Righteousness is an entirely inaccessible goal because of the majesty of righteousness. If you want to succeed in life and know that you have succeeded, you had better not try to be righteous. The next five minutes' pleasure can perhaps be got. To be sure, time will remorselessly make away with your five minutes, and therefore this kind of life has an endless failure about it; but this sort of failure differs from the sort of failure that the ethical seeker must face. Hence, one who doesn't understand the value of righteousness asks, "Why do you ask me to undertake such a process?" And so with interpretation.

An interpretation involves something which may be defined in explicitly social terms in this way: There is somebody whose world–winning idea at a given time means an interpretation. The interpreter must address his interpretation to somebody. Then you have something like what appears in the case of an inscription deciphered or interpreted at a later time: the interpretation in order to have meaning must be addressed to somebody, and the question whether it is a correct interpretation involves three questions: (1) what is interpreted; in the case mentioned, an Egyptian inscription; (2) by whom interpreted; (3) to whom interpreted. All this you must have in mind in order to know whether the interpretation is good.[12]

Is an interpretation true? You must know whose idea or what idea was to be interpreted, by whom and for whom it was interpreted. It is addressed by somebody, the interpreter, to somebody. The consequence is that since you always begin with some expression of an idea in the pragmatistic sense, the interpretation of the idea offered by somebody to somebody leads to the same thing with which the process started. If the interpretation is understood by anybody, then you have as the result a new idea.# It is the translation of the original idea to somebody, but his ideas or the expressions of them will just as much need interpretation as what you started with. Therefore the final interpretation of what anybody says can never be found by anybody in finite time. In conversation we always break off with the process unfinished. The process depends upon those same features.

In the case of self-knowledge, my knowledge of myself is never a completed process, just because it is a process of interpretation. I endlessly interpret my past, addressing my future, whenever I use memory to guide and adapt my knowledge to new situations. The process cannot be finished. The effort to get complete self-knowledge is as hopeless as the effort to get the last moment of time. If I were given all the possibilities of insight that could come to me from some other world, and if the self retained the character of an activity to be interpreted, the process of interpretation would be as endless as the process of the ethical life.

It is worthwhile to add just one inevitable aspect of this, which relates to the certainty of the interpretation. As there is no finality in the interpreting process, so there is no finality in the process of seeking for the true interpretation. You will never get it in finite time. Our knowledge on the highest levels involves just this endless search. #

We may attribute the perfect truth to some divine insight, the Deity; but such perfect truth, if it be for God, is not for the interpreters.[CA] They are on the search for it. There are perfectly definite means for correcting a false interpretation such as will lead towards the detection of falsity.#

You have an excellent right for asserting that by the way of interpretation you are on the way towards the truth; but the process of searching for an interpretation is in the nature of the case a process that involves illusion.

Many approach philosophy with the hope that they will find in philosophical method a finality of certitude.# Many have sought this through the discovery of axiomatic truths whose contradiction cannot be conceived. Such "immediate certainty" would be a certainty that couldn't be questioned. It is an important feature in the study of philosophical problems to have in mind the fact that a final certitude and an immediate certainty are equally impossible to any rational being who lives in time.

Immediate certainties we certainly do not possess. This is one of the most salutary and most comforting aspects of our human undertaking. Such truths would have an abruptness and a dogmatic character which one learns to give up with a certain joy. The same may be said about final certainties.

You often meet with that view of mathematical truths which supposes mathematical science to be based upon axioms which you can't possibly question—immediate assurances. Such we used to hear of in the older textbooks, especially in geometry. But what appears to you as an immediate certainty appears so because you don't understand the subject. Immediate assurance is an excellent sign of probable lack of insight into the topic.

Aristotle in his own way insisted upon the acceptance of immediate certainties in order that science should go on at all. # These were the "ἄμεσα," the *immediates*, not to be found by syllogizing. He mentioned the famous *principle of contradiction* as an example: "*A cannot be A and not A at the same time and in the same respects.*" This principle was a typical case of an immediate certainty. But in telling us that that proposition is immediately certain, Aristotle himself gives a *reason* for believing it, a very pretty reason: If a man denies it, he either makes an assertion himself, and any assertion implies the principle of contradiction (my assertion is not the contrary of what it means); but if your opponent who denies the principle will not himself deny the assertion, then he will not speak at all, and you may treat him as you would a plant.

It is important to know that there are no such certainties as that within reach of the human mind. If there were, they wouldn't be of any use to us. As a fact we are always dealing with a process which *ought to be* an endless process and one that cannot be considered if you regard it as having a goal that can be reached.

This is not to speak in terms of skepticism, but in terms of *resolute purpose* to move towards the goal, just as in the case of righteousness. The goal of complete finality of knowledge is a self-contradictory goal for a being who lives in time.

Nov. 18 The work of the inductive sciences continues in a more careful way the work which common sense begins. The whole matter of the logic of induction has been very much influenced in my mind by the logical theories of Charles Peirce, whose papers on this and other topics are now in the hands of my associates.[13] It is possible that they will bring out a book at a later time.

The inevitable doubtfulness of the single instance of interpretation, and the surety of moving in the right direction, are illustrated in the following examples.[CA] There are well-known sources of error in the processes of perception and conception. The process of interpretation in its actual workings is subject, just as all our rational life is, to a constant risk of error. But interpretation can be so guided that one can say with a reasonable assurance that he is on the road towards truth.

In the scientific community, the third element of the triad,[14] the directly inductive investigators complete the process of testing the hypothesis. Any man who carries on a process of scientific induction is himself a triadic community; he is making a hypothesis in terms of which his past experience can be summed up, and he is submitting this hypothesis to test in respect to the conclusions that follow from it. You may say that the process thus characterized is the process that the pragmatists have made so familiar as the process of following out the workings of ideas, seeing whether they work or not, and so it is the process of making use of working hypotheses. One may say, then, as the pragmatists do, that we mean by the truth of an idea its value as tested by its workings, the results to which it actually leads us.

Probability and Truth

What is, however, very defective about James's account of ideas, and that of Dewey's and the Chicago pragmatists', is that one tries to define the conception of truth as consisting in the working of an hypothesis or idea, whereas the conception that is really defined by the process of induction is the conception of probability, one of the profoundest and most problematic conceptions in the whole range of human thought—a conception to whose use the pragmatists have contributed without recognizing what concept they were dealing with.

In saying that the workings of an idea constitute the truth of the idea, one has failed to recognize the fact that the conception actually involved is the conception of probability. If truth belongs to a proposition at all, it belongs to it absolutely and simply. By absolute truth you mean exactly the same thing as you mean by truth. If I say I was in San Francisco yesterday, the statement is and remains absolutely false. In many cases I may be unable to be perfectly sure in my statements about the truth; we are confined to statements based on interpretation. In such cases, however, the fact that we can get only probability at any time is not at all inconsistent with the view that the truth in terms of which we can define our probabilities is an absolute relationship. The realists and the idealists regard this relation in different ways, but in any case the relation undertakes to be an absolute relation. It is absolutely true or false today that I was in San Francisco yesterday. We can define the historical past in terms of propositions that are and remain forever true or false. The conception of probability is the conception that the pragmatists have mistaken for the conception of truth.

I remember verifying this notion of mine by asking my pragmatist friends in Chicago if they were disposed to think that they ought to express as probability that which they were used to express as truth. I found it quite impossible to interest them in the topic of probability. They had never seriously considered it. James never considered the problem of probability except as a quaintly interesting concept. He disliked mathematical concepts, and probability seemed to him an intellectualistic thing.

You live on probability constantly. It is not the case that we so test the truth of a proposition by the workings of the proposition that we can say like James that a proposition is true at a given time when the idea in question works, but ceases to be true when the idea ceases to work. The truth of the proposition doesn't change. It isn't fair to say that because whatever knowledge we have about the structure of the celestial world through astronomical deductions, and because the ancients found the Ptolemaic theory was consistent with their ideas, it was true then, but that when new facts came to light and we gave up the Ptolemaic view, it thereupon ceased to be true. It would be quite wrong to say the Copernican view is true now because it works. That would be to conceive truth as mutable, which is a profoundly illogical position.

It is perfectly correct to say that the probability of a hypothesis, of an opinion, is a very mutable thing. If a man pays insurance on his own life, he pays on the basis of a probability based on the ground of statistics. One defines the amount to be paid in terms of probability. But one deals meanwhile with matters that are either true or false. The mortality tables are correct or incorrect; they possess that character at any and all times; whatever they are, they have that character and keep it, as statistics. On the other hand, the probability which is represented by the price which a man must pay to insure his life alters all the time; conditions alter; he may be uninsurable at any price tomorrow. The price today might be absurd tomorrow; his likelihood of life is changing all the time.

All probabilities are matters that have to do with a peculiar kind of interpretation. In a world of probabilities something is true all the time. It is an absolute truth now that I shall, or shall not, be alive the first of January next. I don't know; and if the question interests anyone who means to insure my life, it is a matter of probability. The probability itself may shift: that is mutable; but the truth remains immutable all the time. I was alive January last; statements about the past are either true or false; that truth will forever remain; nothing will ever alter it; it is irrevocable. But the probability that I was alive on the first of January 1915 may become in various degrees less and less if somebody has reason to make the historical statement. The acceptance of that statement will depend upon evidence which will be probable evidence. What day was it Julius Caesar was assassinated? You can make an estimate which is more or less probable; but your statement is either true or false. Uncertainties beset us in all connections, but they do not mean either mutability or indefiniteness of the predicates true or false. The probability that a given statement is true is estimated from the point of view of the one who estimates it, and is in general very highly mutable.

The whole discussion of the subject has been confused by the inability to distinguish between the meaning of truth and the meaning of certainty. It is often held that if one is a believer in absolute truth, he must be a believer in absolute certainty. {F. C. S.} Schiller holds that any believer in absolute truth must be in the position of one who believes in papal infallibility: if we believe there is an absolute difference between true and false, there is no reason why we shouldn't burn a man at the stake for uttering false propositions. But so to view the matter is to forget that while the uncertainty of human propositions is a good reason why we shouldn't burn men at the stake, the truth or falsity of the statements is not a mutable matter. We deal with probabilities in all matters of life. The methods of getting at such probabilities as we can attain are the methods of deduction and induction.

Deduction

Some propositions can be inferred from other propositions. There are propositions such that we have related statements in pairs so that if proposition "A" is true, proposition "B" is true.

That relation may be a relation about which there is question. All such processes are subject to the errors of computation. It is false to say: In case proposition "B" follows from proposition "A," then from the nature of the case we can be perfectly certain that if "A" is true, "B" is true. That is false because we cannot be certain that the relation in question is correctly judged by us. "If A is true, then B is true" is a relation of deductive inference. If your deductive[CA] process is correct and if the premises are true, then the conclusion is true. But the person who conducts deductive processes is subject to constant danger of error.

Deduction leads you to conclusions that are certain in the sense in which the premises are certain, and deduction gets to a kind of certitude. It is a certitude which is sometimes spoken of as absolute. Mathematics, it is said, deals with absolute certainties. Its processes are essentially deductive, it deals with necessary conclusions; it is concerned with truths which are in themselves absolute in case they are truths at all. The correctness of the multiplication table as it stands printed in a book is absolute if it is correct at all: 5×7 cannot be 35 today and 36 tomorrow. At the same time we all know that computations which use the multiplication table have always in practice some uncertainty about them. The best you can do in your computations—for example, a bookkeeper's balance—is to get probably true results, although you are dealing with relations which are in themselves immutable. Computing involves a process of interpretation.

The modern standard mathematical tables have been subjected to a scrutiny which makes the probability of error extremely small. The earlier tables of logarithms had a good many errors in them. Those errors have been gradually weeded out, and it is extremely likely that every figure in a well-edited table will be correct; but there is nothing that can be said to be known to be absolutely true. It is only very highly probable that they are accurate. The whole process is progressive. But there is nothing mutable about what is the logarithm of 2 according to the usually assumed base of logarithms.

A believer in absolute truth is not a believer in absolute certainty, if by absolute certainty you mean certainty on the part of a human being. Such a being never gets absolute certainty. # From the very nature of his process he cannot do it. Probably it is absolutely true that a being who lives in time is never going to get absolute truth. If he says it is "immediately certain," it is highly probable that he doesn't understand the subject then in question.

A generation ago almost any philosopher who was interested in the absolute certainty of propositions would tell you that it is self-evidently true that things equal to the same thing are equal to each other. But alas, modern logic has shown that the axiom in question has rather the property of being a convenient <u>definition</u> of certain <u>kinds</u> of equality. The person who cites the axiom as absolutely true has probably not faced the question of what he means by equality. The application of it might lead to error: if A and B play even in a certain way, and B and C play even, A and C may not play even at all. Probably few general statements have done more to confuse the minds of students of {those} complex relationships which can be defined in some form of equality than this essentially confused axiom.

Certainty is not truth. We may be dealing with absolute truths and not be certain that we are dealing with absolute truths.

Induction

Everybody admits that in a greater part of our scientific thinking today we deal with inductions and not deductions. These processes go hand in hand, but a considerable part of our work is of the inductive nature. What guides us in our inductions?

Men, so far as the records go, have always been dying; so one gets inductively the principle, "All men are mortal." The sun has repeatedly risen once in twenty-four hours; inductively one concludes that the sun will rise tomorrow. These inductions are admitted to be probable, but they are based on the principle of the uniformity of nature—what has happened is likely to be repeated. If A has always been B, it is probable that A will always be B. It is not asserted that the conclusion is necessary. Inductions are well enough exemplified by the fact that they depend upon some such principle as the uniformity of nature.

Bertrand Russell, in his *Problems of Philosophy,*[15] abandons the method of regarding the principle of induction itself as a certainty. He says it is a principle which one may regard as simply actually used. He gives it to you in this way: If a large number of instances are known where A has proved to be B, and if no case has been found in which A is not B, then the more frequently A has been known to be B, the more probable it is that all A's are B.

Russell told me that he had taken interest in the topic of probability and recognized its importance. Probability seemed to him an undefinable quality of propositions. In place of "self-evident," the new realists are fond of substituting the word "primitive" or "undefinable." Russell would say simply, "I have no grounds for this principle of induction; but we use it; and it is easy to show (again inductively) that the sciences always use it."

If all swans have so far been found white—this is Russell's instance of induction—it becomes more and more probable that all swans are white. But it turns out that there are black swans. "Well," says Russell, "it turns out to be a false proposition; but all the time until black swans were found it was becoming more and more probable that all swans were white." The probability for Russell increases with the number of instances. I urged on Russell the very obvious objection that if this were the case, and if a man who had seen only white swans wanted to be as sure as he could be that all swans were white, his most convenient method for making the proposition more and more probable would be to breed white swans in great numbers. But as a matter of fact, such breeding would increase the probability that the whiteness of swans is a hereditary character.

The way in which black swans were found was by looking elsewhere for them. Not intentionally, they were found by a Dutch navigator in South Australia at Swan River. The proper method of testing the induction would not be to multiply your opportunities to see white swans, but to search all over the field. We cannot accept Russell's account of the inductive principle. The mere increase in the number of observations of white swans does not increase the probability of the induction. All inductive arguments deal with probability. What is this probability, and where does it appear?

Nov. 20 Russell's instance of white swans is unfortunate for him. In a good many cases we do generalize with a sense of increasing probability due to the accumulation of observed instances. But in natural history other considerations are more important. There are cases where a crucial experiment may be a warrant for a generalization. You could keep looking in the Northern Hemisphere as long as you liked and find only white swans. The induction would succeed uncommonly well up to a certain point, and then become no longer applicable when the black swans appeared.

It is wrong to suppose that induction is usually or principally concerned with probable generalizations. One common account of the induction process has been of that nature. Inductive reasoning, it is said, passes from the less general to the more general—of course, with probability only. Its road is from the particular towards the universal, they say. On the other hand, deduction passes from the more general towards the less general; the syllogism begins with a very general premise and then finds a case that falls[CA] under it. The conclusion is true if the premises are true. In contrast, the conclusion of the inductive reasoning is more general than the premises. But it is not at all characteristic of induction that the conclusion should be any more general than the premises. Often the conclusion is about a supposed or known individual thing, especially about an unknown character of an otherwise known and individual object. There is then no question of generalization at all. One doesn't get the conclusion, "All A's are B," but that this object has this previously unknown character.

That is peculiarly the case in historical inductions, or in those sciences which are concerned with the individual past. Induction has some of its most significant instances where one is concerned with an individual fact altogether. We use induction especially in our interpretations of a social sort. They are assertions about beings or events that we suppose to be individual. Histories are largely made up of assertions about what are supposed to be individual beings or events, and most such assertions are the result of inductions, only probably true, and characterized by the absence of any attempt to generalize. The historian is reasoning about the probability of the occurrence of certain events, say at the battle of Waterloo.

Two regions of study are full of examples of this kind of induction. Histories, including biographies, are accounts of individual events which are at best only probably true. The items are sums of money and such particulars; the data historical; the means are records, the reasoning inductive. Again, dynamic geology is interested in generalizations; but descriptive geology is akin to geography: one deals with historical events which are particular.

There is a curious contrast between the sort of reasoning here concerned and the sort of induction which Russell had in mind in his account of the inductive process.

[Here Royce discussed at length the inductive reasoning connected with Schliemann's excavations at "Troy."] If nature has followed the usual course without the interference of demons, and if nobody has interfered with the hill, {and} if the Trojan war story is in its general outlines true, then if I dig in yonder hill, I shall find the ruins of a city. He dug and found the ruins of a burned city. He found such treasures as the stories indicated. Conclusion: the story has probably a good deal of truth about it. No generalizations are involved in the conclusion. You see what makes the conclusion a probable one: the chances of my finding in yonder hill what I predict grow smaller in proportion as I increase the individual detail of my assertion.

The legends about Minos and the labyrinth at Crete are obviously fairy stories. Here we have (1) a story; (2) an interpretation in the form of a hypothesis that if there is truth in the story, then certain things will be found by digging; (3) agreement between the prediction and the "find." There isn't any generalization, there is an immensely persuasive crucial test.

The inductive method depends on assuming an hypothesis, testing it by an experiment, and thence concluding a probability. The method used in such cases is well-known and it is always to the popular mind an impressive method. The kind of impressiveness that it has is easily illustrated. *Nov. 22*

When eclipse expeditions visited remote places where the coming of the eclipse and the laws of astronomy were unknown, the verification of the power of the astronomers to predict phenomena seemed almost magical. The motive of the expedition is not to find out whether the methods of science are sound, but to observe certain phenomena which could not be predicted—the state of things in the solar corona, etc. At present enough has been seen of these phenomena, and the habit of sending such expeditions has fallen a good deal into disuse. One went to an island in the sea and informed the natives that the sun was to be darkened. The natives had their ideas about eclipses, and would regard the phenomena as having a supernatural background. The astronomers could set the hour and tell just when the spot would appear on the edge of the sun. The phenomena occur as predicted; the sun is wiped out for two, three or six minutes with the sight of the corona, etc.

Observe that there is no antecedent likelihood that if a man makes at random a prediction of the occurrence of an eclipse at a certain moment, the eclipse will occur. On the basis of common information, even the prediction "I shall live to see a total solar eclipse" is probably wrong. Hence, the assertion "The sun will be totally eclipsed at a certain moment at a stated place" is a highly improbable statement. As a fact, a total eclipse couldn't occur except at the time when the moon is on a line between the sun and the earth, and very seldom then. But this statement is made by the astronomer on the ground of the knowledge which he has about the heavens and their ways. The eclipse occurs according to the precise prediction. Conclusion: it is probable that the general information which the astronomer has about the heavens and their ways is true. Here you have (1) general knowledge; (2) particular prediction made on the basis of the general knowledge; (3) the outcome as predicted. Conclusion: the general knowledge is highly probable. The kind of information upon which such arguments are based is very unlike the kind of information that Russell insisted upon in the white swan instance.

Science is still in a position where we can't deal with weather prediction any better than Russell wanted to deal with the white swan case. About 70 percent of the weather predictions are true. The conclusion that in view of this a weather prediction taken at random is likely in that proportion to be true is a matter of probability.

In the case of the eclipse prediction there is more detail. They can tell, not with absolute accuracy, but within a very few seconds, the moment of totality at a given point. The moon of theory doesn't precisely agree with the moon of observation. Precise conformity of the moon to the Newtonian law of gravitation can never be completely discovered. No observation can make that law perfectly true. The conclusion that we get in such cases is that the probability that the laws are correct is very great.

Observe what the process involved is. You have (1) a hypothesis "H" with which you are dealing, and which is to be tested; (2) consequences, computable deductively: if "H" is true, then p, q, r, etc. are such consequences; (3) a fair sample of p, q, r, etc., are tested, and are found true. Conclusion: "H" is (probably and approximately) true. If fair samples are tested, the probability increases very rapidly that "H" is approximately true with the observations of p, q, r, etc. multiplied. All of the physical sciences get that kind of verification. That is why the pragmatic account of the thing is imperfect: the prominence of the probable and approximate is not accounted for in James's account. He hasn't laid stress on the fact that it isn't a question of defining truth in terms of workings, but a question of the degree of probability that the hypothesis is approximately true, in terms of the actual observations.

The process is essentially triadic. What I call the community of science is a community of interpretation consisting of the people that make the hypotheses, the people that put them to test, and the people that deal directly with the facts in terms of which the tests are defined.

It is not the characteristic of induction that it generalizes, but that it reaches the probability of probable and approximate hypotheses. The hypothesis isn't found to be approximately true, but probably approximately true; and the degree of probability and the degree of approximation constantly improve as "induction proper" succeeds.

The moon either does or does not follow the laws of gravitation. But from the nature of the case, the Newtonian law is committed to too fine an assertion about the movements of the bodies to be ever completely verified. It is a numerical hypothesis, and it is too exact to be verified completely by any finite observation. It would involve knowing whether some precise value of an irrational fraction is the value represented by physical quantities.

What happens is that consequences are computed and the computations are discovered to be approximately correct. The probability increases very rapidly with the increasing observations, providing only fair samples are taken.

A scientist like Professor Davis studying the detail of the Connecticut valley with reference to its geological past faces very different conditions. The sequence in which geological events had taken place was in question. What order of the laying down of the strata would explain the formations? What has happened here? After collecting much data by observation, he hit upon a theory of how the formations might have occurred, and from that hypothesis he then proceeded to compute consequences like p, q, and r. There was no probability that any of the propositions p, q, and r were true; the more unlikely they were, the better they were for the purpose: they were fair samples. They had to be worked out deductively. If "H" is correct, then yonder beneath the surface you will find consequences p, q, r. Davis could say to a farmer, "If you will dig a well 30 feet deep in such a spot, you will find certain fossils of a specific sort." And so it would turn out.

In this case you had an unlikely individual fact. That is a typical instance of interpretation. The process of getting at the facts involves the formation and testing of the interpretation of the facts. The total of what we call the inductive method consists of these three elements: (1) a retroduction, or abduction, leads to the formation of "H," the hypothesis to be tested; (2) a process of deduction leads to finding what is probably true if "H" is true. The more such consequences you get, the better, especially if they are consequences otherwise apparently independent and if you have no other reason at the moment besides the hypothesis "H" for believing them true; (3) verification by "induction proper," as Peirce calls it, which depends on testing a fair sample of the consequences of the hypothesis.

The general principle: That which is antecedently predicted when it is unlikely makes probable the basis of the prediction; and with a rapid increase {of predictive success, the probability increases} in proportion as that which is predicted was antecedently unlikely and independent of other knowledge than the hypothesis in question.

In the progressive sciences these processes are left to (1) inventors of hypotheses; (2) deductive theorizers; (3) those who make the inductive tests and specific observations.

You may get a generalization, but you may be dealing throughout with individual facts.

Nov. 27 I have illustrated both the logic and the epistemology of induction. The kind of knowledge that we have of the truths which are reached by the methods of science is essentially a knowledge which includes interpretation. It involves ideas and the kind of synthesis of percepts and concepts that any ideal leading involves. According to the pragmatists, what we know through the working of our ideas is that our ideas work and are insofar *true*. But the fairer view would hold that an induction is of course an interpretation of collected experience in the light of a hypothesis, and by virtue of the actual confirmation of the hypothesis to which the previous experience has led a truth is defined which you can characterize not merely in perceptual terms by reference to working, for it was antecedently probable before the test that the hypothesis would not work. With Peirce's theory of interpretation, and with the theory of induction, one uses at every moment the idea of a truth which is *simply true*, and not at some moments true and at some moments false. Truth is itself absolute; the inductive interpretation is expressed in the form of a probability. The conclusion of the induction is, "Therefore it is probable that the absolute truth is so and so."

There is also a common type of inductions whose essence it is to generalize: "All swans are white." When our business is generalization, then the whole process assumes another form which Peirce calls the *inductive syllogism*. There the reasoning is of this sort: A, B, C, etc., have the character M; but A, B, etc., are fair samples of some large class of objects; therefore, it is probable that the objects belonging to this class in general possess in a large number of cases the character M. The generalizing induction depends upon taking fair samples and judging the whole by the samples. If you want to know whether swans possess a certain color, the reasoning depends on taking a certain number of swans and observing their color. The minor premise runs: "The swans that we have taken are a fair sample of swans." The major premise is: "This, this, this swan is white." The conclusion as Peirce would state it: "Probably a proportion that is approximately the whole of swans will be white."

Samples would have to be taken such that there would be no reason to expect that all of them would be white unless they indeed represent the law of all the swans. The constant use of samples in the *market place* illustrates our usual methods of generalization.

Application of this to the process by which we know about the community: So surely as I have a knowledge of myself, there are in the world selves that are not identical with me. Certain signs come to me which I interpret {as}[CA] suggestions of ideas, some of them in such contrast with my ideas that

I simply disclaim them, "These ideas are not mine." These ideas give you a knowledge of reality which is neither perceptual nor conceptual. Here is my foundation for the interpretation that there are ideas in the world which are not my own. To have any idea about yourself is to know that you have a neighbor. The mere presence of intelligible ideas of your own is the beginning of a knowledge of the *alter.* Every idea is a partial expression of a plan, and all that you mean by your self[CA] is a life lived according to a plan. If there appear life activities, ideas, not your own, then they are as such ideas of an *alter.* The hypothesis "I am not the only self in the world" requires me to define what I mean by myself. I find within my own life a triplicity of present, past, and future selves; and still more, if my account of myself is an intelligible account, it is of a being who responds to communication with companions.

If I see USE NO WATER written on a blackboard, a mind not my own is expressing itself. This intrusive idea calls upon me to bring it into coherence with my own meanings, to explain or reduce the antithesis with all ideas which I now recognize as my own. If somebody else thought this and meant something by it, then what he meant would have some intelligible connection with the rest of his ideas. What did he mean by it? Hereupon one may use all sorts of analogies and hypotheses: Under what sorts of circumstances do I say to myself, USE NO WATER? The process of making hypotheses goes on until you find a coherent meaning in the intrusive idea. In this case there was sizing in the blackboard which water would injure.

Those who decipher inscriptions or ciphers make hypotheses about how certain signs are used, which hypotheses are verified by a coherent meaning.

In a conversation, the other man gives you signals. You the interpreter thereupon set forth your interpretation in a response which represents another idea coherent with it. This goes on endlessly. If the signs don't suggest to me any interpretation, I say I don't understand the man at all. The purpose of the conversation has failed. He is a barbarian to me, or I to him. But if the conversation becomes fluent, then each step coheres as well as we could expect with the previous ideas expressed. Each says to the other, "I follow you." The process is everywhere dual in that there are two people concerned, but it is triadic so far as means are suggested which make the ideas of the two cohere.

The beings whom we interpret as constituting mutually contrasting but mutually coherent lives can, and in a large number of social relations do, cohere with each other in such wise that the whole process has the rhythm of the life of a self with a present, past, and future, whose meanings and purposes have at any one time a more or less intelligible coherence. My assertion that communities are real is simply that they have the same kind of coherence that individual men have. Any man has at least a multiplicity of past, present, and future selves. A rationally cooperating group is then of the nature of a self. The facts which occur there are exactly the same facts that illustrate your idea of your self.

Nov. 29^{U} [Here Royce read from his account of Meister Eckhart in *Studies* of *Good* and *Evil*, pages 261–97, making a few comments as he read.]

Bergson seems to be a mystic with knowledge of the self. The genuine mystics have often put their views into this essentially paradoxical expression that the true knower does not express himself at all. As one Oriental mystic puts it, "Believe not those prattlers who tell you they know God; he who knows him is silent." Notice Eckhart, "When I come into the presence of God, I form no idea."

From Hegel's point of view, any man with desires of his own finds himself unable to express himself alone; he needs a neighbor with whom he is in some sort of contrast. This contrast is primarily contradiction; so the primal state of man is that of universal warfare. {Notice} the "dangerous pair." Then comes synthesis where they end their fight.[CA]

But the triad of my triadic relation is not the Hegelian triad because when a man cannot sell his house but can sell it through an agent, he is not at war with himself.

Dec. 2^{U} In the two volumes of *The Problem of Christianity* this metaphysical side is especially emphasized in the theory of the community.[16] The thesis of Idealism is defined as a thesis that the world is a community. Note the difference between this definition and certain others. You will easily see a certain contrast suggested—a contrast between the world as a community and a world as a self, or that the Absolute has the nature of an ego.

So far as mere exposition is concerned, the exposition of that idea of reality has met with opposition which I regard as opposition due to misunderstanding. This will not take the same form if you approach the question from the distinctly social side, as is done in defining metaphysics in the second volume of *The Problem of Christianity.*

{Having examined the social nature of knowledge as found in interpretation, the next need is to study the social nature of truth.}

Chapter 3

The Social Theory of Truth

Dec. 2[U] cont.

I shall try to show you that the idea of truth is essentially a social idea. There is, of course, the idea that a man can define by himself; a man therefore can think of truth by himself alone, but, even though he tries to do that, the distinction between my past and my future self must be recognized. This is a fact which has a very interesting relation. When you make a judgment, you, as a fact, appeal ideally or literally to somebody. When you assert that a proposition is true, you are actually making an appeal to somebody. The one to whom you make your appeal may be the social order to which you belong. When unable to say that a proposition is true, without making an assertion as to how the thing would appear from a point of view other than that which I now have, I make an appeal to somebody to validate it.

The meaningless ideas cannot be true. In order to possess truth you have to be intelligible. Intelligibility implies a quasi reference, an ideal reference, to the intelligibility of something else. When I suppose my words to be an expression of ideas that are intelligible, that intelligibility has no meaning, unless there are at least possible hearers to whom my words would be intelligible. Absolutely lonely intelligibility is a contradiction. Thus when we assert a truth as true we appeal to somebody else. Thus the idea of truth has this social character.

The idea of reality has, in another way, a social character that is well evidenced in our ideas of physical reality. Suppose a man told me that he was acquainted with a physical object but that this physical object had this peculiar character which only he could verify, and that he possessed some sort of knowledge—call it perceptual or conceptual, for that matter. If he put the case in that way, I should observe that that object had all the character of a dream object. Somebody has a dream; the dream is an experience whose objects are not physical objects. If, on the other hand, the dream world turned into another kind of a world, if these dreams could enter into distinctly social relations of mutual comparison, it would have the nature of our physical world. It is essential to a physical object that it can be appealed to in a social way. Heraclitus noticed this early. He pointed out that when we dream each one turns aside into his own world but when we wake we have a world in common. The reality which belongs to the physical world is a social kind of reality.

The blackboard has a character of social reality. It belongs to the character that makes the physical world what it is for us. There are other kinds of social relations concerning other special sorts of realities. The physical realities have a character of being viewed by us as at least possibly social. The real has to be viewed as at least possibly verifiable by more than one individual.

This is a fundamental reason why no rational being has ever held as a philosophy the doctrine of solipsism—that I am the only real being—even though it has often been played with. The doctrine of solipsism has never been expressed as a rational coherent sort of philosophy; for one would refute it by expressing it. One who held that doctrine would be saying that something was true and would thus be appealing to somebody other than himself.[CA]

For a similar reason, that is why the persons whom I have sketched for you—the mystics—are in a peculiar contradictory position. They are in the position of the solipsist very much; for they abandon social relations. When the mystic approaches his goal, all vanishes. The real is indeed for him a world which loses reality.

Reality is a concept involving interpretation. The world is the interpreter of my problems. The universe contains its own interpreter or is its own interpreter. Thus I have sketched for you the way in which, when we revise our metaphysical ideas, we get a view of metaphysics which has been summed up in the way which I have indicated. This idealism is rather different from the idealism which many of the opponents of idealism have in mind.

Professor Perry has laid stress on a very valuable proposition—the proposition of the egocentric predicament. He has pointed out that the idealism that he regards as the characteristic idealism is due to a false interpretation of, and a false emphasis upon, the egocentric predicament. The type of idealism which he criticizes seems to appeal to this notion: that when I imagine any entity, I can observe that I myself am ideally present along with this object as the supposed knower of it; so that, whenever I try to conceive my world, I am at the center of it. My ideas are viewed as essential to asserting that that world is.

The situation is that which you can observe also in the field of vision. You find the world that you see centered about the ridge of your nose. Of course we observe that this is not an important thing to note about the field of vision. What one wants to know is what the world would be if he were not observing it. Therefore Professor Perry observes that of the two opposed entities—of these two in knowledge where it is at all normal—the entity called the world has much greater importance. While the egocentric predicament always exists, still it has small importance for the discoveries about the world. The "I" then, according to Professor Perry, counts very little as against what is known. Thus knowledge, according to Professor Perry, is a sort of commerce between two sorts of objects. The world on the one hand determines this knowledge and doesn't need his knowledge to exist. To think one's self out of the real world is the normal realistic position. But observe that, in the view of reality that I am suggesting to you, the problem is somewhat different from the position that Professor Perry implies.

Take the case of the physical object. It is essential that that should be our common object. We have the world in common. Now the truth of the assertion that we know the same objects is a truth that requires a good deal of analysis. But it is a truth that is certainly not asserted by one who lays stress only on the egocentric predicament. Hence, there is presupposed not the duality which Professor Perry implies, but a triadic aspect. It is, of course, of decided concern as to what the world would be if the individual self were outside of it. Of course, we are constantly abstracting the subjective as opposed to the objective side of it. The situation is not dualistic, however; it is not a commerce between two entities, but it is always a question about[CA] the relation between at least two knowers and a reality.

Of course, our metaphysic will always be an interpretation. I suggest merely that the doctrine that Professor Perry dreads is decidedly different from that which a social view of metaphysics can give you. For the being which I ascribe to my neighbor is not the being as it appears to me. Of the two—my social world or myself—there are many ways in which you can say it is the former—my social order—that has a higher degree of significance.

Read the lectures in the second volume of *The Problem of Christianity.* Read the chapter, "The Possibility of Error," in *The Religious Aspect of Philosophy.* That chapter constitutes the first statement that I ever gave to my own form of idealism. In that text occurs the expression that my affirmation of the truth of my belief in some assertion is an appeal to a standard view about the matter concerning which I am making an assertion.[CA] This doctrine is essentially triadic. Also consult *The World and the Individual* and make comparisons with James's *Pragmatism* and *Radical Empiricism.*

In my volume entitled *William James and Other Essays*, you will find *Dec. 4*
one essay entitled "The Problem of Truth in the Light of Recent Discussion," originally delivered as a lecture at Heidelberg in 1908. James died in 1910. F. C. S. Schiller of Oxford took part in the discussion, but neither James nor Bergson was present. There was a statement of the principles of pragmatism and a heated discussion followed. This essay is an amplification of what I said there.

All James said by way of criticism of this essay was that he thought it more connected and effectively put together than most of my things, but could not accept it in the least as a correction. In it I mention that the ideas of truth and reality are essentially interpretative ideas, depending upon interpretations.

For a rational being unaware of his past and future and of his fellow beings—no matter how intelligent he was and how clearly he could conceive his propositions—there would be no idea of truth. He would have no way of defining what is meant by truth. He wouldn't have any such idea of truth as that which guides our own thinking, and he would have no use for the distinction between reality and appearance. He would be making assertions about objects, but there would be no meaning in calling them real.

The social aspect is actually inherent in our daily judgments about physical reality. A nature-object that nobody else can observe is no nature-object. To say that this object exists for me only, is to say that this is not a physical object. Heraclitus first mentioned this character of physical reality, which distinguishes it from the dream world: If the object is common, it is of the waking world. It has a community reality.

In my *Studies of Good and Evil,* you will find an essay with the title "Self-consciousness, Social Consciousness and Nature" which bears on this. When we define and make explicit our ideas of truth, we make explicit our idea of its social character.

The Reflective Method as Interpretation

This {procedure} can be brought out in an entirely impersonal way, by an illustration furnished by mathematics. I call it the reflective method. You will find it actually used in the exact sciences where deduction is the principal method employed. Its essence depends upon decidedly impersonal considerations which no longer appear social. I refer to the case where one tests the truth of an assertion by comparing it with another assertion by means of a third assertion or conceptual construction—{as in the} *reductio ad absurdum.*

There are certain relations between propositions which are very fundamental for a logician. One of these is expressed by the verb "implies." It is the illative relation. If all men are mortal, then no immortals are men. One of those propositions implies the other. It is the kind of relation which you express by if and a consequent. It is the relation between the antecedent and the consequent of a hypothetical proposition. It is called the illative relation because it is the one you use when you make an inference (Lat. *inferre, illlatus*). In the syllogism you infer a conclusion from two premises. If all men are mortal, and all the professors are men, then it follows from those two premises together that all the professors are mortal. Here you lay no stress on any sort of triadic relation: the two premises together form a pair which when taken in unity will permit you to infer the conclusion. This is a dual relation expressed by the word "illative."

Let me show you how that relation can be made use of to test the truth of a proposition, although the circumstances are very special under which the test can be employed. Propositions go in pairs. To every proposition, true or not, there always corresponds its contradictory. It is useless to say that there are some propositions whose contradictory is not conceivable. Unless one knew what the contradictory meant, he couldn't understand the proposition at all. You may reject its contradictory and think it false, but you can always conceive it. Now if M implies not-M, M is false in the sense of being self-contradictory—you give yourself the lie; you imply that what you say is false. Or if not-M implies M, then not-M is self-contradictory and M is true. In the previous case, not-M was true. Any proposition stands in the illative relation to itself (M implies M), but every proposition has its contradictory (not-M). The *reductio ad absurdum* is the proof that a proposition implies its own contradictory and is therefore false. Or you can take it the other way and show that the contradictory is absurd and therefore the proposition is true.

A very interesting case of this was found out quite early in the history of the theory of numbers. The prime numbers are very frequent in the first hundred; but as they come, they also determine their products; so, the prime numbers grow more and more sparse. Isn't there a last prime number so big that the previous primes as factors will determine all future numbers? Euclid gives you a proof that the proposition "There is a last prime number" implies its own contradiction. He also gives it to you in the form of showing that the contradictory of the proposition "There is no last prime number" contradicts itself.

Suppose there were a last prime number P such that all whole numbers after it would be multiples of previous primes. But then there would be a whole number that you could get by taking the product of 2, 3, 5, 7 . . . and P. Call that product X. If X exists, there is a number X plus 1, which is prime, because if you try any factor you will always have 1 {as a} remainder. Thus if P is the last prime number, P isn't the last prime number. You imply that there is also a prime number X plus 1. This comes out by what you can call an interpretation. The construction mediates between the proposition and its contradictory. This is an example of the reflective method.

There are many propositions such that when they are set side by side with their contradictories, nobody can see by direct inspection anything self-contradictory in either. There must be in such cases a third proposition or construction such that it stands as an interpreter or mediator of one proposition to the other. This is illustrated in the proposition, "There is a last prime number" and "There is no last prime number." You can't tell by direct inspection which of these propositions is true. To find whether a given number is prime, you must *Dec. 7* try the factors, by what you may call an "exhaustive induction." There are certain general rules which help you in the case of certain factors; and there is a plan for forming the <u>sieve</u> of numbers, by taking the primes as factors and striking out from the table of numbers the multiples which have been thus far found by taking the previous primes as factors. The primes have been computed until the twelfth or thirteenth million. The number of primes per million diminishes according to no particular rule. Nobody can see by direct inspection any reason why the proposition, "There is a last prime number," should be false. The Greeks hit upon the method of showing <u>mediately</u> that the proposition is false. The proposition used as a mediator is this: "Any set of numbers which has a last member has a product"; and also "Every number has a successor."

Another case of the same process. Either Pythagoras or some early member of his school is responsible for this theorem. The comparison of <u>lengths</u> brings us to the problem of incommensurability. We always find two lengths in terms of a common measure; but the diagonal and the side of a square are incommensurate by any considerable unit.

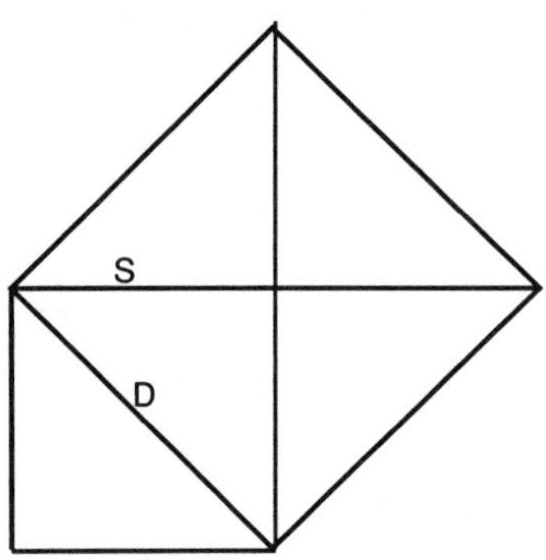

If D is even, let D = 2n
.'. $4n^2 = 2S^2$
.'. $S^2 = 2n^2$
.'. $2n^2$ is even
.'. S^2 is even[CA]
.'. S is even
.'. D is odd

$D^2 = 2S^2$
.'. D^2 is even
.'. D is even ------------------ .'. D is odd
(.'. S is odd)

If there were a common measure, then there would be a pair of whole numbers D and S such that, if you used this common measure, the length of the diagonal would be represented by the whole number D times the common measure, while the length of the side would be measured by the whole number S times the common measure. But both D and S would be <u>even</u> numbers or <u>odd</u> numbers.[CA] For if there were any common measure, it would be possible to choose {another lesser} D and {another lesser} S such that they would have no common factor: then if one[CA] of them was even, the other would have to be odd; {otherwise they would have a common measure}. The squares of odd numbers are odd and of even numbers even.[1] {Hence, in the above columns, by starting downward from the left column's $D^2 = 2S^2$—the result of applying the Pythagorean theorem to an isosceles right triangle—Royce uses *reductio ad absurdum* to show that D and S cannot have a common measure.}

Therefore, there is no such pair of whole numbers, and the diagonal and the side have no common measure.

The Definition of Truth in its Relation to Interpretation.

Dec. 8

If you consider merely the state of mind of a person who expresses an opinion, you can hardly mention anything so absurd that somebody isn't certain that the judgment is self-evidently true. On the other hand, you can hardly find an assertion that is so accurately an expression of truth that you can't also find a person who regards that assertion as absurd.

The absurd may be believed to be true in mathematics, as in the case of the proposition that there is a last prime number, or that there are not two lines which have no common unit. So with the notion that the earth is a plane.

I regard the truth of a judgment as something which is distinct from whether it feels sure to me. One makes a difference between the truth of a judgment as "somewhat" objective and as "somewhat" which one may correctly or incorrectly appreciate. Our whole theory of truth depends upon our making some difference between our state of mind and the truth.

A man often says, "This is so and I know it: I shall be elected; I know it; I feel it in my bones." Afterwards, if he wasn't elected, he has to revise his former expression: "I thought I knew it, but I didn't. I took it to be knowledge but it wasn't knowledge." Then of course the question arises: If you knew it, how is it that it wasn't true? If you didn't know it, how is it that you were sure?

This is the puzzle which James regarded as solved by driving all the difficulties together in one place. He assigns the relations between certainty and truth so that the difficulties are all left for truth, while certainty is taken care of by present experience, which puts you in possession of the living truth. But such truth shifts and is mutable, and the question may well come to mind: Does the effort to put all the difficulties on the shoulder of truth really aid us in our theory of knowledge? You "know" so many things that aren't so, and subjective certainty often runs counter to the truth. Must we not expect to recognize that distinction? I shall insist that truth and certainty may be at any point far apart.# It isn't the purpose of philosophy mainly to produce a subjective certainty. When we seek the truth, we do not mainly seek confidence.

We need a definition of an objective truth which is distinct from the certainty of anyone who at a given time makes a judgment. The neorealists agree with this. The relation between a true and a false proposition is an immutable relation. The same proposition would be always true or false. This for the neo-realist goes along with the correspondence view of truth. According to the neo-realists, you must recognize the subjective meanings of those who assert propositions, that is, judgments on the one hand and objects on the other. Judgments are what they mean; facts are what they are. Truth is a relation between judgments and objects, between a judgment and a fact. The truth-relation is conceived as immutable, though possibly in a given case inaccessible. The relation which constitutes truth is a relation between judgment and fact.

According to pragmatism, truth is fluent; according to neo-realism, it is not. So far I agree with neo-realism as to truth; but its account is inadequate, as we shall see.

The Social Aspect of the Consciousness of Truth.

Dec. 11 In general, I get practically no response to this contention of mine as to the social nature of truth.[2] Russell, in {Chapter 12 of} his *Problems of Philosophy,*[3] states a problem about the nature of the truth of a belief. He mentions two or three different views about truth and the objections that arise about them, and then gives his own adherence to another view. The substance of his position in that chapter is that a theory of truth must permit of possible errors. Since beliefs expressed in judgments go in pairs, to any judgment there always stands opposed its contradictory. Corresponding to every true belief there is a false belief, whether anybody holds it or not. Any theory of truth must recognize this possibility. Furthermore, a theory of truth must distinguish between the belief and its object; and for Russell the problem arises, how is a true belief related to its object?

First Russell discusses the coherence theory. Although beliefs are related to objects, the coherence theory holds that the truth of beliefs depends on the attainment of coherence with other beliefs. The tests of truth are internal. The complete expression of the meaning of an assertion would involve the attainment of a coherent system of belief which would in the end, by virtue of its exhaustive coherence, be true. In Joachim you find stress laid on such a theory. Russell holds it can't be successful. Beliefs may be coherent and form a very considerable system without being true at all.

{In} the correspondence theory, Russell himself defines a form of the correspondence theory, which declares that the truth of a belief lies in its correspondence to its object. He points out that, in its simpler forms, the correspondence theory is open to objections. If the object of my belief is the existence of Achilles, or if I believe that you are a real being, the truth of my belief would be the fact that my belief corresponds to reality. Untrue beliefs would be untrue because there is no such object as the belief sets forth; but as the object of the {untrue} belief is nothing, what does it mean to say that beliefs are not true if they correspond to nothing? Russell's opinion is that a simple form of the correspondence theory will fail. One must consider the nature of the object of belief, and explain false beliefs such as you get on Othello's part in the situation between Desdemona and Cassio.[CA] A true belief involves a certain correspondence with a particular object having a relational structure; in this case the relation is that of love between Desdemona and Cassio. The truth of the belief lies in the question whether there is in the world a complex arranged in the same order as the ideal terms of the belief. In that form Russell himself maintains a correspondence theory of truth. He says if there are in the world certain complexes related in the same way in which the beliefs relate the corresponding ideas, if to certain ideal relations there correspond in the world complexes of reals related in the same order, then the belief is true.

The theory of truth which I oppose to Russell's theory depends upon another aspect of the situation. If a man asserts something to be true, it is very generally the case that he is thinking of some sort of correspondence between an idea and an object. The one who has a doctrine about the world or any object in it, has something which so far as his beliefs are coherent can be set forth as a portrayal of this object, a portrayal which expresses something intelligible to the man who holds the belief. If his belief is clear, it becomes explicit to him. When he says "I believe there exists such and such an object" he is indeed thus interested in some sort of correspondence which includes a resemblance between idea and object. In the real world there is an object which has certain characters which the belief portrays in certain aspects. So, in general, portrayal does enter in. To say that such and such an object is real is to say that to my ideas there correspond certain objects which the belief resembles in some sense or other. So far so good.

But now we come to the critical and neglected thing that I cannot get people interested in. If I have supposed that there is a lion in the corridor and go out and see there isn't any lion there—if my belief about the weather proves false—I not only recognize a noncorrespondence between the belief and the object. I not only declare that a certain correspondence is not present. What I say when I say my belief was a false belief is not merely that I don't find an object corresponding to my belief, but that I don't find a certain object in a certain time and place which my belief had intended. My belief is false only if there aren't lions where I had supposed them to be. There is required not only "correspondence" but the correspondence in question must be the particular correspondence which I myself had actually intended as that upon which I stated my case. There must be the aim of the believer, or there is neither truth nor falsity. The belief is required to possess a specific correspondence to some determinate object. It is this, over and above correspondence, which is in question.

Beliefs are in the position of the acts of a marksman: if there was no aiming, there was neither hitting nor missing. No mere study of the gunshot or the target will tell you whether there was a hit or a miss; there must be knowledge of the intention of the shot. Everybody hits something when he shoots into the air at random.

My judgment is true not merely by virtue of correspondence to some object but by virtue of a specific correspondence to an intended object. If no object was intended, then the judgment has neither truth nor falsity, and no definite meaning at all.

The truth of a belief depends in general upon two factors:

1. Consider the belief and the object. If the belief is to be true there must be a certain correspondence, whatever it is, between a certain relational structure belonging to the belief and a relational structure in the objective world.

2. That {correspondence} doesn't constitute any truth at all. What is necessary further is that there should exist genuinely an aim to hit just that which was hit. In order that the truth-relation should exist, the correspondence must be correspondence to the object which from the side of the belief is meant. The belief must select out the object to which it is to correspond, and it must select the kind of correspondence which it intends to have to that object. Otherwise the belief is neither true nor false.

I cannot suppose that the truth or falsity of Othello's unhappy beliefs concerning Desdemona is dependent on the existence or non-existence of an object in the world whose relational structure corresponds or not to the relational structure of the belief. In order that the truth or falsity of the belief, "Desdemona loves Cassio," should be in question at all, it is necessary that Othello should intend his belief to be true about the real Desdemona. The mere existence of a woman Desdemona loving in the world of real relations a real Cassio is not what determines the truth or falsity of the belief. Othello's belief actually singles out the real Desdemona as loving the real Cassio and defines the sort of relation (loving) which is supposed to hold between the two. If you form an ideal picture of a Desdemona loving a Cassio and there is nobody of the sort in the world anywhere are your beliefs false? No, not unless you were thinking of a portion of the world in which the Desdemona and Cassio of your idea were predetermined.

There must be cooperation of the believer in defining the object in which he is believing, or else the truth or falsity relation doesn't exist. My beliefs are true by virtue of the fact that they correspond to the objects with which they intend to correspond. On the other hand, if although there are no such objects, there is an intention that there should be such objects, my belief is false. Unless one specifically intended the correspondence to be the basis of his belief, of what importance is the correspondence? The truth of beliefs depends not on any relation that can be defined apart from the intent of the believer, which must be taken into account in defining the truth of his belief.

Beliefs are true or false only from the point of view that recognizes an interpreter. The mind of the interpreter is needed as well as the mind of the believer; and the mind of the interpreter must be so related to the object as to be able to define the correspondence of the believer and the object, otherwise there is no truth or error.

Truth is nothing that you can define in terms of a relation which ignores the mind of the believer. I can't stand in the relation of meaning a certain object unless I actually mean it. Every belief has a meaning only from the point of view of an interpreter. Thus every belief is not only a belief about its object, but also a belief about its interpretation, about what it really means. It is an appeal for confirmation to someone who knows what it is aimed at.

According to Russell, if judgments have truth or falsity, it is by virtue of agreement or nonagreement between the ideal portrayal of the situation which the judgments contain and the actual state of things referred to. A judgment if true must be in correspondence with, or if false in noncorrespondence with, an object which the judgment attempts to set forth. *Dec. 14*

Russell points out that there are difficulties in conceiving genuine truth in terms of correspondence with a single object, in view of the fact that a false judgment appears to suppose the existence of an object so that there would be required a noncorrespondence on the part of a false judgment to an object which is no object at all.

Russell tries to state a theory of correspondence which corrects this difficulty. Suppose there is in the world no love for Cassio by Desdemona. The nonexistence of that portrayed object would constitute, according to Russell, an objective falsity on the part of Othello's judgment in question. In case the world doesn't contain something which a certain belief portrays, so that there is no entity thus and thus related, then the belief is false. If there are true beliefs possible, then there must be false beliefs possible. The account of truth must be such as to enable us to distinguish between true and false beliefs.

Can any such an account of truth and falsity (in terms of correspondence) meet the requirements? It omits one fundamental matter. Over and above any relational structure which you may suppose present in the belief as a mental structure, there not only must be a corresponding structure in the world in order that the belief shall be true, but over and above that, precisely that object about which the portrayer intended to make his portrayal must be present in the world. A belief is true only if it so corresponds to an object as it *intended* to correspond to *that* object and to which it corresponds as it intended to correspond. There must be a link between belief and object which you can't express by speaking of any mere degree of resemblance which an idea is required to have to its object in order to be true. Nor can you call an object the object of a belief merely because it *resembles* in its nature the object which the believer had in mind. You can call it so only if he himself would declare, "That is the object that I am believing about." If his belief doesn't correctly represent the object that he intended to represent, then his belief is false. You can't decide whether this was the object about which he believed: that rests with the believer himself or is a matter of interpretation.

[Here Royce read extracts from his *Religious Aspect of Philosophy,* commencing on page 402.] A judgment is a state of mind with three elements. Überweg calls a judgment a "consciousness about the objective validity of a subjective union of ideas." The elements are: (1) the subject of the judgment with the accompanying shade of curiosity about the concrete situation; (2) the predicate which you utter with a sense of its worth as satisfying the curiosity: ("This is a *man*." "13 plus 15 is *28*."); (3) You have a sense of dependence. The value of this act lies in its agreement with something beyond. The judgment is true or false only with reference to that upon which your success in the characterization depends. The intention to agree with the object is contained in the sense of dependence on the object. As a mere combination of successive ideas, the judgment is neither true nor false.

The only object that the judgment has is this imperfectly defined one. Since in such judgments as you make the object is before you only incompletely and vaguely, how can you actually agree with an object beyond your state of mind? We must somehow so define what object we are to agree with that we can either agree or disagree with it. How can you be in error about your neighbor's state of mind? My neighbor is no one of my thoughts insofar as I distinguish my neighbor from myself. I have in my thought some set of ideas which somehow represent him to myself. My judgments are always dealing with my ideal neighbor. The judgment must be able to disagree with its chosen object. There must be some criterion which shows my idea to agree or disagree with the neighbor whom it intends. {Oliver Wendell} Holmes says there are six people who take part in a conversation between John and Thomas. According to common sense, Thomas can never err about the *real* John, for the real John is no part of Thomas's thoughts.

You must always bear in mind in considering the conditions of truth and error: (1) agreement in a complex way with a complex object; (2) intention to agree with that specific object at the time when the agreement isn't tested. Herein consists that aspect of the truth-falsity relation which I emphasize, namely that agreement which one intended to regard as that by which the assertion is to be tested.

It isn't my ideas as they are now whose workings show the truth of the ideas which I had formerly in mind. It is the fact that the ideas are the same throughout. There is this difficulty as to the identity of meaning between the ideas which you had before you tested the meanings and the ideas present in the working. By my assertion of a given judgment I inevitably intend not merely to describe or agree with an object, but with an object which is in a determinate way intended at the moment when I am intending to agree with it.

My judgment has therefore an essential character of appeal to a being who can observe that I have an agreement to the object which I actually intend. The decision as to whether my judgments are true or not could be made only by one at once identical with me as I made the judgment and identical with me whenever I know completely that which I endeavor to characterize when I judge. #

The truth of my judgments depends upon the interpretation of my judgments. They have neither truth nor falsity except from the point of view of an interpreter who knows me better than I now know myself.

The Logocentric Predicament

The general contrast between a realistic and an idealistic point of view is that whereas the idealist is insisting on something that makes him regard the world of reality in mental terms, the realist calls your attention to the fact that common sense well knows that things may be what they are whether this or that mind is concerned with them or not. Therefore, according to realism, we have to deal with the world as if the world could be considered without regard to minds; and realism endeavors to find out what would be true of the world whether minds were in it or not. With reference to those features, they {the realists} say we are able to assert certain things about reality in abstraction from mind. The world apart from mind consists of material atoms; there is ether, space, or whatever you please. That such and such things are real may be a hypothesis which has to be made more or less probable; but the being of these things is such as it is, whatever the minds are. The effort is to abstract from any mental point of view. The idealist thus appears to be one who is misled by, or who misuses, the egocentric predicament. The world for me is always the world as I view it; but according to Professor Perry, I have no right to ascribe a mental character to the real world because of this situation. *Dec. 16*

In Russell's *Problems of Philosophy* he comes to the problem of truth from a different side from that of the egocentric predicament. It becomes explicit in Russell's discussion that a distinctly mental aspect is essential to the very statement and to the very being of the truth-problem: for truths are properties of beliefs. Whatever you say about reality, the truth belongs to a belief. To declare that there is a certain reality is not to say that there is a certain truth. Truth belongs to belief. It is essentially mental in its constitution. The question is not what is real apart from my beliefs and ideas about what it is; but the question is in what sense have my beliefs truth. My ideas belong to me and express me. They take the form of judgments or assertions. They are not definable with respect to a character that they could possess apart from any relation to my mind, for the truth-character belongs to my beliefs.

The problem of getting a realistic definition of true beliefs is a problem with which you can't deal by saying, "Of course, I can't abstract from my beliefs; but such and such is true whether I can or not." The truth that belongs to judgments will not belong to judgments unless they are judgments. The truth that belongs to beliefs belongs to them as beliefs and is not definable in terms of a world in which there are no minds.

The realistic theory of truth tries to say that my beliefs are true in relation to something real. While the truth belongs to my beliefs and they are parties to the truth–relation, still truth may belong to my beliefs in a way which may enable me to say that the situation, which when my beliefs are there, makes them true, may be said to be real apart from my beliefs. The objects could remain possessed of the same character and capable of the same relation to possible beliefs in case my beliefs were left out. Thus they define the truth of beliefs in a way such that the truth is perfectly consistent with the realistic metaphysics.

So Russell finds the essential of the truth-relation to be a relation of correspondence in a form which he finds sufficient. The truth of my beliefs depends upon a certain form of correspondence. The correspondence must be considered as a highly relational one. The judgment has the form of subject and predicate with their supposed or ideal objects. Its truth depends on whether there is or is not in the world an object, relationally so constituted as the idea–system is constituted. If there is, the idea is true.

The question is whether you can state the matter wholly in terms of a correspondence between the belief and some object. My opposition to Russell's theory would be first that it endeavors to deal with the question wholly in a conceptual way. One conceives a certain belief structure and a certain object system. The belief structure and the object stand in a certain correspondence, like a photograph or statue and the man himself. Some relation like this, no matter how complex, is for Russell the thing which determines truth. My whole discussion depends upon the fact that mere correspondence between the mind and object is not enough. Lotze denied that it is self-evident that beliefs must correspond to something not beliefs. Yet he held it may well be that there is something in the purposive character of beliefs which requires that they should correspond with something not beliefs. Since ideas or beliefs are actual live processes, they are inseparable from the ideal leadings which are present to the mind of the believer. They cannot be called true or false by virtue of agreements or disagreements with which the believer has nothing to do. They must be true or false in reference to objects in reference to which the believer wishes them to be true. The true is that in our ideal leadings which conducts us whither we wanted to be conducted: "This is what I was looking for."

Truth turns out to possess a somewhat deeper character than that suggested by Berkeley's analysis.[CA] He defined the world in terms of actual or possible sense–data; the mental character of the world was supposed to be involved in the fact that, after all, your sense data belong to the ideal world; they are mental. But the realists want to consider "possibilities of experience" even in the absence of minds. I say, however, that the truth–character is something that belongs explicitly to your beliefs.

In James's case, the difficulty is the mutability of the whole process of validation. The one who now thinks that he has found Memorial Hall may soon find himself unsatisfied by the object which had satisfied him. But I say truth gets its importance from the fact that success is irrevocable. Truth immutably belongs to the person to whom the success in finding Memorial Hall occurs—the truth, namely, that this validation occurred to him at a certain moment when he found what he then intended.

Thus so far as the mere correspondence theory is concerned, you can't define the truth of beliefs in terms of agreement or correspondence with objects, for the same reason that, in case you merely found a collection of portraits, you couldn't determine whether they truly represented real men. You would have to know what men were to be portrayed; you must take account not merely of the fact that there is a portrait there and that it resembles something or other. What is the evidence that it was intended to be the portrait of anybody? Can you express that element of the situation in terms of correspondence? The point is whether the portrait resembles the man whom it was intended to resemble. If I write certain words in a letter, and if somewhere else in the world somebody else happens to be writing the same words in a letter, does that make my letter a true account of his letter? No, for the intention is lacking. Resemblance isn't enough, no matter how complex the relational correspondence may be.

In vain you declare that the ideas that work are true unless you keep in mind the object to which your belief was meant to conform. There must be an intention of agreement to that object explicitly. All such considerations leave out the pointer element, the marksmanship element, in judgment.

My beliefs aren't truths merely because they find somewhere in the world an object which resembles them or which they resemble. The truth that I demand for my belief can be fulfilled only by virtue of the particular object to which my idea had reference. You must deal with the problem of what object you mean, and this involves the relation of interpretation.

In order to say that my ideas work, my belief must be dealing with an object. Then there must be an interpretation of that belief which tells what object that belief intended to agree with. Then the confirmation must confirm that the belief agrees with the object which the belief intended to agree with. If the knowledge of what object the belief is intended to agree with exists, it exists in my mind or in the mind of another interpreter. Believer, interpreter and confirmer are necessary to the truth–relation. {To portray this process visually:}[4]

Belief	Believer	Coherence of a Self or Quasi-Self
Interpretation	Interpreter	as necessary to the existence of
Confirmation	Confirmer	the truth–relation process.

You can't express the truth-relation apart from a process which is a social process. The world itself must possess the being of a process of interpretation, otherwise none of your beliefs are true and none of them are false.

The world is logocentric. It is itself a process of interpretation.

Dec. 18 Kernan [Russell says:*

We have to seek a theory of truth which (1) allows truth to have an opposite, namely falsehood, (2) makes truth a property of beliefs, but (3) makes it a property wholly dependent upon the relation of the beliefs to outside things. The necessity of allowing for falsehood makes it impossible to regard belief as a relation of the mind to a single object, which could be said to be what is believed.[5]

Othello, says Russell, could have no relation to a nonexistent object, Desdemona's love for Cassio; hence his belief cannot possibly consist in a relation to this object.[6] Russell breaks up the single object into numerous terms. To have truth there must be correspondence between the belief–complex, and the fact-complex. In the belief–complex when Othello believes that Desdemona loves

* This and the next four paragraphs are bracketed because on December 18th, in Professor Royce's absence, his assistant, W. Fergus Kernan, gave this lecture and recommended additional reading for the thesis:

Bosanquet's *Logic* has a very fine chapter on truth and coherence.
Joachim: *Nature of Truth,* chapters I and III.
Russell: *Problems of Philosophy,* chapter XII.

Cassio, loving is a term; but in order for this belief to be true, loving must be a relation which really relates in the factual complex. When loving ceases to be a brick and becomes mortar—a relation and not a term—then the belief is true. Thus you can define truth according to Russell either as a correspondence between a mental complex and a factual complex, or as the reality of a relation.]

[Royce sees the necessity of providing for error, and says with Russell that a judgment taken with reference to its object as an isolated fact is absurd and has no sense. The only way, says Royce further, that you can get a truth is as a coherence in a body. Here we bring in the social consciousness. One must refer truth to some body, to some whole. An error is an incomplete thought which to an all-inclusive mind is known as having failed in a purpose which it more or less completely had. The judgment must be referred outwards to some higher consciousness.]

[Russell tries to break up the world into terms and to consider terms as though they were simply themselves in themselves—atoms. But no term is able to make sense in itself: it has no meaning except as it is related to a whole. "Charles I died on the scaffold" depends for its significance, and therefore for its truth, on the context in which it stands.]

[Bosanquet's coherence is a static description still; there is not enough of process to it, not enough of self-expression.]

[There was some argument as to whether Russell has logically committed himself to detaching terms from the context in which he finds them and attributing significance to terms in isolation.] {Kernan lecture ends.}

Dec. 21 Royce

[Royce next reviewed Russell's theory of truth, *Problems,* chapter 12.] When Othello's belief is true, the relation of loving is objective; when the belief is false, there is no such factual complex unity. A belief is true when it corresponds to a certain exhaustive complex. According to Russell, a relation needs no mind to know it, in order that Edinburgh should be north of London. But he says the relation of belief is a relation of a state of mind to a fact; this relation of belief is thus somewhat unique; it involves mind and fact.

The fact is that Desdemona stands in some other relation to Cassio than the relation of standing to him as beloved. The objects Desdemona and Cassio are not really related as the belief relates them. If such a complex whole existed involving Desdemona's loving Cassio, then the belief would be true; but if the relation is something else, then the belief is false. For Russell, everything turns on stating the whole matter relationally.

I insist that Russell gives us no indication of what it is that establishes the relation of the subject and the object.[7] How is it that Desdemona and Cassio are the objects about which Othello is believing at all? To be object of isn't anywhere analyzed. It is very notable that Othello won't be believing in the

Desdemona and Cassio whose relation is of such tragic importance to him, until he reaches a stage where he holds that the objects in question should have been interpreted otherwise than they first were. The believer always wants to pick out objects that are supposed to be entirely unique. The relation of meaning, of intending, is what Russell leaves out. It can only be interpreted.

My own resulting doctrine is that unless our objects are such that we ourselves recognize them as the objects intended, our beliefs are neither true nor false. True is the belief which agrees with the object which the interpreter of this belief regards as the object intended by the believer. The process of interpretation of our own beliefs is endless. Unless our beliefs form parts of a process of interpretation, they are neither true nor false. If you leave mind out of the world, then none of the beliefs of the mind remain true or false.

The relation of the believer to his own truth and falsity has to be defined in social terms. He can be false to an object only in case the object is his object by virtue of his social relations to the intent of his own belief. My truth turns on an interpretation of what I meant. My world is a world of interpretation. My self is a self of interpretation. You can't discuss or state the meaning of any other world or have any true belief about it.

[To a question from the class, Royce replied]: True is a belief when it agrees with the object which a complete interpretation defines as the object intended by the belief.

The relation of a believer to the objects of his belief is not a relation which you can express in any terms except in terms which consider the fulfillment of the purpose of the believer in defining the object of his belief. That purpose is never completely fulfilled at the moment of his belief.

It is extremely natural to define the idea of truth in conceptual terms. Any such conceptual theory of truth fails, because the truth of a belief is not a character which belongs to it by mere correspondence but it belongs to a belief by virtue of its correspondence to a somewhat with which it intends to correspond. The meaning of a belief must be considered in order that correspondence may obtain at all.

The difficulty in defining a truth when the meaning must be taken into account is one which pragmatism has not taken account of. When the truth of the idea is said to lie in its success, the success must be relative to one's purpose or intention. If this is what I all along maintain, then my present success will allow me to say that this is true. This process of verification has the temporal character—past, present, and future—and it is that which pragmatism neglects.[8]

Take Professor James's well-known example of Memorial Hall. When one sees it, he says, "This was what I was seeking." The assertion, "This is valid," is not an assertion about the moment. The result is one which thus demands an interpretation in terms of one's whole view of time.

Christmas vacation

The truth of an idea comes to be a matter that cannot be defined in terms of a conceptual agreement; nor yet can you define this in terms of perception alone; nor yet can you define it pragmatically. *Jan. 4 1916*[U]

The world of interpretation has this character; it is not a small pool which is ever changing, but it freezes into adamant so far as the past is concerned. Mutability can never be ascribed to truth. The ideal truth from this point of view is one which you can define only in terms of the agreement or nonagreement between the intention and what is intended. The truth has an adamantine character, though you can add new truths to former truths.

If I declare anything to be real, I declare it to be true. Whatever is, is the object of whatever true judgments {intended}[CA] with reference to specific purposes.

When you ask the question "Are my ideas true?" you appeal to a community. This social character of reality has already been mentioned. The world, then, is essentially not the world of this man's mind, nor of that man's mind, but must be defined in terms of the community.

What is this material world in which man has had such success in discovering the laws of nature? It is a process which seems accidental among the natural processes that should have brought into being an individual which has actually created the world of science. The fact is that while nearly all man's intuitive anticipations are wrong still too many of them occurred to make possible the agreement of them by chance.[9]

There is one general principle, essentially vague, which may be called the principle of fecundity of aggregation. Compare Wundt's principle of creative synthesis. He calls his principle a general and of course a vague law of mental life. His point is that in mental processes, synthesis leads to creation. In one's own mind, if you put your ideas together, you get something new. Compare with this Bergson's *élan vital.*

The fecundity of aggregation—the tendency of aggregates to be productive of new features—is even more marked in society. The process is also one which Peirce first suggested. It is essentially at bottom an evolutionary process.

It is the truth character which is at the foundation of the world.[10] If the belief of an idealist is rejected as a false interpretation, it is rejected on idealistic grounds. Just as the statement "This is the last prime number" is a statement which can be shown to be false of its very nature, so with the refutation of idealism. The truth that propositions get is from the fact that they are essentially purposive. A purpose can only be true in that it means to correspond with something. The being of things consists in the truth of propositions or of meanings. The individual stands in the social relation. *Jan. 6*[U]

Even if you try to escape this logocentric predicament by saying that an object is independent of belief, still that very belief that it is independent, has meaning.

Thus the being of the world consists in the truth of propositions about it. This cannot be escaped; to deny it is to affirm it.

Ontological Vocabulary

Jan. 8 [In response to a question from the class, Professor Royce discussed at length the distinction between being, reality, and existence, referring his students[CA] to the "ontological vocabulary" in *The World and the Individual* {1: 47–54}.]

Being belongs to whatever object you can define at all or think of or call to your attention. The objects of a dream have being; fictitious objects have being; round squares have being. Being as being belongs to all possible objects of inquiry or even of denial. The fortune which you don't possess, but think about, has being. An entity is that which has being.

Existence has special reference to time and space. To say "X exists" means X has its place in the time–space world. The sunlight exists: it is yonder now on the snow. Such entities as numbers have being without having existence. So far as the numbers are the objects of mathematical investigation, they have being. They are entities, but they do not exist.

Reality is the name for that which has not merely being, quiddity, or a predicable character, and which has not merely existence; reality is a predicate which applies to the world as a whole, the connected and organized whole of the world. Its significance is distinctly teleological. Reality is possessed by an object which possesses a meaning, a significance, a wholeness, a totality which need not be possessed by an object which merely exists. Reality would be ascribed to the world, existence to this and that in the world.

This about reality is idealistic doctrine. Those metaphysicians whose view has no place for the teleological have no particular reason to emphasize reality as distinct from being and existence. Reality is sometimes used as a name for whatever more may belong to existences over and above the time–space character. Peirce defines the real as that which makes true {one's} assertions about it. A fairly common definition of the real is to use the term as synonymous with the character such that by the reality of the real it is determined whether a given proposition about the real is true or not. From that point of view, the content of a dream has reality, since you can tell lies about a dream or give as faithful an account of it as you choose so far as you remember it. From that point of view, the being of a fictitious entity would have a real character so far as there may be truth in regard to it. If, however, one defines reality relative to truth, the real becomes, as the object of a true proposition, possessed of an idealistic character.

By reality I mean the object of a true proposition. This is a teleological view. Being belongs to the object of a possible concept, without the least regard to how fictitious it is. Existence belongs to objects so far as they have a place in time and space. Reality belongs to objects insofar as they possess characters which make them the objects of true propositions. The reality of whatever there is consists in the truth of the ideas about it which are true. To be real is to fulfill a purpose expressed in whatever proposition or judgment is true about the real. The limitation of the verb "exist" to the spatial and temporal is a very common one. There is one curious exception, in the mere use of words. Further inquiry into the history of the vocabulary would be needed to see how it arose. In saying "X exists," it is very common to use the word "exists" as a predicate applying to God. "God exists," so the theist in general asserts. The atheist denies the existence of God. Here the space-time basis is absent, don't you think so?[11]

Being belongs to any possible object of conception. Existence belongs to space-time objects, the events of today and the facts which are some where. Reality belongs to the possible objects of true propositions. Therefore, reality belongs to all the existences insofar as it is true that they exist described thus and thus. But existence doesn't belong to all the real objects; reality belongs to the divine being and not existence in this technical sense.

Santayana's essay, "Some Meanings of the Word Is," will be part of our work in the second half-year. He lays a good deal of stress on the contrast between essence, which belongs to whatever is conceivable, and existence, which consists of a selection from the essences, some of which exist while some do not. The entities which exist are known to exist, if we know it, by experience; and their existence is spatial and temporal. The whole distinction which he makes is a realistic distinction. The essence of an odd number would be distinct from the essence of an even number. Given an object with an essence at all, you can then make assertions about it which are true or false with respect to the conception at issue; and the essences are real insofar as you can make true propositions about them. Thus, it is true that amongst the Greek gods there were those that were fathers and mothers and sisters and brothers; sex difference was a reality amongst the Greek gods.

Peirce points {out} that although the objects of a dream have no space-time existence, you can truly or untruly recount the dream. The dream object is an object of possible true or false assertions and thus possesses reality.

A physical object, an existence, of which you reported that you regarded it as essentially non-social, would be indistinguishable from an illusion of yours, and the ascription to it of existence could not be maintained.[12]

Intellectual Autobiography, 1871–1883

Jan. 11 I began the study of philosophy before I ever read any German idealism, which was quite unknown to me until I had become acquainted with Mill.[13] I was especially influenced by Mill's examination of the philosophy of Sir William Hamilton.[14] Over against the influence of Mill stood for me the influence of Herbert Spencer. Mill was a critical empiricist, on the whole accepting a Berkeleyan account of the world, though altogether deprived of the theological elements of Berkeley's doctrine. For Mill, the world is known to us through experience, the experience of the outer senses and the inner experience, a world of data of sense or feeling; and all that we can say about it is that these data are such. Mill had a tendency which made William James long after declare in *Pragmatism,* "Were he alive today, he would be one of us."[15] Mill had the interests of a philanthropic liberal and was especially concerned with the fact that dogmatic generalizations about the nature of the world are politically and socially mischievous. He was keenly critical of anything that appeared a dogmatic statement about the nature of things. In that spirit he criticized what he regarded as the dogmatic statements of Sir William Hamilton.

Hamilton was himself critical of the traditional Scottish metaphysics, but he was disposed to decide things by reference to <u>principles</u> supposed to be intuitively known. Mill's own criticism of Hamilton was aided by the fact that a disciple of Hamilton, Dean Mansel, in his *Limits of Religious Thought* (1858), had expounded the Kantian philosophy as a means of modifying the Scottish metaphysics. Here, too, assertions about the nature of reasoning played a large part in the discussion.[16]

Mill found especially obnoxious Mansel's way of stating the case that there are *a priori* reasons for assertions.[CA] His criticism of Mansel is remarkably brilliant. Mill's chapter, "The Psychological Theory of the External World," is one of the most important philosophlcal productions of English thought of the last century.[17]

I became through Mill's influence a decidedly skeptical critical empiricist[18] with this result: We all desire to be guided by something reasonable; we intend to discover what we ought to think and the standards by which thought should be guided. You can never find these in the Scottish way through intuition of first or fundamental truths. If you do, you are always subject to the criticism; "Do you believe these doctrines about the nature of things because you are <u>tempted</u> to? Then they are mere persuasions, they are faiths. Or do you found them on particular experiences? Then they have no necessity about them. Therefore, 'necessary' or 'fundamental' truths must fail as the basis of thinking."

Herbert Spencer's effort to restate the necessary truths on the basis of his evolutionary theory never satisfied me.

It was in such a mood that I turned to German philosophy, to Kant and to Fichte especially, and, by way of an episode, to Schopenhauer. These were the three German philosophers who most influenced me. The years 1875 to 1883 determined my philosophical thinking: this was the time from 1875, when I first began to study in Germany, to the time when I came to Harvard to teach, seven years later.[CA]

Kant seemed to me for a while to have a very definite solution to my problem, but I found it very difficult to understand. In *The Spirit of Modern Philosophy* I have set forth my efforts to get at what Kant had in mind.[19] The neo-Kantian movement was prominent at Leipzig, where I studied; there I heard some of the liveliest of the neo-Kantians set forth their ideas of the problems. I also heard Wundt.

Kant more and more tended to abandon the *Ding an sich*, but insisted that experience conforms to certain general forms which the nature of the knowing intelligence defines, so that the intelligence predetermines in its general form what sorts of objects it can regard as real objects, and therefore the sort of world that we must regard as the real world, though objective.

Over against Mill's empiricism, this doctrine had a certain internal absoluteness about it. Mill left you to the data of sense, to the endlessly shifting variety of the fortunes of experience. This realm of experience as interpreted by science tends to take on the form of law, yet all our laws seem to be of the nature of particular propositions and therefore do not seem to be genuinely universal assertions. Kant thought we could know what it is of the nature of our intelligence to know as real. The forms of the intelligence are impressed upon that which we regard as nature. But that which we regard as nature is a kind of a shadow, a phenomenon, of a real that we can never find. The metaphysical problem is insoluble, according to Kant.

But when I examined this world of Kant, I found always this difficulty about Kant's categories, a difficulty which Wundt never settled for me: the difficulty as to how one should know that the forms of the understanding are permanent forms such that no other forms can guide your view of things. How shall I know that the forms of my understanding are not just about to change? Why should not the categories themselves alter? What would happen to my laws of phenomena if my categories changed?

I was influenced somewhat by the impressive personality of Lotze, whom I heard at Göttingen. He always presented his metaphysic in a tentative way. He was accustomed to say, not "This is the solution," but "It would appear to us thus." He was a thoroughly gentle soul, timid in his manner. The lesson I drew from Lotze was that a man's convictions were not his innate ideas but his postulates.

Fichte's philosophy had that feature: man's philosophy was an expression of the kind of man he was.

When I came to Harvard in 1882 to teach, I brought this: We are in a position of postulates, voluntary attitudes, will attitudes towards the world, and our purpose as philosophers is to reflect on these and to bring them into some kind of union and also to attach them to experience. On so much our philosophy depends.

But the difficulty is that your general opinions, the categories of your understanding, are useful to you so far as they give you views which you state in universal propositions. You want your postulates to tell you something universally true; but so far as you deal with particulars, your difficulty is to attach your postulates to your empirical data. The philosopher must be guided by postulates which he doesn't attempt to verify but only asserts, or which he verifies by verifications which are matters of the moment. A truth ethical or spiritual is never contained in a moment. A general truth is never illustrated by experience and must be defined in terms of a postulate. We want to be guided by experience, but never can be guided by experience except at this and that moment; and hence we never get in experience a survey of the whole, the synoptic view which gives you necessary laws. We are at the mercy of what happens at present. What we want is the right to assert something about the nature of the world. We are always left with postulates on our hands which are statements about what we are not now verifying in experience, and yet we want to verify them.

I felt what an inadequate preparation this was for teaching philosophy. I could say to men, "You actually live on postulates, on voluntary attitudes, treating the world as if it were thus and thus; you act in a mood of courageous assertion. You always want verification, but experience teaches you only what is present at the moment." The difficulty would always occur. If I tell them, "Be bold, be brave, take life at a risk," I apparently left them to caprice; I authorized anything, any absurdity. On the other hand, if I said, "Look at the facts of experience," I had nothing to show them but the present. Scientific men were guided by what they took to be a sort of impersonal experience, what I now call a universal experience. My students would say, "Why don't you go to the methods of science?" My critical response was, "I doubt not your right to your postulates in the laboratory, but what you don't see is that your scientific point of view is also a postulate. You expect your universal principles to guide you in your experience."

Lotze's way of getting out was a skeptical way. He asserted his postulates but regarded this as his own assertion. He qualified his statement of his own metaphysical views by saying, "After all, my assertions about the ultimate nature of things are my view; I leave it to the verdict of a God whom I do not presume to direct. *Gott weiss besser*." That didn't give the kind of philosophy one wanted in order to direct men in the problems of life.

I gradually came in sight of the considerations which I now set forth in connection with the study of the problem of truth and error. They came in the form of a somewhat insistent self-criticism which appeared when I tried to state this very doctrine in a definite form. What I know about the world is that somewhat or other is present in present experience and somewhat or other is postulated. Kant supposed that the postulates could be defined as permanent categories. Try to conceive your world in those terms and what have you? The assertion that there is a present moment of experience. The present moment is the datum; the rest is postulate. The future is postulated; voluntaristically one views the future as if it were to be. Voluntaristically one views the past as if it had been. Space is viewed as if extended indefinitely. If one asks why one makes these postulates, one says that one does so as a voluntary being who simply has to act. But why in this way? No ground appears. Such was my attitude: I had no guarantee beyond this postulating character. This was the central problem for me when I began to teach philosophy here.

If you say the only datum which guides us is the present moment, what do you mean by the present moment? Soon as you try to tell what is your present experience, it has slipped away. There is no present moment: there is a postulated present moment. There is what you would have seen if you had been able to hold it. As Faust says, "O moment stay, thou art so fair."[20] The radical empiricist is always lost when he tries to find the present moment; it turns into postulate. One gets nothing but this endless postulating, with the insistence that one means to be guided by data if they can be found, but finds only postulates.

This led me to the decided reversal of point of view which followed. My postulates may be mere attitudes toward the real. If that is the case, then error is at least possible. But what would be an error? What would it be to err about the past or future? What is it to make a blunder in science? This led me to the doctrine of the nature of error as involving interpretation. I said to myself, this view which I set forth about the nature and conditions of error is true or false. Whether it is true or false, we have here a teleological situation which brings the thought of the moment into contact with a type of consciousness which is not the merely human type.

[Here Royce read from his own notes, written January 11–12, 1883, exactly thirty-three years ago, and rehearsed his doctrine as to truth and error.]

There is a certain value in using the expression, "The being of the world *Jan. 13*[U]
consists in the interpretation of a problem which the world at any time presents to experience." The being of the world involves the interpretation of my problem.[21]

If there were no problem, if there were no interpretation, or if the interpretation were itself given, then the being of the world would be presented to the interpreting mind. But, as the need of an interpretation constantly calls upon me for the finishing of the interpretation, so I can say that the world has, as an aspect of its existence, the fact that it contains the interpretation of the problematic facts. Compare the world of interpretation in *The World and the Individual*.[22] The world then is essentially that which contains the interpretation of the problematic side of experience.

The evils of the world have a character that presents a problematic aspect. Some realistic critics have said that the world is as it is; that the problem of evil is factitious. Compare James, who, in his discussions of pragmatism, spoke in this way. Those who view the matter in this way do not view things from the point of view of interpretation. There is something about the world of evil that you do not understand; the problem is the problem of the restriction of the individual. The problem of evil is not imported by philosophers or theologians. There are aspects of life which we do not understand. But the interpretation of the evil would not be a removal of it. There is a contrast between what we will and what we get.

Note the stress laid upon the term "spirit" in these times of emphasis upon the social. The spirit is often to be understood in the light of the social order. By the spirit in human life, one doesn't mean the aesthetically beautiful or what is meant by the "higher emotions," but <u>whatever brings us into union with the community</u>.[23]

The well-known proverb "To comprehend all is to pardon all" expresses a human view of life which has a good deal of truth about it. To know the world better is to pardon its ills, to be in union with it. So to view the world in this way is to believe that it is a solution of the problem of evil.

Jan. 15 Neorealism lays stress on the comparatively insignificant part played in the account of the world by the place of consciousness in the world. It belongs to idealism to view the fact of knowledge as having a very important bearing on the being of that which is known. Whatever knowledge there be in the world, according to neorealism, does not affect the reality of other objects in the world. Russell says <u>London</u>, <u>Edinburgh</u>, and <u>north of</u> might be, whether there were any mind in the world to know them or not. The world might be what it is if there were no knowledge in it, except that there wouldn't be the minds themselves.

I am willing to rest the case at present upon the point that there is one character of Being which is essentially dependent on the presence in the world of what has the character of knowledge; namely, the aspect of the world that the being of facts involves the truth of propositions. This is a statement which one can prove by the reflective method. Whoever denies this fact reasserts it; just as one who declares that there is a last prime number asserts that the series of primes is endless. Whoever asserts that the world would be the same without knowledge, asserts the contrary of this proposition. Hereupon we find ourselves in a world which can be defined only in terms of interpretation. The truth of a proposition becomes the very essence of the neorealistic conception of Being. This is what I say to the neorealist.

Professor Perry's challenge doesn't apply; namely, that one mustn't reason from his inability to define what the world would be without him to the need of the world that he shall be in it.[CA] It isn't a question of verification or of my own ideas. I suppose that it would make comparatively little difference to the world if my activity were left out. To declare what the world is apart from me is again to assert a proposition as true, and the being of that realistic world consists in the truth of the proposition which characterizes it. Truth then is central in that world.

The being of the world consists in the interpretation of my problem, in the interpretation that it includes or furnishes the problem which the world at any time presents to experience—to anybody's experience.[24] If there were no problem, then one would have no inquiry into what the world is. If the interpretation were itself given, then the being of the world, whatever it is, would be presented to the interpreting mind. But as the need of an interpretation constantly calls upon me for the furnishing of the interpretation and thus forces me to believe in a world, so I can say that the world contains the interpretation of the problematic facts which now occur to me.

My present is problematical. I myself furnish the hypothetical interpretation insofar as I view my present as a process which involves the past and goes on to the future. The world is essentially that which contains and is the interpretation of a problematic side of experience. It has essentially the character of a world of interpretation, a community of interpretation. One cannot define the world in terms of a static absolute conceived as unchanging. One must view it as having the character of a self interpreting a self. That an interpretation has as its very essence something teleological, you can see from these illustrations. That which has to do with adjusting what comes to me from the past to my future plans and undertakings gives meaning to what is otherwise problematical. From that side, the world of interpretation would appear a world in which there is an interpreter, somewhat to interpret, and, by virtue of that interpretation, the problematical side of the world becomes less problematic at each step. The character of winning an end everywhere belongs to the world.

The evils of the world present a problematic aspect. It has been asserted that the problem of evil is factitious: the only thing is the evil and if you can get rid of it, the problem disappears. The practical problem is to remove it altogether. If it cannot be removed, the practical business of life is to remove as much as possible.

This overlooks the relation between the truth of propositions and the being of things. The being of that which you call an evil is essentially the presence of a problematic aspect in this world. There is something about the world of ill that you don't understand. The problem is the problem of the restriction, the incomplete self-expression, of the self of him in whose experience the ill appears. Therefore the problem "Why is it?" is a problem which plays a part in the consciousness of anyone to whom the teleological problem is at all present. It is forced on the attention of everyone as an aspect of life which you don't understand. If the being of the world involves interpretation, then the interpretation of evil will not amount to showing that it is only an apparent evil. It will involve that which for the person who suffers the evil would appear as a reconciling element in his life. There is a contrast between what we will and what we get. If an interpretation of this situation appeared, we should not have removed the contrast but should be reconciled to it.

The "spiritual side of our life" is empirically represented by our social life. In your experience of the world you are taking part in the life of a community. The practical expression of our metaphysic would be a confidence that to know the world better is to pardon its ills, or to be pardoned for our part in its ills. The contrasts are not removed by interpretation; the evil aspects are comprehended and therefore pardoned.

[To questions from the class Royce replied]: If you declare that there is a being which in no sense consists in the truth of propositions, name that aspect and you will at once get a proposition as true. If the world consists of atoms, very well, something is true of atoms or the world doesn't consist in atoms. The truth–aspect and the being–aspect of reality are contrasting but inseparable, like the convex and concave sides of a curve. It hasn't two parts. So the real world has its truth-aspect of being the fulfillment of true beliefs and the refutation of false beliefs, and this aspect cannot be separated from the being-aspect. The being of the world consists in the fact of its possessing and being pervaded by this truth–aspect. You always have to define identity in terms of diversity. You can never say "X is X" without thereby emphasizing a diversity. Just so, I can't recognize the truth of propositions without recognizing another aspect of the world than the truth–aspect, for there must be something that makes it true; but at the same time, this truth–aspect can't be separated from the being–aspect. If I tell you "X is X" I tell you so only in pointing out to you a difference.

Jan. 18 Peirce would sometimes resent a situation in which a "mediocre" person seemed to be understanding too much of what Peirce said; and he would thereupon turn cuttlefish, to the discomfiture of his hearer. According to Peirce, the "scientific method" had two features: (1) Its results were always tentative; there was always something more to be done. Peirce was much offended by the tendency towards finality which characterized the work of the philosophers. (2) At the same time, Peirce was not essentially a skeptic or a doubter: If your method was tentative, it involved a constant and definite progress characterized by the elimination of its own errors. The consciousness of progress depends on recognizing the inevitable. The doctrine of the mutability of truth in pragmatism displeased Peirce. We obtain in our processes a somewhat which when done cannot be undone. Peirce observed that his triadic process was distinctly different from that of Hegel, a contrast which itself needed interpretation.

The world contains the interpretation of its own problems. In order that there should be any world at all, the world must contain reconciliation, an interpretation, of the problem between the presence, from time to time in experience, of the world, and its purpose, meaning, significance, goal. The world of interpretation must undertake to interpret that antithesis between experience as it comes and the goal or purpose of meaning that it has.

Interpretation Encompasses Induction and Deduction

Induction when it is systematically carried on either by an individual who collects and investigates, or by a community of induction (collectors, hypothesis-makers, and testers), involves a triadic process. The induction process passes from less knowledge to more. There is no finality of knowledge, humanly speaking. Every discovery of facts is itself the setting to you of new problems. Every result of the scientific induction or interpretation itself requires interpretation. The more you use the exact inductive method, the more it tends to correct itself; it is of the very nature of induction that it should improve its own method. It may be at any point erroneously put into practice, but it will tend to correct itself if you continue to put it into practice, as in the case of the process of sampling, you tend to vary your mode of taking samples. For instance, take the case of black swans. The process is directed in one direction; upon the facts so far accumulated tentative generalizations are suggested and then the process goes on of testing those generalizations.

The process of conception is the process of actually describing or making clear, of clarifying ideas. This wouldn't be the same as interpreting them, for clarifying is not essentially social. It hasn't the essentially triadic character in the foreground. So also deducing, as in the case of the theory of numbers, discovering what given propositions imply[CA] when assumed as premises is not necessarily of an interpretative character.

It is a process of interpretation when it leads to an endless series of interpretations, as in the case of the reflective method of proof that there is no last prime number, which is interpretative with reference to the contrast of primes with all other numbers. Here the interpretation has a repetitive character, for the construction is seen to apply endlessly to the supposed last prime.

Jan. 20 I don't think it is enough to say that the union of the perceptual and the conceptual is all that takes place in knowledge.[25] If one says that the whole business of thought is not properly to be called triadic, and that what happens is always properly the bringing into connection of an idea and a content, one says what pragmatism says, that a synthesis of idea and brute fact is the success of the idea; live thoughts are neither percepts nor concepts; they lead to percepts, and perception is the cashing of the conceptual banknote, whereby concepts get their meaning.

That account of the merging of the two aspects of knowledge doesn't give us by itself a third sort of knowledge. But the situation is somewhat different when you deal with a process which doesn't mean merely the synthesis of percepts and concepts but the understanding of a <u>contrast</u> between two diversified ideas. Aristotle said there is a tendency for matter to take on form, for the brute content of experience to take on ideal formation. That could be expressed in terms of the union of perception and conception. But when he said that, he didn't speak of a process such as goes on in the social order when men become acquainted or find out how to work together. Here one man isn't brute fact and the other man organized principle. Here there comes into the world the notion of the community. You can't express what {then}goes on in terms {either} of pragmatism or of the Aristotelian alteration of Plato's position.

In unintelligently listening to music, one hears at first sounds; only later does one hear music. The transition does involve the thing which Aristotle opposed to Plato when he declared that the relation between ideas and the content of the world is the relation between the form and the matter of the world. But the musician's insight into music must involve another element, a true interpretation, a knowledge of that wherein the peculiar significance of the composition consisted. He comes to see in music not merely the expression of form in matter, but he perceives how an earlier movement in a symphony introduces and requires a second as the means of leading over to its third theme, as in the sonata form. It isn't merely that one has dealt with a gradual putting of form into matter. One finds the element of contrast, the dramatic element, involved. You have a kind of construction which belongs with indirection. The triadic element must be present in some live way. Antithesis and the third that reconciles them is needed. It appears to me that we are dealing with a fundamentally and genuinely triadic scheme of knowledge and of Being.[26] #

Jan. 22 *Studies in Logic,* by members of Johns Hopkins University, contains an essay by Charles Peirce on induction.[27] There is a passage with regard to the nature of inference and the difference between induction and deduction. He doesn't speak expressly in triadic terms, but this passage gives you a useful view of the way in which interpretation is related to the processes of induction and deduction.

Formal logic, says Peirce in this essay, must not be too purely formal. It must represent a fact of psychology or else it is in danger of degenerating into a thoroughly mathematical affair. He goes on to discuss the dyadic illative relation of inference. "If A then B" should be taken as the typical form of judgments. He also discusses the mode *Barbara* of the syllogism, a triadic affair, as in the situation when a judge applies a statute to a case in court. The cognition of a case is of the nature of a sensation. #

The idea which is in my consciousness, and which is not original with me, is judged to be the work of another mind, by virtue of a direct contrast. Memory is involved. "This is not my idea" is not an assertion about origin; it is a contrast judgment. When I make an assertion, there stands over against me that with which I intend to agree. It isn't mine now. I mean the objective real world. In this relation I am mediated by the insight which knows my meaning; and unless I intend such a thing, I have said nothing whatever, either true or false. Whenever I wonder what is so, the universe is what stands in this contrast to me. My object isn't my present experience, but it is that to which I seek to conform. I truly express it or not.

In my *Problem of Christianity* the thesis is that the success of Christianity *Jan. 24*
has been a social success.[28] The present failure of Christianity is a relative failure to mold humanity in accordance with its ideas. <u>The moral and spiritual authority for me is humanity</u>. That is the essential doctrine.

Dean Mansel's *Limits of Religious Thought* was a book profoundly conceptual in its view of reality and of the problems of religion. He maintained the doctrine of the <u>unconditioned</u> ultimate nature of things {and it consequences}. The human mind cannot grasp the unconditioned. Dogma has to be accepted as revelation, on grounds of experience which actually compels acceptance on the part of the faithful. Our faith cannot be and does not wish to be rationally defended. It defies interpretation. It demands submission. Christianity says, "Accept me as faith, obey as a matter of deed." His God makes the same sort of demand on the soul that the Prussian state makes on its subject: "Obey, follow; otherwise, you are lost. The divine nature is unknowable: you can't judge that what is righteous for you is righteous for God: divine ways are mysterious and you have to accept the mystery."

Mill was interested in religious problems from a humanitarian point of view, and he was vexed by this system of concepts. "If you tell me that I am so ignorant that I can't see the ways of divine providence, I obey; but tell me, as Mansel says, that for the divine being <u>righteous</u> means something that it doesn't mean for me, <u>holiness</u> is different for him than for me, then I revolt. If you tell me that the Absolute means by <u>good</u> and by <u>right</u> something really contrary to what I mean, I won't call those things good nor that God good; and if this God can send me to hell, to hell I will go."[29]

The whole account of Volume I of *The Problem of Christianity* is an effort to interpret the Christian tradition as in essential harmony with the human interests in life. It is of the essence of Christianity as a practical religion to reconcile God and man, to interpret each to the other. That is a progressive process; the insight is progressive; it is not stability, not any fixed dogma. The principle of development is an essentially Christian principle. Metaphysically speaking, Christianity appears, in Volume II, as a doctrine of the universe as interpretation. The ideal of the positive and spiritual union of mankind in the Church is the most fundamental ideal of humanity. The Church Universal has never become visible.

For James, religion is the experience of the homeland which the individual has. That is a distinctly mystical view. For me, the essence of Christianity has been the social element. Harnack, a Lutheran, makes the Church appear as the inevitable mishap, for the sake of teaching the doctrine of the Founder; it involved a falling away from the simple doctrine. Harnack is an antimystic, but he is near to James in this.

I maintain that the essence of Christianity is definable in distinctly social terms. Read my chapter "The Christian Doctrine of Life"[30] and consider that doctrine on the practical side, in connection with what I have to say about the moral burden of the individual, time and guilt, the irrevocable past, and atonement in that volume.

Unless it is to be the case that this war removes humanity entirely from this planet, then some such principle as this of the community must prevail. Germany, the enemy of mankind.[31] {Within the real world of interpretation, Royce's "social approach" to metaphysics, knowledge, and truth has highlighted the striking contrast between the most fundamental ideal of humanity—as yet not realized—and the forces at work in "communities of hate" opposed to that realization.}[32]

End of the first half-year

Part II

The "Logical Approach" to Metaphysics

Chapter 4

Santayana on "Is": His Sharp Distinction between Essence and Existence[1]

{To connect the social approach to metaphysics, the work of the first half-year, with the logical approach of this second half-year, one needs to set both in the context of Peirce's theory of signs. Some time ago, Francis} Galton, in the *Fortnightly Review*,[2CA] suggested how communication with Mars might take place if the inhabitants existed and if their sense organs and interests permitted. He thought of it from our side. In the question on the midyear examination,[3] I put the Mars people in a position of knowing a great deal about us, which would simplify the question. Galton said that if they were intelligent beings, they would have in any case the number system in common with us. He didn't defend this statement, but a careful study of the situation shows clearly that you can't call our number system at all dependent on the laws of our physical world; this is discussed in Phil. 8. If we had no such sense organs as we now have for dealing with the physical world, but had the same intelligence as we now have, the essential meanings of the number concepts might be made entirely clear to us. It isn't a question of the laws of nature, but of laws far more general than those of nature. After you have examined the logic of the number system, you can say that you have the number system in common with all intelligent beings, whatever be the means, sensory or motor, whereby their intelligence gets its expression. The great generality of the number system makes the thing possible.

Feb. 15 Start of the second half-year

Galton didn't think of communicating to them an ordinal number system. He satisfied himself with the cardinal numbers. He would utter the proposition "2 + 2 = 4" by means of flashes in succession. The observers would have to take note of something of the nature of intervals. From the side of the ordinal numbers, there would be various ways of approaching the matter by means of rhythmic beats—1, 2; 1, 2, 3—a drumbeat type of rhythm. The Martians who should communicate to us any rhythm which constituted a repeated system of that sort would impress us and would finally satisfy us that they had ideas.

How far they could progress would be another question. Galton didn't attempt to investigate that. Further development would depend upon the responses. If we began and got an answer to our drum tap, and thereupon we answered, the process of further communication would depend upon the ingenuity of the communicating beings.

Flammarion,[4] in a story, made a suggestion of a very different type. In his story a comet is about to collide with the earth. The astronomers are making predictions that this cometary body is going to be where the earth is before long. A communication is received from the Mars people, who take the simplest method, the iconic method, as Peirce calls it. The absence of mountains and their control of natural forces makes it possible for them to present to us vast pictograms depicting what they will. They use the portion of the surface that happens to be in the darkness, employing rays of vast signal lights which can be read by the telescope. They use what Peirce would call icons, signs which are of the nature of imitations. They know a great deal which we don't know about the comet. The large meteoric masses which are the nucleus of this particular cometary body will strike the earth and do damage; the masses in question are about to hit the earth in the immediate vicinity of Rome. This is what the Mars people want to tell us. To decipher the Mars pictographic signs there is nothing to do but to look; the rest is a mere question of solving what has less complexity than a rebus. They send us a diagram picture of the comet which is shown pointing towards the bootleg of Italy; spots are made in the neighborhood of Rome, and arrowheads are indicated pointing outward from Rome. The sense is, "The comet is about to hit you there. Flee!"

Peirce was fond of his threefold division of signs; he tried a good many other divisions of signs which all turned out to be triadic. His favorite is that of index, icon, symbol.

The index is the sign whose object (to which the sign relates) is connected with it by some kind of contiguity. A weathervane is attached to the wind directions in index fashion. It points toward the wind. A mark attached to things is by its attachment an index. One who blazes a trail in the woods by hacking bits out of the trees and stumps indicates the road by the marks thus made; these indices are attached to the trees or stumps along the road. The connection between the index and that which it indexes (the road, not the trees) is a connection of contiguity, an arbitrary connection.

The icon is the sign which indicates that which it resembles. A diagram is an icon sign, and that mode of making signs is iconic. The sign languages of deaf–mutes, Indians, and secret orders have this general character. An iconic language may be interspersed with symbol signs. Sign languages usually make the icons prominent but use some indexes for indicating the size or shape of the object, or if somebody is coming, for instance, to point to the direction from which he is coming.

The symbol is the sort of sign whose connection with the object is entirely conventional.

These three types of signs differ in the ways of their use and in their usefulness. The index sign is most useful in communicating with a being whose intelligence is of a primitive sort or whose intelligence is unknown to you. You try it with a child and with an animal; you can get some animals interested in the direction in which you are pointing. The icon sign is impressive but assumes a somewhat higher intelligence. The symbol could hardly be used to give evidence of your own intelligence to beings who had not that idea. It it hard to give to symbols the character which makes them obviously expressive of ideas.[5] In discussing the ground of our social knowledge, I have laid especial stress on the entry into our consciousness of an ideal meaning which stands in contrast with our own ideas. Whether index signs or iconic signs were used would depend upon the special empirical conditions. Whether something is for us a sign with a meaning will depend somewhat upon the range of our time span: the light waves and intervals would have to enter into our consciousness. A being with a tremendous time span, or with a span very much less than ours, could not communicate with us.

The whole matter has been discussed wherever teleological arguments are in question. In Berkeley's *Alciphron* he raises the question as to what evidence God could give us of his existence that would satisfy the most atheistically disposed person. In this dialogue, the Skeptic said that he would be content with the writing on the sky of letters which he could understand; the historical evidences and the order of nature do not convince him, but God could easily convince him by writing on the sky. The historical revelation doesn't convince him because he wasn't there and doesn't believe in the story. The Philosopher tries to call his attention to the signs of the visual world. You don't directly see the distance of an object at a distance; you infer it from certain signs which the object gives you of its distance. The various signs of depth are all indirect signs. Nevertheless,[CA] we should be unable to speak of such phenomena as signs. If you put two perspective diagrams into a stereoscope you see a solid object, but this is not because anybody is using that language. The connection between certain visual facts and certain experiences of movement and touch is so uniform that you establish the habit of interpreting as you do the "signs" of the field of vision; but these are not signs in the special sense. This matter comes up in *The World and the Individual* in the Third Conception of Being.

There is an interesting problem as to the difference between (1) the connection between signs and what they signify, and (2) other logical connections which are known in experience. If dawn precedes the sunrise, we do not regard this as the effort of any intelligence to communicate to us. When the sunset presages the darkness, we do not regard this as a sign. The symbolic connections are as arbitrary as the laws of nature; they are determined by convenience. Thus that the symbol π is used for a well-known ratio is a purely arbitrary matter; yet the connection is one of sign and thing signified.

We should all agree that Berkeley was a little too sanguine when he made use of the very interesting psychological connection between the signs of the field of vision and the tactile and physical facts which they indicate as being the same as the connection between a sign and the thing signified in the case of a communication. This is important from the point of view of an argument from design.

The coming half-year's work will be based on the Gifford Lectures, called *The World and the Individual.* From here on my intent is to make prominent the logical approach to metaphysics. The analysis of the metaphysical conceptions and ideas and the synthetic survey of them in their interrelations are our interest. I cannot myself maintain that there is any such thing as an <u>analytical</u> <u>method</u> which can be carried on in distinction from a synthetic method in metaphysics.

The point of view of *The World and the Individual* is in a number of ways different from the point of view emphasized in the first half-year, which was that of the social approach to metaphysics. The triadic theory of interpretation assumed the prominence which it has in the *Problem of Christianity* since the time the Gifford Lectures were given. Yet there are a good many aspects of the argument in *The World and the Individual* which demand the very same structure as the structure which I have been expounding. The real world turns out to be a social world of the same general outlines which are familiar to you from the first half-year's work. I do not believe that my form of idealism has essentially changed; I suppose it to be essentially the same doctrine in both cases, but I hope that I have not merely repeated myself in these two approaches.

Certain conceptions will be discussed which have not been discussed in the foregoing. The conception of the <u>infinite</u> will get an interest for us, and for that very reason the conception of the <u>self</u> is going to be emphasized from here on. At your leisure you may wish to consider what is the relation between this doctrine of the individual self and the doctrine of the community, which I emphasized in previous chapters.

Feb. 17 The positions are those which are natural to one in sympathy with the New Realism.[6] Apart from any direct influence of Russell or of Moore of Cambridge, Professor Santayana had reached his views some time ago. This presentation of the matter is due to his earlier studies in scholastic philosophy. The background of his thought was due to his training as a Catholic and to his philosophical reading guided by that early interest. Santayana has been a keen critic of various expressions of the New Realism.

The issues raised in this paper are extremely elementary, and no complex metaphysical issues are here decided. At almost every point there is opportunity to bring into the field of vision matters which are very critical for the understanding of the idealistic position. [Here the lecturer began to read from Santayana's paper.]

"Some Meanings of the Word Is"[7]

If we take the term essence to designate inalienable ideal being, of which physical or psychic existence happens to realize a part, we may contrast the sense in which being is predicated of essence with some other senses of the verb to be; for there are many.

The terminology of the language is Aristotelian in its origin. Essence is the name of the what of things, that which answers the question "What is it?" "What is it really?" "What is it genuinely?" That character, that feature, that account, that nature of things which answers the question "What is it?" is essence.

"Inalienable" is used in the sense that so long as this thing is precisely what it is, it can't lose its essence. The essence of a thing is that about the thing which it couldn't lose without ceasing to be that thing. This suggests a good many questions, some of which are dealt with later. Taking you as a person, what is your essence? Well, it is your inalienable being: the what about you of such nature that, if you should lose it, you wouldn't be you. Essence is in that sense inalienable.

"Ideal being" is used with no tendency to go over to an idealistic tendency in metaphysics. If you consider the essence of a thing, you have before you the ideal account or the ideal knowledge of what the thing is. Thus your own essence would be that of which one would have an idea who knows precisely what you are. The scholastic doctrine in discussing such matters often had the advantage of the special Christian doctrine called creationism. You are now because God created you. Before you were created you had an essence; that essence is common to you then and now. That is your ideal being. Your essence doesn't belong to you in virtue of your existence as a created being. God has created you, but one doesn't express that when one speaks of one's essence.

"Physical or psychic existence happens to realize a part" of the essences. In advance of the creation of the world, the Divine Intellect, considering what world he should create, faced a world of essences, ideal beings. In that world were contained all the possibilities of existence so far as they were genuine possibilities. They constituted what St. Thomas in his account of the Nature of God discusses under the head "Concerning the Divine Ideas," the facts which the Divine Intellect would face in advance of the act of creation.[8] The world of the divine ideas would be the world of the essences.

That world of essences would have to account for two well-known kinds of being in the world that is. (1) When God creates the world, he creates kinds, species, laws, relations, universal types, sorts of being. Of course, it was a very interesting question for scholastic philosophy what the difference between this kind of being and any other kind of being is. (2) Then there are individual beings. The world of the divine ideas would contain both. Thus the Divine Being knows in advance not only the what of humanity, but also your own individual what. The difference between these two was a very critical question for scholastic philosophy, as it has become again from the point of view which has led to the New Realism. In what sense is there an essence of Man among the essences, and in what sense is there an essence of each individual man? And how does the difference in essence which distinguishes Socrates from Plato differ from the difference in essence between man and beast?

From that point of view, physical or psychic existence "realizes" or brings into the realm of created being a part only of the essences. There are countless things which God might have created and which he didn't create. In dealing with the world of his ideas, the divine Will selected those of them to which the creative Idea gave the particular realization which constitutes the existence of the created world. The general relation is that of part and whole, or in terms as near to ordinary usage as you can get, the real or existent is only a part of the possible, so far as its essence is concerned. Only a part of the essences are existent. There are countless more that might have been, but here are only you and I. We human beings form a part of the beings that might have been evolved.

The word "is" is the copula of judgments expressed in subject and predicate, S is P.

First Meaning of "is": Identity

[Royce continues the reading]:

> *1. The copula properly denotes identity, not merely in the obvious case of* A *is* A*, but in cases where diversity of symbols or of approach disguises the identity of the object meant, so that the discovery of this identity may be important or surprising; as when we say, "This is Odysseus," or "XI is 11," or "12 is 2 × 6." It is in this sense that being is proper to essence; everything* is *what it is. Whenever for the sake of emphasis we repeat a word, saying "No, No," or "Business is business," the effect is to detach and make indubitable the essence we mean, so that attention may be fixed upon it to the exclusion of circumstances, which do not alter essences.*

For "circumstances" the Aristotelian language originally used the word "accidents," although by circumstances one means accidents of a decidedly accidental sort. It does not belong to your essence that you have or have not a hat, or that at present it is or is not on your head. That is a circumstance. There are some circumstances which become from some points of view in which one is interested more or less essential. It isn't a mere circumstance that I have eyes; it does alter something which I should regard as a part of the essence of me. Whether my eyes are open or shut may be said to belong to the circumstances; but if I am a tightrope walker it may become essential whether my eyes are open or shut.

Of circumstances and accidents one may say that these are terms of decidedly variable meaning. It is pretty hard to say what sort of circumstances in no wise alter essences. This difficulty lies very deep in the heart of anything realistic. It exists in the nature of realistic conceptions and in a way warrants the question which I raise at the culmination of the austere argument in *The World and the Individual.* The sharp distinction between circumstances and essences is an important distinction, but it is well for us not to think that this whole matter is clear and easy.

"Business is business" means that while you are in the business mood you have to fix your attention on the what of some one piece of business, or perhaps on the essence of business viewed as a somewhat vague universal. One says "Business is business" when he is interrupted by that to which he doesn't want you or himself to attend: Let's leave out the circumstance and stick to the essence of it. In this case the difference between essence and circumstance is precisely a difference to which one wants to attract attention; one turns away from the interruption; we mustn't be turned away from our goal. But the right to distinguish between what is and what is not business may become a very important ethical question as well as a theoretical question. This all raises the question of the sense in which one can say that circumstances do not alter essences.

[Royce again reads]:

> *In such expressions of identity lies the most proper and literal force of the word is. Hence the term essence, derived from the same root, is well fitted to designate any ideal or logical nature, anything always necessarily identical with itself. Nothing else so truly is as character. By having character things can become candidates for existence; without character their existence would not differ from their absence nor from the existence of something else. Even after things lose their existence, or before they attain it, their character defines and distinguishes them in eternity, so that true and false assertions may be made concerning them, such, for instance, as that they do not exist. What an essence is it is always; and insofar as a thing changes*

> *its character it embodies a different essence and, however continuous its existence or persistent its substance, is "essentially" a new thing.*

"Character" is whatness. "Things can become candidates for existence"—"things" are essences. Unless you yourself have an essence, your existence wouldn't differ from your non-existence. Unless you are you, what is the difference between your being and your non-being? That which constitutes your essence must be such that the world would be different if instead of you there were somebody else filling your place. You can raise the question, "What would that be?" Here, however, we don't answer such questions; we are raising them.

The world of essences was object for the divine Knowledge; the world of divine ideas is the world of the objects of the Logos, the second person of the Trinity. "In the beginning was the Word, and the Word was with God, and the Word was God." That doctrine, as worked out and put in technical theological form, would be the doctrine that in advance of creation there would be the world of the divine ideas, the world of the Logos, the world of the candidates for existence. That world would seem to have a kind of existence of its own. The scholastics were puzzled by that. Was God then limited by the fact that the ideas were there and he had to know them? St. Thomas solved that problem by this answer:[9] In advance of creation the divine Being possessed a Being of his own, a reality of his own, and knew himself to be imitable in an infinite number of ways. These ways in which he could be imitated by a created being were the essences. The divine Intellect knew that, not by a laborious inspection, but by an immediate intuition. In common terms, one would say that the candidates for existence are the world of possibilities which might exist or not. The possibilities have this shadowlike being of their own. They aren't without some sort of fact–character about them. Their fact–character is not the character exemplified by the existence of this or that. When you distinguish between the that and the what of things, between the fact that you are and the kind of character whereby you answer the question what you are, one has then a sharp distinction. There is a difference between the fact that you are (you might not be; you might be annihilated at any moment) and what you are.

But after you have made that distinction, you then come upon the very interesting and puzzling feature of the case just discussed. The whats, the essences, the occupants of this shadowland of being, from which we, the existent beings, are selected, are not a realm of nothings but a realm of genuine possibilities. Then the question arises, what shall we say about these? Wherein does the world of the existents differ from the world of the possibles?

Here one faces two problems which you can get into clear language only by using those queer abstracts: "the whatness of the that," "the thatness of the what." If you ask what it is that distinguishes the possible from the existent, you face the question of the whatness of the that. Further, the world of essences would be itself a world of facts, and you must face also the thatness of the what. There is a good ground for making this distinction.

<u>The whatness of the that</u>: The that of you as distinct from the what of you gives rise to the question, what happened when you came into being, when the merely possible you became the existent you? What difference does it make to the created world whether it is created or not? Apparently it makes a great difference; but the whatness of the that is a puzzling and insistent problem.

<u>The thatness of the what</u>: The world as it would be if all of us were destroyed is a world of essences. Isn't it a world of facts? What kind of facts are they? That is the second question.

Since you have a character, your existence does differ from the existence of something else. If you vanish from the world and somebody else takes your place, that makes a difference in the world; but that difference depends on the fact that you have a character. If there were no difference between you and your neighbor, if both of you had no character whatever, then the existence of one wouldn't differ from the existence of the other. Essence and character are used synonymously for the <u>what</u>.

Aristotle had in Greek the expression τέ ἡστι (what is it?), and he then made himself the word essence, τἄ τέ ἓ̂ξ εἶ̂ξαι (*quid sit esse,* what being is). This means the essential character which differs from circumstance.

The thatness of a thing is its existence. If God created the world, the essences of things were already there in the world of the Logos. That character would in eternity, apart from the coming and going of existence, define and distinguish them. The world of essences is a world of facts, but they are not existent facts. In advance of creation Socrates doesn't exist; but of this being you could make an assertion that was false. Aristotle didn't suppose that the world had ever been created, but he made these distinctions whenever he had occasion.

Change doesn't belong to the world of the essences, but to the world of the existents. When you change in the world of existence, you as existent embody or exemplify that which is the existence of a different essence; but the essence of you doesn't change. The universal nature of man, what Human Being is, isn't changed when you shoot a man. That shooting destroys that man's existence. The essence of Man will remain unaltered eternally. The same would hold of the individual essences; that which distinguishes Socrates from Plato isn't altered if one of these men vanishes. If one man kills another in a duel, or if each kills the other, the two essences remain as distinct as ever. To be dead doesn't change <u>what</u> you are.[CA] Of course, it makes a great difference to anybody who is interested in the question <u>that</u> you are. The same holds where changes are concerned. A thing can change its character. Insofar as it changes its character, it changes its essence. So far as it becomes a part of your essence that you are now to be viewed as a member of Phil. 9, you embody a different essence. Before you took Phil. 9, your individual existence embodied other essences; when you became a member of Phil. 9, your existence embodied that different essence. All changes which occur in the world involve essential changes, but the essences themselves don't change. The existence in question takes on, or partakes of, a distinct essence from the foregoing. The essences aren't changed.

In the seventeenth century the philosophy of the time hoped to get rid of Aristotelianism altogether. Experience showed that it couldn't. I am glad that one neorealist knows how near he is to these considerations.

Feb. 19 In Professor Santayana's paper we have a summary of considerations which a person has to face irrespectively of any one metaphysical doctrine. These considerations lie deeper than the contrasts between realistic and idealistic points of view. Both the realist and the idealist will have to take account of these matters. If you can find out that Professor Santayana's account of the situation is true and adequate, it will be by way of reflecting upon certain aspects of experience or of facts that are known to you. Of course, the kind of cognition which is expressed by Professor Santayana's statement is a conceptual sort of cognition, although perception also comes in, in the portion which we shall take up shortly.

What Socrates taught his pupils to insist upon was an account of what are here called the "essences" of things. That was the Socratic method: "Don't be deceived by the transient aspects of the world; consider instead the essence of things." The essences are exactly what Plato called the Ideas or ideal forms or types. Aristotle preferred the word "forms" for that aspect of the essences, considered with reference to the realm of facts. You, as this being, have a form. You, as you the individual are, are a certain combination of the form or essence of you, and the matter of you. The matter of you is that which is necessary to the condition of your being as this individual in the world of individuals. That the essences, the whats, are substantially the Platonic ideas is the consideration which Santayana has in mind.

The essences exemplify, or are identical with, those possibilities whereof the things which are are the exemplifications. That is what is meant by saying that the things that are realize or express in individual form a selection only of the essences. You are an example as an individual of what the realm of possibility, apart from your realization of it, otherwise contains. You exemplify certain possibilities: If you change, if you live and pass from state to state, that means that you as individual exemplify now one possibility, now another.

Thus essences do not change, but the individuals which exemplify them change by virtue of the fact that they now partake of this essence, now of that. They partake, exemplify, share, are embodiments of, now this essence, now that. Physical or psychic existence happens to realize a part of the inalienable Ideal Being which constitutes the realm of possibility, the realm of the Platonic forms or ideas. When the essences get thus realized or exemplified in the realm which we ourselves occupy (so far as we are the beings that we are), you have the contrast between the individual on the one hand and the essence which at a given time the individual realizes. This contrast is prominent throughout all Platonic discussions of such matters. If you would not be deceived in your estimate of the world by your passing impressions of the facts of the world, be sure that you take account of what essences or possibilities are realized. Your reason is perfectly capable of taking account of these essences by themselves. And then, of course, you will see that the various individuals which realize possibilities do so by partaking now of this possibility and now of that.

Meanwhile, all along here is mentioned the relation of inherence or the relation of partaking of. Insofar as it belongs to your essence now to be a human being, you inhere in or partake of the essence of Man. Sometimes this relation is read in the other direction and it is said that humanity inheres in you. The facts can be discussed only by taking account of these distinct aspects of the situation. The essence which you realize belongs to the world where essentially nothing changes and all is eternal. As for the individual exemplification of the essence Man, you can illustrate it rather than readily understand it, for the problem of the individual is indeed a puzzling problem.

Permanently puzzling for Aristotle was this problem: Are the essences by themselves essentially universals, so that it belongs to their nature to be the essences—each one—of an indefinitely great number of individuals. Is it of the nature of Man that there might be a great many men? When you speak of this shadowland of the possibilities, wherein do they differ from the individuals which exemplify them? And as for these individuals which may partake now of one essence and now of another, wherein do these individuals preserve their individuality? You can express the problem in the form of various distinctions which are as puzzling as they are familiar. What is the difference between two individual men, Socrates and Plato? It is not a difference in essence so far as they are both men, but some other essence might be exemplified, the man of some calling or nationality or language. On the other hand, so far as they have the same essence, they are two examples of the possibility called men or Man. Are individuals distinguished by their own essence wholly? Could there be two individuals the same in all essential respects? Then what would be the difference between them? One in vain endeavors to escape from these problems by declaring that one has given up these scholastic distinctions and futilities. These problems arise again in whatever way you turn.

If you ask about multiple personality as seen from Santayana's point of view,[CA] I suppose we should have to call that a case of some individual partaking at different times of different essences. For Aristotle, the world consists of individuals; each individual exemplifies some form or essence, or is a combination of some sort of essence with some matter, some means whereby some form is exemplified. That which goes on in the world involves a change according as now this, now that essence is exemplified.

Aristotle was always conscious that he differed from Plato as to the sense in which the realm of possibilities have themselves a place in being. Aristotle represents Plato as thinking that each essence has its own inalienable being, so that it is as good as if it were a reality, whereas the individual beings of our realm of common sense are more or less fantastic or not genuine. Aristotle is proud of the fact that for him everything that is is individual. Nevertheless, he sometimes speaks of the essence of the individual as being more real than the individual is. The relation between the two is one of the puzzling problems of a Platonic or Aristotelian metaphysics. Professor Santayana for the moment presents to you the distinctions and does not here solve the problem.

William James studied the remarkable case of a carpenter named Ansel Bourne[CA] who drew his savings one day and disappeared.[10] Some months afterward a Philadelphia shopkeeper, who had said that his name was Brown, waked up and demanded that people explain the thing to him: he was Bourne. The whole situation was incomprehensible to him. The Society for Psychical Research took it up. Hypnotic methods were used to get the two personalities side by side and compare them. By these experiments Bourne gained a certain amount of memory of what had happened. No pathological phenomena such as characterize an ordinary case of insanity were involved. It was a case of exaggerated absentmindedness; he forgot who he was and who he had been.

Santayana would have to say that Bourne changed his essence during those times, although the Brown essence and the Bourne essence would be in each case the essence of an individual. In what sense the character of the psychical processes would make such an effort to explain the facts adequate, you must yourself judge.

"This is Odysseus" refers to the surprising identification of the poor old beggar going about the court, recognized at first by nobody but his dog and later on by various people gradually, until Telemachus says, "This is Odysseus"; then Penelope says, "This is Odysseus"; and finally, the suitors have to say, "This is Odysseus."

In the Ansel Bourne case, James's comment is that, as far as he can make out after a careful analysis of what could be discovered in the hypnotized patient, Brown was a sort of dwarfed and very much reduced edition of Bourne as he had been. It was only a piece of him that forgot the rest of him and went off to a Philadelphia suburb.

Second Meaning of "is": Designation of a Property (or Quality)

[Royce continues the reading from Professor Santayana's paper:]

2. The copula is also used, in predication, to designate some property in what has other properties as well, in the form A is B; a formula which, if being always means identity, would be self-contradictory. Wine is wine and red is red, but red is not wine nor (in the sense of identity) can wine be red. When we say it is so, we mean "has the color red." This use of the word is remains ideal and relative to character only; it does not transgress the sphere of essence, logically or esthetically intuited, but it marks only a part of the essence embedded in the whole. We see in this that essences may be complex, many essences being included in one, as the essence of red wine includes the essence red, and the essence red, perhaps, the essence extension. Every quality in actual or possible objects is a fundamental and separate essence on its own account. The fact that some essences are used by us as subjects and some as attributes in describing existing things is due to the actual constitution of nature, in which some qualities happen to be deeper and more constant that others, as the mass of a body is more constant than its position. In the realm of essences every distinguishable element, and every possible system of elements, is equally primitive and indestructible.

When we say "Wine is red," this use of the word "is" doesn't refer to the puzzles of the realm of the existents but to the realm of the possibilities or essences. In the realm of mathematical analysis one is studying the nature of complex essences. The concept of a prime number is a concept of a complex essence with different aspects which must be considered by reference to what it is to have factors. All this belongs to the realm of the essences. According to this second section, essences have a complex character from certain points of view, although in certain respects they haven't such complexity, according to Santayana.

Third Meaning of "is": Existence in Time and Space

[Continuing the reading:]

3. The word is, however, has another totally different acceptation when it means exists. Existence adds no new character to the essence it hypostatizes, since the essence of any existing thing is its full character; but the hypostasis is temporal and caught in a mesh of natural relations (as even one part of physical space is in contrast to any other part) to which the essence hypostatized is impervious. When the word is designates existence it claims for the object a place in some natural context, amid external variable relations, such as the essence embodied could not have in its own dialectical and eternal medium. Whether such a claim is just can never be determined by analyzing the essence of what is said to exist, but only by exploration, through experience or evidence, of the flux of nature, until the essence invoked is discovered embodied in the suggested context: for it is idle to say that a thing exists or does not exist, if we do not say when or where. Existence exhibits things in a situation and with an emphasis which their mere essence could never have had. Things generate one another, and their flux, by catching the dye now of one essence and now of another, becomes varied and describable. Something is, in the sense of exists, when it figures in this changeful and selective illustration of essences.

Existence means the realization of essence. You the individual being exist; that means you have an essence, but your essence doesn't constitute your existence. The what doesn't determine the that. Existence, as an abstract noun, is a general name for the fact that somewhat is, but with special reference to the matter that the thatness has apparently the character of being individual.

The realm of the essences, of the possibilities, has its own curious sort of fact–character such that if everything which exists were to vanish, still the essences would remain unchanged, for their being is inalienable. On the other hand, the thatness is certainly different from the character belonging to the essences.

Hypostasis is used for a substantially present instance of an essence. Substance is the equivalent of hypostasis. A hypostasis is an individual exemplification of some essence. The fact that you exist adds no new character to the essence of you. Your existence doesn't distinguish you from other animals, which have the same existence as you. Before we were, we were possible; our essences are unchanged by existence. Existence itself doesn't belong to the realm of characters.

When Kant studied the ontological proof, he discussed this matter and said, "Existence isn't a predicate which genuinely belongs as a character of the object that exists." You have to deal with this problem whether you deal with an idealistic or a realistic view of the world.

"Dialectical and eternal medium" refers especially to the feature upon which Plato laid stress: how do you find out about the essences? By a process of analysis which you can best carry out by asking, "What is this?" and best continue by a process which the Socratic dialogue exemplifies:

What are you?

A statesman.

What is a statesman?

Hereupon you enter upon the dialectical process.

In the realm of the Platonic ideas nothing changes; each essence is what it is and identical with itself and different from all others. To be sure, there are complex essences there, as in the case of the essence of red wine, and here special problems of the complication of essences are involved. The essence of prime numbers may involve the essence of factors. The whole theory of numbers is a theory of a very complicated world. Nevertheless, the realm wherein all these essences have their place isn't changed by anything that happens in time. What happens in time is that now that individual realizes a certain essence, then another essence. All these considerations are on your hands in any case, whether you agree with realism or with idealism. Santayana is disposed to emphasize the materialistic features of realism; he is a Platonic materialist.[CA]

I haven't as yet found any less hostile and polemical mode of approaching the contrast between realism and idealism than this essay furnishes. It has the character which people so inadequately call by that much abused word "suggestive." It is full of challenges and of indications of interpretation. *Feb. 24*

Under {Santayana's paragraph} "1," stress has been laid on the fact that the word "is" expresses identity. How problematical an affair identity is you have already begun to see.

[Then, rereading paragraph "2," Royce interspersed comments]:[CA] The "characters" of objects are the <u>whats</u>. Thus, when water exists, it is an existent which embodies or exemplifies some essence; but in this essence there are various characters, some of which in the existent water are more subject to change than the others. The chemical constitution of the water may remain unchanged while it undergoes changes of temperature; but in case of a chemical change such as decomposition, the essences of other elements take the place of the compound called water. Under ordinary temperatures and under the pressures with which we are most familiar, water is a liquid; it is or for a while remains a liquid. An existence which embodies or exemplifies a complex essence has some characters which are more transient than others. If you are telling what sugar is, you characterize it in terms of the characters essential to, constitutive of, sugar. But when the sugar exists, without ceasing to be sugar it is soluble. When you dissolve it, it exemplifies still what is essential to sugar. The important point is that in such cases <u>is</u> stands for what is no longer identity but is used to mean "has the attribute, the special character of." Sugar is soluble. The complex essence is taken as the subject, whose part, some one of the essences included within it, appears as predicate.

[And rereading "3"]: In another usage of the word "is," this paper exists, this desk exists, you exist. Existence adds no new character to the essence it hypostatizes, to the essence to which it gives the thatness in question. When you exist, that makes no difference to what you are; you are the same in respect to your essence. The difference is in the <u>that</u>. The essence hypostatized is impervious to, unchanged by, this change which occurs when somewhat exists. Existence involves you in a relation to other existent objects, but none of that network changes what you are. That network is temporal.

But change can be viewed from another side. When you change, it may be that you take on a new character. Insofar as you do, then you exemplify a new essence. When Woodrow Wilson is elected President of the United States, his essence is the essence of the same man, but he takes on a new essence. He now exemplifies what the Constitution, the law, and in part the customary usage of the country recognize as the characters of the President. The situation which appears when he is elected and inaugurated involves existence—now a President of the United States exists and that President didn't exist as President before. An individual existent man has taken on the character of President at the moment of inauguration, and he assumes thereupon that character or essence. Another man has taken over the functions of President. Meanwhile the functions of a President don't alter when that person becomes President. It makes no difference to the essence of a President of the United States that now this man is President, now that. It makes a good deal of difference to the man. The man himself before he was President was a citizen; he had the essence of a citizen, not of a President. In order to be President, he has to take on another essence, that of President. The hypostasis, the existence of a President, is temporal. The President is "caught in a mesh of natural relations" (and political relations); but to these the essence hypostatized (the character and office of a President) is impervious. Thus the President Woodrow Wilson exists in some context amid external variable relations, but the essence of President couldn't possibly have those external relations in its own dialectical medium when the dialectical method finds out what it is to be President. That essence doesn't change even when the existent President is no longer Roosevelt or Taft but becomes Wilson.

The constitutional President of Mexico doesn't exist. Mexico may have a constitution which defines the essence of a president, but that doesn't assure Mexico of having any constitutional president.

For a while Jefferson Davis was the existent man who was President of the Southern Confederacy. Today, the President of the Southern Confederacy doesn't exist. There is no such person and presumably there never will be. Even were the lost cause revived, it would not be the old Confederacy. But the words "President of the Southern Republic" were defined by the agreement of the Confederate States. The President of the Southern Confederacy, the Emperor of France or of Brazil, have essentially individual being, although in the realm of existence there might be no such beings. Only one man could exemplify the essence: there can be but one if there is any. This gives what I call a "class of one." This class might have no existent representative. There is but one constitutional President of the republic of Mexico, in the sense that there could be no two; but there needn't be any; and as a fact there is none.

There is but one President of the United States. There can be but one. The right of Hayes to be the one was seriously questioned. If the validity of the election and resultant inauguration of Hayes had been brought to issue before the Supreme Court, the question would have been "Who has this essence?" This is the kind of question from which Mexico has suffered so often. What individual existent embodies the essence? One faces the question with the knowledge that the essence can be embodied by but one man; what one must be determined from the side of the essence.

When you read the Constitution, you learn what the President is, not who he is. When you elect him, you bring this essence into existence. If you make a contract with a man whereby a corporation or firm or partnership is brought into being, you define in the contract an essence; but by defining the essence, you don't define an existent. It is possible that a legal entity of a corporate nature should be brought into being without any of the objects in question being themselves existent. The constitution of any sort of organization does not itself assure anything in the realm of existence. As soon as the constitution of a club is set down as a plan or project, in essence there is such a club. The constitution doesn't make the existence; it is some further act. When the officers are elected, something occurs which belongs to the realm of existence. You can't say that the essences remain nothing at all until the existence is there. The essences are a good deal; they are precisely what we are interested in when we consider plans, projects, agreements, constitutions, and laws. When we try to get something done, we face the problem of how to give to a certain essence a certain sort of existence. When we get it done, nothing happens to the essence, for that was in our mind when the plan was started.[11] The distinction between the existents and the essences is a conceptual distinction. The new character happens to the man who writes the essay, not to the essay. The essay hasn't done anything.

If you want to know what is the constitution of the essence before it comes into existence—well, make a promise or agreement, sign a contract. Then you are acquainted with an essence which may or may not come into the realm of existence. You ask what the essence is before it gets embodied or exemplified. Just contrast what is present before the project is carried out with what is present when it is carried out.

For idealism, of course, there is an intimate connection between essence and existence. For idealism, the reality of things consists in the fulfillment of certain purposes. Your plan in the [aforementioned] instance is changing all the while until its execution; it is a different plan as you go on, and at the point where the existent is certainly there, the plan itself gets completed. I shouldn't think, however, that this made insignificant the distinction between essence and existence. In the realm of interpretation, the essence and the existent go together more intimately than in the realm of conception, and the distinctions get mediated in various ways. To understand the distinction between essence and existence means to find a certain inadequacy in it. Here, Santayana relieves one of mere polemic.

If one asks whether there is not a distinction between an essence and the essence of an essence, I answer that there would be a certain essence which would make a man a president. To get at this one asks, "What is essential to the office of a president?" "What is the essence of the essence?" The realm of essences is full of relations. To be a president involves a standing-in-relations—relations to the electors, to the voters, etc. It is essential to the essence of a president that he should be a person so known to the country that people should vote for him. That essence of a president is something that we prize very much. It will be our votes which will determine whether Wilson shall be re-elected or not.[12] The electoral college embodies a decidedly different essence from the one which the founders expected it to have. It was very soon found out that that whole plan was impracticable. A change occurred which was a change in essence, although the essential feature of the change is not written in the Constitution. We pledge in advance the persons whom we nominate as electors, and we regard ourselves as voting for the President.[13]

Whenever you form a deliberate plan, in accepting the plan before you do anything, you define and understand an essence for whose existence you hope. Whatever carries it out is quite distinct from the plan itself. It has been objected that sometimes the carried-out plan is different from the plan undertaken. That will concern us at another time.

Fourth Meaning of "is": Origin or Substance of an Existent

Feb. 26 [Royce continues the reading of Santayana's paper]:

> *4. The word is, in a looser sense, often serves to express the substance or origin of a thing, as when we say, "This spark is a firefly, not a star." Essentially a spark is simply a spark and a light a light; but in the natural world a light may be the effect or the appearance of many different things. A sure sign of this improper naturalistic use of the word is may be found in the phrase, dear to so-called critical philosophers, "This is nothing but that." Thus we hear that a house is nothing but bricks and mortar, the mind nothing but a bundle of perceptions, God nothing but a power not ourselves that makes for righteousness, the material world nothing but a permanent possibility of sensation. Such assignations of specific origins or substances to the things of daily discourse might possibly be correct physically or his-*

torically: the whole substance, the full ground of what is analyzed, might be given in such an analysis. In fact, this sort of analysis is seldom adequate; in none of the four examples I have just given, for instance, is even the substance or origin of the things in question assigned correctly. But even if it was, the essence of each of them would have been missed and left standing, and in spite of the critic would remain the very essence that it always was. Things are never merely their whole substance nor merely their whole cause; they are what they are, having an inalienable physiognomy and essence of their own. To say they <u>are</u> what they are made of or what brings them about, when this is something wholly different from them in essence, is to use the very <u>to be</u> in a confused and confusing way, although the poverty of language may render such speech inevitable.

Santayana is himself a believer in naturalism: his world is a naturalistic world. I have heard him say that he never could sympathize in metaphysics with a man who wasn't in essence a naturalist. The word {"naturalist"} may have a great many meanings in its theoretical definiteness. One may prefer to call himself a mechanist. What is meant by naturalism is that ideals, wishes, purposes, desires, interests—such as we human beings know and value—don't determine facts. Facts come and go as it is their nature to. They come as they will. The world as a naturalistic world is determined by an order which is independent of desires, wishes, ideals, values, and such affairs. It is a world of a sort that people commonly call mechanical. In Santayana's *Life of Reason,*[14] he makes use of the word "mechanism" freely. The meaning of the world is not determined by virtue of any of those interests or ideals which we human beings regard as rational: the world is irrational; it is whatever it is its nature to be. Lucretius the Epicurean, in accepting naturalism, found that freedom which he regarded as the goal of the wise man, freedom from superstition. The existent world has the character of the atoms which fall through the void; matter moves as it is its nature to move. That fact proves of great importance for one who wants to free himself from all superstition.

The natural order is what we have been calling the existent order. You discover it by discovering not what things are but that they are. Its complications are such as Aristotle tries to catch by using the category <u>substance</u> versus quality, quantity, etc., which are the categories of <u>accident</u>. Santayana does not go into the distinction between substance and qualities, quantities, or relations.

Santayana here points out that, in talking of the natural world, one has occasion frequently to lay stress on certain aspects of facts which tempt one to an improper naturalistic use of the word "is." As a scholastic, Santayana is somewhat offended by this, because it isn't a fixed usage and is never quite adequate. In your natural world there are certain facts called "substances." They are things; for a materialist, they are atoms; for an Aristotelian, they might have decidedly other characters. In any case, in the natural world these substances appear now here, now there; now in this way, now in that. A chemical element is a substance and may appear as a solid, a liquid, or a gas according to conditions which have to do with the element in question. In such cases we are likely to use the word "is" and say, "At normal pressures and temperatures hydrogen is a gas." In any such case we have this improper use of the word "is." What we mean is "appears as," or "is of such-and-such a nature," "has this substance or origin." Substances come into existence and go out of existence; therefore there are origins. Also there are appearances and seemings. When we want to express such things, we use the word "is" in this sense. The only justification is that the poverty of language makes it inevitable; we haven't any other verb that will do as well. Santayana regrets this usage. He doesn't refer it to the defect or confusion of any group of philosophers, except that he says the so-called critical philosophers are likely to emphasize this improper use in such expressions as "This is nothing but that."

The great point is to distinguish this use of the word "is," proper or improper, from the other usages, especially from that use which expresses the genuine essence, what it is.

[Royce concludes the reading:]

> *Whenever, then, the word is though used with literary propriety, seems to cover some ambiguity or (as in the ontological proof) to lend itself to some obvious fallacy, we have but to ask whether it is used essentially, meaning "is identical with this," or attributively, meaning "has this property among others," or existentially, meaning "has a place in the flux," or naturalistically, meaning "has this substance or origin." If we substitute the last three phrases whenever they will fit, the cases in which the word is alone remains appropriate and sufficient will be those in which it serves to denote an essence, to give that essence a definition, or to call it by some synonym of its proper name.*

The main matters on which Santayana has laid emphasis are the distinction between essence and presence in the fact–world, the essences versus their embodiments or exemplifications. In close connection with this you get a definition of existence. The other point of the paper is the question about the nature of identity. The members of the realm of essences have being, but this being is different from the sort of being called existence. The two realms have some close relation. Amongst the essences, the great relation is that of identity, and the word "is" expresses identity. The nature of identity and identification brings up various puzzling questions which we must take up later.

In the final paragraph Santayana uses as synonymous with the meaning "exists" the expression "has a place in the flux." The flux is the order of nature, the world of existence and of changes. What exists has a place where it exists and a time when it exists. For a materialist, an atom exists all the time, unless the world had an origin; but at any time an atom would exist in a place. From this point of view, existence presupposes an interesting triadic relation (not however a mediating relation) of this sort: Let Q stand for an existent. Q is in the place P at the time T. An existent always stands in this triadic relation. There would be always a triadic relation of Q and P and T. Let R mean the relation of being in a place at a time, and you get a shorthand expression: R(QPT), which means Q is at the place P at the time T. The world of existence is full of objects which always stand in such triadic relations. The subject of the relation is always some existent; if it is a determinate and definite existent, it has a place at any given time; and there is a time when it is at any given place. If we substitute blanks for these three, we can reduce all propositions about existents to "Blank is at place blank at time blank." Give me a place and a time, and name me the existent which is at that place at that time, and you will have expressed the characteristic relations of existence. What we know about existents depends on filling out these blanks. One term is the existent itself, the second the place, and the third the time. Santayana isn't especially fond of these logical technicalities, but this is in accordance with what he says.

Places and times have no part in the realm of the essences. If you ask "When is redness?" there is no way of answering that question. Redness is eternally, without reference to time.[CA] Where is redness? Nowhere. It is out of space, out of time.

The realm of the existences is in space and time, but in this curious way: an existent may change its place, and you may consider it now at one time, now at another. But if you take a proposition telling the truth about an existent, it will always be one that fills out the three blanks. Here and now is this piece of chalk. This chalk is in relation to Emerson Hall, to this room. It is also in relation to time—11:35 A.M.

A relation is a feature about an object which it has when you view it in some sort of set or group or class. When a man belongs to a group, he has relations to the other members of that group. When you are here in this class, you stand in relation to the other people in this class. Relations are characters or qualities or features belonging to a member of a collection. The relations in general are forced upon a thing by the order of nature, by the existence to which it belongs. If you took a fact all by itself, apparently you would get rid of the relations, though there are obvious difficulties in the way. That this chalk is here in this room at a certain time is for you a relation in which this chalk stands to its environment. Propositions with reference to this condition are triadic. The relation is a relation of the object to other things in space and time.

Since an atom always was and always will be, according to atomism, in {the} last analysis the proposition would be one that said something about all the time, so as to say something about the single time on the basis of the law.

The atom would move through space but at any given instant it would be at a very individual place. The natural order is such as to determine where a given atom is at a given time. The moon is just now in such relation to the earth that tonight it will rise or set at a certain time. The moon is a peculiarly unchanging body; it wasn't always so, it had a history. If you try to tell the truth about the moon, you always have to have these propositions at a given time, at a given place. You can't get rid of these propositions and tell physical truths about the moon. They are relational truths about a place and a time.

A piece of chalk embodies in existence an essence. The existent piece of chalk always has its time and place. The existent chalk isn't identical with the essence. Whenever an object exists, it has to be at a place and time. These propositions can't be asserted about the essence.[CA] If I took the chalk all alone by itself and omitted the consideration of everything else, there wouldn't be any place at all. The chalk hasn't any inherent place. No somewhat has an inherent place. The actual places are always relations. Kant regards space–relations as such that various objects can coexist in the same space; when they do so, they do so at a time. I don't know any basis for speaking of inherent place as something that wouldn't involve spatial relations.

Santayana is talking about a world of essences which are very numerous. If the world of essences contained but one, whether that could now exist and now not exist, I suppose from Santayana's point of view it could. Existence isn't merely a relation amongst the various essences. Existence doesn't get into the world of essences at all. As to the relation between the essence and the existence, I must refer you once more to the opening paragraph of the essay, ". . . existence happens to realize a part." The whatness or the what of the chalk is its essence. There is an irreducible difference between the realm of existence and the realm of essence. To existence belong objects which stand in these curious triadic relations: each one of them has a place and a time for its existence in such sense that if you are going to say "exists" and to know about its existence, you have to know about its time and place. "It is at a place P at a time T" will in general refer to a definite place and time, so that, if you were to refer to another place or time, the proposition wouldn't be true.

In paragraph 4, by "origin" Santayana means simply the beginning of existence.[CA] Some things originate: Up to a certain time, a certain chemical compound wasn't in the realm of existence; it began to exist at a certain time. In an atomistic world, that would be true of compounds of atoms. Things have origins very generally. Various naturalists would work out these considerations very differently, but all these people would agree in Santayana's distinction between existence and essence.

{After this exposition of Santayana's four meanings of is, the question arises whether Santayana's distinction between essence and existence is as sharp as he insists.}

Chapter 5

The Relational Form of the Ontological Argument

Existence doesn't involve relations which you can call mere relations amongst the essences. The problem of existence is well raised by the discussions about the so-called ontological proof, which assumed its classic form through a monograph of St. Anselm. He gave as a proof of God's existence the fact that by definition God is such a being that his essence implies his existence. He tried by analyzing the essence of God to show that God exists. He stated his proof in the form of an address to the Deity. The atheist is one whose misbelief is foolish. Why then is one certain of the existence of God? *Feb. 26 cont.*

Anselm propounds this divine answer: It is foolish, it is essentially irrational, to deny the existence of God; for what do you mean by the Deity? No matter how you came by the idea, if you have such an idea at all, you define God as the being than whom no greater or more perfect can be conceived. The question isn't how you came by this idea: the very definition of God requires his existence once you have got this idea of him. There are two ways in which you know the essence or definition of God. You can say his existence has its place only in the mind of one who thinks of God. If God existed only in the idea of the person who formed this idea of him, then God would have an *esse in intellectu.* But God can have an *esse in re*, an existence proper, outside the mind of the definer of God's being.

The question is, is God's essence such that his *esse in intellectu* is the only being that he has? Or has he also an *esse in re*? Anselm hereupon says it is obvious that if God is the greatest or most perfect possible being, then he must have an existence outside of our conception or idea of him; for a being that has existence only in the intellect can't be as great or as perfect as a being who exists both in the mind of the one who thinks of him, and in fact. God can't lack existence outside the mind. His essence is such that he must exist. To be the all-perfect being he can't be existent merely in the mind. He must have a place also *in re*. The very perfection of God's nature requires his existence.

Anselm had a very high opinion of this proof. One of his contemporary critics wrote *A Book on Behalf of the Fool* ("The fool hath said in his heart there is no God")[1] and declared the whole proof to be fallacious.

This question tends to bring to light in a marked way what you mean by existence. Is it possible that the existence of a thing could be proved by defining the essence of it and then by declaring that this is the sort of thing that couldn't fail to be?

Feb. 29 Santayana mentions that his survey of the meanings of the verb "to be" will aid you to clear up the situation of the ontological argument in which the word "is" has an ambiguous usage that escapes you. The gist of Santayana's opinion is contained in his words that the essence of a thing is not affected by its existence: "Existence adds no new character to the essence it hypostatizes, since the essence of any existing thing is its full character." Sooner or later, if you are going to take any position about metaphysical questions, you find it necessary to face this matter. There is no more important issue between realism and idealism than this. I don't think you get a fair view of idealism if you think of its issue with realism merely in terms of Professor Perry's egocentric predicament. It is not the most important feature of idealism that it appears to be committed to an insistence upon the importance of what Professor Perry calls the egocentric predicament, viz., that the being of things—whether of God or man or the physical world—is a being in the mind of some thinker. That isn't the most important feature of idealism. The really most important feature is exactly the issues here concerned: does the existence of anything make any difference to its essence? does the essence of anything make any difference to its existence? is it any part of the essence of a thing that it exists?

I am now trying to set forth not the idealistic but the realistic view. It is essential to Santayana's position to assert that the existence of a thing adds no new character to a thing. It is an essential feature of idealism—a difficult thesis and not the one most commonly made explicit—that there is a connection between essence and reality which Santayana doesn't recognize.

When you approach Anselm's proof in the spirit of a realist, you see a great deal of reason for rejecting the proof and to state the case as Santayana does. By making this negative assertion, you don't exactly find out what existence is: but it seems plausible to say that the character of a thing is not altered by its existence or nonexistence.

[Here Royce reviewed the argument of Anselm's *Proslogion.*] You can't rationally deny the existence of God; it would be a self-contradiction; the word "God" means a self-existent being. Anselm's definition of God, as I remember the phrase, is *id quo majus cogitari nequit*, the most perfect possible being.

Anselm makes the distinction between essence and existence but his vocabulary is different from that of Santayana. Anselm says there are two kinds of being, *esse in intellectu* and *esse in re*. When you form a plan of any sort—a plan of a house or of an essay—then your plan has *esse in intellectu*; it has being in a mind or in the mind. So far you get when you understand what the plan is. If you carry out the plan, then it has *esse in re*, being in fact or in reality.

If God has *esse in intellectu* alone and not also *esse in re*, says Anselm, he would not be that which by definition or by essence he is; namely, that than which no greater can be conceived. The divine being must therefore have factual being. *Esse in intellectu* is not as much as *esse in intellectu* + *esse in re*.

The author of the tract *Liber pro insipiente* (A *Book on Behalf of the Fool*) did not himself maintain atheism, but could not regard Anselm's argument as sufficient. His way of discrediting it was to exemplify the fact that you could prove the existence of anything you wanted if only you permitted yourself to add to its definition some type of perfection which should be the highest possible type. The islands of the blessed wouldn't be nearly so blessed if they had only *esse in intellectu* and no *esse in re*. This author suggests in passing that this argument has a very dangerous result: the worst possible devil wouldn't be quite so bad if he had only *esse in intellectu* and not *esse in re*.

Kant, in the *Critique of Pure Reason,* says (as does Santayana) that *Sein*, factual existence, is no real predicate: it doesn't tell what the nature of a thing is. Kant's example is that there is no difference between a hundred possible dollars and a hundred real dollars, no difference in their nature, in their essence. It makes a great difference to me whether I have the hundred real dollars or the hundred possible dollars, but it makes no difference to the dollars. How could I plan to earn $100 if I didn't know what $100 is? Does that change when I earn the dollars? If it does change, I don't get what I worked for. It is of great importance to get them in reality, but if their essence changes while I get them, then it wouldn't be carrying out my plan. These commonsense instances could be multiplied. "If wishes were horses, then beggars could ride." The beggar knows what the essence of riding is well enough to want it. Will, purpose, intention, desire, these all (so far as they come to consciousness clearly) include the consideration, and possibly the longing consideration, of some essence, of some what; but you in vain think of what it is that you want unless you have some means of getting it. It may be that things come to him who waits, but they don't come to him who merely thinks about their essence.

Yet there is something very captivating about the Anselmian argument. Anselm himself supposed it to apply to one case only, the case of the all-perfect being, and he would have declined to accept the wishes of the beggar as fair to his case, or the hundred possible dollars.

Hegel, in his *Logik,* says in answer to Kant that the ontological proof is not intended to apply to beings in general. In Hegel's opinion there is at least one case, the case of the nature of God, where the essence of the thing does involve its presence in fact.

Whoever fills out a check writes out the essence of the thing so far as he can express it. The problem of the contrast between essence and existence is closely analogous to the problem about the relation between the check and the account. The check made out and honored is worth more than the check only made out. If somebody taken at random fills out the check, you will have the essence but not the existence in question, and the bank will probably return the check stamped "no account." It occurs to one that the probability of this will be likely to be increased by the size of the check. If it were possible to define the greatest possible amount that one could write out on a check, that would hardly guarantee that the check would be honored.

The ontological argument appears to have this fundamental absurdity about it, and has repeatedly been thrown out as utterly insignificant; yet it has a fashion of returning. There always remains in my own mind an incident which had its own pathos, which may illustrate the absurdity of the ontological proof. A Maine farmer traveling west was induced by confidence men to exchange his greenbacks for worthless counterfeit "gold." The farmer had never seen any gold money and said pathetically, "I thought gold was so precious that it couldn't be counterfeited." In a way he had taken the essence for the existence. That which appeared as gold, in view of the preciousness of it, must have that character.

You can say that that is the pathetic situation of Anselm: God is so perfectly perfect that he cannot not exist. The *esse in intellectu* cannot counterfeit the *esse in re* because it belongs to the essence itself to be so perfect. That seems to be Anselm's position.

Santayana's phrases, ". . . the word *is* . . . seems to cover some ambiguity," {and} "Existence adds no new character to the essence it hypostatizes," bring before you the essence of the ontological proof.

St. Thomas asserted in the thirteenth century that God has indeed the character of *aseitas*, the character of being such that he cannot not be; but our human intellect is not able to grasp such being by any necessary process. God knows why he must be. A being whose essence involves existence is one thing and there is only one such being. But a being so known to you that from your knowledge of his essence you can conclude his existence—that is absurd. There might be a gold so precious that it couldn't be counterfeited, but we can't find out enough about gold to know that it can't be counterfeited. It may well be the case that there are some things that have to be so. Perhaps the world is such that good triumphs and has to be; but we can't say, "Of course it is of the nature of the good to triumph."

So much for some of the assaults upon the ontological argument. The more recent realistic discussions leave it in worse shape even than this. I am not giving you the idealistic side of the matter at present.

March 2

Over against these obvious objections, we are using something like the ontological proof all the time. Aren't you using at the moment something like an ontological argument for supposing that there is a real world and why there isn't rather nothing at all? You reply that something has to exist; some such a somewhat as you take to be the world must needs be; you know there is a world from the nature of the case, from the very definition of the world.

Other instances come in sight. Surely the past belongs in some sense to the realm that has being. But since your memories are always fallible, why not have it all some sort of dream? Why not say there never was a past and there never will be any future at all? Perhaps there is nothing whatever that represents the fortune which we face with such interest. Is not your answer to such hypotheses somewhat dependent on something which you are likely to call the very nature of the situation?

Inductive inquiry can give only probable results. In the realm of history there are no propositions which are better than propositions of a probable sort. Historical propositions may be highly probable; they aren't certain. Nevertheless, being, reality, existence, the world, the past, what is to come in the future, must have some reality. One says a day must bring forth something. Even if the conception which you have of a day is one whose application to the future has to remain always merely probable—as Browning says, "Who knows but the world may end tonight?"[2] nevertheless, if the question arises, "Why anything at all in the place where tomorrow will be, if it comes?" "Why not suppose that there is nothing whatever there?" your answer is that somehow the nature of the case seems to forbid this. It is of the essence of the past that it was; it is of the essence of the future that it will be. Here then is a case of essence which seems to be somewhat differently related to the ontological predicate than the cases which Santayana puts before us.

The contrast between the essence, which is impenetrable to the changes of existence, and the existence itself, thus appears to us in certain respects inadequate. When we view the past and the future, the situation is not merely the conceptual situation which Santayana lays down in his contrast between essence and existence.

The ontological proof has after all a kind of immortality about it. You see how vulnerable it is when you deal with such things as the pathetic fallacy of the poor old man who thought gold must be so precious (must possess such an essence) that its existence couldn't be counterfeited, that what furnished you with the essence of gold must furnish you with the existence of gold. But if you think of the past and the future, you view the ontological argument in a somewhat different light. Perhaps a study of the reflections which this situation suggests will somewhat alter your view of the sharpness of Santayana's contrast between existence and essence.

Let us return to Santayana's account of the facts:

> *When the word <u>is</u> designates existence, it claims for the object a place in some natural context, amid external variable relations, such as the essence embodied could not possibly have in its own dialectical and eternal medium. Whether such a claim is just can never be determined by analyzing the essence of what is said to exist, but only by exploration, through experience or evidence, of the flux of nature, until the essence invoked is discovered embodied in the suggested context: for it is idle to say that a thing exists or does not exist, if we do not say when or where.*[3]

This passage expresses Santayana's classic abstractions in a very persuasive form. It also shows you their problematic character. He says you can't find out existence by consulting essence. You can't prove propositions involving existence by abstract reasoning. On the other hand, propositions which involve essence you can prove by abstract reasoning: for instance, the proposition about the prime numbers, the assertion that the side and the diagonal of the square cannot possess a common measure, can be proved by abstract reasoning. The field of mathematics is full of propositions which are proved from other propositions. The question, "What are the axiomatic propositions—or are there such?" which cannot be proved, is an interesting problem; but in any case the situation is familiar. So also you can prove what would be the behavior of a planet in a world which consisted of a sun and a planet and where the laws of gravity were different from those of the natural world. The phenomena of such a world would be very different from those of this physical world. All such propositions can be proved from given premises by following certain general logical rules of inference. But by such means, so Santayana points out, you can never prove that anything exists or <u>is in the time-space world</u>. To endeavor to demonstrate existence by such abstract reasoning would involve the fallacy from which one is safe if one has once been clear about the contrast between "is" as relating to essence and "is" as relating to existence.

The justice of the claim that an object exists cannot be determined by analyzing the essence but can be found "by exploration, through experience or evidence, of the flux of nature, until the essence invoked is discovered." The evidence will be derived from what is called "the flux of nature," presumably by examining it. The evidence in question is for Santayana empirical evidence, founded on fact.

What light can experience throw on existence? According to Santayana, I can't prove that God exists by analyzing his essence. As with the old man's counterfeits and the beggar's horse, it is experience, if one has it, which shows existence. I wait or hope for something, knowing what I hope for: knowing the essence doesn't assure me of attaining that for which I hope. When the $100 come into my possession, if they do come, I have an experience. Then what sort of a judgment does experience warrant?

Experience, as I am accustomed to say in an elementary course on logic, leads me to, or warrants, or assures me of, the truth of what a logician would call particular judgments, judgments of the sort exemplified by some such assertion as "Some A is B." It is by experience that I can discover that some A is B. Or simpler still, I discover by present experience that there is some light. If you sat in the dark, your knowledge of what light is wouldn't give you any light, but experience gives you some light when you look about you. Experience warrants the particular judgment, "There is some light." That judgment refers to what you ordinarily call existence. You don't discover existence by abstract reasoning but by experience insofar as your proposition "So and so exists" refers to something which can be expressed in a particular judgment and insofar as a particular judgment can be warranted by experience.

In the analysis of a particular judgment, the judgment "Some A is B" substantially gives you this sense; viz.: there is somewhat which is both A and B. Here the sort of thing which you describe both in terms of A and of B (the A that is a B or the B that is an A) is different from nothing at all. A particular proposition can be expressed symbolically by a non-equation to nothing at all or zero. $AB \neq 0$. Somewhat of the sort there is; the AB kind of a thing has presence which experience can find, detect, exemplify. Just as the judgment "There is some light" is warranted by our experience of the light so that particular judgment "Some light is colorless light" is warranted by the experience of colorless light. If you consider the color that exists about this chalk rubber you can say, "Some chalk rubbers have red strips on them." The experience gives you the existence of the particular. So then you can define what experience can warrant in terms of what for the logician is the ordinary particular judgment.

Opposed to the particular judgments are the judgments which are characterized in logic as universal judgments. They, to be sure, are not judgments involving any empirical existence, although sometimes particular and universal judgments are united in a well-known way. The essence of the universal judgment is that it declares of a proposed or considered sort of a thing "There is nothing of the sort." The judgment may be true or false, but it is a judgment that is negative with reference to existence.

If I say to you, "There is no horse in this room," I say what you might think to be self-evident. The evidence, whatever it is, isn't quite empirical. What you can find by experience is this judgment, "Whatever I observe is something not a horse." That, experience warrants. The particular judgment of experience can be warranted only by an experience in the strictest sense: you can prove that there are red colors or that in the existent world something of that kind can be found, only by experience. You can't prove it in the abstract; no amount of reasoning about the essence of red shows that there is any red in the world. In revenge for this limitation of the particular judgment, you observe this interesting limitation of the universal judgment. In the sciences and in all that part of our life where we are dealing with judgments about right and wrong, the universal strictly so called can never be proved by experience.

I defy you to prove by experience that there is no horse in this room. You will probably not take the trouble to look for the evidence. If you are pressed for the evidence you will say substantially that you don't see one. But there are a good many things one doesn't see which might turn out to be there. You would see the difficulty of proving that there is no pin on the floor in this room. The proposition "There is no horse in this room" involves a good deal of confidence in our power to know about the realm of existence which does transcend our power to know about the contents of experience. To say "I don't see a horse" is positively to be expressed "What I see is not a horse; I see not-horses; I see things that do not belong to the class Horse. I see coats, blackboard, etc." But the assertion goes further: it declares that no examination of experience, none whatever, would reveal horse; there is none here to see. To assert this is to assert something which you can never prove by mere experience. Your actual commonsense proof follows this course: I see no horse here and if there were one here I would see him. This is probable only by virtue of principles about horses and your vision, which experience can never warrant.

Universal assertions do involve negatives. They are essentially negative in their character. Their form may be positive. If I say, "All men are mortal," my assertion is twofold: I mean that the immortal men are not to be found. That is a genuine universal; it is negative. Accompanying that assertion is the assertion deriving from experience, "There are men." If you are asked how you know there are any men at all, you say your warrant is in experience. The empirical side of such universals is particular, and vast numbers of the so-called universals of commonsense are compounds of what would be logically considered universal propositions with what logically considered are particular propositions. If you confine yourself to what you have in mind when you assert simply the universal, or better still to that to which one who expresses himself in universal terms is at least committed, then you have just negative features belonging to the essence concerning which your proposition makes some existential judgment.

The typical universal is the assertion "There is no horse in this room." It is negative and experience cannot prove it. You can't experience its absence in the sense which enables you to make the universal proposition, just because you can't prove the negative "That whose existence we experience here is not a horse."

The assertions which we actually make fall into two classes: (1) The universals, which experience cannot prove although we use them all the time in dealing with experience; (2) the particulars, which if you sufficiently limit their meaning to the objects of experience taken as they are presented to you, then experience can prove them. On the other hand, they can't be proved by abstract reasoning.

There are some deeper connections, with which we don't deal here, between essence and existence. The contrast in any case is there to consider. Essence seems to be the proper object of rational consideration, for you can understand the nature of an essence; and if it is a complex essence, you can take it together with other essences and make them the subjects of universal or rational demonstrations. You can show, for instance, by presuming certain fundamental principles, that it is of the essence of a triangle that the sum of the three angles shall be equal to two right angles. You can show that it is of the nature of the whole numbers and of the diagonal and side of a square that there is no pair of whole numbers such that . . . [etc. incommensurability]. But so far as you deal with existence, the existence itself has the particular character which experience can show. When I speak of existence, I speak of that which can be mentioned in particular terms and can have its presence in the world of fact and can be expressed by a particular judgment, which in turn can be warranted by an experience—a circular process of definition.

If the question arises "Are there any men?" owing to the complexity of the idea, the answer (given in terms of experience) is not quite as finished and satisfactory an answer as we could desire. Experience shows that there are objects which, with the ordinary tests of existence, you regard as sufficiently exemplifying the essence of man to enable you to say "There are men because I have met them." It seems to be experience which shows us that there are physical objects.

On the other hand, the laws of nature can be expressed only in universal propositions. Just as in the case of there being no horse in this room, the laws of nature express themselves negatively, and so cannot be proved by experience. Experience seems to prove that the sun has risen today. The general principle that the sun will go on rising daily forever you can make only probable.

You see that the relation between experience and existence is very close. By an existent we mean somewhat which is an object of experience or somewhat which experience evidences to us or brings to us. The sharp contrast between object of experience and object of abstract reasoning is clear enough so far as we confine ourselves to these simple considerations.

But unfortunately the case can't be closed by any such simple contrasts as that. More deeply we must go into the consideration of things. The world of existent objects which we deal with is a world which has other characters than you can exemplify by the cases so far taken up of horses, men, light, etc. Experience can show you that there is a chalk mark on the board, provided your experience enables you to assert that this is a chalk mark and your vision shows you the mark. But the objects you talk about have another character. Exactly how far you can deal with these other characters in terms of mere experience is a well-known philosophical problem, a problem which is brought out by considering a matter about objects which doesn't at first attract your attention.

Unavoidability of the Relational Form of the Ontological Proof

It is customary to suppose (and Santayana unquestionably supposes) that the existent objects we deal with in the realm of space and time include objects which are of the nature of so-called individuals. Their case is that of the proposition "This is Odysseus." That proposition is a little different from the propositions such as "This is a horse," made by someone who sees it.

The proposition "This is Odysseus" involves a very curious union of the universal and the particular. Our existents are amongst other individuals. Any man would be regarded by us as an individual. You certainly can't prove that John or Odysseus exists by a merely rational demonstration. It isn't of the essence of a man to exist. There was a time when you were not, and there will be a time when you will not be, as man, and so you as the human being are somewhat whose existence certainly does not flow from its essence. Even if you insist upon your immortality, you will still admit that you needn't have been at all. That you are a contingent being is a universal opinion. So far, then, your existence doesn't follow from your essence and needs proof. Either experience or the evidence must show it. You find an existence not by examining its essence, says Santayana, but by consulting experience, or consulting evidence.

Hereupon comes the question "What evidence have you for the existence of an individual man as an individual man?" If I strictly examine the evidence on the basis of which I assert that I stand in the presence of an existing individual man, the evidence appears to take on a somewhat different appearance. When you say "I met my brother today," what evidence have you for the assertion? You first say the ordinary empirical evidence: "I know my brother well; I have met him all my life; I met him today and I saw him." Yes, you met somebody who resembles so much of your brother as corresponds to what you then recalled of his essence; but what evidence have you that the man you met was your brother and not his double? Your evidence isn't merely empirical. To say "I saw my brother" means I saw somebody so like my brother that I can't tell them apart, and I am sure of their individual identity. One may feel very sure on what Santayana calls the evidence.

If common sense is asked, "But what evidence have you that this is your brother and not merely somebody who looks like him?" you would have to answer, "The evidence I have certainly goes beyond experience: this is very like my brother and there can't be anybody else who looks so much like my brother."

You now have to state the proposition in general terms—and what evidence have you for such a proposition? The evidence would take a rational form, a form which common sense would state by saying, "There can't be anybody else who looks so much like him as this; my brother is essentially one; there can be but one of that sort; there can be but one man who looks and speaks so much like him."

Whoever says that concludes that a certain existence conforms to a certain essence. He declares that there is some essence or nature such that this world cannot give it any embodiment unless an individual embodiment, and that the world does give it this individual embodiment. Whoever uses arguments of that sort concludes an existence from an essence. Whoever says the evidence shows the existence, holds that the essence gives some light on the existence. Otherwise, you couldn't be warranted as well as you think you are in holding that you saw your brother. That assertion involves holding that there can be none but he who is so like him. Whoever appeals to evidence for existence is using some form of the ontological proof.

Is there anything whatever in the sort of reasoning which is represented *March 4* by the ontological proof? I suppose this question to be of very critical importance for your whole view of the method of metaphysics. The fact that Anselm was using that proof in reference to the God of Christianity is a historical accident. The argument has numerous idealistic contexts and uses. Our discussion here concerns no one technical issue: it is a question of your whole conception of reality. We have to make up our minds more or less as to whether there is anything in the ontological proof which needs further examination.

According to Santayana, whether anything exists can never be determined by analyzing the essence of it. I remember when Emerson Hall was an essence; gradually it came to exist. The only way we can find that Emerson Hall exists, according to Santayana, is not by inquiry into its essence "but only by exploration, through experience or evidence, of the flux of nature." That seems good sense. Empirical exploration isn't the only way which Santayana mentions: A good deal of what we know about existence depends on "evidence." Here, however, Santayana thinks you are not using the ontological proof in any shape.

The nature of a triangle can be characterized and defined in terms of already established principles, theorems, or whatever they are. Supposing the principles of Euclidian geometry, I can discover some of the properties of a triangle and show that no Euclidian triangle can exist unless the sum of its angles is equal to two right angles; but that doesn't show me existence.

Strictly construed, universal propositions are negatively existential propositions. The evidence depends on previous universal propositions. I know what I mean by a horse; I look about the room and see various non-horses. "There is no horse in this room." What I see is not a horse. I do not experience that there is not a horse. I experience the presence of something not a horse, and that is what I get from experience.

Try to demonstrate by experience that there is no pin on the floor. Usually we get our existential negatives of the universal sort by the process of giving it up. That is good sense but it isn't demonstration. The strictly construed universal proposition is a negative existential proposition not demonstrable by experience without the aid of universal propositions already accepted.

Experience can be characterized as the source of positive existential propositions of the type that we may call particulars. Open your eyes and you experience what you classify as light. What you mean by light is what you now experience. If I speak, there is some noise. If you classify it as a human voice, your assertion is empirically warranted in your own meaning. All that is needed is that you should have the experience. You hear what you mean by a human voice. That assertion could never come from any mere combination of universal propositions: it is warranted by experience.

But apart from universal principles, experience does not give us the individual existences in which Santayana is evidently interested, for he mentions Odysseus as a recognizable man. No experience gives you that. Your recognition of a man involves assertions which go beyond merely accepted sense–contents. By experience you cannot prove that you saw your brother this morning or that you see him now.

It is no matter of current experience that something happened last Thursday. What I mean by current experience I simply illustrate: You hear the human voice. That is no hallucination as long as it persists; you might afterwards call it a hallucination. The dreamer, so far as he is aware of the sense of his dream, has his dream and experiences what he experiences in his dream. Current experience is well represented by a human voice as you now hear it. But you don't experience that I am the same person who lectured to you last Thursday.

When does memory experience the past or the future? Verify now last Thursday's lecture as you verify the sound of my voice—you can't do it. You can be confident that your memory is correct. You have evidence that last Thursday's experience was what it was. It isn't experience in the sense that the sound of my voice is experience. I think you are quite warranted in asserting that it is the same lecturer, but you and I can't prove it by current experience. It involves memory.

I have already told you in the first half-year's work what I mean by saying that I am the lecturer who lectured to you last Thursday. My meaning is that I am considering a certain coherence of my past with what I view as my present. When I have sufficiently recovered my coherence, then I am sure of myself. That is using evidence and not using the current experience.

Santayana gives you the alternatives "through experience or evidence" for finding where the existent exists in time and space. Evidence you are constantly using. I am not wishing to raise any doubts in your minds with regard to that evidence on the basis of which you are confident that your account of your past has its well-recognized grade of correctness. But there is no moment when this is experienced. Experience is illustrated by the sound of my voice as you now hear it; evidence by your confidence that it is the same lecturer.

In a story of Talmudic origin, King Solomon had a wonderful signet ring whereby he compelled demons without parting with his soul. It was doubtful then whether he had a soul anyway but he did get his demons. They made the temple for him and taught him his wonderful wisdom. The demon came to feel that he had done his share of the temple building and also that he had taught Solomon about as much as a mortal man ought to know. He begged that he might borrow the signet ring and sit but a moment on Solomon's throne. Solomon incautiously handed him the ring. The demon at once took Solomon's robe, flung him into the desert, and himself taking on the guise and appearance of Solomon, sat down and called in the court. People had no hesitation in recognizing him as Solomon, but they noticed a sneering manner, a cynicism of language, an incautious confidence about him which made them say, "It is Solomon but he has changed somewhat." He was a much worse ruler than before. It was the false Solomon who married the 5,000 wives and brought the manners and customs of the kingdom into a degenerate state.

Meanwhile, the real Solomon wandered in the desert and became a cook in the palace of a distant king. There he attracted the attention and finally the love of a princess. In the mouth of a fish was found the signet ring which the demon had hurled after him into the desert. With the princess Solomon wandered back to the court, entered and went to the demon, to whom Solomon then showed the signet ring. The demon gave the appropriate sounds and vanished.

This story raises metaphysically the highly interesting problem of identification. You identify not merely your lecturer but you identify or suppose capable of identification material objects of all sorts. For atomism every atom is an individual entity persisting through time.

Russell, in his book *The Scientific Method*,[4] one of the principal documents of current realism, says that the identification of a physical object has to be ideal identification which one doesn't actually accomplish in one's own case. To accomplish what the court in the case of the substitution of the demon for Solomon never attempted to accomplish—actually to accomplish the identification of an individual physical object—would involve an actual watching of a certain series of transformations of current experience, looking at the object (this desk) at various angles, getting countless perspectives, testing the physical object for its properties in various ways, and then observing a continuity of such experience, as when the table continues to feel solid to your touch, as you suppose yourself to observe.

If the court had been fully able to get such experience, they would have seen Solomon thrown away by the demon. The identification of a physical object would involve a very long series of experiences of the object. (Which is my hat? Which is my coat?)

The general rule would be that something involving a long and continuous following of a sequence of experience would be necessary for identifying an individual. The legend of Solomon, by the very wildness of its story, illustrates how little it is that we experience of the individuality of a door, of a blackboard, how little we experience of the identity of a friend from day to day, in what we commonly call our experiences of individuals.[CA] It is plain that your experience of your brother or anybody whom you identify from day to day would have to have a complexity, a richness, in the following from moment to moment, a closeness of detail, which the mythical case of Solomon and the demon brings to our imagination. Vast would be the scope of the experience which was an adequate experience of the list of the objects which you find in the world, if it was to be an experience of their individuality.

Whatever principle is going to enable you to weave together all these experiences and identify Solomon or an atom from day to day, from year to year, from kingdom to desert, from this world to the next, the range of experience needed would be prodigious. Plainly then, the evidence we use is evidence which if it were sufficient evidence and evidence in terms of experience, would be evidence of a very vast range of empirical contents.

If for this experience we substitute, as we inevitably do, what Santayana calls "evidence," we do it in terms of principles whose questionable character you can easily see—not that I want you to conclude that they are invalid, but to examine them. They involve knowing a good deal. "There are no two different men who look so much alike as my brother resembles the man whom I just saw." "There is nobody else delivering lectures who," etc. These principles are easily accepted; it is inevitable for common sense to accept them; but they show you a connection between knowledge and reality which surely needs a somewhat watchful testing.

Suppose you somewhere found the evidence you need that, if you had been present all the time, you would have seen that same Solomon sitting continuously on the throne, or that you would have seen the same lecturer moving about continuously, in ways that warranted the identification. Of what nature would those evidences be? They wouldn't be data of momentary experience at any point. What you experience is that something like a human voice sounds. Such experience you have, and that shows you existence; but it leaves unsolved the problems about identification. It is experience of the now, not of yesterday or tomorrow. The evidences which you need for your identifications of men, of Emerson Hall, of yourself, the evidences which you need if you are going to assert the continuity of the physical world, will consist not in presentations but in general principles.

Such general principles you are using all the time. You are quite sure that the world of existence is one in which men are not transformed as in fairy stories into wholly different objects. There is continuity, there is persistence in physical nature of the sort that permits us to identify objects. But what is the evidence? It is inductive. These principles become more and more probable as we continue to test them. The continued testing leads to such agreement between hypothesis and fact as pragmatism likes to set forth in terms of the working of ideas. You mean, however, not only that they are working but that they have worked and will work. The coherence of past and future which inductive investigation constantly uses is not merely a present working; it is something which belongs to our interpretation of our past and our future. We are always aiming at something not now verified, not now presented, which we view as probable.

You can never get rid of one feature in any account of the inductive probabilities. They refer to a coherence of a past and present which we verify neither in the past nor in the present but by interpreting our relations to a past and a present. The world of matter persisting through time, of individual men who have some coherence about them, this is a world never directly verified but always obtained by an interpretation of the meaning, the sense, of the past and the future.

If one wants to fix one's attention upon just one centrally important point, there certainly was a past, and the past in time has some sort of coherence with the present. This past existence on which the inductive side of our study of nature and of man depends—why do we affirm it? The question isn't why we ought to feel confident of it as we do but on what logical ground do we assert it? Well, something that you know about the nature of the past excludes from consideration the hypothesis that the world has just begun to be and there never was a yesterday. The past at least you know to be real from the very essence of the past, from the very essence of the time process, from the very essence of the situation upon which you depend at every moment of your interpretation. You are using an ontological proof of the past. The hypothesis that there was no past at all, nothing ever happened, all memory is false—that hypothesis is excluded in your opinion from the very nature of the case. The past was whatever it was; the very nature of the past forces on you that there was some past. Whatever happened happened.

Your identification of this and that object in your material world may be founded on false observations; but the past experience which you are always presupposing as the basis of whatever you have to say about the world inductively judged—that existed. The very essence of induction depends on presupposing that the essentials of your account of time—the past with its irrevocable character, the future with its yet expected character—these represent existence. Your evidence about nature and man and whatever else you are dealing with involves the ontological proof. Wherever you use evidence at all as evidence for the existence of somewhat not now experienced, you are dealing with that which comes to your knowledge in such wise that its essence involves its existence.

Although the ontological proof is so easily refuted, you use it all the time. It underlies all your notions of all reality. In any case, the nature, the essence, of the time–process is an essence which corresponds to the most significant feature of the real world, the feature which gives it its character of a flow in time. You in vain make light of the ontological proof. Applied to mere conceptual objects, it is indeed vulnerable. Applied to your experience, you use it all the time.

March 7 The matter comes to this: Whoever says he can prove the existence of somewhat by certain evidence, inevitably, when he tells you what his evidence is, sets forth the essence of something. If the question at issue is "Does X exist?" the evidence which logically requires that X exists must be sought in some essence. Now we are supposed to be clear that there is no being whose own essence implies its existence. The essence in question will not be the essence of X. That which gives genuine warrant for asserting the existence of X must involve some relation in which X stands to the rest of the world—a relation, such that if you know enough about the rest of the world and about this relation, you have that which insures the existence of X.*

You go outdoors in the morning and see in the snow the foot tracks of a human being, a cat, dog, or whatever it is, and thereupon you make an existential judgment, "A cat or dog or man has been finding its or his way through the snow." Robinson Crusoe in the story is fascinated and terrified when he discovers the human footprint on the beach; not that he has discovered a being "Man" whose essence implies his existence. He has discovered the existence of a foot-track; and owing to the laws of nature or to something known about the world, it is the essence of foot tracks to imply, not the existence of foot tracks, but the existence of some animal adequate to make them.

A familiar principle is often supposed to warrant assertions of existence, viz.: Whatever exists or comes into existence must have a <u>cause</u>; there must have been somewhat to cause it; the character or essence of the situation (when somewhat comes into existence) implies the existence of the cause.[5] In any case, whoever makes use of evidence like the footprints inevitably makes use of what you might call a <u>relational form of the ontological proof</u>.

When you try to take a conceptual object all by itself and explore its essence in order to warrant the assertion that it exists, you meet the difficulty which Santayana points out, which makes the ontological argument appear so vulnerable. But in the relational form of the ontological proof, the essence which you employ is not the essence of that whose existence you now prove. The proof is: In view of the essence of a relation, some object of the sort in question must exist. I use the ontological proof in this form if, observing the

* The crucial assertion.

light, I go on and say, "This shows that something is the source of light." Of course, I may fail to identify it.

Relations such as causation by known or presumed laws of nature—however you define them—bring in an ontological proof. In the light of relations which are supposed to be known to you, you get evidence that there is a man speaking, or that an animal has been here and made this track in the snow. The prerequisite knowledge is knowledge of the essence of the relation of the datum to somewhat which is not the datum.

The data of experience do indeed illustrate to us the present, but they are meaningless without a supposed past and an expected future. All my memory may fail me in detail, but one can always say there was a past or there wouldn't be any present; there will be a future or there wouldn't be anything going on at the present time.

Defining the past and the future in terms of their relation to the present, the essence of that relation, together with the datum of the present, is declared to warrant the assertion of the past existence of the past and the future existence of the future. Granting the relation of the past and the future to the present, the essence of that relation in view of the present requires that there shall have been a past and that there will be a future. To assert that there was a past and will be a future is to use the ontological proof. This is only an extreme case of the inevitableness of the ontological proof in this relational form. Every reasoning on the basis of evidence to something not supposed to be a datum is a use of the ontological proof.

When asked whether the essence of X is identical with the sum total of its relations, I reply that you can't say that the thing is merely the sum total of its relations; but I think you can say that if you know all the relations of a thing, you know everything about that thing. I am on the whole on the side of the believers in internal relations. Yet there is a place for the individual which involves somewhat external to the relations. It is no part of this argument to define that.# We shall deal with this question later in the course.

[Royce here replied to other questions]: The nearest you come to the immediate is the presented insofar as it is the presented, but everything else is more or less relational and you know it mediately. One doesn't know one's own being or essence immediately. Schopenhauer was in the right about the Self in an anecdote which he told of himself. During the busiest period of his youth, he was wandering in the *Tiergarten* in Dresden, talking to himself and more or less to the flowers. An officer was concerned about his abstraction and asked him somewhat authoritatively, "Who are you?"—"I wish you would tell me; I don't know." He was right. My essence isn't known to me; it is too near, just as I don't see my eye. The problem of the *Atman* or Self will come up in connection with the metaphysical basis of Mysticism.

We can't begin our study of the world of essences with the essence of the self, for that is a highly indirect knowledge. Assuming your knowledge of what you mean by light, you open your eyes and you see what you mean by light. So far you get a verification which shows you the existence of the presented somewhat. That is as near as you get to the immediate, normally. That is the "knowledge of acquaintance." The instant you make use of evidence, you deal with the quasi- "immediately presented" and with a knowledge of its general relations—the cause or whatever it is which brought it into existence, its relation as a present datum to the past, etc. None of those essences of the relational system which you use seem to be completely known to you, but you use them.

I am not attempting to give you evidence for a particular kind of existence. I am pointing out to you that if Santayana says that evidence can logically warrant our assertion of the existence of somewhat, his evidence, as soon as it is something more than the presented knowledge ("somewhat shines"), will consist in the acceptance or assurance of a certain relational essence.

In that sense we know that in some sense there was some past and there will be some future, or since everything has some cause or other, the tracks in the snow are evidence that there has been something here.

State if you can a use of evidence so as to make this evidence prove the existence of somewhat without declaring that the essence of some relational system warrants the implication of the existence of the object as belonging to the real world. Where would there be any such evidence without the ontological proof?

You cannot get the ontological proof to apply to the divine being in Anselm's way or to the counterfeit gold; but unless there is somewhere an ontological proof which holds, then indeed we have no logical proof of any existence and there need be no real world at all.

Essence and existence can't be as independent as Santayana supposes them. The essence and the existence may be in much closer touch than this abstract discussion has tried to make plain.

The word cause means so many things, one has so vague a meaning for it, that we do well to speak in terms of other categories—relational categories to be sure. I shouldn't myself hold that the Kantian account of causation is definitive. There is one way to make it pretty exact, the way Howison employed when he spoke of causation as the illative category, the category in terms of which you infer existence. That would be an effort to give precision to the ideas which Kant wanted to use. Whenever you use an already accepted existent supposed to be already there as an evidence for the existence of some other "what" which isn't in the field of what is already accepted, as when you use a present existence as evidence for a past existence, then you use an illative category in terms of which you suppose yourself warranted in inferring the existence.

A presupposed existent gives me evidence of another existent. The relation between that which gives me the evidence and that of which it gives me the evidence is a causal relation. If we define causation in that way, it is indeed in terms of causation that we do infer existence. My whole point is this: Whenever one existent is supposed to give you ground for inferring another existent, then the ontological proof is used, insofar as this relational system, of which the evidence and that of which it is the evidence form parts, is a system such that the world cannot but contain it. When I say "The track evidences the animal" I mean to define some illative relation: in the end, I have to say there couldn't be such tracks unless there were an animal to make them. It is essential to the system consisting of track and maker of track that that existent should belong to the world.

Certain foot tracks in the Connecticut sandstone long assured people that there must have been an animal which made them, an animal of which there remained no geological trace whatever but his tracks. This illustrates how problematical the connection may be.

Question: What is the status of Santayana's "inalienable ideal being" before it becomes "hypostatized?" These types, forms, universals, have their own kind of being which you can only illustrate. What bravery is doesn't change when the brave men die or when the cowards run. You recognize that essence is real in a sense in which existent beings aren't real.

If you say the essence is a meaning in a mind, the realist declares that red would be red whether anybody saw it or not; so also bravery remains bravery whether any one appreciates it or not: It isn't mental being. Certainly it isn't physical being or existence in time or space. Thus it is its own kind of being which can only be illustrated. Socrates discovered the essences: they are only there, but they are there in a sense peculiar to themselves. You can distinguish the bravery of a brave man from the existence of a brave man. The bravery of brave men, according to realism, doesn't need the mental existence of the admirers or experiencers of bravery—just as two and two would always make four. The world of essences is as independent of mind, from the realistic point of view, as is the physical world. Santayana only illustrates essence to you and declines to admit that it is mental.

For Example, The Principle of Individuation

I have so far stated the general grounds for holding that you do not in experience find individuals. While Santayana does not here discuss the nature of the so-called principle of individuation, it is fairly clear that he holds that ex- *March 9* perience presents to you existent facts. A fact which exists is so presented that it is at a given time in a given place; it is some where and some when. From that point of view, experience would present to you an instance of a triadic relation of something somewhere somewhen, which would be precisely what you mean by the existent.

As against that view, I pointed out that experience certainly does not present to you the individual which you usually regard as no doubt present. Experience doesn't give to you the lecturer who delivered the last lecture, the individual person who gives this course, nor does experience present this individual person to me, since, as I tried to characterize to you, I am for myself the object of an interpretation of the meaning, coherence, significance of the process of my life. A certain coherence of past and future is exemplified by current experience, one may say; and on the basis of that coherence, I regard myself as this self. But for me that is an interpretation. Who I am, or what it is that I mean or have in mind as myself, I do not find presented. I am in the same position in that respect as Schopenhauer was from his own point of view when he had his passage with the officer. It is, of course, a somewhat mystical point of view that Schopenhauer was expressing: but while the mystical side of the discussion will interest us later on, negatively speaking, Schopenhauer rightly enough stated the thing. You yourself are not an experience to yourself if your experience is like mine. You are for yourself the object of an interpretation. It is a theory, a view, a doctrine about your life which enables you to characterize the meaning or the person meant when you speak of yourself.

So also, in following the lecturer from one lecture to another, you would be using not the presented experience of any moment, which indeed gives you a particular, such as the light at this moment when you look, but does not present the individual.

Since Santayana unquestionably means by the existent object an object which is at a determinate place when a determinate time is selected for the consideration of the question where it is at that time, it appears to me that Santayana does not make out that experience can find that the existent has its place.

If mere experience doesn't present to us those existents which are individuals, such beings may be furnished to us as the result of evidence. But insofar as you use evidence for an existence, you use the conditions which are supposed to belong to some relational system, and you know that this relational system itself belongs to or is bound up with existence. That the use of evidence for an existence involves an ontological proof was just set forth.[CA]

There is a matter which has been kept in the background in this discussion. While no one experience presents to us an individual, we all of us hold that there are individuals. No discussion is more prominent in the current presentations of the realistic view than the discussion of the "inevitable necessity" that this world should consist not of generals, universals, types, essences taken as Platonic ideas, but of individuals.

In the realm of the Platonic ideas there are in any case many universals, sorts, types—light and sound and color, pain and pleasure, joy and sorrow. Those are all essences. Experience can exemplify them at a moment so far as experience possesses or presents characters. All that one can indeed verify. One can verify that a meaning, an essence is present. No doubt in order to do that, one has to be able to grasp the meaning in terms of which one identifies this essence. It isn't the problem of the existence of these essences so far as these are universals. If I now mean anything by light, then I do indeed see light now. If I mean anything by "sound of the human voice," then I can verify the fact that experience now presents the sound of the human voice. So far experience carries us.

Yet very frequent is the assumption and assertion that what experience shows us is always something individual. In any case, if you ask what is really there when the light shines and is observed to shine, the answer comes, "That which is there is an individual."

In realistic discussions, statements of that kind are very frequent, and no part of such discussions appears to be more prominent than the thesis, the opinion, that the real world consists of individual entities. When we ask ourselves how an individual is identified, we then come to a matter which is worthy of further consideration than we have so far given to it, the so-called principle of individuation.

It is worthwhile perhaps in passing to glance at a proposition which Santayana does not utter. I am not sure myself how at present he views that proposition; I very seldom have heard him give his opinion about the principle of individuation. But since he declares that the existents must be somewhere and somewhen, he seems to hold that the world is made up of facts each one of which has its own (its individual?) time and place. I am not sure what his actual position about that is.

In any case, many realists will say that this world is made up of things or facts, each one of which has its time and its place determined so that at a time it can be only in one place and at any time it must be somewhere, and of such individuals the world consists.

What I have already said would show you the difficulty involved in making this assertion. When it is so trivially self-evident in appearance, so easy to make light of the ontological proof, it is curious that one of the most notable uses which is made of the ontological proof—not about God but about the real world—is the use which you will find repeatedly made by realist writers, so far as you can make out their intention.

The assertion that this world consists of things, each one of which is individual, is often made as though it represents the modern point of view, the only sensible point of view, that which any man who can think clearly is going to take. Often you find people who are not acquainted with scholasticism, scoffing at the doctrine that the world contains anything but individuals as the doctrine invented by the schoolmen who, unable to think clearly and unacquainted with the study of experience, were accustomed to speak as if there could be leoninity and humanity, whereas it should be clear that this world consists of individual things.

Good examples of such assertions are to be found in Aikins's *Logic*. He is a realist and says the world consists of individual things. When he comes to discuss the idea of the uniformity of nature, he lays stress on the distinction between things and the relations or circumstances in which they stand or to which they are subject. In terms of set considerations based on this analysis, he then maintains the principle that granting the same things and the same circumstances, you must have the same results. This principle of the uniformity of nature he uses for the logic of induction.

Aikins is fond of making sport of those muddleheaded people who will use such expressions as "A smile went round the company." There can only be a number of people who smiled. One of the simplest logical rules for such a writer is one which Aikins uses when he speaks of terms which pretend to have absolute meanings. Only concrete terms have a meaning. "Humanity" is abstract but "this man" is concrete. An individual is that which you know to be there. Of the individual you may speak. The danger of failing to remember that is one which Aikins considers a danger to the clearness of thinking. The risk of supposing that there are universals appears in many modern theories of the State or of Society.

Professor Sumner of Yale, who wrote a book on what social classes owe to one another, made part of his argument turn on the fact that most of those who undertake in a benevolent spirit to appeal to the State or the social order as the governor or guide of the individual, speak as if Society existed, as if there were really somewhat which we can call the State or something of that sort. The State merely means all of us, and the doctrine that the State should take charge of this or that social matter means that the majority of us should overcome or keep in subjection the rest of us. This doctrine, revolting to the principle of human liberty, Sumner rejects, and thinks it would be easier to reject it if you saw that there is no such thing as Society. The world consists of individuals—so far as men are concerned, of individual men.

For the time being I don't wish to return to the discussion of the reality of communities in the earlier part of our course. I point out that Aikins and Sumner have taken as an axiom the proposition that the world consists of things whose situations and time and place and relations may change, but whose individuality makes each one of them itself and no other individual.

If one asks what is the basis of this assertion that the world consists of individuals, the answer commonly given is that it is an assertion which appeals to clearheaded people. The others who suppose that smiles and families and states and such abstractions have part in the existent world, well, that comes from confusedness. Think clearly and you will know that the world consists of individuals.

This doctrine has been known as nominalism. The doctrine is no more and no less scholastic than the doctrine of realism. Both doctrines grew up in the course of the history of the peripatetic philosophy in application to the special problems of the Christian theology.

The contrast goes back to the discussion between Plato and Aristotle. It is notable that while Aristotle on the whole insists that the individual is the being, the real, Aristotle is not a mere nominalist, for he has the universals; they have their place in reality also. In his polemic against Plato, however, he attacks Plato for supposing that the realm of the Platonic Ideas possessed a being of its own which had existence. Certainly the question at issue can't be settled by appeal merely to Plato or Aristotle.

When the scholastics themselves reconsidered the whole matter, they found on their hands the question. What do you mean by the individual? Their definition was much influenced by considerations furnished them by the data of their theology. So far the discussion belongs to the context which Christian theology suggested. They had to account for the presence in the world of human beings with souls and bodies, and also of incorporeal beings, angels. All these created beings were distinct from the Divine Being, who possessed that mysterious *aseitas* or self-existence which was a peculiar possession of the Divine itself. Consequently, they were obliged to consider what they called the principle of individuation. If the world consists of individuals, what makes the individuals distinct individuals? Wherein does one individual differ from another? Plainly, in some respects, in some essence. On the other hand, evidently this distinction of individuals has something to do with time–space relations.

That "something" becomes important in the light of some considerations which you might call trivial, though they were grave enough for the scholastics in view of the theological situation. Man is both mental and physical during his earthly existence; then there is a separation of soul and body at death, and a reunion at the resurrection. This principle required careful consideration.

The case of the angels presented a particular problem which led to the result that the problem of individuation was very carefully discussed by the theologians in their angelology. How one angelic person would differ from another was discussed. After all, whatever you may say about the theological basis of the doctrine of the angels, an angel had been defined as an intelligence in abstraction from sense organs. The angels had a character which we regard as belonging to ourselves so far as we get a notion of the pure ego, the being that has an aspect of its life which isn't determined by physical conditions. It is a perfectly genuine philosophical problem.

The scholastic discussion of the individuals couldn't cease with the trivial statement that the world consists of individuals. When you ask what constitutes an individual, you find that the definition of an individual is an extremely hard problem. It can't be a self-evident problem that the world consists of individuals. You have to consider the meaning of the statement if you are going to accept it. Sumner, to whom nominalism is a perfectly obvious doctrine, well, such a writer shows himself not aware of the problem.

The current nominalism is certainly not identical with realism in metaphysics. I am not sure that Santayana wants his statement to be interpreted nominalistically at all, and I suppose he is not a nominalist.

Russell has maintained that, if it is a question as to whether universals, types, essences in the general sense have themselves a being, then we ought all to be on Plato's side: the essences certainly are in large number universal. The universal term has then a perfectly real meaning. It is not absurd to say that there should be a realm of universals, for the essences are in large part such.

It is precisely in the realm of essence that the difficulty about individuals would arise. It is easier to say, by virtue of the difference between the essence of a triangle and the essence of a circle—both universal essences—what you mean, {than to say} that an individual triangle has existence in the realm of space. But if you want to tell what constitutes the essential difference between James and John or between two individual atoms, then you have difficulty.

Russell has long been a person who is not a nominalist, for he says, on the one hand, that the universals are just as real as anything else from the point of view of the essences; and on the other hand, I understand him not to be a nominalist from Aikins's point of view.

If you suppose the proposition "The existent world consists of existent individuals" to be true, the question why you regard it as true is one which would bring you back to the ontological proof. Aikins has no difficulty in pouring out these propositions about what the existent world consists of. These are the sort of propositions which a clearheaded man would accept. The world consists of beings such as men who are individuals, not of caninity, etc.

If this proposition is accepted, it can't be accepted as a self-evident proposition, for it is hard to know an individual. You would have to know that what the legend narrates about Solomon and the demon is untrue; the legend isn't self-evidently untrue, but only because you have good inductive grounds for holding that such myths are usually false stories. A very little consideration of the matter would show that the proposition is not self-evident. Why do you believe it then? Why is it so sure that the existent world consists of individuals?

Put that proposition in any form and I submit that the acceptance of that proposition can only be on grounds which require the thesis that it is of the very nature of the existent world (the whatness of the that) that it must consist of individuals. The proposition that the existent world consists of individuals can only be proved by logical inquiry.

Whenever the nominalists say in their lighthearted way, "Any sensible man knows that; only the poor scholastics with their muddleheaded difficulties could believe that universals had a place in the world of the existents," he points out to you a proposition which he holds to be true because he holds that the essential situation set forth in that proposition must be exemplified in the real world. Why shouldn't humanity or mankind be represented? Why shouldn't the community be real? You can answer, "It is of the essence of a community not to be what it is of the essence of the world of existents to consist of." But prove the proposition without an ontological proof. Why shouldn't mankind exist? You can easily answer, "For my part, I haven't yet met with the community; I don't find it in experience." But that doesn't give you any warrant for the assertion. Most of you who rejected the community as no reality had reasons which had to do with the essential characters of the situation: it is of the essence of things which are existent that they should be individuals; humanity and mankind are the sort of objects which essentially can't exist, but individuals are objects of the sort that the world has to be made of.

My thesis is this: The principal users of the ontological proof, not about God but about the world of common sense, are the nominalists. Nominalism is a doctrine depending on its own form of the ontological proof. The only grounds which you can give for the assertion that this world consists of individual beings, depends on saying, "It couldn't be otherwise, it is of the essence of existence that the existents should be individual. The world of the Platonic Ideas may have its own shadow of reality, but the world of the existents must consist of individuals." You will find that your ordinary common sense is in possession of some such proposition as that. And if you are asked for the reason of the proposition, you must declare that which you don't generally like to make too explicit, but which any nominalist such as Aikins constantly uses—the proof, namely, that to be existent is to be an individual because it is of the essence of an existent to be individual.

The nearest Santayana comes to that assertion in this paper is where he declares:

> *Existence exhibits things in a situation and with an emphasis which their mere essence could never have had. Things generate one another, and their flux, by catching the dye now of one essence and now of another, becomes varied and describable.*

> *. . . . Whether such a claim (that an object has a place in some natural context) is just can never be determined by analyzing the essence of what is said to exist, but only by exploration, through experience or evidence, of the flux of nature, until the essence invoked is discovered embodied in the suggested context: for it is idle to say that a thing exists or does not exist, if we do not say, when or where.*[CA]

The proposition is a proposition about what it is of the very nature of existence to demand, namely the possible answer to the question when and where. To say that is to say that of course time–space existence must in its nature be determinate as to time and space and that the existent world must consist of objects about each one of which you can say that at a given time it is at a certain place. If you determine a time, then you must determine a place.

One of the favorite theses of the classic scholastics, held by St. Thomas in particular, was the thesis that for all beings of the nature of human beings, all corporeal beings, the principle of individuation is the time–space principle; that which distinguishes one individual from another is that an individual is here now.[6] This principle, that time and space furnish the ground for the individuation of things, is a perfectly statable principle, and it is of this principle that Santayana appears to be speaking here. It suggests a nominalism of its own. So far as the world consists of such determinate objects, then indeed the world of existence does seem to be a nominalistic world. The essences can be exemplified and may be universal. An existent may change its essence as it moves in time and space. It may now be red, now green. The fortunes of the existent involve changes from one universal character to another. But the existent, so far as the principle of individuation is a time–space principle, is individual in its nature, since it would always have a here and now which would characterize it at this point. So far Santayana would seem to be a nominalist. The existent world he seems to view nominalistically.

Why? Santayana gives you his own carefully shaded version of the ontological proof: "It is idle to say that a thing exists or does not exist, if we do not say when or where?" That is, you couldn't mean anything unless you were ready to add the time and place. This is to say something about the whatness of the that—nothing can exist unless its space and time have this determinate character; and this space and time character, as the principle of individuation, will give you always individuality; and so existence will give you individuals.

But why can't a thing exist otherwise? Because it is of the nature of existence to reject existents not determinate by time and space. Nothing can be in various places at the same time, but a thing must always have a time and place. These two propositions are not identical propositions. Both of them are propositions such that if you accept them, you accept them on the ground that no other sort of existence can be. Whoever says that is essentially using an ontological proof. If from every point of view the argument of the old man about the gold were wholly absurd, one is dealing here with an absurd argument.

Here existence and essence come together; existence cannot be other than existence in time and space. Santayana seems to be committed to this despite his cautious expressions. He has said elsewhere, not in this paper, that it is absurd to think of any existent world not subject to natural laws. It is necessary that things which exist should possess this or that character—an instance of the ontological proof. Whoever says this is now dealing not merely with the essences, or merely with the existents, or merely with experience. He is dealing with <u>the essence of existence</u>. He is declaring to the Being who, prior to Creation, faces the essences in advance of existence, "You must create that kind of world if you create any world at all, for it is the essence of that world that it alone should exist if there is to be any existence." He is then addressing an ontological argument to the Creator. We all do it all the time whenever we seek to prove existence from evidence.

The nominalist is the principal user of the ontological proof.

Whoever takes his existents as space-time individuals has on his hands the problem of the identification of individuals {—the problem next to be investigated}.

Chapter 6

Identity and Identification

I now pass over to the discussion of such propositions as those which Santayana mentions where he is giving his first examples of the word "is":[1] *March 11*

> *The copula properly denotes identity, not merely in the obvious case of A is A, but in cases where diversity of symbols or of approach disguises the identity of the object meant, so that the discovery of this identity may be important or surprising; as when we say, "This is Odysseus," or "XI is 11," or "12 is 2 × 6." It is in this sense that being is proper to essence; everything is what it is.*

Insofar as the conception of an essence can be by mere illustrations made precise and defensible, I suppose that conception is now before you. The distinction between essence and existence is a conceptual difference. We have several times got warning that from the point of view of interpretation, the essence might not be so fixed, so impenetrable a state as we had been led to suppose. Nevertheless, I am trying as far as I can to cling to Santayana's distinction.

This is a classic distinction; it came out in consequence of the dialectical method of Socrates, the Platonic Socrates. The world of essences is the world of the Platonic Ideas. The doctrine itself got changed in the hands of Aristotle, which led through a long process to the distinctions on which the scholastics laid stress. There was then the sharp contrast between the world of the divine Ideas, the possibilities which might be created, and in contrast there was the world possessed of the sort of being that the created things have. To be sure, you remember that in that world there is a being, a reality, namely God himself, for whom in the classic scholastic doctrine (as St. Thomas defines it), the fact would be statable that, from God's point of view, an ontological proof would hold; for as a fact his essence does require him to exist. But although this is not to be presented merely as a theological but also as a metaphysical doctrine, it is to the natural intelligence of man, according to St. Thomas, not directly knowable, although there are several indirect proofs which St. Thomas gives, or at any rate, there are various less direct proofs than the one which St. Anselm gives, for holding that there is a being whose essence does require his existence; namely, God. But according to St. Thomas, we don't know the divine essence in any direct way, and therefore we cannot see why he cannot fail to exist, although St. Thomas thinks we can prove that there is such a being. There is then in the world of St. Thomas a being whose essence does imply his existence, although we can't know that fact; while for created beings there is a sharp contrast between their essence and their existence.

Anselm's form of the ontological proof is easily to be rejected. In Santayana's opinion, the analysis of this {alleged} travesty is made easier by the examination of the meanings of the word "is."

It appears that the classic distinction between essence and existence (which is now a commonplace of many different philosophical discussions of such problems and a distinction very interestingly revived) has itself some difficulties, as some of your questions have brought out. Those difficulties especially appear in view of the fact that something in the nature of an ontological proof appears to be uttered by anyone who asserts any such metaphysical thesis as that of the nominalist. The doctrine that all beings in the world are individuals, or that this world consists of individual things, persons, etc., and that universals, Platonic Ideas of the type of universals, have no place in the realm of existence—that doctrine is advanced by nominalists with that appearance of self-evidence, against which I have warned you as always a suspicious circumstance. It is somehow "self-evident" that everything must be individual. If so, the essence of individuals is such that the essence of the world requires individuality as the character belonging to being. To maintain that is inevitably to maintain that a certain kind of existence is required by the essence of being of the things that are to exist and by the essence of existence.

At the point where one inevitably returns to the problem about the essence of existence, the nature of what it is to exist, at that point one sees that the classic distinction is in danger of wholly or partly failing or requiring modification.

So far we have got in our discussion.

The Identification of Individual Existents

Santayana's first meaning of "is," is the assertion of identity, an assertion so obvious that Santayana doesn't want to lay great stress on it.

> *The copula properly denotes identity, not merely in the obvious case of A is A, but in cases where diversity of symbols or of approach disguises the identity of the object meant, so that the discovery of this identity may be important or surprising, etc.*

Santayana suggests that mere identity, if it were presented, would not be surprising and important but disguised identity, which you have to discover, may be important and it may be surprising. Further down he gives his own examples:

> *Whenever for the sake of emphasis we repeat a word, saying "No, No," or "Business is business," the effect is to detach and make indubitable the essence we mean, so that attention may be fixed upon it to the exclusion of circumstances, which do not alter essences.*
>
> *In such expressions of identity lies the most proper and literal force of the word is. Hence the term essence, derived from the same root, is well fitted to designate any ideal or logical nature, anything always necessarily identical with itself. Nothing else so truly is as character.*

The "identity" may mean identity in essence or in individual existence. When an identity is somewhat disguised and it is important that it should be discovered, that whose identity is disguised may be an individual: then the thing becomes surprising. Again, the identity may be an identity of an essence; I shall speak of that case soon.

I have mentioned to you the difficulty there is in saying that we know at any one instant the identity of an individual whom we suppose to find presented. The side from which I approached the question was the side which leads us to emphasize the fact that our experience presents to us always the general, in the sense that you experience what you mean by the human voice or by the light. But sometimes the matter is approached in another way.

A famous approach was the one that the sophists used in advance of the appearance of the Aristotelian logic, as one of their favorite puzzles. A veiled person is presented: you don't know who this person under the veil is. The veil is taken off; he is your brother. Conclusion: You don't know your brother. We commonly suppose ourselves sure of our identifications; but if we fail of an identification when it ought to be a commonplace that it should be made, our surprise over the failure may lead us to say that we haven't the knowledge that we ought to have. That is the sophists' puzzle.

I needn't consider the ordinary way of treating this fallacy or puzzle in the textbooks. When you look at the matter more closely, instead of being surprised that this person fails to know his brother, you can instead of that be surprised that he claims to know him at all when it involves so much.

[Here Royce recounted the return of Odysseus to the court at Ithaca as a beggar, and his identification {in turn} by his dog, by his son Telemachus, his queen Penelope, and the suitors.] The test which is accepted, that he can draw the bow of Odysseus, involves the problem of the identification of a physical object. Odysseus is identified for the poet by what is felt to be the coherence of his purpose. The queen is faithful to him by a conventional and established marriage tie which the gods have sanctioned. But what Odysseus means for her is also what we in more modern terms might choose to call the spiritual unity, or in primitive universally human terms, the soul of the man; and he means for her, when once the recognition has come, the coherent process, the one who took part in the quest for Helen of Troy, who through not only wanderings but through vicissitudes of heart and soul (so that for him faithfulness didn't mean what it meant for Penelope) had sought something coherently throughout. This notion involves interpretations and therefore something else than what you can state in terms of the mere characterization of the essence of this individual Odysseus.

The sense in which "This is Odysseus" is the sense that presupposes and includes a temporal process, the process of the wanderings, the heroism, the marvelous works, and the home-seeking of Odysseus. The identification is not a merely conceptual identification. It is the identification of the sense of a process: this man who defiantly faces the suitors fulfills and expresses the purposes of the life of Odysseus. The expression of purpose is however a process. The identification isn't the mere identification of an essence. That is because you are dealing with the self, although the same sort of consideration has to occur in dealing with the identity of the individual thing.

Hegel, in his *Logik*, discussed the principle of identity in a fashion which constitutes one of the most crabbed and at the same time one of the most significant of the theses of the Hegelian *Logik*. The thesis in question, which you can hardly tolerate if you regard knowledge wholly from the conceptual side, but which is, so to speak, essential to your very view of knowledge if you are thinking of a knowledge by interpretation—not only knowledge of, but through and by means of processes in time—is this: identity is inseparable from, implies, is in unity with, yes (if you like to use the word "is"), identity is difference.

Hegel, who had his own version of the dialectical method, was fond of annoying the popular mind by putting his paradoxes and leaving them there. The barren Understanding separates the essences and views the universals as having nothing to do with each other. The Reason, which carries on the process which we have been calling the process of interpretation, regards the variation of essence as of its very nature. It is never engaged in dealing with a mere distinction and identification of essences. Identity is difference if it is recognizable identity.

I hope these very considerations which we have been discussing have more or less prepared you for what Hegel put in this paradoxical form.[CA] Santayana regards this doctrine, I am sure, with especial abhorrence; it would seem to him to be "essentially and characteristically" not only false but barbaric, the doctrine of a barbarian. I shouldn't object at all to the thesis that there was a good deal of a barbarian about Hegel. He was a decidedly cantankerous and worrying person. He expounds Kant always polemically in a wrangling way, tearing him to pieces but making his own progress in this fashion. Hegel needn't have expressed his doctrine of interpretation in so hostile a fashion or so as to stir as much hostility as he did.

Look at the matter a little further. Taking the thing as conceptually as you can and stating the puzzle just as a puzzle, you might express the matter as Whitehead, a very different thinker from Santayana or from Hegel, has expressed it. He has come out as one of the new realists, an intimate friend and fellow worker of Bertrand Russell. In the introduction of his *Universal Algebra*, in characterizing the formulas which are most used in algebras of all sorts, Whitehead calls attention to the familiar form of the equation.[2] Without regard to its customary use as the equation of "quantities" in elementary algebra, the equation appears in many branches of mathematics, and you have all sorts of equations on your hands; the relation is one that varies enormously. Sometimes you will find the equation using the sign = as a symbol for identity. Sometimes you will find it used as in the ordinary algebras where equality of numbers or of quantities is concerned.

Whitehead remarks that an equation is at once the expression of a truism and a paradox. The two sides of the equation are sharply sundered as right side and left side, and it is therefore paradoxical to make the approach to identity. But at the moment you declare the equation, there is some respect in which values, numbers, or whatever else you are talking about are identified, and to express the equation at all makes the thing something of a truism. But the fact that there are after all two makes the quasi-identification of them somewhat of a paradox.[3]

Santayana's own illustrations are good: "12 is 2 × 6." In symbolic form, that would be expressed by using the sign of equality, "12 = 2 × 6." Whitehead says any such equation is at once a truism and a paradox. This is what Hegel insists upon. If "2 × 6 = 12," at the moment when you have known this and seen why, the matter becomes a truism. Why mention it? Does twelve mean anything from this point of view but twice six? On the other hand, if you approach the matter from the other side, it is a paradox. Twelve is a number, has its own unalterable individuality in the world of numbers, and stands here as not twice six.

However you put it, if you turn to the incessantly fluent and constantly changing character of the kind of knowing that we have called "interpretation" as giving you the basis for comprehending or grasping the nature of this union of paradox and truism, or whether you try like Whitehead to point out that there is here a somewhat mysterious matter which the student of algebra has to put up with, or whether like Santayana, with classic repose of manner you quietly ignore the paradox by declaring that the identity is an identiy and that anybody can see that, but that the identity can be veiled from the human being so that it seems surprising when discovered—however you deal with the thing, there stands the fact.

Take the case which Santayana likes to pass over as briefly as he can: A = A. What I am asserting is asserting a difference [not an identity, unless identity is difference].[CA] After all, the beggar who has now drawn the bow is different from the Odysseus who left Ithaca, different from the beggar, different even from the monarch whom we now recognize, for he is about to slay us, the suitors. Difference there is in all sorts of forms; we face difference, and yet we identify.

Now oddly enough—and this Hegel liked to hurl at the poor Understanding—this is what you get even if you try to confine yourself to the most common truism, A is A. [Here Royce wrote on the board.] But this A isn't this A; I wrote it twice. Moreover, you wouldn't understand the proposition unless I wrote it twice or unless you spoke the word twice. What is then accomplished by this <u>twice</u>?

Santayana says, "Whenever for the sake of emphasis we repeat a word, saying 'No, No,' or 'Business is business,' the effect is to detach and make indubitable the essence we mean, so that attention may be fixed upon it." But it is hardly the way to fix attention on it, to leave out something that it is. Which is the A on which you fix your attention, the A on the left or the A on the right?

After all, you are dealing with facts viewed in the light of a process. Whether in the case of Odysseus or in the case of a more abstract object in algebra or in life, the object appears as holding an identity which is the identity represented by and through the interpreted coherence of a process, a sense, a purpose, the fulfillment of an idea. From that point of view, then, the paradox and the truism are indeed inseparable.

Approaching the matter from the side of the truism, when you are just about to get complete identity, you discover that you haven't said anything. From the other side, you are impressed by the difference. From Santayana's point of view, you are impressed by the puzzle: isn't it after all a debatable matter? Perhaps he isn't Odysseus, perhaps he is not sufficiently identified, perhaps many could have drawn that bow. Perhaps the whole process may belong to the world of Solomon and the demon rather than to the world of the Odyssey.

But we who read the poem regard the world as not so made. We who identify 2×6 with 12 accept our theory of numbers and are sure of this thing. It isn't then a mere question to be avoided by saying that identity can be disguised or forgotten and then you need to emphasize it. Every assertion of that kind, "This is Odysseus," involves . . .* The fact called identity is perfectly inseparable from difference. Hegel's paradoxical language is somewhat ill chosen, but you may be guided by such considerations as the thought that simply conceptual language can't express your thought; you are dealing with what is essentially in its nature a process.

March 14

We have now seen something of the complication that underlies any assertion of individual identity. Something further regarding that problem may be said by way of illustration of how in practical life we test assertions [of personal identity. The proposition usually appears in connection with][CA] some statement about a much more complex individual, from our human point of view, than the hero of the Odyssey. Identity is something that every man wants to keep and to use for the purpose of being able to carry on his practice, including his business activities, with reasonable success. He needs to identify himself in order to cash the draft he carries. To define his status in the business community, to deposit his funds in a bank, identification stands side by side with some more or less practically important comment in which other predicates than the predicate of identity appear. A man must be identified as so and so, and characterized as a person thus and thus responsible.

One uses Kant's well-known classification of judgments into <u>analytic</u> and <u>synthetic</u> (or ampliative). By it a judgment is analytic if the predicate is simply found in the subject as when one says, "The red wine is red," or "The red wine is wine." On the other hand, a judgment is synthetic or ampliative in case something is predicated which is not to be found in the subject. In "The sum of the angles of a triangle is two right angles," a somewhat {appears} which you can't find in the subject itself. When one uses this familiar Kantian classification of judgments, what we have now seen is that there is a sense in which, strange to say, while we suppose the judgment of identity to be the most analytic of judgments—if we say, "A is A," where we seem to predicate nothing not found in the subject—it proves that in the case of individuals this assertion is an extremely ampliative or synthetic form of judgment. "I am I," or "Odysseus is Odysseus"—what is an easier thing to say? But when you are dealing with the individual of daily life, the concrete individual who is supposed to be hardly found in experience (which presents to you only light, sound, character, etc., not the individual), the individual is assumed by the very method which Santayana employs as—well, the characteristic being, so that whatever is, is in any case an individual. Well, if you speak of the concrete individual, then the identification of an individual as a certain individual proves to be something most decidedly involving synthetic judgments.

Is it a commonplace that this beggar is a king? The suitors don't think so

*Here RWB writes, "Notes incoherent."

when he begins to draw the bow and turns upon them with the arrows ready and the weapons now brought out by Telemachus and the others who are in the secret. They don't think the proposition is merely analytic when arrow after arrow clangs and they fall, or when they meet together at the bank of the river as ghosts and make note of the fact that they are now dead and he killed them.

It appears a synthetic proposition in common life where the use of it involves matters so commonplace but so stupendously important to the individual. Suppose the question arises, are you the man that you say you are? You present the draft calling for payment to A.B. You are quite ready to write your name on the back of it; but are you A.B.? As you well know, the bank may require identification and demand it by means of devices which appear to you strangely arbitrary and which are so (for what tests are to be accepted is a matter of practical decision).

One might say that the case thus approached is an ideally natural instance to illustrate pragmatism rather than realistic metaphysics. But one doesn't yet find identified all that the conception of the individual would demand. The bank treats you as A.B. if you give it sufficient warrant to do so. The plan may be found to work under such circumstances, but that it is not an infallible plan the bank knows. Every now and then the bank is surprised by some person with a new mode of swindling, making use of an identification in order to cash worthless paper. But when the bank says, "This must be A.B. because he produces the acceptable marks of identification," it doesn't mean merely that such a hypothesis works, that fearlessly one faces the consequence. It means that it is <u>true</u> that this is A.B. One knows that one is not actually certain that it is true, and that the plan one uses is insurable. The risk is such that in the long run with well-trained bank officials, the bank loses so seldom in accepting such identifications that the advantages accruing to the bank are sufficient to warrant the slight risk. The bank accepts on grounds that are not so much pragmatic as statistical. The costs of doing such business are less, including the actual cost of the sums paid out, than the advantages accruing.

Identification is founded upon assertions which intend to be true propositions and not merely pragmatically so. So few of such propositions are false that the expense involved in acting as if this one were true in each case that comes up is covered by the advantages, under very close restrictions.

The identification is intended to be such that it involves true propositions, yet exactly wherein this truth consists (apart from inductions from the consequences) is as hard to see as it is impossible to dispense with the assertion: that such methods of identification are sufficient to present what is in most cases a true identification of somebody.

If the case is sufficiently novel to require new kinds of evidence, then you will embark upon one of the most difficult inquiries with which the practical human mind has to do. As soon as you have left the beaten track where the identifications which on inductive grounds are accepted in conventionally established ways fail, it is extremely difficult to discover new ones. The mythical case of Odysseus would hardly give you a sufficient view of the enormous difficulty involved in such cases.

In the famous Roger Tichborne case,[4] the heir of an English country squire had gone to Australia and could not be found. The person who was to be the heir in case R.T. was dead took over the estate. After many years there appeared a person who declared himself to be the lost heir. He showed marks by which he was to be identified. Old family friends and neighbors said he looked like R.T. He told stories about his youth. Most persuasive of all, he used a means of test which one would be very much disposed to regard as well-founded. The universal proposition that an individual man is a man who can be recognized by his own mother after a lapse of time, and that one who can thus be identified must be identical with the individual for whom the mother in question identifies him, looks like a very reasonable universal. This claimant was recognized by the mother of the original heir. To be sure, she was very old, her memory was failing, and she naturally longed for her lost son. It was maintained at the trial that her intelligence was inadequate to meet the problem. In any case, she accepted him before she died. The defense asserted that this person wasn't R.T. but Arthur Orton,[CA] a butcher, whose career in Australia they undertook to trace. He had become intimate with the real R.T. and had learned his story. The question before the court, as it was reduced by the two so-called theories of the plaintiff and the defense, was "Is this R.T. or A.O., the butcher?" In the trial a Chief Justice of the time won a great reputation by his charge to the jury in which he reviewed the evidence.

The contest was a hot one and people were divided. Very characteristically, the popular sympathies didn't go with the individual as individual, but with the more universal or general aspects of the supposed essence of the individual. The case became a sort of conflict between the classes of those well placed in social position and the "plain folk." The people saw a plain man asking for the chance to assume the position of an upper-class man. They were quite willing to insist in a prejudiced way that the claimant belonged to the upper classes, in order that they might vindicate the right of anybody you please to be anybody you please. If the defense declared that this person was a butcher, that was all the more reason why he should be a squire. Thus the individual identification became complicated by the desire for the triumph of a member of a given class. In romances, the important thing to discover is that the poor boy or girl turns out to be an empress or prince in disguise.

In the end the case went against him, and after another long trial he passed a fourteen year sentence of penal servitude for perjury. He survived it, brought his defenders more or less together, and never withdrew his claim. He died leaving the matter as it was.

You see where you would be if, when you came home, they suddenly declined to identify you. How would you prove it? All the tests would depend for their objective validity and sufficiency upon negative universals easily asserted but very hard to prove. Is this A.B.? He behaves like A.B., he looks like him, he speaks like him. An identification sufficient in its workings to meet a reasonable amount of success is a test of handwriting: he writes as accessible evidence shows that A.B. does. But the identification involves more than that. He writes as A.B. does, and nobody but A.B. writes just as A.B. does. Such universal negatives we generally regard as probable and do not undertake to prove them.

Sometimes you find that those who cash travelers' checks are dissatisfied with the single signature test and like to make the matter a little more probable by using a numerical test. Once at a Scottish bank the paying official asked me to do what the check requires; namely, to write at the bottom of the check a signature to be compared with the signature which I had written on buying the check. But on the whole he preferred not to settle the matter with that Wouldn't I endorse it on the back? He preferred to have me write it in another place without opportunity to make the comparison myself, before his Scottish skepticism somewhat gave way. He was a realist and a skeptical realist, but he accepted the identification and I got the payment.

The identification, you can easily see, of course depends on two propositions, one of which is an especially doubtful proposition. (1) This person makes the signature which is written for identification on the check presented. (2) Nobody but the original signer could do that. There is no necessity here. I suppose there are a good many forgers skillful enough to look at a signature and then to write it offhand without appearing to copy it. The skillful forger who was a good visualizer might do what the Scottish bank official had me do. No tests of identification are empirical tests. You are in the region of metaphysics when you cash a check.

When from the sea you look landward and say "Land," you mean "This looks like land." You can go further on the general grounds of physics and say with Russell, with strict inductive warrant, "Nothing looks so much like land as that without being land." One may be deceived by a fog bank, but on the whole such judgments of identification are pretty successful. But that is in the nature of a particular judgment. If, however, when you first see land, you say, "That is Cape Cod," that involves saying, "That looks like Cape Cod and no other piece of land looks so much like it." So of Emerson Hall. That second proposition is the one in which, if you miss your way, you are most likely to be deceived. "That is my hat"—the grounds for differences of opinion are numerous.

So much for the problem of the identification of the individual from that point of view. The lesson of it all comes into sight when we consider all those matters about the identification of a person in the light of what one says about oneself. When the long-absent king said, "I am Odysseus" and meant it, his identification of his self, like your own from day to day and from hour to hour, depended on something which was not purely conceptual. In the analysis of my own ideas and feelings, I do not say that I find contents which agree with my conception of myself; I don't say that alone, for I mean by myself one whose life is the expression of a purpose. When I declare that I am the same person who lectured to you last time, I am doing it with reference to a plan of lecturing; numerous and intricate as the stages of that plan may be, still I see something coherent about it, and it is in terms of that coherence that I identify myself as that lecturer. My sentences hang together by virtue of that purpose with which I began them. What I mean when I say, "This is I," is that what I am now doing is coherent with what led up to this. Exactly how complete is my warrant for saying this, we shall see. But what I mean by myself is the fulfillment of a purpose, the carrying out of a plan, the living of a life. When the bank clerk fails to identify me, after all he doesn't know what I am about. I know. It is this orderly coherence of what I am doing with what led up to it that gives me the grounds for my self-identification.

This is closely involved with the fourth conception of Being in *The World and the Individual*, reality as the fulfillment of a purpose, an individual reality as the fulfillment of a purpose whereby a somewhat is distinguished from all others and from the world.[5] This is in the end a super-social view of the nature of reality.

A somewhat similar consideration appears to me to hold in the case of the identification of a physical object. That identification can be made only in purposive terms: what the thing is now is a further expression of the same idea or purpose whereby the thing was characterized, was distinguished from others in an earlier stage of experience. That I shall try to show you further on.

The Identification of Essences

I may well conclude this discussion by calling your attention to the fact that a somewhat similar problem arises in a very intimate relation to its own solution in the case of the other kind of identification. Santayana's cases, XI is 11, 12 is 2×6, are cases of the identification of essences. Santayana speaks of those as if they were cases so familiar as not to need much further comment. But identifying the two essences involves the same paradox that we have mentioned, the paradox that Whitehead describes when he speaks of an equation as a unity of a paradox and a truism. $2 + 2 = 4$ is a truism; it is also a paradox solved only by a study of the nature of addition and of the numbers themselves.

There is an instance which Santayana might well have used as an example, for he respects greatly the philosopher who uses it, and I think he would regard it as accurately stated. It shows you how much is involved in the identification of essences. At the close of his *Ethics*, Spinoza leaves this as his final proposition:

> *Blessedness is not the reward of virtue, but is virtue itself; nor do we delight in blessedness because we restrain our lusts; but, on the contrary, because we delight in it, therefore are we able to restrain them.*[6]

Blessedness and virtue are surely essences. The proposition comes after a long discussion of how the highest good can be obtained. It depends on restraining one's lusts, the human passions, the source of irrationality. People usually suppose that something external, perhaps the control of a guiding providence, the will of God, the order of the world, sees to it that good comes to you if you do well or if you control your passions. But Spinoza sees deeper than that. Blessedness is not the reward of virtue, as if God or the order of human society found that you had gained virtue and thereupon gave you blessedness; but blessedness is virtue itself. Because we are in possession of this supreme insight and self-possession, therefore we are able to restrain our passions.

He conceives this power partly as the mystics view the highest insight which comes from union with the divine, and also as the Stoics viewed the possession of wisdom which gives a man self-control. Spinoza writes in the same place:

> *We see what is the strength of the wise man and how much he surpasses the ignorant who is driven forward by lust alone. For the ignorant man is not only agitated by external causes in many ways, and never enjoys true peace of soul, but lives also ignorant, as it were, both of God and of things, and as soon as he ceases to suffer ceases also to be. On the other hand, the wise man, in so far as he is considered as such, is scarcely ever moved in his mind, but, being conscious by a certain eternal necessity of himself, of God, and of things, never ceases to be, and always enjoys true peace of soul. If the way which, as I have shown, leads hither seem very difficult, it can nevertheless be found. It must indeed be difficult since it is so seldom discovered; for if salvation lay ready to hand and could be discovered without great labor, how could it be possible that it should be neglected almost by everybody? But all noble things are as difficult as they are rare. (Finis.)*

For the sake of the identification of the two essences, self-control and blessedness, Spinoza lays emphasis on the contrast between them, the contrast between that which would make life elemental and that which would make it perfect. You insist upon difference whenever you identify.

March 16

I just used Spinoza's closing proposition in his *Ethics* as an example of the identification of essences. There one is in the distinctive world of essences and consequently free from the difficulties and ignorance that complicate the problem where individual identification is concerned. In any case, in dealing with essences your reasons for the identification must depend on a knowledge of what the essences are. The situation about them is one in which, to borrow an expression which Charles Peirce used, "You are potentially omniscient about the essences." With respect to essences, there is something which enables you, if you have any grounds whatever for approaching, recognizing, acknowledging, making use of, analyzing, identifying the essence, there is something which gives you warrant for your assertions about it. The essence does not, like the individual object, in our absence behave as it chooses. It behaves as its definition requires or as its relations to other essences determine; and these relations at least are definable.

In this world the range of human knowledge is most impressive and encouraging. The mathematical sciences move in the realm of essences. Vast and numerous and complicated as are the problems, the means for solving the problems are in the hands of those who set them. The definition of the problem predetermines its answer, although you may need to work for centuries before you can give its answer.

In the world of essences, you aren't baffled in the case of an identification by the fact that you are ignorant of data which would determine the identification if you had it. The claimant to an estate may be difficult to identify because of the difficulties of the world of existence; but the essences so far as you define them are your own so far as you are a definer and define them with significance.

In quite a different context, in considering our fourth conception of Being, we shall return to the same problem when we consider the problem of possibilities; for, as we have seen, what Santayana calls "essences" we can regard as capable of being named possibilities.

In the world of the essences an identification then is made upon grounds that ought to be open to a pretty definite reflection. Spinoza's identification of blessedness and virtue is an interesting instance of that. You can easily see what on the whole it is.

Spinoza began his philosophical reflections with the problem in mind of which he tells us in a remarkable essay which he partly wrote and left in fragmentary shape, the *Essay on the Improvement of the Understanding*, an essay suggested by the Cartesian *Discourse on Method.* It was Spinoza's attempt to state a philosophical method. In the introduction of that essay, he tells what interest guided him when he attacked his problem. He sought to deal with the problem from its practical side by strictly rational methods. The practical problem was the problem of defining the way to supreme or perfect happiness or blessedness as distinct from whatever mere fortune determines.

The multitude seek worthless things; the philosopher is interested in seeking that which is the highest good, that whose attainment would be a supreme and unending happiness. Spinoza undertakes to define this. Briefly and in a calmly pessimistic manner, with that deep insight into values which constitutes the mystical side of his nature, he states the vanity of human life as ordinarily lived, and the search for goods that can be won only through conditions which involve an evil greater than the prize. The power of a man is infinitely surpassed by the power of external things, and we are therefore, except by chance, powerless to obtain any particular good that we are looking for. If we are in the position of the wealthy or sit in the seat of kings, we generally say we can get the good if we want to; we demand it, we pursue it, we get it. But after all, as individuals we are infinitely inefficient as against the world, and sooner or later the world will break down this fortune, overcome this mere individual activity, reduce to powder this machine that we have been making. Our power is infinitely surpassed by the power of external things; therefore, that which the multitude seek is not on the whole good.

That which is a good, however—well, it turns out to be something which one gets not by fortune, but by a certain attitude, a certain way of taking life, which proves for a thinker of Spinoza's sort at once stoical and mystical, a way of taking things which involves an endurance of fortune with resignation, a peace in the midst of the tumults of the world, a spiritual success which is more than efficiency. Spinoza's definition of that in this *Essay on the Improvement of the Understanding* is a monument of the kind of philosophizing in question.[7] Schopenhauer said that if you wanted to cultivate that attitude, which he also found an antidote for pessimism, that attitude which he called the resignation or abandonment of the will to live, there was no better work to read than the introduction to this *Essay*.

The idea is one which Marcus Aurelius also addresses to himself very often when with resignation he comforts himself for the annoying and tedious fortunes of being even a Roman Emperor, by virtue of the fact that the Emperor, if he is wise, has power to look at the perfection of the nature of things as well as of a slave, to contemplate the perfectly perfect that never passes away, the good that we have always with us, whatever the insistent misfortunes of barbarian warfare or the annoyances of the fools of the world at court. The attitude that is needed is the attitude of not undertaking to change the detail of the world, but undertaking to take the attitude toward it that finds it everywhere the expression of the divine will.

Spinoza was a man influenced deeply by some of the medieval Jewish philosophers, himself a fine example of the religiously disposed type of the Jewish nature, a man who in another age might have been a prophet; while side by side with this depth and stoical resignation, this love of pure wisdom, there is something of the mystic glow, something of the mood that we shall have to study from another side. Meanwhile, Spinoza possessed that fine shrewdness that makes his work so characteristically and thoughtfully Jewish in its keenness of insight, so that for instance Santayana, who so classically detests the romantic type, finds a permanent interest in Spinoza, an interest which certainly involves different motives from those which usually appeal to the mind trained either in Hellenic ideals or through scholastic ideals.

Spinoza had an advantage somewhat analogous to that which is so marked in a very different thinker, the Apostle Paul, in whom you find side by side the keen hardheaded common sense and intelligent self-criticism of the best minds of his people, while his religious experience had the mystic background of the doctrines of Charity and the Universal Community.

So then, when Spinoza is talking of blessedness, he is talking of that ideal object of an unchanging felicity which the stoics and mystics both have repeatedly attempted to define, and for which Spinoza had his critically determined and shrewdly analyzed account. In dealing with the special problems of life, Spinoza treats them throughout the *Ethics*, especially in the third and fourth parts, subject to the practical principle that the passions of men are not to be laughed over but to be understood. He has his own theory with regard to human passions, a theory closely connected with the psychology of this time. His principle is mercilessly applied, with an almost cynical turn, to the vanity of what the man who doesn't understand himself views as his happiness.

The shrewd critic sometimes turns from the mechanically necessary but endlessly varied play of the human passions to the consideration of the true good which comes from seeing the divine perfection in everything, the "substance" in everything, what the stoics called "nature," everywhere. This, the genuinely rational attitude, is the one which one readily approaches if one thinks of taking life with resignation. This side the realistic mind can easily comprehend. So in Bertrand Russell's recent essay,[8] he has declared that while one may and must abandon entirely all traditional theology, one has still left a religion which permits and includes some things which tradition has emphasized: acquiescence, resignation, the turning away from the troubled world to the peace of the eternal. The eternal appears to Bertrand Russell in a somewhat decidedly symbolic and mathematical form, being capable of expression in the laboriously wrought-out formulas of the *Principia Mathematica*, although he thinks it should be made clear to the plain people. When he comes here next year, I take it he will endeavor to make an acquiescence doctrine, resignation, a pacifism, and social radicalism too, comprehensible to the plain people. There are some ways in which Russell touches Spinoza or in any case has analogous opinions.

Here in fact is a region where the idealistic and the realistic views may come very close together, in a way that has a metaphysical significance, where it is a question of the purposive side of the world—that, namely, which constitutes the purpose, the value, the worth, that for which things are.

Well, this is a digression, but it helps us if we take note of the sense in which Spinoza makes his identification of virtue and blessedness. We are dealing here with essences. The search for the good leads men for various reasons to the idea of virtue. Virtue is that which all men or gods approve, or which prudence admires or extols. There is a way of life which is pleasing to men or gods, if you have any gods, or to those to whom you are responsible or with whom you have to do. In the end, it is said, virtue gives you success in life. So long as you view things in this way, you are likely to have some such maxim as "Be good and you will be happy." If there are gods in your world, and if you define your virtues conventionally in terms of them, you are likely to say that if you are good, the gods will reward you. If more skeptical consideration shows you that the evil are not devoid of prosperity, you may still say that the virtuous man may look to his family, his friends, his community to sustain him; if you are virtuous, men will stand by you and you will get the reward which their support and help will give you. Virtuous activity then becomes like any other skillful activity; it is skill in pleasing the gods or your neighbors or perhaps yourself which you show in your virtues, and you get as the reward of it the satisfaction which comes when the gods bestow their favors on their own, or when men speak well of or reward the doers of the good, or when man has the satisfaction of a good conscience.

One distinguishes virtues and the goods which result from them or accrue to them, and so is likely to say, "Blessedness is the reward of virtue";—possibly (in case you so believe) because the gods see that the virtuous are happy;—possibly because you see that the social order secures that good things come to those who are good servants of the social order;—possibly because a man's conscience is his constant companion or may become so, and he may well look for the reward of a good conscience.

But another point of view guided Spinoza when he began to write his *Essay on the Improvement of the Understanding*, the point of view which Marcus Aurelius assumed as his own. You are very imperfectly able to control your fortunes, and the definition of the good simply in terms of the loyal identification of the true self with the aim and purpose of the community does not in general form part of the consciousness of the stoics or mystics or of Spinoza. He didn't think of the thing in those terms, for good reasons; for his own life as a thinker began with entirely undeserved misfortune, an outcast from the synagogue and equally hated by the Christians of the old church and of the various new sects, who all held him to be an atheist. He was dependent on the fact that the Dutch government tolerated all sorts of faith; he was free from persecution if he left political matters alone. It was natural that such a man should define his life in lonely terms.

The result was that Spinoza neither regards virtue as leading to good through some process, nor thinks of life in that way—as virtuous action pointing towards a good result because of gods or men or one's own conscience. Spinoza is very clear that you don't know what a day will bring forth yet willing enough to try the device of escape from entanglements in a solitary way since the faiths of the various churches do not appeal to him. He seeks for the good of life by viewing from above, looking down on the whole situation.[CA] That survey can be guided by what the Stoics called the appreciation of the universal wisdom, the identifying of the self with the divine wisdom that is expressed in nature and that is independent of particular fortune, so that whether it is a stormy day or fair, you know that it is always good, for all is so determined. The god that you deal with is the pantheistic deity in complete possession of everything, allied also with the mystical deity. That which you deal with is that which Russell deals with when he says that, to be sure, human lives are generally very tragic but the mere review of the inevitableness of the tragedy has itself for the thinker an element of comfort. The contemplation of mathematical truth is itself a comfort. This mind that, so far as fortune is concerned, is so bounded in a nutshell, can count itself king not merely of space but of all the spaces, Euclidean or nonEuclidean; its realm is the realm of the infinite assemblages, the infinite order systems or whatever else the logician or mathematician may choose to contemplate.

Spinoza finds that to be the case. You may or may not sympathize with that point of view. The mystical attitude may seem to you, in the form which Russell adopts, fantastic or unreal, or again it may seem to you coldly repelling. But, in any case, if you are to understand the Stoics, Marcus Aurelius, or to view things as Russell or Spinoza or the Hindu mystics view them, then you must become acquainted with the attitude which Schopenhauer called "the denial of the will to live," an attitude of resignation which, when contrasted with the attitude of the one who seeks to get goods through virtue and so is engaged in the agitated search for a tolerable state of things, is the possession of a supreme good, cold, intellectual, eternal.

The essence which is here in question ("good") is remote enough from the essence known to common sense. Even Spinoza has to say that the wise man, insofar as he is such, in possessing this {good} is scarcely at all disturbed. This is an attitude in which one surveys life and the good as one who looks down upon a vast landscape from some great eminence, and loses sight of the differences between good and evil because one sees the supreme connection. That attitude may involve an abstract indifference to things, a turning away from the contents of life. So mysticism seems sometimes to pretend that it doesn't take notice when it does; but then, those are matters of the application. As an ideal, this view was expressed by Marcus Aurelius; and Bertrand Russell's "A Freeman's Worship"[9] is an intelligible expression {of it}.

This view faces one of the sharpest differences in practical life, the difference between search and attainment, between the quest and the goal, and since we don't always get our goals, the closely related difference between good and evil is in question; but this view ignores that difference. One looks down and sees the connected whole, and hereupon one makes an identification. The identification is one that one makes who says that the wise man is in some sense always at the goal whatever happens. Yes, life is tragic, but a really wise man who has got the grasp of his relation to the Platonic realm of the eternal beings, such as the mathematical infinite—well, knowing that is comforting, over against the constant experience of the human individual in his merely natural aspect. Nature is regarded as not the divine, but as the place where the natural human individual commonly supposes himself to be left in the chaos of fortune. If you take the natural man not in the stoical sense, but as the creature of fortune, then he is constantly wavering between good and ill, hesitating in the search, agitated but always failing in the quest. But from the other point of view, these diversities partly fade and are partly brought together into some perfect unity.

One expresses this matter technically when one uses this joining of a negative assertion with an identification:

> *Blessedness is not the reward of virtue, but is virtue itself; nor do we delight in blessedness because we restrain our lusts; but, on the contrary, because we delight in it, therefore are we able to restrain them.*[10]

For now the virtue in question, the virtue of the Stoic, the virtue of wisdom, of insight, is a new kind of virtue, which consists in this uniting, this holding together of quest and goal, purpose and object.

Every identification is this curious union of paradox and commonplace. How paradoxical such a view, and also how commonplace, the closer study of stoics and mystics will show you. Paradoxical it is, for it is often asserted by a man who is much a victim of misfortune, but nevertheless in ideal he can find comfort in taking that point of view. On the other hand, if there is anything in that view, then it ought to be a statement of a commonplace, something that hardly needed to be mentioned; for if this is wisdom so to know the eternal that nothing different from the eternal has any genuine significance, well then the identification would hardly need to be mentioned. If the acquiescence is attained, why argue it? This will meet us when we study the mystical views. Every mystic holds that the union with God, the possession of the eternal, the insight into the fullness of being, the union with the origin of life, always tends to defy[CA] mere expression; it is silence that best expresses it. On the other hand, the doctrine always seems remote from ordinary life.

A classical expression of this paradox is to be found in Schopenhauer's *The World as Will and Idea*, where he points out the vanity of the quest for fortunes, since they can never satisfy, and then gives as the solution of this pessimism the attitude of resignation and the denial of the will. He points out how that attitude has been repeatedly exemplified by saints and sages. At the close of the first volume he points out how paradoxical the whole situation is; those who stand without say that his resignation is a mere nothing, a false attitude; but to the one who has won the true denial of the will to live, it is our so varied world with all its stars and milky ways that is nothing. And with that word *nothing*, Schopenhauer closed this presentation of his metaphysics.

It turns on recognizing a varied realm of contrasts of good and evil, quest and goal, and then indicating a point of view from which all these become nothing. The identification in such cases shows its distinctively purposive character; the proposition "A is B" (essences) means that A fulfills from some point of view the purpose of B. It is essentially teleological, not a mere statement of fact, but the expression of a purposive view. It means that the purpose that I have insisted upon thus far when I have distinguished A and B is fulfilled by not distinguishing them any longer. With reference to the purpose in question I find from my new point of view that they are the same; I cease to note the difference. That is what happens in such cases when one identifies. If I say, "6 + 5 = 11," the two sides of the equation are quite different; but for the person who understands the purpose of summation and its outcome, this difference becomes insignificant, vanishes, passes away; it is the same number, which you can call 6 + 5, and 11. You are dealing with a difference, which you at first emphasize. So long as it is a problem, what is the sum of 6 and 5, you keep them sharply apart. The moment when you make the identification, you say, "I can substitute one for the other." Henceforth, there is no reason for dwelling on the difference. For this purpose the difference is null, destroyed, laid aside. So with Spinoza, blessedness is virtue itself. Common sense sometimes says A and B are practically identical; they are as good as the same thing; to all intents and purposes, A is the same as B. Thus you see the practical character of this paradox.

Up to a certain point, I may have made a diversification between the two essences, blessedness and virtue. At a certain point I discover a unity of purpose, a calming of the will to live; and hereupon what has been opposition becomes identity for me. If I forget what made me draw the contrast, I do not recognize the identity. I had thought that blessedness and virtue had the great difference of the reward that you get for a certain action, and that which brings the reward; but I now occupy a point of view which I say is the looking down upon the connection:[CA]

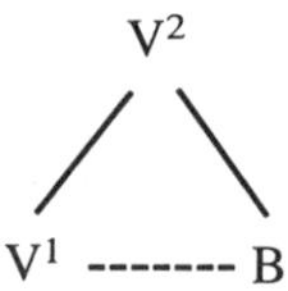

Now I emphasize the identity; but I shall cease to see that, if I forget how diverse they were. This is what we see when a given process reaches its attainment, its fulfillment. The fact that a certain identity couldn't be expressed because it would be to express a difference is what Hamlet says at the last when he has made his supreme resolve: "The rest is silence." So far it has been diversity. Now it is silence; silence is identity.

March 18 The problem of identity in cases of essences brings out the teleological character of the relation. When you identify essences, you do so because you find the same purpose fulfilled in that which seemed at first approach to be a diversity. One essence fulfills the purpose of, accomplishes the meaning of, proves to be the fulfillment of, all that the other had intended, promised or purposed.

Identification of Natural Objects

The question of the identity of natural objects still remains. In this case it is fairly easy to see that a good many of our ordinary identifications are of the nature of recognitions of diversity together with a remark, sometimes rather abstract, sometimes highly concrete in its significance, that despite the apparent diversity, the oneness of purpose of the objects supposed to be diverse warrants or sufficiently authorizes the assertion of their identity. Very frequent indeed in the world of common sense is the situation where, speaking of what one supposes to be an individual, one says, "This looks as if it were different; it is the same." Sometimes the relative surprise, and also, as you will notice, the satisfaction, which come at the moment of the identification in discovering this teleological continuity or identity, gets expressions quaint enough in their character, but showing you at once the presence of a distinction where there is an identification, and revealing a process which means a sort of overcoming of the apparent diversity. "I see you are the same old John, the same old fellow." Here the usage of the verb to be to express identification is characterized by a now wholly popular and untechnical reference to the fact that recognition is accompanied in this case with a sense of separation in time, the identification being the identification with the old. The home feeling is itself characteristically agreeable apart from particular reasons why it should be; the wanderer in a strange land has his loneliness impressed upon him by virtue of the fact that things do not give him the home feeling. On returning, he has it; the identification is accompanied by a characteristic sense that the identity is welcome. "This is the same old place"; "old" suggests a reference to a past time. This is not the same, for it is the now; whereas that to which one refers belonged a good way back there in the past; but there is such connection that one sees that this is the "same old" whatever it may be, for that which is now presented has the welcome character of the identified, of the recognized.

Recognition then is accompanied with the sense of the fulfillment of a purpose; for amongst other things one's purpose is if possible to recognize. The quaintness of the expression "the same old" is due to the motive which leads us to associate familiarity with union of endearment and contempt. The loving mother abuses the baby and calls it a rascal; so the identifying person makes light of that which he identifies by calling it the "same old"— "old" having the well-known association of being after all decrepit, worn out, no longer with the importance of novelty; "old" expresses the sense of endearment, and endearment constitutes an aspect of the identification.

Of course, if I declare that the identity of the individual is for the identifying person an identification of the purpose of the individual identified, then the same problem arises about the identification of purpose. But the reason is that identification in the case of individuals is not simply an expression of the nature of an essence. It isn't simply anything conceptual. Identification then is not mere identification of concepts. Mere concepts are not mere concepts when we identify them. Identification is an act of interpretation. Our purposes, like the rest of our lives, shift with the moment. What we are now doing is certainly not what we are doing at another time. What we now purpose changes with the situation. Novelty is at once the fate and the quest of life. I don't propose to do what I did before, and if I did I couldn't. This is the only time and context that I have to do this deed. But while life is full of diversity, the knowledge of the self is a knowledge of the coherence that underlies and overarches all its diverse purposes, always acting anew yet still always itself together with its past. I am the same self with the self of yesterday so far as I am conscious of carrying on in its present stage the activity of yesterday. It was a forward-looking activity and demanded change and novelty; now I have the change and novelty, but this is coherent with the foregoing.

I mean the same at the end of my sentence as when I began it, although it isn't normally the case that we know at the beginning of a sentence how it is going to end. That which you can introspectively discover with regard to the coming portions of a sentence will confine itself to a few words or emphases, to faint tendencies or fringes, to distinctly transitive and not substantive states of consciousness. Some ideas are in mind; those are what you are going to introduce in what you are going to say. Just how you say the thing—well, that changes all the time. No matter how much you think over what you are going to say, unless you actually commit your words to memory, you cannot predict what you are going to say; and hence the endless, on occasion the fascinating, novelty of conversation, the surprises of the situation. The dramatic temper is satisfied with its varieties. And yet he indeed converses ill who doesn't hold himself together, doesn't keep himself to the point, doesn't in any wise get the conversation so that throughout any section of it there is something which is the issue, the topic, the interest, the concern. The connection may be called identity. "What I intended to say I have said." "What I began to say was this," and I may now mention the end of the sentence. But on the other hand, what I end by saying never is what I began to say. My whole life is a life of change—in conversation that is peculiarly prominent—but the identity in question is an identity entirely subject to, interwoven with, or expressive of coherence. There is a purpose, an ideal, an intent which the whole conversation or sentence fulfills. The end of it is as necessary as the beginning; every part of it is needed for the whole. The totality having the sense which the beginning sets, nothing less than the end of the sentence would complete the sentence. The sentence, however, is the whole of which you might assert that it is the same throughout, because it isn't merely the same but is precisely the whole. "The same as" means something that you can express only in terms of interpretation. The sameness means the teleological unity of the whole.

Physical individuals are identified in a similarly teleological fashion. The table is the same, although at any moment it presents to you sense-impressions which are likely to be changing or which would be changing if your own point of view changes at all. The physical world has the Heraclitean character of endless fluency; you never step into the same stream twice. This character is one to which Bergson has given a fresh interest by his skillful analysis of the fluency of the facts of experience. Nevertheless, identification runs through it.

Is that entirely expressible in Santayana's terms as a realm of essences, wholly changeless, simply eternal, entirely impenetrable to the flux, a world where all is and nothing becomes, a changeless world? Is its relation to this fluency simply the relation which Santayana points out: that what changes is the essence which an individual physical object exemplifies; that what you call this table exemplifies now this, now that essence, and this exemplification may involve extremely rapid changes. Is that the whole story? In that view, the essences do not flow, but fluent is the partaking now of this essence, now of that. This view would leave us, on the one hand, the world of essences, where the identifications could never be expressed because the essences are what they are and never change; on the other hand, the world of existence has all the changes, but they can be understood only by saying that when a thing exists, it catches the dye now of this essence and now of that.

So, to state the matter simply brings us the old difficulty in a new way. In what sense does the existent partake now of this essence and now of that? Whether you try to express this in terms of mere identity, or in terms which recognize fluency, you have the same difficulties. Perhaps one can gain a good deal by recognizing that one is dealing with a world of changing facts, facts which are partly facts of existence and partly facts belonging to the realm of the essences. The realm of the essences is not so abstractedly to be sundered from the real of the existents, as Santayana supposes. His paper is a classic, beautifully clear in its distinctions, and yet one may well doubt whether so wealthy a realm as ours can be expressed in these terms.

A few examples may help us to see the complexity of the issue. There are a good many things in the world that present themselves to us as so profoundly changing in their character that it appears as if change belonged to the very essence of the thing. Not all those things are often recognized when we speak of physical objects, so that one doesn't often speak of them as realities, real existents.

You have heard that no two of us see the same rainbow. If we are interested in rainbows and look out after a shower in the mountains and notice our rainbows, we are decidedly disposed to suppose that if perception is to be trusted, each of us sees a rainbow; and the assertion that no two of us see the same rainbow appears artificial. It is only when we consider cases like the rainbows in the Niagara spray that the assertion seems more reasonable. When the sun is sufficiently down on the Horseshoe Falls from the Canadian side, the spray in which the rainbow apparition appears is so close that two persons side by side will be placing their rainbow in different points, so that they do not see the same.

Nevertheless, the perfectly simple case of identifying your rainbow is a case which will illustrate the difficulty. How long do I see the same rainbow? When does it become a different rainbow? From a distance and with a relative slowness of change of the approach, one would be led to say that the same rainbow stayed for some time; one holds on to the identification for some moments. As a result, the poet Shelley is able to use with certain winning persuasiveness the words of one of the spirits who comforts Prometheus as he lies bound on the mountain, "A rainbow arch stood on the sea, which rocked beneath, immovably." He tells how the clouds were driven between by the tempest, and that becomes a little difficult to follow; but even in a storm a distant rainbow might give you that impression; the rainbow arch stands on the sea, the sea rocks beneath, but {the arch} doesn't move.[CA] It seems to have this paradoxical movelessness about it, usually only for a short time. Here you have the case of a change in which the identifications which you try to make are all the time broken up as you try to make them.

Observers at sea will seldom notice a certain apparition. With the sun high up, you stand with it at your back; waves are steep-pitched and the wind strong enough so that the foam hisses from every square inch of the water; and all this foam is occurring on the background of a strong sea. As you look, there are certain effects which may be very magical. The waves, with the sun at your back, may get a very dark seeming by contrast with the foam; the foam itself is rushing before you as you look. (We must suppose the wind across your field of vision.) The wind is driving the foam high everywhere; and now as you look at this scene, the white foam and the dark water give the effect of jet-black water; but the relation of the foam to your eyes is somewhat like that which gives you the spray relations of Niagara in the late afternoon.[CA] You are pretty nearly between that spray and the line of the sunlight. The rainbow effects may be quite brilliant and in contrast with the black waves, the white foam, the rushing of the water, and the strong wind. The effects will be very striking: black waves with glittering white foam and spray rainbows. That is an effect which is constantly changing before you—a very impressive one worth looking for when you happen to be at sea, if the morning is bright and the waves are pitched high enough and the situation is such as I have characterized. It is one of the sea beauties which many people miss, even in many voyages.

The case at once illustrates a problem of identification. Generally, you aren't disposed to do much identifying as you look; it is a Heraclitean world; things flow; it is once for all a fluid world. Yet this and that rainbow may catch your attention and then it has a kind of permanence. In any case, diversity is mingled with identity in most curious fashions. The rainbows place themselves on the waves; and what is <u>this</u> wave as to its extent? How long is it the same wave? You quickly make the distinction between one sea and the next one; you individuate the waves; and that effect you have in very different sorts of seas. That involves the question as to what is the identical wave. The rainbow was on this wave, but what is this wave? And when does this wave become the next wave?

A system of waves of this sort may be and often is at just such times crossed by another system. The sailor generally is fairly interested in a practical way in cross seas, and generally individuates and identifies such seas. What are the bases of this practical identification? Each sea has a more or less determinate and recognizable direction. A wave motion is a rotary motion, and the direction of the rotary motion is different in different seas. The particles of water are rotating in this way or that, and the result is the direction of this sea. With less wind and in much smoother water you can have cross swells of various sorts. When a hurricane approaches, it shows itself by a ground swell which crosses the prevailing seas, and it is easy to recognize the direction of the swell and know where the seas are coming from, and thus to identify the single one.

Those are cases likely to be neglected in metaphysical discussions, but they are practically of great interest to navigators or artists or mere observers of nature. Those are cases of identification and diversification which demand attention. A cross sea is worth recognizing by a navigator and may have a very important effect upon his ship. The principal danger of hurricanes is that, as they pass, there are so many seas. It is the variety of the seas that does so much damage; in cross seas things happen that don't happen otherwise. That was found to be the case on the *Campania*, crossing the banks of Newfoundland in our direction after a considerable gale. When the wind changed to the northeast, there was a strong sea. The second-cabin passengers happened to be out on the companionway watching the sea in the weather. A cross wave swacked the vessel on one side. She went over until she had time to recover. When the sea went off, six of the passengers had gone off with the sea. Thereafter, I suppose the Cunarders, always careful of their passengers, were a little more set in their ways about not letting people out in such times. This illustrates that a cross sea is important because it has a very significant effect on what may happen.

The phenomena in question illustrate the whole problem of identity and change. The mountains give you a great deal of it. The identification of a cloud involves a very fascinating problem. Large clouds which pass well under the light constantly suggest the words "the same cloud," but the cloud is shifting. How long is it the same cloud? Those who have a tendency to identify clouds metaphorically with mountains and shapes sometimes amuse themselves with watching the change: "It is an eagle"; "No, it is a dragon"; "No, the dragon is a king; an old woman with an umbrella." These shiftings, if you like, belong to the realm of appearance; but they suggest to you what the situation is.

The world of the clouds, the seas, the rainbows, is a world which gives manifold exemplification of the problems of nature. Now remember that this world of the perceived objects differs from the orthodox physical world largely with respect to the kind of diversities that are there and the practical importance of what happens there. A large range of observations could be made which would hold of the world of the mirror and not of the world outside the mirror. Whenever you look into those large mirror globes that some tastes make prominent in the ornaments of estates, you deal with similar phenomena of identification.

When we speak of "the same physical thing," we are dealing with that which has a great deal in common with the spray and the cross sea, and one must be prepared to deal with that sort of thing when one makes his identifications. Our identification of a physical thing is an identification that is wholly unintelligible in terms of mere fact. It must be made in terms of the coherent fulfillment of a purpose.[11]

Concluding Critique of Extreme Realism

March 23 [Royce called attention to his exposition of the metaphysical vocabulary in *The World and the Individual*, Vol. 1, pp. 47–52.]

The topic of metaphysics is the true relation, the difference and the relation, of the two aspects of the fact-world, which can be expressed as the what and the that.

The word "being" is used for the character common to any and all grades of reality.

Instead of the Four Conceptions of Being, I should now say the four Ideas or Interpretations of Being. An idea is an expression of an interpretation.

I suppose you will be disappointed in the discussion of what I describe in this book as Realism. The realists have always complained that what they meant by realism isn't properly characterized by what I insisted upon as the fundamentally realistic view of what it is to be real. The third lecture, "The Independent Beings," has been criticized as one which didn't show a fair attitude toward the doctrines criticized.

Neither of essence nor of existence can you give any purely perceptual or purely conceptual account. Santayana, following an Aristotelian scholastic model, has held that the meanings of the word "is" can be best characterized by calling attention to the sharp and irreducible contrast between essence and existence, regarding the existents as examples which somehow or other simply put certain of the essences into what the world is, while the essences belong to the realm that I have been trying to get before you. I think that you will see that I have done whatever I could to defend and expound Santayana's sharpest distinction between these two realms.[#] When you seemed to find difficulty with this distinction, I tried to defend it as far as I could. But we have exemplified in this discussion the fact that you cannot adequately state the facts about reality in terms of this contrast. The essences turn out to be not merely the static, changeless, Platonic conceptual entities that they were to be. The very fact of identity that we try to express as the most characteristic meaning of "is" (per Santayana) shows that the essences in their very identification involve a differentiation. Identification appears as the result of an interpretation. Blessedness turns out to be itself virtue, not a reward of virtue. The interpretation isn't merely an event in the mind that thus interprets, but an event that is itself a metaphysical event. It is of the very nature of what constitutes blessedness and virtue that these should be distinguished but identified. From that point of view, that which is an essence is not a mere essence, it is an interpretation, it has the character of the interpretation of an essence. You are dealing with a process, something fluent. This fluency pervades the whole world of the essences. One's insight into the essences depends upon and involves interpretations, because it is of their very nature to be interpretations.

All the difference between reality and unreality can be defined in terms of what I characterize as ideas, the point being that an idea is not a conceptual or perceptual entity, but that which is experienced, found, noted as a fulfillment, so far as it goes, of a purpose, so that the idea changes as the purpose develops. The idea is expressed as itself a purpose, while the expression of the purpose is never completed.

Santayana's world of essences is not the fixed and changeless world that it was to be, or else you could not make any identifications in it. The situation is Heraclitean; you cannot step into the same stream twice. To escape this flux, Plato defined the essences, but he so illustrated them that he once again defined the flux. Aristotle, who developed the contrast which Santayana uses, developed it in such a way that the only genuineness in the essences was that they were always expressing themselves in the life process as its goals at the same time when they were endlessly restating themselves, so that his doctrine was throughout of an evolutionary sort. Where he couldn't recognize the growth of things, he failed to deal with the problem they presented to him. The various essences of natural kinds had their being in that they were the forms in which the potentialities of nature tended to get fashioned, so far as the world has its reality at all.

You cannot express the difference between real and unreal in terms of any one distinction between essence and existence. The world turns out to be describable only in terms of fluent topics of interpretation. The world of the essences is itself the world of fluent meanings, fulfillments of purpose.

Existents, as distinguished from essences, are of course known through perception, experience, or through evidence. Any use of evidence requires an interpretation of the essence of existence; it requires considering that the grounds why things are in the world of existence are grounds that are due to the essence of existence. We must make some use of some sort of ontological proof if we are to have any reason for believing that anything exists. Experience presents to us types, universals, characters, sorts, and therefore entities that are not merely perceptual, but entities that are also infected by the conceptual character.

Realism can be characterized as that view which Santayana gives expression to when he declares that the great metaphysical distinction is that between the essences and the existents, a distinction which can be defined in terms of perception and conception. The existence of things and their essence are mutually independent in this view; the ontological proof must be abandoned because essences and existents are independent in the sense that whether a thing exists or not doesn't depend on its essence. That kind of independence seems to be the very essential feature of the realism that Santayana exemplifies. The consequence of viewing the thing in that way is to insist upon a certain independence of the existence of things from[CA] the question whether they are known or not.

Mysticism is an interpretation of the world in terms of perception or immediacy. It says that it is of the essence of reality that if you are to know it fully you will perceive it directly; it is properly the object of an intuition.[12]

March 25 The question at this point is not of expounding my own theory but of becoming acquainted with the various ways of taking the Idea of Being. Here is a difference between what is real and what is not real. It is a difference which is in a way represented by the difference between the existent and the nonexistent of scholastic terminology, only, as we have seen, the difference between that which exists and that which does not exist is not the only difference of which we have to take account.

In the realm of the essences you already have a difference, such as would have some significance from the point of view of a being that considered the world apart from its creation: there would be the difference between what is genuinely true of an essence and what is not genuinely true of it. From that point of view, the idea that is involved is in part the idea of truth; but there is some sense in which you would make distinctions if you were considering the nature or the essence of an entity which you regarded as being as ideal as any entity could be.

There is some sense in saying that the Achilles of the story did really kill Hector. It belongs to the essence of the Achilles[CA] of whom the Homeric poem gives you an account that he is in some more or less individual way, at some more or less individual time, the slayer of Hector. That which is reported of him has this character, that a question can be raised about what really belongs to or is characteristic of a being that is treated as known to be a fictitious being.

Years ago I remember that an author played with the idea of taking the account that Shakespeare gives of Desdemona and the account that he gives of Ophelia, and making up a dream within a dream with regard to what might have been. One would like to know what would have been the case if Juliet, supposed to exist in some realm—neither the Shakespearian realm nor the realm of essences—had not met Romeo at the time but married somebody else. Under other circumstances Hamlet would never have met Ophelia and that tragedy wouldn't have been in question at all. With these alterations as a basis, the author worked out a very interesting account of an idealized realm in which events were different.

In such fancies one deals with a realm which has the quasi-existence of the poet's framing. One cannot deal with the problems of any such altered world without giving an account of things which involves a decided alteration of the story that is accepted; but it has its own distinctions between the true and the false, its own character, which you can define in terms of the hypothetical propositions. It is a realm with which we shall deal especially when we take up the judgments that take the form of the hypothetical. Grammarians call this realm the realm of hypotheses contrary to fact, yet the "fact" to which these hypotheses are contrary may be a very hypothetical world in which one can say, "You know Desdemona did love Othello; Juliet did actually love Romeo." That world is a world in which the hypothesis that it needn't have been so, is well in place; but the conceptions of Being involved are such as one has to deal with afresh.

Santayana's realm of essences has its own difficulties which cannot be dealt with in merely conceptual fashion. The consequence is that in order to deal with the problem of reality at all satisfactorily, you must take account not only of the realistic distinction between the existent and the nonexistent, but also of those distinctions which relate to a realm of truth that has certain gradations about it, which we needn't attempt to define otherwise than by considering the way in which they arise in the mind. When we study mathematical truth or poetry, we find reason for having such considerations in our minds; and we shall analyze them as considerations that have to do with the sort of being whose essence consists in the truth of certain propositions. This is not precisely Santayana's realm of the essences as he has defined it. The world where there is some distinction between what truly would have been Desdemona's fortune if she had never met Othello is a world that has a being whose general nature is definable in terms of the truth of certain propositions. We shall have occasion to see later on in how many ways that sort of realm comes to us. Nobody can sufficiently consider the problems of metaphysics without considering this realm. The scholastic study of the problem of Being had to do with that realm also and often dealt with the problems of it. {First, however, one needs to examine the position of those who identify Being and experience, the mystics.}

Chapter 7

Mysticism

Mysticism: The term is one of many uses in the course of the history of philosophy. People commonly associate mysticism with an idea about what are the special beings present in the world, rather than as an idea of what it is to be. It is usually taken as a very vague and variable doctrine concerning things, rather than as a metaphysical doctrine as such about the way in which what is real differs from that which is unreal. It is usually taken as a doctrine concerning some beings that are said to be real. To say that a man is mystical in his opinions commonly means that he believes in ghosts, or he consults astrologers or fortune-tellers, or in his opinion the beliefs of such and such a so-called mystical creed are correct. He is a partisan of some faith-cure group or Christian Science, or in some such way as that, a mystic. This is not a mystical doctrine as such, because it isn't so far a doctrine about what it is to be, but about beings that are said to be, although the doctrines in question often do involve in their expression a mystical conception of what it is to be. The characteristic feature of mysticism is not that you are guided in your life by this and that special opinion, but {is} a doctrine that to be real means a somewhat that you can define in terms of a certain attitude toward what is, as distinct from what is not. *March 25 cont.*

In the second lecture of *The World and the Individual*, I have illustrated that attitude in a general way, and in the fourth lecture the mystical doctrine is the subject. Mysticism is the view that to be real means to be what I have called "immediate," as distinct from being discovered through the examination of evidence or from being definable in terms of some articulated and precisely characterized aspect or mode of experience.

The mystic isn't interested in deciding determinate issues, as when one says in the pragmatic way that so-and-so must be viewed as existent for we find it in experience. The mystic has a hunger after certain issues that are not definable. You can't find out exactly what is the issue with him. He doesn't study the special tests which one is accustomed to apply. Common sense grows increasingly critical in submitting to experience that which is to be tested; but the mystic takes refuge in a certain indifference to sharp tests.

But this is after all the external view of mysticism rather than its internal spirit. Whenever you state special issues or look for a test as to whether a certain hypothesis is true or not, you are using what is for the mystic indirect or mediate evidence. But when you deal with reality you simply abandon such distinctions; for the real is that with which, if you are acquainted with it at all, you are directly acquainted, so that your test is not that of definition but of acquaintance. Your attitude is that of perceiver and not that of knower about.

The mystical view depends on substituting an extremely rich acquaintance with the real for various attempts to define whether certain ideas are true or not. The mystic is impressed with the fact that all your efforts to deal with the real, except by immediate acquaintance with it, are efforts that lead to error, to delusion. You must transform your self as well as your object if you want to get any genuine acquaintance with things. Common sense uses an utterly inadequate instrument. That which grasps the real is somewhat which viewed as knowledge belongs to a state of mind which is essentially incapable of definition from without or in any terms but its own. The real is the object of a certain immediate acquaintance. On the whole, you may be able to define what the knowledge of the real would be if you could get it. Everything but immediate acquaintance with the real must be illusory. The real is such that if it were known, there would be nothing but the immediate left; there would be just the presence left. Anything definable is illusory. That which is real has to be above definition.

Bergson has emphasized the inadequacy of the intellect to grasp the nature of the real. In all your definitions, to find out whether a certain hypothesis is true, your attitude is that of one who contrasts one object of the understanding with another, tests one essence to see whether the evidence shows that that is or probably is. In general, one is dealing with the categories of the intellect. Bergson is not a mystic in the sense that makes him a person appealing to the mystical experience as the one that he counsels, in the sense that some of the sages counsel it. He has made the mystical point of view at once a popular and a very significant and effective metaphysical view for those who in his time have been weary of the contentions and abstractions and inadequacies of various theories.

Bergson, in the Oxford Lectures,[1] defined the issue as one between perception and conception. All our ignorance about the world is an ignorance of perceptual content; the real difficulty is that you haven't what you want in the way of perception. Pragmatism is that point of view which seeks for the solution of special doubts and difficulties and always deals with special problems. The pragmatic method, insofar as it succeeds, tells you about what is real so far as it tells you what concepts can be verified perceptually. Insofar as it does this, however, pragmatism has always in its special thesis the truth–value which James so emphasizes. That which you can verify is good as a fragmentary means of finding the real; thus you constantly make use of such fragmentary knowledge; but in every such case what you discover is the solution to some *special* question. But Bergson, leaping over all the intermediate stages, supposes in a fashion deliberately fantastic the being for whom the question, "Where is Memorial Hall?" never arises, a being such that, before he defined the issue in conceptual terms, the answer was already before him.

Reality is that which is known by a being possessed of that sort of knowledge, a being all of whose questions were answered before they were asked, not by the special perceptions that guide us in our conduct, but by an acquaintance with that which would furnish in advance all that we seek to define. Only an ideally perfect knowledge of acquaintance would be a knowledge of the real.

In James's *Introduction to Philosophy,*[2] the case for pragmatism is stated entirely in terms of the observation that we are always lacking the knowledge that we seek, and we are guided, as we have to be, by the methods of a science—the fashions of inquiry that belong to our research for the real. But just as Bergson defines this, to us practically inaccessible, ideal of a personal *acquaintance with*, so James speaks of all our practical knowledge as an endless effort to get what is coming to us of a sort of knowledge that, if we possessed it in the sense that we wish we could possess it, would no longer be the solution of a special problem.

We must sharply distinguish between the mystical idea of what it would be to be acquainted with the real, and any special opinions of the mystics of what beings are real. It is the question of the *that*, not of the *what* of reality. For the mystic, the nature of reality is to be such that acquaintance alone presents to you the *what* of it; but this acquaintance is an immediate acquaintance which presents to you the fact *that* it is. We here have a peculiar union of the *what* and the *that*.

Bergson is not a person who revels in mystical experience. He starts from a commonsense contrast between what we have and what we want, the perfection of insight which we never obtain, but which when we define it as an ideal does give us a view of what it is *to be*.

The mystic is not to be answered by saying that his views are fantastic. He is dealing with the nature of what you are trying to find when you test hypotheses. We are always looking to find out what hypothesis is true. The mystic is aware, as James was well aware, that what one would want if one could get it, in place of this endless search about the truth of a particular hypothesis, would be some acquaintance with fact, which acquaintance would be above all special issues that are raised when one inquires into the truth of this and that hypothesis.

The woman of Samaria at the well,[3] hearing that after all there is a living water such that, if one drank it, one would never thirst any more, turns from her world of pragmatisms, from her efforts to find this and that quenching of the thirst, and begs for "this water, that I thirst not, neither come hither to draw." The mystic, perceiving that we are thirsting for satisfaction, declares that therein lies the very defect of our view of what it is to be. We shall be in the presence of Being whenever it occurs to us how so to solve the problem of Being that we taste the living water so that we "thirst not, neither come hither to draw." This is how the mystic states the mystical problem.

March 28 The mystical view comes to one as a significant view so far as there comes to his mind that the approach to the real when we deal with the relations of things is not the view that gives us what we want, while there is a hope that if we could get more into touch with a perceptual view of the world, we should reach what we want.[CA] It is perfectly possible for one to be himself a mystic, to say that the real is to be known by perception, without himself having the perceptual experience; to maintain, as Bergson does, that if we had perception in an unlimited degree, it would acquaint us with the real in a fashion that would relieve us of any need for conception. This immediately affects his attitude toward a great number of problems, although he may not himself be possessed of such a point of view. At any rate, whatever we affirm that presupposes a conceptual point of view will not be satisfactory. One doesn't have to be a practical mystic in order to take that position.

Of course, it is very natural that such a theory of Being should have been especially characteristic of faiths, doctrines, movements, and tendencies that themselves have been disposed to hold the position that their adepts or the extraordinarily privileged were acquainted with the mystical experience. Occasionally you will find a person who says that he himself has it. Such thinkers there were among the Hindu philosophers, who were pantheists with a strong tendency to regard the world as one, to think of the world in terms of the unity of Being, to be with strong emphasis monistic in their views.[4]

March 30 No view is more plastic, more mobile, more of a nature to furnish you with surprises than the mystical view. From another side, indeed there is something that appears at times as a very great monotony about the mystical story. One reason why one gets weary of it is that one tends to confound the accidents with the deeper features of a mystical view; then one holds that a mystic is a person of some queer experience and that the mystics are an uncritical and extremely simpleminded lot of folk.

Professor Leuba of Bryn Mawr, who has contributed a good deal to the literature of the psychology of religion, takes his mystics from the point of view of the man who is interested in mysticism merely as an experience which is subjectively, or more or less also socially, exalting or interesting to those who have it. They find comfort in that experience and are sustained by it and live lives that are more patient or enduring or inwardly successful than other lives; so that just as a person might exercise in a gymnasium or study some foreign language or take any other intellectual or moral tonic, so possibly one might be a mystic. According to this writer, the great mystics have been simpleminded to the point of relative absurdity. They are dreamy folk. What is attractive about them is that they have often combined with this softness of intellectual fiber a great moral vigor. They have been reformers and persons who were practically quite successful. That is a matter of curiosity to this writer. But so far as these people have supposed that these experiences were throwing light on any subject, they have failed to see that {ordinarily} evidence is based on data that tend to prove so and so; but the mystic has no data that he can analyze. His field is a field of amiable incoherence so far as concerns the mystic's efforts to express a theory. Mysticism is an inadequate effort to take the world richly. The problematical importance of mysticism turns upon the fact that these people who are so ineffective as thinkers are so practically important.

Bergson's account of the nature of the ideal form of knowledge, the purely perceptual type, enables us to see how mysticism looks from without to a very alert and critical mind certainly not disposed to take for important fancies merely as fancies.[CA] The considerations which make Bergson defend a point of view which is essentially the mystical point of view are not considerations dependent upon the prominence of the mystical experience in his life. His antiintellectualism is a perfectly articulate doctrine.

James's point of view was decidedly similar. The mystics whom he met personally attracted him very much. His patience in listening to "cranks" and his efforts to help them made him very keenly awake to the value of such people. He valued them for their originalities. He was especially struck by the writings of a Mr. Blood, a pluralistic mystical writer. In his *Varieties of Religious Experience*, James treats the mystics deliberately from without, in the sense that he lays no claim to mystical experience, while as a skeptical person he can still say that the experience appears noetic. In many cases he was rather alienated by the tendency of most mystics to insist upon the absoluteness of certain data, but he was always looking for that which would make important for people the existence and the work of mystics. He would find much less interesting some of the things that I shall make important.

My desire is to make clear what is essential and what is accidental to the mystical point of view. The essential thing to me is that for reasons that we can call dialectical reasons (reasons due to their own objections to explaining the world in terms of mediation), the mystics are persons who define what it would be to know the real if we could know it at all. In daily life and in scientific experience we do not know the world, because it is some intellectualism or some practical motive that leads us to view things so and so. The main matter is that instead of interpreting the world mediately, instead of analyzing the world's constitution as Santayana has been doing, instead of taking such mediate or intellectualistic or practical methods, the mystic holds that if we could get the real, we should have used a method which Bergson illustrates in his *Introduction to Metaphysics* when he says, "There is one being in any case that we have to know, if at all, immediately, namely the self." So without emphasizing these quaint or exotic forms of mystical experience, Bergson can quite deliberately counsel you to put yourself inside the object, since you see that all knowledge of the self—the illustration which constantly recurs—except immediate knowledge would not be knowledge of the self.

{Notice} Deussen of Kiel University, *Sixty Upanishads of the Rig-Veda*.[5] Professor Woods of Harvard has translated Deussen's account of the technical philosophy, the Hindu scholasticism.[6] The Self has to be described as "it isn't so, it isn't so."[7] Fichte calls the Self a deed, and for him this deed is indescribable.

April 1 I had the great satisfaction some years ago of telling Professor Deussen for the first time in his life about Tennyson's contribution to the literature of mystical experience. It was at the philosophers' congress in Heidelberg in 1908. Deussen would not have found his heart enriched and helped toward the mystic vision by what has happened during the war.

Tennyson

Tennyson's *In Memoriam* is rather less known than it should be. The habit of speaking of the older Victorian period as "outgrown" has tended to deprive the younger generation of Englishmen of one of their best opportunities to understand the temper and the thought of their own time. Tennyson is sure to be heard of again when the generation comes to itself. There are obvious inadequacies and limitations about Tennyson, but what he had to say he could say. Although he told it at great length, I cannot say that I think it was ever at too great length. It seems to me that we shall always have a great deal to learn from Tennyson.

A personal intimacy of two young college men, an intimacy broken by death, is preserved by this poem, which records not merely the keeping of a formal faith, but a profound and significant intimacy of spiritual companionship under the idealizing conditions of memory and death. This poem records a long series of phases of growth and experience of the poet as he remembers his friend. At first he tries to distract his mind, then expresses the need of getting the friend from a new point of view and giving him a tribute that was just to his powers. Then the poet more and more considers all that the friend's life had meant, so that the interest becomes that of the community of mankind in a valuable friendship and in the friend that represents it, so that the poem is very greatly universalized.

Tennyson writes at a time of doubt. He was much influenced by the conflict between religion and science in the form in which it began at the period when he was an Oxford undergraduate, so that the poem has a great deal to say about how far faith has at its fundaments a foundation. Since feeling, emotion, is very prominent throughout the experience that is to be considered, the poet has an opportunity to discuss the metaphysics of the emotions, and he does so in a way which is very living, very charming. So far his work is allied with that of Wordsworth, who presents things to you that are at once philosophical and poetical in their meaning. It is a mystical poetry that is never obscure, never hard to read, and that grows upon you the better you know it.

Tennyson had a certain amount of mystical experience of his own. He has given some account of it in his autobiographical statement. His son has told briefly the facts. It was a perfectly genuine and natural thing for Tennyson to have under certain circumstances an experience of that sort of absorption which the mystics have always regarded as of the nature of a revelation. The mystic experience recorded in this poem is one that actually occurs.

The passage begins at XCII of the *In Memoriam*. The poet has been considering the possibility of some sort of personal communion with the dead. He long deals with its difficulties and very carefully voices what he regards as its dangers; he wants his beliefs about the dead to be founded in genuine experience and not in superstition. On the other hand, he wants to receive the full importance of the cult of the dead. At this point the poet raises the question, what would be an experience that brought me into touch with my dead and gave me some acquaintance of the actual survival of death. The poet is quite cautiously speculating on the possibility that one could be sure of a revelation from the dead. He is dealing with the phenomena of psychical research, but in perfectly general form.

Here you have an approach to mysticism through skepticism, a perfectly natural affair. Raising the question, "Have we experience that shows us that the dead survive?" the poet tends to answer it quite negatively, with skillful mention of the perils, doubts, difficulties. Then he is led by that very fact to associations which suggest to him that it is possibly we who cut ourselves off from the dead by wrong types of experience. Possibly a transformation of the moral defect of our own stage of life might make intercourse with the dead a live thing. Addressing ideally the dead friend, the poet says {in stanza} XCII:

> If any vision should reveal
> Thy likeness, I might count it vain
> As but the canker of the brain;
> Yea, tho' it spake and made appeal

To chances where lots were cast
   Together in the days behind,
   I might but say, I heard a wind
Of memory murmuring the past.

Yea, tho' it spake and bared to view
   A fact within the coming year;
   And tho' the months, revolving near,
Should prove the phantom warning true,

They might not seem thy prophecies,
   But spiritual presentiments,
   And such refraction of events
As often rises ere they rise.

Satisfactory evidence of psychical research[CA] must not be expected in dealing with anything that is supposed to indicate actual relations with the dead. Whatever comes in the form of "psychical experience" is subject to doubt. What would make the intercourse with the dead what the psychical researchers call veridical? The immediate research is subject to doubts which the poet summarizes; an immediate apparition wouldn't prove that this is the dead man.

Then comes the thought that perhaps the difficulty that makes the barrier so hopelessly insurmountable may be due to our own attitude. We ourselves may be the source. This view comes at this stage of the poem very naturally, first in the form of the general suggestion that if there were any revelation, it would mean an inner transformation, only it would have to be something profoundly convincing.

XCIII

I shall not see thee. Dare I say
   No spirit ever brake the band
   That stays him from the native land
Where first he walk'd when claspt in clay?

No visual shade of some one lost,
   But he, the Spirit himself, may come
   Where all the nerve of sense is numb;
Spirit to Spirit, Ghost to Ghost.

The genuine skeptical point of view is to say that if there were an experience, it would be a transformation of the experience which psychical phenomena exemplify. It is the touch of spirit to spirit, ghost to ghost, that is needed.

O, therefore from thy sightless range
With gods in unconjectured bliss,
O, from the distance of the abyss
Of ten-fold complicated change,

Descend, and touch, and enter; hear
The wish too strong for words to name,
That in this blindness of the frame
My Ghost may feel that thine is near.

If the dead friend were to reveal himself to me, that would mean that I was changed. As I am, I am incapable of such experience; it would need a change in me.

XCIV

How pure at heart and sound in head,
With what divine affections bold
Should be the man whose thought would hold
An hour's communion with the dead.

In vain shalt thou, or any, call
The spirits from their golden day,
Except, like them, thou too canst say
My spirit is at peace with all.

They haunt the silence of the breast,
Imaginations calm and fair,
The memory like a cloudless air,
The conscience as a sea at rest:

But when the heart is full of din,.
And doubt beside the portal waits,
They can but listen at the gates,
And hear the household jar within.

Here is a thought that is presented to you somewhat in stages, the thought that an inward preparation is needed for that kind of union with the dead which one longs for. The transformation involves that which is so significantly indicated as assuming the attitude of the one whose soul is at peace; of course that couldn't be assumed voluntarily. The imagery of the poem is very frequently that of English country life.

XCV

By night we linger'd on the lawn,
  For underfoot the herb was dry;
  And genial warmth; and o'er the sky
The silvery haze of summer drawn;

And calm that let the tapers burn
  Unwavering: not a cricket chirr'd;
  The brook alone far-off was heard,
And on the board the fluttering urn:

After all, in the approach to this experience of perfect insight one insists upon a concentration which leave some perfectly capable of critical watchfulness and always doubting observation of detail. One is not disposed to a blur of sentiments. Clear everything must be. There is a very interesting increase of clearness of vision and skeptical alertness in a curious union. The poet thinks how doubtful we are about the dead and looks for the light.

And bats went round in fragrant skies,
  And wheel'd or lit the filmy shapes
  That haunt the dusk, with ermine capes
And wooly breasts and beaded eyes;

While now we sang old songs that peal'd
  From knoll to knoll, where, couch'd at ease
  The white kine glimmer'd, and the trees
Laid their dark arms about the field.

But when those others, one by one,
  Withdrew themselves from me and night,
  And in the house light after light
Went out, and I was all alone.

A hunger seized my heart; I read
  Of that glad year which once had been,
  In those fallen leaves which kept their green,
The noble letters of the dead.

And strangely on the silence broke
  The silent-speaking words, and strange
  Was love's dumb cry defying change
To test his worth; and strangely spoke

The Faith, the vigour, bold to dwell
On doubts that drive the coward back,
And keen through wordy snares to track
Suggestion to her inmost cell.

A very characteristic expression of that kind of mystical approach. One faces the doubt, it is the sort of doubt that keeps the coward back. One is very watchful. There is a sense of constantly increasing energy of thinking and clearness of insight.

So word by word, and line by line,
The dead man touched me from the past,
And all at once it seem'd at last
The living soul was flash'd on mine.

And mine in this was wound, and whirl'd
About empyreal heights of thought,
And came on that which is, and caught
The deep pulsations of the world,*

Aeonian music measuring out
The steps of Time—the shocks of Chance—
The blows of Death. At length my trance
Was cancel'd, stricken thro' with doubt.

Vague words! but ah, how hard to frame
in matter-moulded forms of speech,
Or even for intellect to reach
Thro' memory that which I became:

Till now the doubtful dusk reveal'd
The knolls once more where, couch'd at ease
The white kine glimmer'd, and the trees
Laid their dark arms about the field;

And sucked from out the distant gloom,
A breeze began to tremble o'er
The large leaves of the sycamore,
And fluctuate all the still perfume,

* {The crucial lines.}

And gathering freshlier overhead,
Rock'd the full foliaged elms; and swung
The heavy-folded rose, and flung
The lilies to and fro, and said,

"The dawn, the dawn," and died away;
And East and West, without a breath,
Mixt their dim lights, like life and death,
To broaden into boundless day.

There you have in brief the whole story of the mystic. You see the essential feature. It is a form which has nothing to do with any one creed. If you stand outside of it, you can say, here is a man who feels things in his mind that are of great interest to him; the experience doesn't prove anything except that he had it. Whatever statement of that sort you may make is external and stands apart from it. But this vision, if it came, alone would show the real. This is the experience which is essentially metaphysical. The poet came upon what is. That experience comes only when he no longer experiences his dead or this or that event, but when all is transformed into that which is. This experience reveals. It gives the entire change of attitude towards experience which would be needed in order that the light should come.

One of the most impressive lyrics of the poet William Blake—although the popular mind thinks of such things as the well-known "Tyger Tyger burning bright"—but where he reached his highest was in a group of verses which appear among the *Songs of Innocence*. Here one has an extremely simple expression of experience, with a background of death and longing as a means of approach. One has fancies of which one can say when he is awake that the experiences have nothing congruous about them. The poet doesn't believe these things to be revelations, but they suggest the transformation which is the distinctly mystical transformation. There is first increasing consciousness of our inability to find out by any touch that we can get in life that touch with the dead which we want. Then suddenly, the revelation of that which does reveal.

The Land of Dreams[8]

Awake, awake, my little Boy!
Thou wast thy Mother's only joy;
Why dost thou weep in thy gentle sleep?
Awake! thy Father does thee keep.

"O, what Land is the Land of Dreams?
What are its mountains, and what are its Streams?
O Father! I saw my Mother there,
Among the lilies by water fair.

"Among the lambs, clothed in white,
She walk'd with her Thomas in sweet delight.
I wept for joy, like a dove I mourn,
O! when shall I again return?"

Dear Child, I also by pleasant streams
Have wandered all Night in the Land of Dreams;
But tho' calm and warm the waters wide,
I could not get to the other side.

"Father, O father! what do we here
In this land of unbelief and fear?
The Land of Dreams is better far,
Above the light of the Morning Star."

It is worthwhile to notice that Tennyson himself in *In Memoriam* does not decide in favor of a mystical view of the solution of the problems of *In Memoriam* itself. The problem is that about the other life and our relations to it. Appeal is made to another form of solution which has an interesting and, I think, unquestionably a technically intended relation to the doctrine asserted and the point of view emphasized by Kant. There is no word in the text that indicates whether Kant was the philosopher whom Tennyson had in mind. The expressions are so technically Kantian that it is interesting to look at the matter from that point of view. *April 4*

Kant is profoundly opposed in spirit to mysticism. Where this tendency approached something, he found the tendency evil,[CA] so what Kant has to say about mysticism in any of its forms is polemical. Kant's own solutions of the problems of immortality and God are in ethical terms. These are for Kant not the objects of theoretical knowledge, but of rationally justified and rationally inevitable postulates. To put the thing in fairly easy and obvious language, for Kant it is "as if" there were God. That is the rational view to take with regard to the problem whether the world is divine or expresses the divine; it is rational to view the world as if there were a God. Theism has a kind of validity whose nature we shall analyze under the third conception of being. In the case of immortality, that is the object of a postulate. We ought to view the human individual "as if" he were the expression of an endlessly significant task, so it is "as if" man were immortal.

Now in a very interesting fashion at the close of the *In Memoriam*, Tennyson expresses that {"as if"} conclusion, not the mystic conclusion at all. When he is summarizing the result of these years of thought, inquiry, scruple, puzzle and mystic experience, what he has to say is that we get the best point of view when, looking over our life and its result, we hope:

CXXXI

That we may lift from out of dust
  A voice as unto him that hears,*
  A cry above the conquer'd years
To one that with us works, and trust

With faith that comes of self-control,
  The truths that never can be proved
  Until we close with all we loved,
And all we flow from, soul to soul.

If the mystic experience comes in fulfillment of that cry, it would belong to another life. In this present life our solutions must be in terms of "as if."

[Here Royce read and commented upon several Hindu Upanishads concerning the question what it would be to know the Self.] It would be to identify subject and object, to overcome the difference between the Self and the Other, so that one no longer would be seeing or knowing another. The completion of self-knowledge would be the vanishing of consciousness. The search for the complete Self is the search for that which is in some way its own extinction. So the sage Yâjnavalkya to his wife Maitreyi.[9] But when Indra, the god, learns from Prajapati, the highest god, about the true Self, the teacher reaches a stage in his exposition where he depicts the perfect self-knowledge, not as absence of consciousness, but as the sort of freedom allegorized by freedom in the form of immediate knowledge. The complete Self would be incidentally omniscient but would care nothing for that detail. Its completeness would consist in that freedom.

Thus complete self-possession has a type which is repeatedly characterized and best expressed by absence of difference between Self and not-Self, and so by the completion which is of the nature of an extinction. On the other hand, you can express this—and in figures that have some truth about them—in the form of that kind of fulfillment that is simply in possession of, and utterly free from, not at the disposal of, whatever experience you please.

* {Royce emphasizes the "as if" character of this appeal by stressing "as unto".}

In the hymn "Jerusalem the Golden," the mystic paradox is expressed in somewhat similar shape, with stress laid on the negative side of the thing. "It isn't thus, it isn't thus," so the hymn says, "I know not, O I know not what joys await me there." In that form of mysticism, you notice the sort of expression of immediacy which you might call the free or fluent sort. The hymn sets forth a wealth of experiences; the author uses wealthily the forms of sensuous immediacy: "There stands the throne of David," etc., recognizing that none of this is literally true, but thus we can depict for ourselves what the completeness would be.[10]

The emphasis is laid on the fact that the state of the complete Self is a state at once free from the variety, opposition, contrast between ego and non-ego, and at the same time a state of complete fulfillment.

Emerson got his *Brahma* from Hindu sources.[11]

If the red slayer think he slays,
   Or if the slain think he is slain,
They know not well the subtle ways
   I keep, and pass, and turn again.

Far or forgot to me is near;
   Shadow and sunlight are the same;
The vanished gods to me appear;
   And one to me are shame and fame.

They reckon ill who leave me out;
   When me they fly, I am the wings;
I am the doubter and the doubt,
   And I the hymn the Brahmin sings.

The strong gods pine for my abode,
   And pine in vain the sacred Seven;
But thou, meek lover of the good!
   Find me, and turn thy back on heaven.

This is what you know when you know the Self simply and completely. It is also the being that these various sages have been describing, the state of mind that Tennyson found for a moment when he says, I "came on that which is, and caught the deep pulsations of the world."

Meister Eckhart

April 6 Eckhart I first heard of through my own reading of Schopenhauer when I was studying in Germany, at about the same time that I heard the metaphysical lectures of Lotze. My attention was attracted to him by some remarkable passages in Schopenhauer's *The World as Will and Idea.* Then I procured the edition of Eckhart's sermons in Pfeiffer's *Deutsche Mystiker* (1857). Until about the time when I {read} this paper in 1894,[12] Pfeiffer was an authority on Eckhart's type of mysticism, and the comments and discussions of this type which you will find in Schopenhauer and von Hartmann were based almost entirely on the data contained therein. Since then there has been a considerable addition to the collection on which that book was founded. Pfeiffer dealt almost entirely with the Middle High German text of Eckhart's sermons. Denifle collected the Latin writings and considered them from the point of view of a trained scholastic writer, and restated a good deal the aspects of Eckhart's doctrine on which I have been led to lay stress in this paper. If this essay were republished, I ought to take account of Denifle's researches, and in particular of the fact that much of Eckhart's doctrine was actually worked out in Latin as part of the work of a scholastic Dominican author, and one whose views are put in somewhat a wrong light if you think of them merely in view of the sermons collected by Pfeiffer.

I found that when I had once grappled with the difficulties of the Middle High German text, Eckhart soon became very fascinating. The language is highly preferable to the philosophical language that developed when in the later history of German thought the terminology of philosophy received its technical form. Middle High German is especially fitted for translating scholastic writings and for expressing philosophical thought. I have often regretted that Middle High German did not become the triumphant power in the history of modern German thinking. The differences are, of course, not for me to characterize philologically; one can only say that Latin, turned into the Middle High German vernacular, gives an expression to philosophical thought that is in many ways to me very fascinating.

Eckhart {died in} 1327. In the sermons he appears much less a technical philosopher than in his Latin writings. His sermons appear {to be} the record of a soul alone with God. The highest truth of religious experience, thinks Eckhart, is that the Godhead as such simply cannot be revealed absolutely to any form of rational insight, human or divine.

> *On the contrary, it is of the very essence of reason itself to be dependent upon something that is not reason. . . . The salvation of the soul depends upon a certain act of rising above knowledge to what is beyond knowledge (268–69).*[13]

The doctrine that all our knowledge is founded on what is essentially beyond knowledge gets on occasion for Spencer a slight mystical flavor.[14] It seems quaint enough to think of Spencer as a mystic, an extremely prosaic thinker, devoid of a sense of humor, unable to read Homer with any interest, because after all those Greek stories were so barbarous and untrue; yet Herbert Spencer sometimes approaches to the mystical point of view. For this doctrine does somehow help to reconcile religion and science. For science doesn't know, and religion doesn't know; and in such ignorance they have a common basis for such grasping of the truth as belongs to man.

But Eckhart's Unknowable is something that he often speaks of as the *wüste Gottheit*, or wilderness of Godhead; it isn't Spencer's Unknowable, but rather the One above knowledge of Plotinus or the neo-Platonic mystic Dionysius (270). It is owing to the need of transcending all duality that the highest knowledge becomes identical with the deepest mystery.

[Here Royce read with deep appreciation the sentence from Eckhart regarding the "unborn reality" or "nameless nothingness" which God may be indifferently said to possess]:

> *Du solt alzemale entsinken dîner dînesheit, unde solt zerfliezen in sîne sînesheit unde sol dîn dîn in sînen mîn ein mîn werden also genzlich dass du mit ihm verstandest êwiglîche sîne ungewordene istigkeit und sîne ungenanntem Nihtheit.**

I suppose that although I shall use a little repetition in making this statement, it is worthwhile to point out to you once more how much these positions that we have been illustrating in Meister Eckhart are identical with the very view about the nature of knowledge and its object with which we have become acquainted through Bergson.[15] The speech is very different, and Bergson in the practical sense is on the whole no mystic, for he views all this as a modern man does. Bergson himself regards the intuition which ought to take the place of scientific forms of knowledge or inquiry, not as a special possession to be gained through a form of insight which belongs to a peculiar class of adepts. But when he says, in the way that he has so often varied in his popular expression, "If you seek for knowledge, enter into the interior of your object," and when he defines the goal of knowledge in terms of pure perception (which, though we can't hope to get it, yet if our knowledge had perceptual completeness, would leave no place for conception and therefore no place for the kind of truth that you can express in conceptual terms)—when Bergson says these things, he sets forth what in an entirely different language Eckhart sets forth in his sermons. *April 8*

* For a translation, see p. 191.

When Eckhart was telling us in his proverbial expression about the knowledge which one might believe the angels possessed—that knowledge which they had instantaneously at creation, for they were angels—when Eckhart was telling us that, he was of course using other language for the same sort of thing that Bergson speaks of. When Eckhart says that the angels with their intuitive knowledge of the divine had never understood how it is that the Father, Son, and Holy Ghost are in this mysterious relation, since the more one knows the less one understands, this sounds capricious of course and scholastic, or again, as the speech of a medieval preacher.

But though the language is very different, what is at the heart of it? This statement that the more one knows the less one comprehends is the statement that it isn't conceptual knowledge that you want: it isn't the dealing with the world that Santayana has depicted as the world of the essences: it isn't that that you lack in your ordinary search for the facts about reality. What you need is the perceptual; and had you the perceptual, then you would be in the angelic position. Comprehension belongs to the conceptual side of things, to making the distinctions between one essence and others, {and to} raising all those problems about identity and difference.

Hereupon, if Eckhart, approaching the matter from another side, is making use of those strange paradoxes about how those who tell us about God show that they are prattlers—they lie and commit sin (278)—whereas, on the contrary, one should accomplish that task of losing all one's individual or divided selfhood and sink away into the divine nothingness which is also the fullness of being—what is this but another way of approaching the same consideration? The perceptual is what you want. Then, are words needed? Words bring up concepts, and concepts are not what is needed.

The puzzles will grow only the more considerable if you consider existents over against the realm of the essences. Whether it is experience or evidence that gives you your mode of getting at this <u>existence</u>, such a mode acquaints you with, or reports to you, the fact that—well, certain existents are known—you feel sure of them—but that again isn't the perfect knowledge that you seek. If you say you can't get it, Eckhart and Bergson agree to that. Nevertheless, all your search is governed by the ideal that you never attain, the ideal that if you found the truth, that truth would be silent, as when Yâjnavalkya says of the true Self, "Neti, Neti; it is not thus, it is not thus."[16] Only negatively you can express it.

What then do I gain by this confession of helplessness? Eckhart might reply, "Here you get at that idea, if you will, in terms of which we define the limits of our knowledge. If you ask for the goal of knowledge, you can only define it in terms of regarding it as a limit, and so treating it that of course you do not get this knowledge. It belongs to practical mysticism to regard the goal as something that the seer intends. But then your whole view of the metaphysical problems will be altered and guided by this view of what the goal would be if it could be attained." In this way the most paradoxical expressions of Eckhart become natural enough from this point of view. Keep in mind that this is exactly what Bergson would be saying if he were turning his mind in this way and giving a practical account of what the mystical attitude ought to be.[17]

St. Thomas is peculiarly skillful in dealing with the difficulties about the doctrine of the Trinity. Of course, one doesn't look in one's Aristotle for any decisive knowledge about that, but to the Church some features of the knowledge of the divine nature are revealed and are above human knowledge, although St. Thomas finds that good reasons can be given why there is nothing self-contradictory in these doctrines. But the matter goes beyond knowledge. St. Thomas is very skillful in choosing his terminology, suiting his terminology to the problems as they had developed, but is also clearly aware of the need of great caution in what he says about it. But Eckhart is concerned with matters that he must preach to the people. He takes a fearless attitude which he regards as genuinely orthodox—although in the end the Church was about to condemn his position at the time when he died. We can say that this has features which we should regard as unorthodox (279 ff.).

Our mystic is fond of making the distinction between God and the Godhead (280). You can easily see that when one uses the word "essence" about the divine being, one isn't using the word which you use when you speak of the essence of this or that, or deal with those problems which Santayana dealt with. The divine essence differs from the other essences in being the essence of an uncreated Being, the essence which differs from all the other essences in that all the other essences somehow depend on it. Of this essence you can indeed say that it is very genuine, but it isn't an essence that definitely differs from existence. Scholasticism is committed very largely to the view that it is of the nature of God to be. For the divine being himself the ontological proof would hold so far as he comprehended his essence. St. Thomas would say that while the ontological proof of God's existence would be obvious to God, it isn't obvious to us, because we don't know the divine essence completely. But Eckhart says you must abandon all your private views and special ideas.

> *You shall always sink away from your selfhood, you shall flow into his self-possession, and your very thought of Yours shall flow into his Mine, and become there his Mine so completely that you with him eternally apprehend his birthless fullness of being and his nameless nothingness"* (278).

To say of an essence that it is unborn is to say what Santayana says, that the essences are changeless and eternal. But God's essence differs from all others in that it also has the nameless nothingness. Its absence of name consists in this, that it isn't defined by its distinctions from other essences. It is that which if apprehended at all would be apprehended by direct perception, and therefore it wouldn't be apprehended by naming it. All names are false of it. Thus you can say in Eckhart's terms, it is above every *Iht*, and at the same time that it has *Nihtheit* (291). So also Yâjnavalkya of the true Self, and so Bergson of reality, if he continued discussing the matter in that sense.

The technical distinction between *natura naturans* and *natura naturata* (279) is not in itself a heretical distinction. In God as the highest, however, you have according to Eckhart an essence that is above all special essences. God as the Trinity, the "natured nature," is secondarily derived from the very Godhead, the "unnatured nature." So then, Eckhart feels no fear in saying that the nature of God, so far as God is the Godhead, the genuine God, is above the nature of the Trinity, a derived aspect of the divine nature.

Eckhart is sure, if you really want to come into communion with the Absolute God, to get the *Atman*—what Bergson conceives as this complete perception—if you really want that, then even the Holy Trinity can never suffice you (290). Here Eckhart was in danger from the standpoint of the Church. The Trinity can never suffice you if you want to know God, for that is the revealed God, the explicit God, the God that is mainly conceptual in its character. You must get past God the Trinity, past the God with whom in the beginning was the Word; for that God is a being only relative to the objects of his omniscience (280). God, as a relative term, is relative also to even the creatures; I am in a sense the cause of him just as much as he is the cause of me. This problem was one with which St. Thomas often dealt. In order to be omniscient, God had to know me. What is that but to give me a share in the divine being? The pantheistic tendency of such considerations is evident.

Just as for Bergson this perception that we never get is the goal of our knowledge, so also for Eckhart, who seeks the thing in terms religious as well as scientific, just as for Bergson, though he can't get it, this perception is the goal of our knowledge. According as you look at it, God appears now in this way, now in that (280–281). So when you considered the essences in Santayana's case, you had that curious puzzle of identity and difference in a way that always leads you to view Santayana's realm of essences as if something happened there. Only the Godhead (vs. God) has fullness of being. The difference is that between the absolute and the relative. In imagination Eckhart transfers himself to this position in advance of creation. One considers anybody you please, any essence you please, with reference to its genuine source. All the distinctions from other essences fade away. All that which is in the Godhead is One. The term "God" is a relative term, a term relative to the term creature (281); it doesn't meet this essence which is always presupposed. Why is it that you cannot by any study of Santayana's realism or any other form of intellectualism get at the ground of these various problems about essences? It is because their solution lies in a kind of Being which you can't express in relative terms. "All that which is in the Godhead—that is One, and thereof is not to be spoken" (281). Now Eckhart speaks in language which is in part borrowed from Plotinus. The God of revelation, the Doer, God as the creator of the world, these are only relative aspects. Here again in vision for the sake of edification, Eckhart supposes himself to pass through the created world to the place where this insight is grasped. "When again I come into God, if I form no image, my rewinning [of the Godhead] is nobler than was my issuing forth" (281).[CA]

From the point of view of one who has turned away from all this conceptual knowledge to this genuine insight, it is as if this very imperfection never had been. Schopenhauer, at the end of his *World as Will and Idea,* says that for the transformed seer who has abandoned all the delusions of this world of Will, all this world so full of varieties, with all its stars and milky ways, all that is *nichts*. So Yâjnavalkya, so Eckhart, so any mystic must say.

Think of yourself as coming out of the realm from which you sprang, the realm of the divine ideas, as resulting from this mysterious deed whereby you are created (281). Suppose yourself returning through the apprehension of what the essences are, through the grasping of that which lies beyond your essence or your existence, namely, the true source of it, the Godhead; then it is as if "nobody had missed me when I departed thence" (281).

Now all this in Eckhart's mind has an intensely practical application. The life of a practical religious devotion is an effort to win this goal (282), and whoever stops at this or that stage of growth, saying, "I will serve God in this way; this is enough," is in a position which Prajapati assigns to Indra,[18] whoever stops with that Upanishad, he will be essentially deceived.

The best aspect of one's soul, the biggest guidance that one gets from one's inner self, the spark or glimmer of one's soul, that takes no contentment in the Trinity, in the world of the Logos, exactly the world that Santayana described. Just as the definition of knowledge in perceptual terms which Bergson gives doesn't solve any special problem of science, but does determine an attitude which is central in characterizing and in estimating all scientific knowledge, so for a practical mystic like Eckhart, while it doesn't tell you anything about special dogmas, it does enable you to solve problems when they arise (285 ff.). A mystic of this sort escapes at once from everything in the nature of pragmatism. The knowledge that you look for isn't found by verifying special hypotheses, but belongs to a form of perception which lies beyond all forms of knowledge. Good works would be essentially pragmatic; but "Your righteousness must issue, like the Trinity, from the very Godhead itself; else all your striving is in vain" (285).[CA]

"Hence only religious experience can really touch the truth" (286).[CA] In any case, the mystic knows the sort of thing, the what of the absolute knowledge and insight, and if that has entered into his life, he can and must speak with fervor of that. It is so. This he sees. That, you remember, is what Shandilya says, "Who knows this, he in sooth hath no more doubts."[19] To Eckhart's followers he appeared as "Master Eckhart, from whom God conceals nothing" (286–287).

The practical danger, yes, the curse, of the doctrine, as taught by many mystics is that of Quietism (287). But Eckhart is no quietist; you must put off the world by overcoming it by the power of God. Eckhart, so long as he is in this world, simply means business; viz., his life's business, though he is far from being a pragmatist. Union with God is his whole aim; you must learn to turn away from every practical "good" that you have been seeking apart from God (288).

Eckhart's power as a teacher lies in this union of spiritual freedom and of rigid self-discipline (288). You are dealing with a mystic who now appears on a side of his nature remote enough from that which the Hindu mystics exemplify. The words are those of a man of the Rhineland—the Germanic soul.

April 11 The soul of man, for Eckhart, has various higher and lower powers, or faculties, of which, of course, the intellect and the will are the most significant (288). Eckhart's psychology, like that of the classical scholastics, is based on a union of Aristotelian and Augustinian terms—the more theological side of it being much affected by Augustinian formulas. Eckhart's Fünkelin or Ganster, the soul-spark, "the uncreated essence of our created soul" (288) in its origins is rather Augustinian than Aristotelian; it corresponds partly to Aristotle's Creative Reason and partly to the various aspects of the central mental life which you will find emphasized in the Augustinian account. The "uncreated essence of our created soul" is that which was the essence of the individual in advance of creation (281).

To be, by virtue of one's spark, united to the Godhead would constitute the essence of salvation, which is not therefore a matter of the special fortune that happens to one (289). In that union with the Godhead our individuality is not to be wholly lost (289). Here is a feature whose consistency with the rest of Eckhart's doctrine we need not further criticize. Here the rugged temper of the man appears. "I will respond as it seems to me," etc. (290). Here you have rather the man of personal experience than the scholastic speaking. A quietistic mystic simply ignores the individual, but Eckhart maintains individuality (the Fünkelin or spark). This saving of individual immortality through the emphasis upon the very mystery that seemed when it was first stated to be a mystery wherein all varieties are lost (i.e., in the Godhead) is very characteristic of Eckhart. Absorption into the divine is never a finished thing. The familiar metaphor of the absolute haven is not used by Eckhart, but is my own effort to express the sense that he seems to have in mind (290). I think that this, though not Eckhart's expression, is a reasonable way of rendering the spirit of some of the passages in his sermons.

Our every effort to express our relation to the simple and ultimate mystery involves a duplicity of terms, and in fact of mental attitudes (291). That is what Yâjnavalkya says: Consciousness seeks another and another than what is now wholly present.[20]

The surrender to God is for Eckhart always as much a positive as a negative process. There must be an absolute union of spirituality and of daily activity—distinctly a motor attitude throughout. Eckhart condemns all the "wild" mysticism of his time, all merely antinomian tendencies. He does this not merely as a teacher of the Church, but as a practical man (292).

Eckhart says some things about vows that would not be approved by the casuistry of the scholastics generally. The private vow has a character that they often insist upon. The public vow (e.g., marriage) does bind one by a public obligation, but Eckhart insists upon a freedom with regard to the inner vows. In case you find such vows to be a hindrance to the higher life, you are free (292). As man is lord of the sabbath, so one is lord of his spiritual life, if he is sure that he keeps the spirit of the vow in a new and better way.

It is with temptations as with sorrows. They are the nobler incidents of the life of the outer man, if only the inner man is at peace. Then comes a word that is often repeated; I suppose that Eckhart may have been the first user of that word; it becomes a frequent mystic word, a saying constantly used in sermons:

> *That a man has a restful and peaceful life in God is good. That a man endures a painful life with patience, that is better; but that a man has his rest in the midst of (and through) a painful life, that is best of all* (294).

Our will surrenders itself, then God acts on us—in us and through us—and that is why this is no quietism (296). The divine life as thus expressed appears very active indeed. God might choose, even in this world, to grant the peculiar grace of mystic ecstasy itself (296). St. Thomas Aquinas discusses that very frequently. The classic instance used generally is the word of the apostle Paul about being caught up into the third heaven where he heard the unspeakable things which it isn't lawful for man to utter. That the Apostle was speaking here of mystical experience is commonly recognized.

The authenticity of the tract, *Sister Katharine*, has been questioned by Denifle, on the basis of his use of Eckhart's Latin writings and his general comparative study of Eckhart's work. It is in the opening part of this tract that you have the account of the laborious discipline by which a soul gets its freedom—penance being merely an incident. After this first section another stage comes; Schwester Katrei far transcends her teacher and attains the place where she can say to him, in the fearless mystic speech, "Rejoice with me, for I have become God," a passage that very much struck the attention of Schopenhauer

(296). "Become God," at one with the divine essence. That is precisely what Shvetaketu learns: "*That art thou.*"[21] Thus the Hindu says, "I am Brahm." In this mystic speech, God means now the Godhead; nearness means union (297).

Bhagavadgita

April 13 The work on which Emerson founded his "*Brahma*" is the Hindu poem called the *Bhagavadgita*. "Gita" means song, and the first part of the word means substantially "sacred," so that the name means the Sacred Lay. It is one episode of a famous epic full of long sections that originally were written as more or less separate poems and then traditionally worked into the scheme of the epic as it stands. It was one of these episodes to which Emerson's attention was attracted. It is a favorite Hindu document. The *Bhagavadgita* or Sacred Lay tells a story that introduces a philosophy, and the philosophy is incidentally a mystical philosophy. The special philosophical system concerned is not precisely the one that has become a classic representative of this sort of thinking in the Hindu thought. That classic system into which the Upanishads developed is known as the Vedanta system. It received a kind of scholastic form of its own. Its principal commentator, Sankaracharya, at the period when there was a revival of Hindu thought after a period of Buddhism, stated its principal doctrines and told in his opinion what was meant by various puzzling assertions in the Upanishads. It is this Vedanta system as set forth by its principal commentator that lies at the basis of Denifle's discussion of these matters. Professor Woods was a pupil of Denifle for a while, and he has translated some of Denifle's contributions. The philosophy of the Vedanta, the classic Hindu mystical scholasticism, is very accessible and is expressed in a very learned and, so far as the state of the case permits, a very exactly formulated and clearly stated form.

There is no doubt that in their own way the Hindu scholastics had a very precise and clarified way of thinking out their thoughts, so far as the thoughts could be regarded as clear at all. The difficulty of the Hindu Vedantism is not the difficulty of confusion, but the difficulty that you have had exemplified by those expressions that I have cited from Meister Eckhart. The simplicity of the whole avoids any mere confusion of idea; but this very simplicity is a simplicity of mystery. However skillfully stated, the central thought always appears as having this central difficulty. The easiest way of appreciating this difficulty is the way that I have suggested: Follow the clue that Bergson has given: what one is looking for is the definition of a realm of complete perceptual knowledge. Were perception unlimited, so that we had no need of conceptions, then we should be relieved of the difficulties that pragmatism emphasizes or that conceptualism or realism has been emphasizing for us. We should be in presence of that which Tennyson characterizes: we should come on that which "is." All that one says about what "is," is of course essentially inadequate to the expression of the thing. The perceptual knowledge would be the sort of knowledge that Tennyson has so eloquently exemplified for us, that which in his case came in the mystic vision of the night.

But one could have a perfectly definite view of what it is to look for such perceptual knowledge, and one would from that side have perfectly definite ground for saying that if one comes on that which "is," one can tell in advance that which it is to be. There is no puzzle about what would be your experience if you experienced the absolute, except the puzzle that belongs to the very center of a perceptual doctrine. You would have the immediate; you would stand in the presence of that which "is."

What do you learn about the world by asserting such a doctrine? Well, you have learned what illusion, what error, what deceit is, what it is to be misled by phantoms or by phenomena. You have got beyond the point where you look in the false direction. You see: why the difficulties arise that we so elaborately exemplified in dealing with Santayana's so richly complex world of the essences and the existents; why those difficulties arise and why they lead to the paradoxes of that world; why you go about in that round of the essence having some mysterious difference from the existence, while, on the one hand,[CA] the existences cannot be deduced from the essences—you can't prove them by any sort of general demonstration—while, on the other hand, it is plain that essence and existence have some deeper connection if the world is in any degree a rational world where evidence counts, where you can hope to prove anything. These difficulties point in a fashion to the permanent need of a kind of knowledge which isn't this conceptual knowledge. On the basis of the mystical view of what it is to be, we can see why the conceptual realm will never content us, why in that realm one is always dealing with illusions. If one heaps up the brilliant and varied figures of the tropical jungle, as Shvetaketu's teaching does, or if one deals with the varieties of Santayana's essences, one is dealing not with that which "is." That which would present Being would have to be experienced; but nothing that the pragmatist looks for renders you at any time the cash value, for what one always gets in the realm of experience is the transient, the relative, that which sends you somewhere else: I point to the real, but the real is somewhere else. It is that observation which constitutes the central observation of mysticism.

As a final instance of the mystical point of view, I bring you back to what the *Bhagavadgita* happens to contain. The writer is not strictly speaking {as} a Vedantist. His own position has aroused a good deal of controversy. The Hindu commentators differ somewhat as to their view of his actual position amongst the schools and his relation to the classic Vedantism. The episode of the *Bhagavadgita* is a very favorite part of popular teaching both in India and elsewhere. Most of those Hindu teachers who have visited this country are very fond of the *Bhagavadgita*; it is one of their topics of instruction. Most of the so-called Swamis teach the *Bhagavadgita*. Those who grow enthusiastic about Hindu thought are likely to be enthusiastic about that.

It influences you especially by laying stress on narrative and giving this narrative a symbolic meaning. The topic of the whole *Mahabharata*, of which the *Bhagavadgita* is an episode, is a warfare between the various branches of a certain great family. The epic had some basis or other in the facts of some great warfare amongst the reigning families of India, leading to events which were remembered long after in a form which crystallized into this. The families in question have various great wars, and most of the episodes of the *Mahabharata* have to do with that.

In the *Bhagavadgita*, at the beginning of one of the great battles (which those concerned supposed would be decisive), a prince Arjuna leading his own branch of the family and his own partisans—a vast array—was approaching the battlefield. The battle was about to begin. Then there came over the mind of Arjuna, who was an experienced and otherwise a brave warrior, a terror which was now a moral terror. He wasn't afraid of his own death, but there came over him a great pity for the hosts of those who were to be slain on the behalf of his family, a sorrow which he expressed by saying, "And shall all these die for me and mine?" With this there came a horror of this bloodshed and carnage about to take place.

All this moral terror of the great prince is picturesquely contrasted with the scene of the approaching battle. The elephants and the trumpets, the drums, the cymbals, all the sounds of coming warfare are presented. Meanwhile, the people in general are joyously looking forward to the conflict on both sides. But Arjuna hesitates for a time and holds back. Now Arjuna had a charioteer, and it chances that the charioteer was one of the incarnations of the god Vishnu, a prominent figure in the Hindu pantheon at the time, something like Indra. This incarnation of Vishnu is the charioteer of the prince, and the prince does not know it; he knows him to be a wise and skillful person. The charioteer addresses the prince and asks him why this horror. Then the prince warmly expresses this pity and this sense of guilt which goes naturally with the responsibility of devoting to death {many} of these for the sake of the family and the individual prince.

The charioteer replies in a reply which runs substantially thus: "As a fact you are mistaken. This world upon which you gaze is a world that you comprehend not. It is a shadowland, it has no true being. These are phantasmata; there is nothing here happening that is real. <u>Real</u> is only the God, the *Atman,* the Self; yes, real am I." (The charioteer as the incarnation of Deity can thus speak.) All these here exist as my transient embodiments. Since this is so,

If the red slayer think he slays,
Or if the slain think he is slain,
They know not well the subtle ways
I keep, and pass, and turn again.

I am this; I am the only one in all this; this realm is my own. I am all this; nothing then really happens here; nobody is slain; no man's death amounts to anything. Therefore (and this is the result of the long conversation), O prince, fear not, care not, strike boldly, slay. The slaying is fated. The dreamworld has to appear thus. Nothing really happens here. Self, readiness, is all. Take it as you find it, accept it, live it, and fear not. Why should you fear, when nothing happens through all this battle but the expression of the Absolute, the Self? Be free from all care, and thus enter the fight as these do, careless of what is going to happen. Nothing is decided but that I am I, the Self is the Self, the Absolute is the Absolute. The red slayer does not slay; and the slain may think he is slain, but it happens not. The situation warrants a complete indifference to fortune.

The strong gods pine for my abode,
And pine in vain the sacred Seven;
But thou, meek lover of the good!
Find me, and turn thy back on heaven.

That word refers to another episode of the *Mahabharata* in which there is a story of a hero who for heroic reasons takes an interest in the fortunes of certain persons, and finding that these persons for offenses against the gods have been consigned to hell, declares that if his friends are there, he is quite willing to go there too, and fearlessly descends into the uttermost hells and he is quite indifferent, for he has found what he wants: union with his beloved friends. He shows his triumph in the form of a mystic independence of fortune. With that episode in mind, Emerson was led to that part of the word of the Brahma.

The other poetical figures which Emerson uses he also got from the *Mahabharata*. The sacred soul of the Brahmins themselves is somehow a direct expression of the Absolute, of which they speak—"And I the hymn the Brahmin sings." You will remember that the power of prayer, as a magic power, is identified with the Absolute. That too, you can easily see, would conform perfectly well with the otherwise far distant view of Meister Eckhart. You remember how for Eckhart the act of the religious soul, if it is a real act at all, is God's act. The *Abgescheidenheit*[22] isn't something that does a work of its own apart from the Deity. It is simply the calm resolve that God's will shall be done. That resolve is identical with the divine. Hence far apart as the figures are, the identity of thought is present in all these cases. This coming on what is leads to the same result, however you put it.

In the case of the *Bhagavadgita,* the triumphant joyous result is reached. The hero turns to the battlefield and wins a great victory, a victory in and through indifference to fortune, utter contempt for death, also utter indifference to pity. For after all, what is there to pity, because there is nothing to happen. That part of the poem is an immediate changing from the extreme pity which on the whole characterizes the Hindu mysticism, to its very reverse. Why not ruthlessness? After all, nothing can occur. That note isn't common in Hindu doctrine, which appears in the pitiful form, just as in Schopenhauer; but there is a close connection between this ruthlessness joined with pity and the general paradox of the whole mystical position.

A long story is the *Bhagavadgita.* The episode has episodes within it. The discussion is tangled with many threads. The question about the connection between good works and spiritual perfection appears in various shapes.

Before I leave altogether these illustrations of mysticism, there ought to be said some further word about the relation between this mysticism and various tendencies that you can recognize in art and in poetry. There is, of course, a rather large realm of mystical poetry. That poetry has played a considerable part in the hymnology of the church. It has also expressed itself in various forms of musical art, and dramatic art is naturally very readily concerned in the development of this sort of thing. From time to time when a mystical movement appears in other branches of literature, you will find it influencing art. Possibly at the next time I may be tempted to call your attention to some passages from Dostoyevsky which illustrate the mystical point of view in art.

Wagner and Bach

If you look for the mystical point of view in art, it is interesting to be reminded of the place where it has been made very prominent in recent art and music. That union of motives in the *Bhagavadgita* appears in the works of Wagner, who is obviously a mystic; but the place that mysticism occupies in Wagner's mind cannot well be characterized except in terms of a conflict.

The *Tannhäuser* remains the most popular of Wagner's dramas; before people can understand Wagner otherwise, they can understand Tannhäuser. The story of Tannhäuser you remember: the man swept away by a literally demonic passion, the victim of a demon lady, escaped through some return of manhood, a longing for the real world. Returning to the world, he finds himself at odds with it. He has broken with the church and with the world; he is lost in the hands of a demon. Elizabeth is his one hope. For her he has a romantic and a mystical passion. She represents a mystical point of view, which she develops in the course of the drama. That which she expresses in the last act is exactly the mystical point of view: he might be saved by some intervention of the divine, and to that end she hopes to save him by an act of complete resignation.

Wagner was very much under Schopenhauer's influence when he wrote the *Tannhäuser*. Wagner independently came on the mystical point of view and was glad to see how near to Schopenhauer he was. The solution of the problem is the solution which Schopenhauer expresses as complete resignation, the denial of the will to live. It is that which Tannhäuser reaches as the outcome of the whole struggle. In the Pilgrims Chorus, that is the motive. The tragedy of life consists in the struggle of passion not only against fortune but against itself; while salvation, if it could be found, would come in the form of some resignation which was an inevitable surrender—a dwelling which would be eternal if one could find it. The musical drama of Wagner differs from his earlier expressions insofar as it is a mystical rather than a romantic type. The solution is found in the entire resignation that is salvation.

Of course, there are many other poetical expressions of that kind of view of life and of its meaning, and there are many other expressions in Wagner, but this is a characteristic one. The idea, you see, is that of a mysticism approached tragically with the sense of disappointment and defeat, such tragedy and failure as that which drives Tannhäuser in hopeless search for salvation to the Pope; the relief comes magically and mystically.

The relief has received a notable expression in those very remarkable verses of Edgar Allen Poe, *For Annie*. The poet, who is not thinking in mystical terms any more than it was inevitable for Poe always to think, gives you this sort of solution of the situation in his dreamy notion of a life after death in which the lover of the poem is at peace. The general thought of the poem is easily expressed in words that give you the relation to the mystical approach. Poe's lover lives a sort of life in death; in a way he lives despite death, but how happy and peaceful, for there has been a reconciliation with fortune and with the beloved. The lover is contented in a kind of Nirvana because all passion is over. The great feature of this peace is that one is relieved from precisely what Schopenhauer insisted upon, the torment of the will.[23]

For Annie

Thank Heaven! the crisis—
   The danger is past,
And the lingering illness
   Is over at last—
And the fever called "Living"
   Is conquered at last.

Sadly, I know
   I am shorn of my strength,
And no muscle I move
   As I lie at full length—
But no matter!—I feel
   I am better at length.

And I rest so composedly
   Now, in my bed,
That any beholder
   Might fancy me dead—
Might start at beholding me,
   Thinking me dead.

The moaning and groaning,
   The sighing and sobbing,
Are quieted now
   With that horrible throbbing
At heart—ah that horrible
   Horrible throbbing!

The sickness—the nausea—
   The pitiless pain—
Have ceased with the fever
   That maddened my brain—
With the fever called "Living"
   That burned in my brain.

An oh! of all tortures
   That torture the worst
Has abated—the terrible
   Torture of thirst
For the naphthaline river

Of a water that flows
   With a lullaby sound,
From a spring but a very few
   Feet under ground—
From a cavern not very far
   Down under ground.

And ah! Let it never
   Be foolishly said

That my room it is gloomy
   And narrow my bed;
For man never slept
   In a different bed—
And, to sleep, you must slumber
   In just such a bed.

   Of Passion accurst—
I have drunk of a water
   That quenches all thirst—

My tantalized spirit
   Here blandly reposes,
Forgetting, or never
   Regretting, its roses—
Its old agitations
   Of myrtles and roses:

For now, while so quietly
   Lying, it fancies
A holier odor
   About it, of pansies—
A rosemary odor,
   Commingled with pansies—
With rue and the beautiful
   Puritan pansies.

And so it lies happily,
   Bathing in many
A dream of the truth
   And the beauty of Annie—
Drowned in a bath
   Of the tresses of Annie.

She tenderly kissed me,
   And fondly caressed,
And then I fell gently
   To sleep on her breast—
Deeply to sleep
   From the heaven of her breast.

When the light was extinguished,
   She covered me warm,

And she prayed to the angels
To keep me from harm—
To the queen of the angels
To shield me from harm.
And I lie so composedly,
Now, in my bed,

(Knowing her love)
That you fancy me dead—
And I rest so contentedly,
Now, in my bed,
(With her love at my breast)
That you fancy me dead—
That you shudder to look at me,
Thinking me dead:—

But my heart it is brighter
Than all of the many
Stars of the sky,
For it sparkles with Annie—
It glows with the light
Of the love of my Annie—
With the thought of the light
Of the eyes of my Annie.

That is the sort of peace that Tannhäuser seeks and finds; it is that which Elizabeth in her view of the problem seeks for him in her farewell words of hope; it is that of which the Pilgrims Chorus tells him.

That is by no means the only sort of expression of this thing in Wagner's case. His most elaborate effort to express it, you find, of course, in his concluding work: *The Ring* gives you the problem of deliverance in the form of the self-destroying and world-destroying act of Brunhilde, who ends by deciding that rights and contracts and duties and whatever you speak of as definite or mediated—all these things—cease entirely in the perfect future.

In strong contrast with this feature in Wagner, you also find the other feature: the vigorous, ruthless life which is characterized in the Hindu *Bhagavadgita*. Only in Wagner this appears in distinctly Germanic form: the life of those who delight in war and vehemence. The solution of this curious antithesis has countless forms, from the case of *Tannhäuser* to the case of *Parsifal*. It is a solution that takes a mystical form, though I have never been able to find in *Parsifal* a perfect expression of mysticism, for from my own point of view Wagner is too elaborate in *Parsifal*.

The *Parsifal* solution is at any rate on a much higher level the expression of the same view. Parsifal also drinks of the water that quenches all thirst. As in the case of Tannhäuser, the solution comes with finding out how to quell and quench altogether the thirst for the napthaline waters of life.

All through the Wagnerian operas, apart from this resignation, you will find a set of characters who do precisely what they want to and nothing else. There are two ways of living, from the Wagnerian point of view: Do what you want to do; be sure you want to do it, do it recklessly, and take the consequences; without the least hesitation, do what it is your will to do. It makes little difference whether it is the glorious Siegfried or whether it is one of the dwarves: so long as one's will is alive, one does what one wants to do. No "moral scruple" appears in any Wagnerian drama. Wagner himself, as a dramatist, was unscrupulous. But there comes a time when the world can no longer endure its own horror, when one must take the mystic drink and end it.

The one thing that you never find in Wagner, was, in the musical art of Germany, best expressed by a man who was far beyond mysticism, although he took up all that was significant in mysticism—Bach—particularly in the Passion music: the expression of the word and attitude of the angels that excel in strength. That is something which might be called "a going beyond mysticism to another realm."

It seems natural to bring to some kind of provisional close what I have *April 15* been saying about mysticism, its various forms and its significance. I just made a special and somewhat literary reference to the musical and dramatic art of Wagner. I was making certain remarks on the mystical spirit that Wagner illustrates. These Wagnerian forms have a German setting which is important in view of their history. They have an important relation to the medieval German mysticism which Eckhart has illustrated for us.

Eckhart, a German of the Rhineland, of the Dominican order, a product of the general philosophical cultivation of his time, a graduate of the University of Paris, a result of the scholastic movement on the whole, while illustrating in many respects the same sort of mysticism that has been illustrated for us in Hindu thought, in Tennyson and in others, also has for the coloring of his mysticism something very different from what you can call quietism.

One does not sufficiently get the whole story by approaching the matter from any one side. Unquestionably, there is a strong tendency in the mystical point of view to lay stress on quietism.

One can say that the attitude of perception is a receptive attitude. The mystic is one who is finding immediacy, not creating anything, not interfering with anything, not doing anything which involves a falsification of the real by making use of special activities of conception; the mystic is in a sense a quietist, in that he does assume the merely perceptual attitude. But in the life of the man who is a mystic, the hope is the mystical experience. Dissatisfaction with mediation expresses itself in a change of attitude, an effort to reform the self, something that appears in the individual mystic as self-discipline, which prepares the way for this vision of finality, by means of processes which certainly are not themselves a vision of the finality, but which involve a progression toward it. So without dwelling particularly on the case of Eckhart, we can say that throughout the whole history of mysticism we find a strong tendency toward the decided elaboration of the mystical states. There are stages of approach toward the final goal which must themselves be viewed as having a distinct significance for the mystic. Were he at the goal, then indeed his position would be the one expressed by the word that those who know the truth—well, they are silent. If they are silent, then as Yâjnavalkya told us, it is as if they said nothing.

On the other hand, in practice, the mystic is actually living; so he is not at the goal, but approaching the goal. The approach itself is an approach through something that involves change—not, of course, the planning and effort to attain various practical goods, but the effort to attain spiritual self-possession and peace, an effort that always leads to something that the mystic himself will always express in terms of a process. The self is to be preserved, it is to be accepted, it is to be found; and so the mystic is the lover and the follower of some kind of a process. As in the teaching of Shvetaketu, as Shandilya says (in his brief account of what the goal is when you obtain it), not merely, "Let him whose soul is at peace worship this Self," but also obviously says, "This is the way; look hitherwards if you seek for peace," so the mystic is always speaking in terms of this quiescence, but his position is always that of recognizing the goal.

In the beautiful symbolism of the fourth gospel, in the story of the woman at the well in Samaria, when the woman gets the word from the Master, who is also the Logos, the Word that promises the coming of the complete insight, she begs that she may have it "that I thirst not, neither come hither to draw."[24] The very antithesis emphasizes the thirst. So it belongs to mysticism to have this thirst.

On the side of the strenuous activity, we saw examples of that in Eckhart, so the mystic didn't appear in practice as a quietist, but looked for a goal through some very strenuous search for perfection. This appears throughout the history of medieval mysticism. It is always a quest, and this diversifies mysticism and makes what would otherwise be this dreary story of speechless and utterly uninteresting silence something that after all is human.

Quite recent students of the mystical experience have been led to lay stress on the practical aspect of the matter. Evelyn Underhill has written two books on practical mysticism, one of them a very valuable collection of illustrations largely derived from medieval mysticism.[25] There are several other recent works in which you will find a great deal of this.

Nevertheless, there are those to whom, whether as ethical teachers or as philosophers of life or as artists, a quiescent goal, a quietism, comes out as after all the deepest lesson that mysticism has to teach to a distracted age, to a soul in pain, to a world in which there is so much restlessness. Amongst those who have viewed the matter thus and, for that very reason, brought out the more glaring and more irrational contrast between the mystic goal and the real life that even makes it attractive to the suffering soul, is Wagner, and so I gave you examples from his musical drama, where the glaring contrast is a very noticeable feature.

In an essay on German Ideals, Professor Francke[26] pointed out a paradox that had often interested him during his long acquaintance with the German mind {both} as the student of literature knows it {and} as the American mind has come to contrast it. In his characterization, Professor Francke lays great stress on a contrast that has played a large part in German life between the motive of "living oneself out" stated as one's goal, and the self-restraint which all thoughtful people, whether Germanic or not, are accustomed to recognize. In his account of American life, Professor Francke somewhat kindly has insisted upon the statement that the American traditional training has always represented to him a very much more self-restrained person than he finds prominent in the more restless literature of Germany; it would offend the American mind trained in the Puritanical ideal to find itself letting itself go. From that point of view, instead of regarding us, as some foreigners have done, as more impulsive than other peoples, Professor Francke finds we have a somewhat inhibitory self-restraint from the Puritanic side.

Scherer, in his *History of German Literature,*[27] has noticed a significant shifting of motives in German thought. At the beginning of his compendious portrayal of German literature, he says that our literature has been characterized by great reactions, not political as in France, but farreaching moral and social reactions. A given tendency for awhile takes possession of the field, then comes the reaction. The tendency which has seemed to express the whole ideal, the whole devotion of the nation, is now played out—a back number. For that there is no understanding any more; for that, this age has no place; this is not a time for that.[28]

Now, of course, all nations speak in that way; that belongs to the changing type of human nature in general; but the feature has been more marked in the history of German than in other literature. You find more continuity in the history of English literature during the Reformation; even in Scotch literature, the ballads, and Sir Walter Scott; not such vast and intimate and deep moral shiftings as you find in the German literature. In French literature you have vast political revulsions and tendencies, but the Germans have had these vast moral revulsions. That change in experience type, or in the coincident form of the social order, we have exemplified when we spoke of the antitheses within the mystical development or in the mind of Wagner. But whether you take these antitheses side by side or occurring in successive times, you find them very markedly present in German literature.

One is reminded, says Scherer, as one looks over our literature, of Siegfried's forgetfulness of Brunhilde; it is so with us in "our" literature; we have again and again drunk the forgetful drink, then comes the new age and one has no understanding of the old ideas.[29]

The contrast between the quietistic aspect of mysticism and the more strenuous aspect is inevitably there. The Hindu doesn't give it to you in a form that is for him socially and morally so prominent. He is on the whole a quietist, and he is content to be such; but after all, he stands in a contrast to the world about him that makes the forest sage incomprehensible to the soul of one qualified to be a disciple. So long as the mysticism remains merely passive, its tale is not all told. It has another meaning for life; it demands a transformation of life, a transformation needed for the mystical attitude itself. We shall want to know what after all the mystic has told us. Has he simply done what Yâjnavalkya did to Maitreyi, "Thou hast bewildered me"? What is the significance of this antithesis?

In the history of thought, such better understanding of the matter is prepared for us by various considerations. Plato had a great antithesis to deal with, between the moveless being of the Eleatics, which if it were capable of being viewed as anything would be viewed as a changeless somewhat, and the restless flow of the world of Heraclitus. Plato's solution was indeed an incomplete one, but everybody knows that it is the essential problem; and insofar as Plato solved that problem, it is his accomplishment to bring together a realm which is a realm of pure concepts—and so far a realm of those essences such as Santayana describes—and to bring that together with the world that is the world of life, to show that these ideas actually live. Plato is always trying to do that, and insofar as he is always trying to do that, his philosophy is in the modern sense an idealism—not merely a doctrine that things exist merely as states of people's mind, but that the world is the world of a divine insight, a divine self-possession, a divine life.

The neo-Platonic philosophy has often been accused of letting the Platonic philosophy degenerate by viewing the Ideas merely as the thoughts of God. It remains a problem of philosophy today, as before for idealists, only it is recognized as one of the permanent problems of philosophy[30] —the task of bringing the pure being, the essences so far as they are without movement, the changeless so far as in Santayana's phrase it is impenetrable by the flux of life, into some genuine contact with the flux of life. It is the problem of our Fourth Conception of Being. I have already approached this very feature from the social side by saying that the genuine cognition takes the form of an essentially social interpretation which is also temporal, constructive, creative.

Though not a mystic, Goethe is capable of appreciating the mystic approach. He can speak not merely in idealistic terms but in pantheistic terms, as when Faust addresses Marguerite. Goethe, on the whole, appeared with a certain triumphant peacefulness of assurance about the reasonableness of life and of the world, an assurance that lay very deep in his heart and produced the best of his work.

Santayana, in his *Three Philosophical Poets,*[31] is not attracted by Goethe's type of thinking, finds a much greater sympathy with Dante, and is most of all attracted by a great deal in the thought of Lucretius; but the book contains a beautiful and fair characterization of Goethe.

Deeply influenced by the crisis of the time,[32] Santayana has since been moved to express himself in a much more austere way; nevertheless, it is a very interesting thing that immediately before this crisis, Santayana spoke with such fairness and clearness and coolness and, within his own range, with such strong sympathy with certain aspects of Goethe, though those features that he could not tolerate are clearly enough emphasized in his account.

I have no right to pass judgment on any musical question, surely no privilege to assume that you[CA] are either familiar with or decidedly interested in musical art. Whatever I say about it is extremely ignorant in the sense that must be true of one who is merely a lifelong listener. The close connection between the musical art and the means that the mystical spirit has to approach its own expression is fairly obvious. Music does not always speak in mystical language, of course, but it has natural affiliations with that expression because of the very general character of the thing. It is an art of highly intelligent perception, an art that watches rather than interferes or even sympathizes with interference. Much more than architecture, which suggests the conceptual approach to facts, and decidedly more than plastic art, which indirectly portrays some aspect of life, music seems to appeal directly to something that has to do with immediate experience and which if it could be purely immediate, would present being. In some sense, the lover of music can say, "I came on that which is." Music appeals deeply to sentiment and emotion, yet it is a wholly objective thing. The trained mind finds its detail inexhaustible, for such an approach characterizes any technical treatment of the musical art; but, on the other hand, the experience in question is the experience of an immediate.

So while it isn't at all fair to say that music of all the arts is the most mystical—that I shouldn't for a moment attempt to assert—it is perfectly true that it has very genuine relations to that sort of spirit in the search for the mystic union.

The contrast between the passive perceptual {attitude} and the watchful attitude, the further contrast suggested by the difference between the performer's and the listener's attitude—these things are obvious enough in music. When it is a question of musical art itself, it is worthwhile mentioning the sense in which musical art partakes of the mystical spirit as the art of a composer has dealt with the matter.

In some of Wagner's work, he is explicitly an exponent of the mystical point of view; in that case he is dealing with the tragedy of the relation between the finite and the infinite. In *The Ring*, or in the despair and defeat of the lovers in *Tristan*, or in *Parsifal*, this appears.[33] But *Parsifal* has never seemed to me as much the highest intended expression of Wagner's art as it seems to the regular Wagner admirer. I sometimes feel that after all, with all its beauty, *Parsifal* shows traces of having been written by a man who lacks a certain sense of humor; for there, after all, you deal with a danger which can easily attend the expression of mysticism. It is a dangerous test for a mystic: has he a sense of humor? Eckhart, you will recall, warns the faithful: "You must remember that God has done much better for the world than if he had merely saved you, and you had better show your appreciation by doing a little saving on your own account." Mystics are sometimes in danger of being a little too demure, taking their approach to peace with too rapturous contentment.

It is difficult for me to hold the whole illusion of the scene in *Parsifal* when the temptations are prepared for the wondrous hero whom nothing can tempt. When the diabolical magician brings up, as the expression of his greatest power, the being who shall be forced to tempt to the betrayal of his faith, honor and Grail, the hero of the play, this temptress appears as a person expressly qualified for the work in a statement which lays great stress on her vast age and the number of persons whom she has misled. I find difficulty in hearing this account without being bored and decidedly doubtful whether anybody who is about to be influenced by such a person could be very dangerously tempted. As a fact, the temptation turns out to be somewhat inert, and somehow the converted being who takes the place of the temptress appears not only peaceful but (to me as a mere watcher of the play) somewhat dilapidated, and I find myself somewhat in tedium. This feature of the play goes side by side with the mystical vision of the Grail itself, with its most elaborate array of color, form, and beauty; but, after all, these are but stage effects and they are somewhat tawdry. It is the more grotesque parts of *The Ring* that impress me more deeply.

Brunhilde attracts when she mystically resigns the world, or she would attract if she became really a mystic at the moment and didn't give you too elaborate an account of what is going to be won. The lady protests too much. At that point, the matter grows less impressive.

Of the two poets who happen to tell the story of Siegfried, the one who has got the story in the most immediately attractive form seems to me to be William Morris, whose story seems to me a much better form of drama than the Wagner trilogy, though that meets my mind much better than *Parsifal*.

I call attention to the art of Bach. Bach was forgotten entirely; the world had neglected him; he suffered long from the forgetfulness of the mind of the German people. Then he was revived—the discovery being made on the whole by Mendelssohn. Then he spoke for himself.

There you have what seems to be by far the highest work of the musical art in modern times, all the more clearly of the highest grade because the music itself has to be based on what is now a very simplified form of art, in that its means are comparatively crude, without the great modern orchestra or the technical equipment of the modern musician at the control of the artist. Greater than Beethoven who is always striving for something, where Bach is always in the region of his own perfection, Bach seems to me to speak what is in some sense the last word in music. Whoever can appreciate genuine music has only to go to Bach to find this attainment of perfection in the form that makes you say, "How easy it is to be perfect!" You have only to open your ears and hear, open your mouth and speak what the spirit forces you to speak without regard to your time at once a work of perfection. "I could write Shakespeare's plays if I had a mind to." So you could write Bach's music if you had a mind to. But nobody has had a mind to since he wrote it.

The greatest of musical drama—more profoundly mystical in the sense that the vision is much completer but the vision doesn't anywhere suggest to you passivity—is the *Matthew Passion* music of Bach. Now the tragically bad taste of the public has led to indifference to this: "This is queer old music, all in the minor key." This is the highest reach of dramatic musical art. It has characteristics to which I have made some reference in my chapters, "Time and Guilt" and "Atonement," in Vol. I of *The Problem of Christianity*.

Bach's music is always full of activity, and yet of the activity of a mind that is always at the goal. The perfection that it constantly expresses is of the type that Aristotle suggested in his great account of the perfection of the mind of God, though Aristotle was the very reverse of a mystic, full of interest in the concrete and in natural history. But how can such immediacy have any commerce with that sort of variety? It is precisely in such commerce that genuine interpretation consists. When the understanding of life takes the form of a process, a process every stage of which is irrevocable and at the same time constitutes a progress beyond that which has been already attained, a process guided by the chronosynoptic vision of the whole, then you are dealing with that which is beyond mysticism and that which is at the same time the fulfillment of mysticism, the union of satiety and activity, of triumph and peace in triumph, the kind of union which Paul depicts in I Cor. XIII: "For now we see through a glass, darkly; but then face to face. Now I know in part; but then shall I know even as also I am known."[34]

Spring recess

Chapter 8

The Third Conception of Being

I have already pointed out to you in various connections the significance of the third conception of Being, viz., that we always deal with Being indirectly through the truth of propositions; an assertion about Being is inevitably an assertion about Truth. This is a predicament which is hardly Professor Perry's egocentric predicament, but it is involved in a very interesting way in any use in metaphysics of the *reflective method*. As the mystics have shown us, our metaphysical statements inevitably have this highly mediated character about them, in that they involve this reflexive aspect. You say, "This is,"—that is, you say, "It is true that this is," and consequently your statement is inevitably reflexive. What the result is for your metaphysic, you can only make out by considering the matter further; but this reflexive aspect of the world of Being becomes prominent from various points of view that I have thrown together under the "Third Conception of Being," whose expression would be the formula that the Being of things, the Being of the world, the Being of whatever you regard as real, consists in the truth of certain propositions about them. *April 25*

That Third Conception of Being is one that we have already met with several times as our study of the reflective method has led us to the threshold of that consideration. There is an interesting relation between that way of taking metaphysical problems and the one that Russell has made use of in his recent book on the *Scientific Method in Philosophy*, as we shall see.

What I have to say about idealism will be largely founded upon and illustrative of what I said in the first half-year. Two topics will need some illustration: (1) the idea of Time, Lecture III of Vol. II of *The World and the Individual*: "The Temporal and the Eternal"; (2) the question as to the sort of Being that one attributes to the natural world, Lecture IV of the same volume: "Physical and Social Reality."[1]

When I presented this course simply using *The World and the Individual* as my text, I devoted a good deal of attention to the ethical problems, the problem of evil, and its relation to an idealistic metaphysic. Here I shall have to be very summary but I shall hope for some sympathetic enlivenment of the course by your own interest. # There is a sharp contrast between the point of view about life that ought to be prominent in the treatment of ethics, and the point of view which is usually emphasized by the mystics; but the contrast involves also close relations. No thoroughgoing discussion of the problems of ethics and the religious aspect of experience, and the relations between religion and metaphysics, will be possible in our time in this course.

Try as well as you can to find your way to the connections of the various parts of this book. You can help yourself in that by asking yourself especially, "What is the contrast between realism and mysticism"?

You must feel that there is a strong contrast between Santayana and the mystics, a contrast that is obviously temperamental, but also of great technical importance, a contrast that neither the mystic nor Santayana would be likely to express adequately. The mystic would be unappreciative of the contrast between essences and existents. On the other hand, Santayana has no sympathy for mysticism, except from the literary point of view. So far as I know, Spinoza is the only man to whom it is fair to attribute a really definite mystical tendency. It is he whom Santayana has thoroughly and highly respected. Santayana respected those medieval mystics (of that Church which at the start was his) precisely because through their Orders they were contributing to a life that Santayana regarded as important from the viewpoint of community and the values that men can attain and enjoy together.[CA] The medieval mystics contributed to the life of their Church, to their community, and to what Santayana justifies and applauds in that life—namely, the life of reason. But for Spinoza he has words of thoroughgoing respect.[2] He is very careful in his use of language there. One very notable characterization of Spinoza has been given in an introduction that Santayana wrote to a translation of Spinoza's *Ethics,* which appears in *Everyman's Library*. But Spinoza is a mystic only in a strictly limited sense which involves the positive acceptance of all that Santayana holds most in respect: that whole realism whose outline you read in one of its classic forms in Santayana's paper on "Some Meanings of the Word Is." That doctrine thus set forth is a doctrine that of course historically is affected by Plato, expressed in part by Aristotle in the scholastic point of view, worked out also in connection with materialism; and granted all that to be as true as conceptual truth can be, then Santayana is prepared to respect the one who has something further to say that doesn't involve some vague and romantic attitudes; he finds it a rare privilege to speak in terms which aren't directly expressive of the life of reason in conceptual form.

Spinoza had his own right. He accepted a version of the relation between existence and essence which would be, from Santayana's point of view, the very central thesis of a realism. Having accepted that simply and plainly, having been what you can call a materialist (for on the side of what he calls extended substance, Spinoza is a materialist), having undertaken to disregard entirely the teleological side of things as something that throws no light at all on whether a thing is or not, having "taken the world as he finds it," Spinoza is able to adopt an attitude which Santayana can characterize as an attitude involving a certain reconciliation with reality and therefore a certain eulogistic attitude toward the realm of reality, and therefore one that has a certain kinship with the mystical attitude. Spinoza was able to limit himself to just the little that one has a right to say who remains strictly at the point of view that Santayana's life of reason would demand. Surveying the whole, such a man can find, without excess of interest in the teleological, a certain reconciliation with reality which Spinoza finds. For that reconciliation Santayana feels a certain interest which makes him as tolerant of Spinoza as of anybody else who has ever taken a somewhat mystical point of view.

A further aid in dealing with this problem of the contrast between the mystical and the dualistic can be found in a review of those passages in Russell's *Scientific Method in Philosophy* in which he speaks, as he does in the first lecture, of the relations between scientific method and mysticism. The relations between Russell as a philosopher and the mystical point of view are more varied and in some respects more puzzling than those of a man like Santayana. They are both of them realists with very different training and tastes, a difference which they feel in practical as well as theoretical matters. The whole background of their interest in civilization is contrasted. For Russell, the Aristotelian element in philosophy is only incidental, but for Santayana it is a fundamental element in cultivation. For Russell, mathematical analysis has proved to be of final importance, whereas Santayana has only a cool respect for mathematics but is quite willing that Russell and other people should look into it. Santayana obviously feels a frequent suspicion of a certain romanticism and barbarism in the interest {of some} in curious mathematical matters, whose connection with idealistic metaphysics would make it indeed suspicious, were it not that a thinker of Russell's caliber had that interest.

I shall be very curious to find out in what phase his {Russell's} own attitude toward the mystical problems is now passing. His treatment of the topic is a puzzling one. His essay, "A Free Man's Worship," has some very notable, mystically disposed passages which involve an interest in the mystical attitude toward the problems of life, an interest which stands in a curious contrast to the rest of Russell's position. Russell strictly maintains in the general statements of that essay that no light is thrown on the real, so far as we can hope to get at it at all, by any methods but the scientific methods, which are very distinctly not the mystical methods. He wouldn't agree that they are the pragmatic methods, and he would strictly reject the doctrine of interpretation. We can get into touch with reality only by the scientific method. Yet the mystical method has a basis in human experience, so that every deeply considerate man has a power to appreciate mysticism which Russell tries to characterize. The whole question of Russell's relation to mysticism is an interesting one.

In the essay, "A Free Man's Worship," Russell gives an interesting variation of an attitude toward this mystical problem. The modern man, so Russell puts it, the man who has rejected traditional creeds and who is strictly set against fantastic solutions of his problems, such a man seems at first sight devoted entirely to things that appeal to him by the clearness of their logical expression, as in the case of the objects of mathematical research, or again by the clearness of sense–data. But a man who is thus free from superstition has a right to take note of a fact which belongs to the objective world as much as any other fact, although it is a fact about the human mind or about the "spiritual world." The latter is a phrase that Russell would not care to use; he prefers to speak of that world as colorlessly as he can. But after all, this world of man's mind has a right to recognize its own dignity, significance, yes, insight into some sort of genuine and mental truth—ideal truth if you like; it has a right which is not taken away from it by any application of the scientific method and not forbidden by any aversion to the mystical. After all, says Russell, the human mind has in its power to comprehend the infinite—and here the lover of the modern mathematical theories of the infinite speaks—and in the light of mathematical theory (which includes the theory of the infinite) to deal with the wealth of the facts of nature. The mind that thus surveys the larger connections of the empirical world shows its own superiority to fortune by having a certain spiritual fortune of its own, a fortune that it gets in the self-possession of a relation to knowledge. In the realm of knowledge, then, we have a world which is our own world, and this gives us a certain freedom.

Russell cannot speak of that freedom entirely in a Greek way, for it isn't a Greek who is speaking, and he is a modern man. But this realm of theory is a realm where {as in} Aristotle, something happens; viz., the spiritual self-possession of the knowing mind and its union with its objects—objects such as the temporally everlasting. There is something in that relation which Russell regards as genuine, significant, and valuable.

In the light of that view of the world, the modern man has a right to certain aspects of religion which in the past have been very highly important, perhaps amongst its most important features—acquiescence and reverence, superiority to fortune, communion with something real and significant—all that belongs to a point of view which is still rational.

The result is an outline of a relation to truth and reality which is a relation indeed to a realm of Being. Being is rather of the third kind, the Being that belongs to the third conception of Being in *The World and the Individual*. Nevertheless, there is a certain kinship with the view of Spinoza and with the kind of superiority to fortune which Spinoza regards as the essence of blessedness; there is a certain kinship between the view of Spinoza and the view that Russell insists upon.

A person is likely to say, "There is something mystical about this; it supposes some kind of transformation of experience whereby one views from a different point of view the realm that knowledge ordinarily faces." One would under those circumstances ask how far does Santayana follow in this. How far in him too is the Spinozistic union with substance, which involves a certain kinship between Platonic idealism and mysticism—how far is this present in Santayana's mind? It appears that on the whole there is a certain hostility between the view that Santayana himself regards as his own, and the expression that Russell has given in this and one or two other essays. Part of the difference is confessedly temperamental on both sides.

Russell says that he has found irreducible the contrast between the Protestant and the Catholic type of civilization and belief. When Catholic and Protestant come to speak of fundamental matters, neither understands the other, on the ground of that contrast. "I do not believe," declares Russell, "that any one brought up as Santayana was, will ever view such matters as a Protestant does." The contrast has to do with the very matters that come up whenever you try to evaluate the place of the mystical in life.

Santayana, in his latest volume of essays,[3] has given a very keen criticism of Russell's latest discussion of the religious problems. You may well consider this contrast, which gives you two important versions of the realistic point of view.

To Santayana, this way {of Russell's} of indicating the objective significance of an ideal world as a world of values seems fantastic with a tendency towards the romantic. On the other hand, for Russell, this search—in the adamantine land of the shadows which the mathematician studies—for something ideally valuable seems a genuine refuge. Thus each has his own kind of idealism, although they stand in curious contrast as to the place where it appears.

As a pacifist, Russell has something akin to the mystical once more. A word of his well expresses the problem of the mystic in a new shape: "Those who are with me are now in a place in which nobody has been since the days of the early Christians, the place of being utterly opposed to the very heart of the civilization in which they belong, and yet seeking a peaceful way out of this." The solution of the early Christians had something mystical about it, and Russell's own problem has something of the mystical in it.[4]

Recursus to the Basis of Extreme Realism

April 29 The discussion of realism in the third lecture of the first volume of *The World and the Individual* has been much and very naturally criticized on the ground that surely no realist means, when he says that the Real is independent of knowledge, an independence so abstract, so austere, as the assertion that the real and the knowledge of it have positively nothing to do with each other. The argument of the third lecture is an entirely futile argument: it attacks not merely a man of straw, but a thinker who doesn't resemble any serious thinker sufficiently for it to pay to refute him.

It is extremely easy to say, "The real world is independent of knowing; it needs not the presence of knowledge." Knowledge then contains nothing that of its own nature surely throws light on the real. The assertion that one knows the real is an assertion that doesn't come from anything that one knows about the essence of reality and the essence of knowledge. It is an assertion that has to be tested by induction, or possibly by deductive methods, but tested by itself.

It is extremely easy to say that, but very difficult to mean all that that assertion appears to imply. It is hard to state the nature of that independence without going beyond what you mean, without admitting a kind of relation between knowledge and reality which is hardly the relation which commonsense realism means to insist upon. The mind is not merely there in the context of the world, but is so bound up with it that when a man reflects upon the content of his own mind, that reflection somehow throws light on the real. How could that be if the relations were not in some respects mutual relations which go rather deep in some respects into the heart of Being?

To say too emphatically, with too much wealth of insistence, that one's beliefs are true is to make the assertion that the existent world is itself a rational world, an assertion against which the realistic mind revolts, for it seems to a thinker like Santayana precisely like what the idealist wants to emphasize. It is altogether too much like what the superstitious or the dreamers want to emphasize. One wants to know what the real world is apart from one's hopes or desires. So, one ought to say that human reason is wholly incapable of determining the reality of things—the reality which is after all wholly independent of the presence of rational beings.

Yet in practice the realist is always making use of a principle which seems to involve the conviction that what he views as reasonable is indeed of a nature to determine in some respects the nature of things. My realistic colleague or friend, who never can tolerate these views which doubt the universality of mechanism, holds that when one doubts that the world is a mechanical world, he takes at once a subjective or private point of view and seems to have an unwillingness to accept things as they are, an unwillingness which ought to be regarded as abnormal. The opponents of a mechanical view of nature seem to such a realist in an insane position; they are trusting their own sentiments; certainly they are not scientific.

Whoever says that has a point of view which he regards as reasonable or scientific, and this point of view enables him to see that the nature of things must itself conform to that view.[CA] How should one know that unless one is in a position to know that the nature of things is reasonable? How can one say, "I am a believer in atomism because I perceive that to be reasonable" without substantially asserting that it is the nature of things to be rational? If one's deepest reason for believing in a mechanical view of the world, or in the assertion of the universality of natural law, is that, after all, reason requires one so to believe, then is not one holding that reality is something else than independent of our reasoning process?

Evidently then, when one rejects some special idealistic view on the ground that it is unreasonable, one seems to have some ground for holding that the nature of things is in some respects reasonable. But reason, especially as the realistic believer in the reality of his assertions conceives it, is a character that has to do with the character of the human mind. There may be a distinction between the real reasonableness of things and our states of mind when we make our statements. "Of course," says the realist, "your reason doesn't itself determine the nature of things; but if you want to tell the truth, it is of great importance *to you* that *you* should be reasonable. Human reason can copy or comprehend things, but things of course are independent of the reason."

If one says *that*,—after all, one's guide is the principle that the reasonable view is more likely to be the view that reflects reality. How can this be, unless the very reasonableness that the thinker himself is striving to get when he tries to think things out will somehow have to do with the nature of things? The assertion that reality is independent of knowledge seems inconsistent with a thoroughgoing account of things in terms of an utter independence existing between reason and reality.

All that suggests that it is difficult to know *precisely how much independence*[CA] you are going to ascribe to the Real when you say that it is independent of whether it is known or not. Some deep and characteristic relation between the real and the process of reasoning appears to be involved in your confidence in reason which guides every inquiry of the materialistic sort which has to do with the assertion that the world is a mechanism. And of course it becomes fair under those circumstances to ask *how far*, *in what sense*, is the world independent of your knowledge?

After all, if the real is independent of your knowledge, how do you know that it is independent of your knowledge? It isn't merely that accidentally, of course, you have to know about the world in order to make any assertions about it; but you imply an assertion of the validity of your knowledge about the world, and that validity has to do with the essence of reality which must conform to what argument can make clear and reason detect by dealing with the processes of a being with a mind. To know the fact of independence would be knowing a kind of dependence; namely, that what one says about the world is true. These considerations may serve to show you that it is worthwhile to examine how far the world is independent of knowledge.

If you are to know that the world is independent in nature of you, you must know that it has to be so, and thus that something which you assert for a reason is true about it. Asserting this truth about it is, of course, by itself asserting a relation which is a relation which involves a dependence in certain respects of what the world is upon the state of the knowing being.

How could you know it to be independent unless you know it is of such nature that, whatever your state of knowledge, "the world is what it is"—{that is} unless you could give a reason for it? Then you argue; you give a ground for it.[#] Your grounds are mental grounds, and your thesis is that the world has to obey and conform to these rules of thought. Why should it, if it is utterly independent? And if you know it is utterly independent, how should you argue that your views have any basis in reality? The relations of truth and error and reality are bound up. One wants to know what that tie is.

If you took your independence quite seriously, why should you say, "My opinion is well-founded"? If you say your view is reasonable, you make a comment on your state of mind and declare that the real is determined by this kind of thinking. If you say this, however, you seem to recognize some kind of dependence of the Real on a state of mind. It is surely worthwhile to inquire what the independence is.

The discussion becomes more hopeful and promising when you definitely turn it into the discussion of what is the noetic relation between knower and known. How far is it a relation involving something in the nature of independence? You can hardly go on without some sort of dependence which enables you to examine your state of mind and thereupon have an indication which is valid of the nature of reality. The total independence seems suspicious.[5] Everybody who gives a reason for the truth of his beliefs gives a reason why the real conforms to the requirements of the knowing process.[6]

You are in a world of complications, desires, longings; you want to escape from that world. Your escape must be by analysis and discrimination of fact from knowledge. What you want to see are the facts, even of your own mind. They are quite independent of you, the knower. As soon as you recognize that independence, you in turn become independent. If the facts don't depend on my mind, I am independent of the fact-world. The world of the real cannot affect me so far as I am a pure knower. One thus gets a kind of wisdom, a complete independence of fact and fortune. One returns the compliment of indifference: the world cares nothing for me; but so far as I discriminate, I care nothing for the world. When one reaches the goal of recognizing the complete independence of knowledge and Being, and recognizes it from both sides, one gets the Sânkhya salvation. It consists in freedom from illusion; and the last illusion is that you, the knower, are in any way dependent on the world. The world in its reality can do nothing to you, the knower. You and the world are independent of each other. That gives you a kind of peace, a freedom, which resembles the Stoic doctrine.

The Sânkhya doctrine is antimystical, profoundly rationalistic, in type something like the doctrine of Russell, with its own kind of religion, the religion of one who is free from the world just because he knows that the world is independent of our knowing. Therefore, he is able to devote himself to what doesn't involve the eager quest for Reality but does involve the contemplation of that which the free soul chooses to contemplate. According to the Sânkhya teacher, the mind of an unenlightened person supposes that knowledge is due to an impression made by the real world upon a knowing mind, and consequently is disposed to define the whole thing in terms of causal relations which entangle the mind and the world. But this is illusory: the rational mind isn't affected by the real world; pure reason isn't the victim of the real world. The wise one is he who makes that discrimination complete and thereby escapes from the entanglements of fortune.[7] The world, in the presence of a wise man who has made the complete discrimination, behaves like the dancing girl who perceives that her arts are no longer effective; the princes of the court have seen through her arts and devices; she says "I am detected," and she turns away. So the world turns away from the wise man who says "You have nothing to do with me," not as the mystic says "You are nothing," but "I can't be affected by you."

Such is a suggestion of this possibility of a realism which depends entirely upon distinctions. There is one other instance at least of realism where a similarly mutual independence of knower and real seems to be made out, the realism of Herbart.

Herbart, better known possibly by his work in psychology and especially *May 2* by its indirect influence on education than by his philosophy, was an extremely productive philosopher, a contemporary of Hegel and in a great many respects the polar opposite of Hegel. He was minute, very dialectical, very carefully grounded in the history of thought, disposed (insofar much like the new realists) to an analytical method, and very merciless in his criticism of common sense insofar as he deals with matters that need technical clarification. On the other hand, he was very fond of empirical studies, much under the influence of the physical mechanical group of sciences of his day, his ideal both for philosophy and for psychology being very much affected by his knowledge of mechanics. He advanced hypotheses which he proposed to test by experiments which would introduce the mechanical method into psychology. The theory depended entirely upon a mechanics of elementary mental states or tendencies and upon hypotheses of how these work, in terms of highly complex processes of association, which couldn't be directly derived from observation but could be tested, like Newton's law, by experience. Herbart applied his law to a large number of problems of elementary education.

Here you have the union of a mathematically disposed mind with empirical interests. Herbart's speculations were to be tested indirectly by experience; they were to be derived by elaborate analysis; and the hope that inspired him was to bring philosophy into touch with the empirical sciences in a new way.

All this was in great contrast with the methods which came to him by the tradition of idealism. He was especially disposed to attack the idealistic theory of the Self in all its forms. He laid great stress on the contradictions which various views involve, and he used the principle of contradiction like the famous razor of Occam: you can prepare the road to philosophical knowledge by exposing and eliminating the various contradictions of experience.

Unfortuntely, some of our most familiar commonsense opinions cannot bear this test: only indirect experience, experience restated in the light of his hypotheses, can bear the rigid test of his method. Consequently, Herbart is like the Eleatic philosophers in declaring that our experiences of color, sound, etc., do not bring us into contact with the real. The real can be defined only by an elaborate process of elimination. In the end, Herbart's world appears strangely transformed by considerations which force one to say that our ordinary experience cannot be showing us what the Real is, although that there is a Real is something beyond all skepticism. His motto is, "As much appearance as there is, so much indication is there of Reality." You must follow every indication of Reality, but you must do it by a keen analysis of experience.

There are many reasons why it would be of advantage to the new realistic method to revive an interest in Herbart. Austere, original, paradoxical, influenced by the methods of physical science, his contribution to psychology was genuine, although his hypotheses haven't had the fortune that it seemed at one time they might have.

Schopenhauer, as you wouldn't be surprised to hear, was deeply offended by Herbart and skillfully characterized him as a man that put on his understanding hind-before. That characterization is not just of the true Herbart, but it is very natural for the mystic to make it. Herbart was also rather offensive to James, though James found more life in him, more serious things in him from the psychological side.

The transformed realm of Herbart gives us some of the more difficult problems about the real world that belong to a thoroughgoing realism. Herbart meant much more than is usually meant by independent and, although his solution is not precisely identical with that of the new realist, he showed a keen observation of the problem of the relation of independence which can well be commended to all of them.

One who studies the theory of realism must bear in mind two central questions: the sense in which there can be a one-sided or unsymmetrical dependence, along with the sense in which dependence involves something symmetrical or mutual. Isn't all dependence in a certain respect mutual? Can it be true that this independence of the Real and of knowledge is a mutual relation? May it not be a one-sided relation? Isn't it perfectly common sense that it is a one-sided relation? It makes a great difference to the knower what there is to be known, but does it make a difference to the world whether there is a knower or not, unless the knower is indeed a being with a power himself to affect the world by other means than by the means of knowing? You would nearly all of you be ready to make that objection, I suppose.

When I say that the real is totally independent of knowledge—so the realist may insist—I don't mean that the independence can be of that shadowy abstract mutual kind which you try to reduce to absurdity. It is true that in the Sânkhya system it appears that the knower is as independent of his real world as the real world is independent of the knower, and in the kind of discrimination which consists in knowing this fact consists that which the Sânkhya system regards as so important for the salvation of man from the entanglements of existence: but this is obviously a special and not a commonsense view. When Herbart rejects the relativity of the physical world—so the realist may say—he is deliberately artificializing his view of the world. This is not common sense. It is common sense to say that we are very dependent on the world we know for a great deal, but the world is, in just such ways as that, independent of us; and all this has a perfectly plain commonsense meaning.

The challenge of my text[8] depends on emphasizing that it is very important to know what you mean by independence, and whether a one-sided independence can be defined without reminding yourself of the very sense in which you speak of independence, and whether if there were complete independence it could be anything but mutual independence. If independence were entirely mutual in all respects—well, of course, one sees that there the situation would be paradoxical enough and one wouldn't be surprised to see that a realism committed to that would find itself in difficulties.

But, it is said, no such realism is a live realism. A realist regards knowledge as dependent on the object; he well knows in commonsense fashion that the object isn't dependent on knowledge, but he doesn't regard the independence as one that would have to be mutual.

Allied with this problem is one that has played considerable part in recent discussion. It was always made prominent by William James whenever he took this course, and it is prominent in all his discussions of philosophical matters. It has been made still more so by the discussions of the New Realism, a discussion that Russell put into definite statement at the point where he finally broke with his earlier interests, with the philosophical positions of Bradley. Relations are not necessarily internal relations; they may be external relations. Of course, there are internal relations; that is, relations that so make a great difference to the object related that if the object ceases to be in the given relation, its nature is profoundly altered. The relation of friend and friend is of that sort. The friend, so far as he is absorbed in the friendship, ceases to be what he was if the relation entirely ceases. The relation there does alter or affect the being. Such relations are more or less internal; they belong within the related being. A man's emotionally interesting bonds are part of himself; if you alter them, you alter him. Such relations are internal.

But some relations—so Russell insists; so James was fond of insisting—can be external. The lamp can be here on the table or there on the floor; and James used to illustrate this so that the class might have an empirical example: Does the lamp change when I change it from the table to the floor? It is the same lamp; its relation is external. You can judge by experiment whether there can be an external relation; it is easy then to mention external relations. So James held.

Now external relations involve a certain independence. Common sense notices this. To speak of my personal independence is to speak of relations in which I stand to external things. To speak of my internal relations to my world is to speak of dependencies which are involved. As between me and you, my class, there is mutual dependence in certain respects and internality of relations.

The New England countryman proverbially expresses independence in a well-known phrase. He says that an independent person is as independent as a hog on ice—an expression excellent in its choice. The hog put out on the ice is indeed possessed of a certain independence, but it isn't an effective one; he can neither advance nor retreat with facility. His position is not one of power. Independence he has, but this independence means an externality of relations which is here unprofitable, and is thus used in order to show the character of the externality in question. The one not as independent as the hog on ice would have ties and relations.

Now the question whether there could be wholly external relations is a perfectly possible question. It seems easy to answer it empirically. It may be that it is useless that one should be as independent as the hog on ice, but there can be such externality of relationships: if you don't think so, you have only to find the hog and put it on the ice. Externality, so it may be said, is possible; and there is a great deal of it in the world. The relations of the atoms in an atomic philosophy, supposing no mutual forces present, would be external.

Most familiar is the characterization of external relations in this way: the same object can be in various relations. A man can belong to this course or that course, this group or that group, be acquainted with this man or that, in Cambridge or in Boston. The same can be in various series or orders. Professor Perry lays emphasis on that in his *Present Philosophical Tendencies*.[9] There are grounds to which I soon have to call your attention, for I doubt how far you can get on external relations. The question is closely bound up with the problem of the mutuality of dependence.

Logicians speak of unsymmetrical or intransitive relations—before and after, greater and less—relations which are not mutual but are positively asymmetrical. If A is greater than B, B cannot be greater than A. So of "ancestor." Now when we speak of "dependence on," we generally speak of a nonsymmetrical relation. We generally mean a dependence such that it is a one-way dependence. Common sense is rather various in its use of the word "depend," but in general we mean by the word some sort of lawfully definable relation between a pair of objects. When I ventured to speak of "interrelation," you may think that I begged the question, since all relations are in some respects interrelations.[CA] A chart may help:

The Problem of "External Relations"

$\bar{\text{A}}$ = "not-A" (e.g., A absent or "not working," or "out of place")
("If A, then B") = ($\text{A}\bar{\text{B}}$ = O) = ("If $\bar{\text{B}}$, then $\bar{\text{A}}$")
"Dependence" = Lawfully definable interrelation of a pair, e.g., A & B

If A is related to B, B is in some respects related to A. This matter of symmetry or mutuality of relationships interests us, because in general it holds true that if you take objects and consider them in one "sense," they are quite different from what they are if you consider them in the other direction. The relation of buyer to seller is very different from the relation of the seller to the buyer. There is no purchase if there is no sale; but the relations differ according to the order in which you take it. When two people play for stakes, it is very different whether A wins from B or B from A. At the same time, there couldn't be a winning without a losing, so that though in the very nature of the case the question who loses is important, there still remains always but one such.

If one happens to be interested in this mutuality that underlies even the most violent differences, one is in the mood of the Pasha of Persia whom James mentions. They invited him to go to the races. A race, unless it is a dead heat, means to see an unsymmetrical relation of winner and loser. The Pasha wasn't excited: "It is known to me that one horse can go faster than another";

and he declined to go to the races. The same comment reduces to insignificance all instances of unsymmetrical relationship, because it calls attention to the mutuality. Nevertheless, that very fact has a certain interest for one who wants to consider certain notable cases of unsymmetrical relation. Independence has a certain unsymmetrical character that interests us as such. Isn't the relation of knowledge to its object a one-sided relation?

When *The World and the Individual* first appeared, Professor Montague, now of Columbia, wrote me an interesting criticism in which he pointed out that it seemed to him that my chapter on realism had wholly failed to consider what everybody knew; viz., that what is called the *ratio cognoscendi* is different from the *ratio essendi*—the ground of one's knowledge is different from the ground of being. I had simply neglected that difference. Of course, one may say, "The ground is wet because it rains"; and one may say, "I know it has rained because the ground is wet." Here the dependence is a one-way dependence. The wetness of the ground makes known to the observer who is familiar with certain rules of nature that the rain has occurred; but the wetness of the ground doesn't bring on the rain. Isn't it plain that that is the true relation of knowledge to its object? It is a dependence but in one way. The real world makes the knower know what he knows; but the knower's mind doesn't make the world real in any sense.

One technical point. Because of a very simple, well-known, but easily neglected or forgotten character of what is often called the hypothetical judgment, you can say this: In case a dependence, a lawfully definable interrelation, exists between things, then to every dependence which you read in one way, and which ought to be read in one way—which leads you from one of those objects to another, and not backward—there always corresponds another dependence just as genuine as the first, generally having another practical interest, a dependence of the other object on the first. Wherever A depends on B for anything, B always depends on A for something. If the one dependence is a lawful relation, the other dependence is a lawful relation. The two are generally bound up so that you can reason from one to the other. What you know about the one enables you to say, "If A depends on B *secundum quid,* then B depends on A *secundum quid*." The matter in question is one that requires a little closeness of thinking, so that one can easily make mistakes about it; and a great many mistakes of that sort are made.

Closely connected with that fact is this: Independence would mean absence of any lawful relation. If there were no law of a certain kind that would determine how A depends on B in a certain respect, if there were no such laws, then the independence in question would be a mutual independence. Independence if complete would be mutual. If A were wholly independent of B, B would be wholly independent of A.

The Miller of the Dee rejoices: "I care for nobody, no not I; and nobody cares for me." The completeness of the carelessness on the one side is met by the completeness of the carelessness on the other side. The world in which I really care for nobody is a world in which, if I know my mind, nobody cares for me.

In the old days of the horse–cars, a friend of mine, now a well-known professional man, was riding in Boston. The driver was careful to mind his own business and felt that he ought not to be talked to. This absence of intercourse is a mutual relation. He was in the habit of breaking off the asymmetrical relation of quizzing. My friend had endeavored to break the law but had received only monosyllables in response. The driver established the mutual relations at last by this ingenious device. My friend, looking forward at one of the horses drawing the car, said, "Your horse interferes, dosn't he?" (= clicks his hoofs together). This question came after a little interval of silence and so was a new intrusion. "Ain't interfering with nobody but himself." One can hardly conceive a more effective manner of establishing the mutual relation of independence which those two persons had during the rest of their travel.

It is a general logical fact that wherever a dependence exists which you *May 4* can express in one direction, there is always a corresponding relation which you can express in the other direction. Relations of dependence go in pairs, and in that sense there is always mutuality about there being any definite sort of dependence. If A is dependent on B, there is always some sense in which B is dependent on A.

If there were such a thing as total independence, or if you could define total independence in certain respects, such absence of lawful relation would constitute a mutual relation. Independence is therefore mutual. Dependence is not in general mutual; dependence is a one-way affair. Mutual dependence in a given respect would be a purely symmetrical relation which by no means always exists. But where there is a dependence in one direction, there is some dependence of some sort in the other direction.

There is a sense in which the subjects of an absolute monarch are very much more dependent on the monarch than the monarch is on the subjects, in a great many respects. The members of a tribe may depend for their continued existence as individual men upon the will of the chief. A great deal of slaughter is tolerated by some tribes without rebellion; and unless the chief goes beyond what happens to be the limit of tolerance, no rebellion is excited. The subject under these circumstances would be in general prevented from having much influence over the life of the chief.

But it is mere common sense to notice that after all, the most absolute of monarchs is dependent upon his subjects for their submission and obedience, whether from custom or from loyalty, blind habit or choice. He is not wholly independent of them, for if they weren't disposed in some way to obey him, he wouldn't have any obedience to his command and would not be the ruler of those subjects.

The relation of ruler to slave is so far a mutual relation. Of course, the relation isn't a symmetrical one, so far as you consider it as a particular relation of master and servant. But in order that one should be master of a slave, it is necessary that there should be one who is capable of being a slave. Consequently, as a fact, slavery has been limited in its extent in the world by the characteristics of races. The American Indian was much less frequently enslaved than the Negro. Those who stole Negroes from the Gold Coast of Africa found that they could be made slaves. The Indians of the West Indies did not remain slaves in any considerable body for the very good reason that they had to be killed before they would become slaves.[CA] They were very freely killed. The result was a population very full of Negro slaves but the Indians were largely absent from the scene.

A man might be capable of being made a slave by good-humor, optimism, absence of violence of temper; but the master would be dependent on the nature of the slave for being able to have a slave in this man. In an early book, *The Phenomenology of the Mind* (*Die Phänomenologie des Geistes*, 1807), Hegel discusses the master-and-slave relation as a characteristic primitive relation, as being the basis of other social relations, on the ground that the mutuality is such that master and slave are in a way dependent each on the other, the slave-captive being in the abstract dependent on the gift of life that the master has given him, while the master is dependent on the slave for his willingness to serve. The slave gets the advantage of a certain form of cultivation and in the end proves to be rather better off than the master. In those civilizations where slavery has existed for a long time, the slaves tend to get socially the advantage.

Such relations are in general of the character that while the relation itself is not symmetrical, there is mutuality of relations, insofar as, if A is dependent of B, then B in some other respect depends on A, and where one dependence is present, the other will also be present.

Suppose you were considering the behavior of two people who happened to attend this class. On the basis, let us say, of the attendance records of a certain number of meetings of the class, you wished to discover whether there is any law which relates the attendance of A to the attendance of B, whether the presence or absence of one of these men is dependent on the presence or absence of the other. If there is such a law, it is logically probable that it would be of one of these four forms: Some conceivable class of possibilities will be equated to zero, and that will be the law. {To put this graphically:}[CA]

Let A mean "A is present."
$\bar{A}$: "A is absent."

AB = O "If either is present then the other is absent."
A$\bar{B}$ = O "If A is present, B is present."

$\bar{A}B = O$ "If B is present, A is present."
$\bar{A}\bar{B} = O$ "If either is absent the other is present."

Suppose that the law of the behavior of A with respect to B is such that A and B are never present at the same lecture, so that all the attendance records show that. We could express this in this symbolism: that the AB case is equal to zero. One doesn't say positively what happens, but only that they are never present together. In that case, which one is the dependent one?

Suppose the law is, "If A is present, B is present." To find out that is to find that the cases where A is present and B is absent are not to be found: the logical product of $A\bar{B}$ is zero.

What you would call the reverse of that case would be expressed $\bar{A}B = O$. Of course, you wouldn't call this the same dependence as the preceding one.

If they are never both absent, so that if either is absent, the other is present, this can be expressed in two directions.

While those laws are laws of dependence, you are comparatively free to state what you mean by dependence, that is, which is dependent on the other. But about one thing you aren't free. Wherever one of these dependencies is present, then another dependency is present which can be read in another direction. To say "If A, then B" is equivalent to saying, "If B, then A." Thus when an *if* proposition can be read in one direction, there is always an *if* proposition which can be read in the other direction.

All this enables one to approach the issue: What is meant by saying of A and B that in their attendance they are independent of each other? That would involve a mutual independence. Logically we should have to express this by saying that no one of these four possible equations to zero is true; the contradictory of each one of those propositions would have to be true. Only in such a case could you say that their attendance at this lecture is demonstrably governed by no law. True independence would mean absence of determinate law.

You also get a kind of logical instance of what you would mean by pure chance in respect to a certain feature. People sometimes say chance is inconceivable; but one could conceive that the presence of two members of this class was demonstrably of that character. When one had once shown the occurrence of instances of those four cases, there you would have genuine absence of law in a certain respect. By chance you mean absence of law; and absence of law you exemplify by presence of facts which would furnish grounds for contradicting all the lawful assertions of relation. If any law governs, then {at least} one of these four possibilities must be shut out by the facts (= O).

Independence in the abstract can be exemplified well enough. A chance world in which law is absent is abstractedly definable by equating some range of possibilities to zero. If you consider the two propositions, "This man is drowned," and "This man falls into deep water," and ask about the lawful connection between falling into deep water and getting drowned, and if you find instances which shut out all four equations to zero, then the two propositions are not lawfully related. Whatever laws of nature are concerned, they are outside the realm of the universe of discourse.[CA]

A world of chance would be a world of relations of mutual independence. Total independence would be a relation that could be defined only as a mutual affair. <u>If Being were independent of knowledge then knowledge would be independent of Being</u>, precisely insofar as the independence were total.

Are chance and mutual independence at all possible? My critics say, "You speak as if the dependence between knowledge and Being had to be entirely a mutual dependence: surely according to common sense, knowledge is dependent for its knowing upon the fact that something is under the conditions which make it possible for one to experience that something is: but the states of the mind of the knower are not such that Being depends on him."

But my argument consisted in showing that if Being were wholly independent of knowledge, then knowledge would be wholly independent of Being. Dependence is in general a nonsymmetrical relation; the relation runs one way only: but the mutuality that is involved is the mutuality which the hypothetical propositions of the logical textbooks bring out. In case you state anything in the form of law, "<u>If</u> . . ., <u>then</u> . . .," you use an antecedent and a consequent. If the consequent of the hypothetical proposition is said to be dependent on the antecedent, then the situation is such that a dependence in the other direction would go side by side with a dependence in the first direction.

Part of the difficulty of the text of *The World and the Individual*, Vol. I, Lecture III, depends upon the fact that I regard the nature of a thing as so closely bound up with its relationships that I repeatedly say that if things were totally independent each of the other, then they couldn't have any qualities in common, any characters that were real characters really in common. The world of total mutual independence would be a world where these things which had no relations would also have a certain absence of characters that is very puzzling. Or they wouldn't have the characters that in the world of common sense seem to be constantly recognized in the objects about us.

The argument depends on saying, "What a thing is, its essence, its qualities, its character as this thing, depends upon its relations in such wise that if you changed the relations of things, you would change their character." My argument assumes that this is the case.

My critics insist that it is the opinion of common sense that the same object can have different relations at different times. Can't you attend this lecture or another, be in this room or another, take different courses in different years? Aren't you capable of belonging to an organization and then ceasing to belong to it? Isn't it perfectly possible that the same thing can be in different relations? It is empirically obvious, said James with his drop lamp, that it is the same object all the time, now on the desk, now on the floor. Don't you see that a thing is quite independent of the relations in which it stands? At any rate, it is very largely independent, one is disposed to say.

It is very easy to illustrate the fact that many of our relations are in such wise internal that we admit that, if in those respects you change our relations, you change our characters, our qualities. In case a friendly relation is important to you, to change it is to change a value, a status, an important feature. It is the business of the teacher to hope, and so far as he can to bring to pass, that your relations in this course shall make some difference to what might be called your essence. It makes some difference to me whether the class [is] here present or not; that is a social relation and enters into my life as a social being.

But one may say, "It doesn't make any difference to the piece of chalk whether it is on the desk or on the table; therefore, at any rate, some relations can be external relations." The common realistic opinion on that subject is that in any case there are some relations of things—for realistic purposes, the most important relations—which are external, such that the thing can be unchanged and be now in this, now in that relation.

Are there any relations of a thing which are in no sense so bound up in the nature of that thing that if the thing changes its relations, it is itself unchanged?

In Santayana's paper you may remember that portion of the discussion which dealt with interesting questions of personal and other {kinds of} identity. The discussion of those questions brought us to this dialectically interesting and easily illustrated fact, that the assertion, "This is Odysseus," or any other assertion of identity, always involves a curious paradox. Of course, it is impossible to recognize this person as Odysseus unless you have at any rate some motives for finding the recognition difficult or perhaps doubtful. The whole matter is one of the most controversial topics in the theory of the nature of reality. Whenever you assert an identity, you assert a difference. You remember the case I brought up: If I am going to explain what I mean by identity, I meet the paradox about identity which Hegel made prominent in his *Logik*. I can best tell you what identity is by illustration: A is A. Here A is either the chalk mark or the meaning that I have in mind. Whenever I say "A is A," this A isn't this A, for this A is subject and this A is predicate. Furthermore, this letter A isn't this {other} letter A: there are two of them. They aren't the same. So when I say "A is A," you can well ask me which of these A's is the other A. Whenever I assert an identity, I assert a difference. This comes up whenever the questions of personal identity appear.

If anybody says, "I will show you an external relation," if he gives me the example, if he says, "Look at this piece of chalk: it is the same identical piece of chalk, now on this desk, now over there on the blackboard"—yes, but I pointed it out to you at two different times. Something has happened. I explicitly pointed out to you the piece of chalk here; that is a piece of chalk somewhere. They are the "same": Which did you mean? Which of these two shall be the same? The differentiation happens to be in time. Change is going on all the time; you never step into the same stream twice. This piece of chalk does change.

Thus one can defy you to show a case where anything remains the same in different relations. It does make a difference to anything as to whether it is in these or in those relations; and whoever denies this, contradicts himself.[10]

May 9 The rest of the treatment of the extreme realistic conception I shall now have to make very summary. All that I have intended is to let you see the matter on which, at the time when I discussed these four conceptions of Being, I wished to have present to the reader's mind. A relation of total independence of object to knowledge would involve the paradoxes that Lecture III set forth {in *WI* 1}.

If the lecture is criticized by saying that nobody thinks of the relation as one of total mutual independence, I can point out first the historical instances, the Sânkhya system and the other cases mentioned, where such a conception was at least approximated. I can give also the frequent instances where total independence of the existence of the knowing being from the Real is actually asserted of the Real, although one doesn't intend to take all the consequences of this. I can then justify the argument of Lecture III on the ground that most of my critics are not themselves conscious of the sense in which they want this independence to be taken.

In a way, the third lecture is vindicated even from the point of view of the New Realism, in that the assertion of independence is more and more modified by the New Realism. Whatever conception of Being you have, the only chance to make that conception consistent will be to make use of the Third Conception of Being: To say that you mean by the Real precisely that which is independent of knowledge will not help you unless you tell what independence you refer to. The only consistent way to tell what independence you refer to is to make use of the Third Conception of Being. It is notably more prominent in realistic discussions than it was when I wrote these lectures, that the Third Conception of Being is the one into which the realist transforms his position if he has become sufficiently aware of the difficulties.

Critique of the New or Critical Realism via Two of its Extremes

If you look at the matter historically, the highly developed and Critical Realism is that of Santayana's realm of the essences and existents and that realm is defined by abandoning the effort to characterize with any definiteness the distinction between the existent and the nonexistent, by saying as Santayana says, that it is an irreducible difference; it is simply so. There is a good deal of realism that has no conception of what it is to be. Or the realism may take the form that has been expressed in Russell's *Scientific Method in Philosophy*, which would be secure enough against any attack on the abstract assertion of independence.

When one says, "Surely the real doesn't depend on any ideas, but would be the real quite apart from any knowing being," and when one for that reason throws aside the mystical point of view and all the motives that one recognizes as belonging to ordinary idealism, then one has no resort except to speak in terms of that classic and fine analysis originated by the Platonic Aristotelian discussion and illustrated to you by Santayana, or else to say as Russell does, in terms very closely similar to those of recent psychological discussion, "I mean by the Real that which under given conditions would be experienced thus and thus." The Real consists of what Russell has skillfully called *sensibilia*, when speaking in terms of sense impressions and discussing physical reality. The Real consists, not of the sense–data that are present at a given time, but of the data that <u>would be</u> there under given conditions.[CA] So if you are speaking of matters of experience, the Real consists of whatever would be present to the appropriate kind of experience under the appropriate conditions. The Real thus defined is defined under our Third Conception of Being; and thus the realism that is significant within modern controversy is of that type.

This involves nothing of a dialectical demonstration but it is for us a useful result to have found that one is led around to such views, either as the ones which Santayana has expounded to you, or to views about what the Real is which Russell has summarized for you. Now it might be well to say that those latter views are views for which the classical realism has no place. When people, once turning away from the mystical union with Being, desire to clarify the real, to deal with definite propositions, and to accept or reject them with clear knowledge of what they are, then one stands in the presence of the alternatives which Santayana and Russell represent.

The substance of our criticism of Santayana's paper was that hereby we were left without a definition of what it is to Be, except in terms of a dogmatic distinction between essence and existence, a distinction easily illustrated, but incapable of satisfying us. What the realm of the divine ideas in advance of creation, the realm of the possibilities before they were the facts, was or would be, that remains mysterious. In what creation consists—that from the scholastic point of view remains mysterious. The realism here in question is anything but a merely commonsense realism; it is a very highly technical one.

It is a question of undertaking to clarify one's analysis of the situation. We can't say that thus we learn what it is to Be. There is a wonderful transformation of the essence into the existent which is exemplified whenever you consider the coming or the going of a real fact. But how hard it is to characterize that transformation! It distinguishes the fact that happens from the fact that doesn't happen; but if you attempt to define this, you are driven to emphasize how the essences remain moveless and eternal, but yet are so bound up with what is, that every change is an essential change. A man is hungry and then is not; such a transient fact involves an essential change, for there is an essence which the hungry man exemplifies in existence. The eternal world is itself not changing, but the existents are taking on, now the "color" of this, now of that essence. That taking on troubled us.

In short, this conception of Being has at once a beautiful classic definiteness about it, but an abstractedness which is much more than merely cold. This way of taking the thing involves really an abandonment of the effort to make out what it is to Be. Essential reality involves first the reality of the essences, and then the reality of the existents which is still harder to express and explain.

The difficulty is removed if you turn to the other extreme of the recent realism and consider the *Scientific Method in Philosophy* {of Russell}. There at the very time when the realist is doing his best to get free from the trammels of sense, free from the limitations of the mere mind, free from the definition of the Real in terms that entangle him with the experience of the thinker, he is constantly dealing with an account of things which, though distinct enough from Santayana's account of things, still gives you the same problem. Russell's world is a world where that which we feel and see and touch insofar as that world is a matter of experience, is transformed into the world of the possibilities of experience. This realm is precisely that of my Third Conception of Being.

Historically, then, the discussion of realism in *The World and the Individual* has had its own justification, from the fact that those who rejected this distinction into the four conceptions of Being and declared that they stood otherwhere, have gradually centered their own views about one of the positions which I endeavored to analyze in my own way, the one that is discussed especially in Lecture VI of the first volume of *The World and the Individual.*[11]

Precisely insofar as Russell intends to emphasize the conceptual side of experience, the side which you define in terms of your conceptions of physics or mathematics, as revealing that which is—the truth or the nature of what it is to Be—precisely so far, the doctrine falls back into an abstract realism. The real world is for Santayana the world of the essences, possessed of a certain reality; but it isn't after all the reality that we want, for our world is a world of change, of progress. That world is abstract. Russell's world is a world not exactly of the coherent whole of experience, but of possibilities of experience; and it arouses problems which are essentially identical with those brought to our mind by the extreme and austere forms of realism which I have, as my opponents claim, too readily refuted.

We who deal with experience and with the problems of life are dealing with a realm of reality whose nature we shall grasp only so far as we get at the coherence of experience. Surely that coherence is not a matter of your mind or of mine. We must abstract from our private point of view. Whoever says the world is only the contents of certain minds understands neither the minds nor the world, and his doctrine surely doesn't satisfy us. We all seek to find out what the world was before we came into it. We are endeavoring to abstract from the trivialities of private experience but we don't make that abstraction successful merely by leaving out mind, {or by} leaving out the process, or by putting ourselves where the pragmatists in Mr. Dooley's skit would put themselves. The world that we endeavor to grasp is not the world merely of the transient, but the world in which something coheres. It is characterized by the unity of a time–process which is throughout mental but superindividual, the object of a chronosynoptic consciousness.

Life daily puts before you the problem of where you shall find the next stage of the self-expression in which you live and of which your whole appreciation of your world will consist. All that a course of metaphysics can do will be to make this process a little more coherent and selfconscious than it would be otherwise.

Granting that the world isn't simply the mystic's world {nor} simply the world of the austere abstract realism, it isn't exactly that world which could be wholly discussed in terms of Santayana's account of the scholastic world. It must have reality such that it doesn't cease with our minds; it must be superior to our caprices in its truth, so that it is much more significant what that world is than what we merely take it to be. We must subordinate our private interests. The idealism that regards the world as our whim is constantly refuted by tragic experience.

What can this world be? The realistic movement in its revived form has tried to emphasize the fact that one feature which the world must contain may be expressed by saying that the world is to be defined in terms of whatever <u>would be</u> if we weren't there. Since all independence is relative and limited, what you believe about things does make a difference to what they are. Hence, the world should be defined in terms which are realistic in the sense that we must try, so far as possible, to abstract from the subjective, the limited and the accidental in the way of experiencing that is characteristic of human beings.[CA] The realistic movement in its revived form has tried to emphasize the fact that one feature which the world must contain may be expressed by saying that the world is to be defined in terms of whatever <u>would be</u> if we weren't there, in terms which are realistic in this sense, that while it does make a difference to what things are, what you believe about them, since all independence is relative and limited, we must try so far as possible to abstract from the subjective, the limited and the accidental in the way of experiencing that is characteristic of human beings.

All the recent realists are agreed in this. The differences which arise when they endeavor to express their position are extremely interesting to us, not because we are disposed to make merry over their differences of opinion, but because the more you try to deal with the realistic world, the more you see that neither perception nor conception will serve. The world is a process that aims to become coherent, so that what the realist insists upon is more or less an expression of the fact. Never is the world at any instant rational; but as the pragmatists insist upon it, its essence is to aim to be coherent; and the complete understanding of that is precisely that in which a metaphysic consists.

Such a position turns out to be not so far away from the position of the New Realism as some of the new realists endeavor to suppose. Absorbed as they are in the effort to define their own conceptual order, and disposed as most of them are to reject the kind of collective social coherent reality that we have emphasized in the first half of this course, they find themselves deeply, as they suppose, out of sympathy with all idealistic tendencies and extremely fond of emphasizing the polemics against those tendencies. From their point of view, the business of the Scientific Method would be to apply to metaphysical questions the same method of procedure that is proving so successful in the various sciences.

But this is a matter of team play, not merely of polemics. It must depend upon cooperation, so that if it is a scientific method, it is essentially a method of interpretation; but that isn't so consciously realized by the new realists. Their world, however, is a world of interpretation, not the world of a magnified natural man but the world of a social order. Of this the new realists are comparatively unconscious.

If you give up mysticism and {that} so austerely abstract realism which I regard as refuted in the third lecture, then what is it to be? It will have to be defined in terms of the sort of proposition that you will have to state when you are dealing with an empirical concrete problem, and it will have to meet the sort of test that we use in the empirical sciences. What is that which such a test shows you to be true? What is the true proposition? Here we come to the Third Conception of Being, which says the reality of things not merely is consistent with, but consists in the truth of certain propositions about them. If you only know what it is for propositions to be true, you know what it is to be real.

It is very interesting to me to find that after most elaborate efforts to define the truth–concept as secondary to the Real—an effort that he has repeatedly made—Russell at last in this expression of *The Scientific Method in Philosophy*, in this attempt to free himself from the annoying burden of the philosophers who use malicious logic and bad dialectics, who have mystical tendencies and are under the traditions of the priesthood, in this elaborate effort to show how these philosophers are to view Being, Russell comes back to this interesting position: instead of defining the True in terms of the Real, he defines the Real in terms of the True. The world consists not in sense experiences; the world isn't the world of the colors that you see, the tones that you hear; but it is the world that he has repeatedly characterized in terms of possible experience. This is to say that there is a proposition about experience that is true. It is to regard the truth of propositions as a fundamental idea, and in terms of that to define the reality of Being.

That I think is a very interesting metaphysical conception. I suppose it to be one that inevitably brings us back to exactly that view of the world which an idealist finds.

The Analysis of Possibility[12]

The main problem furnished by the Third Conception of Being is one of the most puzzling metaphysical ideas, the idea of possibility. What is a possibility? *May 11*

There are moods in which we greet the use of the word in conversation or in the accounts that people give of things with a certain scorn. We want to know the facts, not the possibilities. A man might have written poetry: He is a possible poet. That may suggest gently tender reflections like those in Gray's Elegy about "some mute inglorious Milton"—he is a possibility. The man that lived historically was some obscure villager, a forgotten person; certainly he wasn't a poet, a Milton.

Elegy Written in a Country Churchyard
Thomas Gray (b. 1716)

Some village-Hampden, that, with dauntless breast,
The little tyrant of his fields withstood,
Some mute inglorious Milton here may rest,
Some Cromwell guiltless of his country's blood.

Th'applause of list'ning senates to command,
The threats of pain and ruin to despise,
To scatter plenty o'er a smiling land,
And read their history in a nation's eyes,

Their lot forbade; nor circumscrib'd alone
Their growing virtues, but their crimes confin'd
Forbade to wade thro' slaughter to a throne,
And shut the gates of mercy on mankind.[13]

The poet continues that opportunity has so much to do with a man's field.[CA] There are good and bad possibilities involved in such a case as that. Your impression as the observer of the records of the country churchyard may be that these people were greatly limited. Their lot in the village was something that determined what they were. But on the other side of the thing, their possibilities might have been much worse. The historical and the possible Cromwell are here contrasted.

Of course, the reflection comes that one says little for a man if one insists upon it that he is a mute inglorious Milton. We can all be that and remain so as long as we please. Is a possibility a label that a man or his neighbor can put upon him?

You do tell something more about the life of the villagers when you remember what wonderful possibilities were hidden in the village life. Whatever happened depended on what could happen. What the Cromwells and the Miltons were depended upon what they were capable of being. The poet's mood emphasizes the possibilities of men and lays stress on the fact that these possibilities have a kind of being which may be very significant; and for the poet's mood, our appeal to history, to fame, {and} to the glories of the world rather hides from us what the man is, and keeps from us the understanding of a very important part of being.

We are reminded of that when we turn to the world of existence, which has its own character revealed by history, by what Santayana calls "evidence." The world of the possibilities has a character that is significant: It has the interesting relation to the existents that, by stripping off the accidental surroundings which belong to some existent, we can always define its possibility. The great poet couldn't have written that poem except by virtue of features, characters, inherent in his nature. It does help you to remember that a man doesn't produce a great poem merely by accident. It grows out of his essential nature—exactly that which Meister Eckhart discussed as the *Wesen* of God and of created beings. We owe the great poem not merely to the fact that the poet and the world working together produced a certain thing, but to the fact that he had that nature. We can see that he could have written more. When we lament the fact that a youth is cut off in the beginnings of high promise, we remember that there belongs to him a possibility, a nature, a *Wesen,* a character, an *essentia*, which now we inevitably universalize.

So to view things is to take account of matters which concern everybody who estimates his neighbor's character. You don't value your friends merely by the words they speak or the deeds they do. You regard that kind of evidence as inadequate. If you have done these deeds, that is an interesting fact; but the deepest interest lies in the fact that they could do these things. They show their possibilities. Of course, we can express that by saying that they could do these things again. The young man reminds us in death that he has shown that he could do these things. As to living men whose actual future deeds we do not predict, we still value them as our friends not merely by their literal words and deeds, but by this *essentia*, this essence that they have shown. Almost any letter of recommendation will refer to the man's capacities. On that basis we get our promotions, our appointments, our elections, our friendships. In the case of your friend, of course, you don't forget what he did in finding that in him which makes him your friend; but you regard a literal account of what he did as very inadequate as an account of what you value in him, viz., the fact that he could do these things.

The conception of possibility thus enters into our view of the nature of things in a fashion which you get first illustrated by that case of Gray's "Elegy" and by whatever you value in a man. You estimate men by their possibilities.

But there is the other feature about possibility which leads us to view it very scornfully. There comes a time in the development of many men when they lead us to ask the question as to how far what they have done allows them to make the claim which they have made based on possibilities. Men don't always live up to their possibilities. A man is perhaps the son of a father of national note: such a man may often feel the burden of the greatness which he inherited as a possibility and which the community demanded of him by way of actual accomplishment—the burden of this ghostly possible self.

There are biological reasons why the period of age comes on sooner than one intends. But a small proportion of young men of promise before they are twenty-five live up to the promise; the experience of having good promise and then finding that promise not lived up to is fairly common. It is right that on the great academic occasions we should officially express to our young men that now their institution greets them with high hopes of their future. But then statistically we have to remember that the number of people who live up to their early promise is small. We all of us have to live with that kind of burden. So you see how large a part of us lies in the realm of possibilities. This possible self amounts to a good deal. Part of one's good fortune is to look back upon the number of crimes which one was mercifully prevented from committing. We all have occasion to see that we are capable of much worse things than we actually do, if we are at all tolerable people. One can say, I have not lived up to my possibilities, but I have not been as bad as I could have been.

All these things serve to emphasize the problem of the possible. What is this possible self? One regards it as due to heredity, as affected by environment, as the object of training, as that on the basis of which you get a degree, an appointment, a business opportunity, a standing in the community, and on the basis of which you earn and keep your friendships. What is it?

It becomes pathetic if a possibility remains a possibility. There are people whose poetic possibility is recognized by their friends and who remain mute inglorious Miltons. That sort of thing may seem to warrant a certain scorn towards these possibilities.

One way to meet the puzzle is an austerely realistic way. One then says all the possibilities are fictitious imaginings of those who do not view the facts as they are. When you are ascribing praise and blame (as in the case of a game lost by bad coaching), why speak of possibilities? Why talk of what might have been? The question is, what were the facts. There is a clear difference between speaking of what somebody actually did and what the possible results of different conduct would have been. To say that somebody died who would have lived if he had been a little cautiously treated is different from saying that one actually murdered a man. This comes up in the case of an automobile accident. When we speak of blame, we do make a difference between the deed and the possible deed. Owing to these possibilities, there is a realistic mood in which one tries to get rid of everything but the actual facts. A friend once said that he had resolved to leave out of account every expression which took the form of saying that so and so would have been, under certain circumstances, that such and such was the possible thing. The friend in question spoke once of the actual death of somebody who apparently might have lived, and the practical question was asked, "Do you think that the patient could have been saved?" "I don't know; he wasn't saved. Let us confine ourselves strictly to facts." It was a proposal to get rid of the Third Conception of Being.

Surely it appears realistic and sensible to want to consider things in that way, to want yourself to be judged by your deeds and not by your possibilities, and to take this attitude toward other people. Here one has to use something like the reflective method. Can we get on without using terms of possibility? What would it be to reduce ourselves to the barren statement of realistic fact?

The realist who says, "That of which I speak is a fact," is reporting something as fact. But what is there in heaven or earth whose essence you can characterize, whose nature you can set forth—what is it of which you can say that it is of this or this character whether a poet or a Cromwell or a driver of an automobile—unless it is an entity defined by its possibilities? Leave out the possibilities altogether from your account, and what have you left? What is the significance of this life on which you look back when you look into the past, except by its reference to possible lives? You inevitably contrast the turning to the right with the possible turning to the left before you met your friend; if chance hadn't brought us together, all those possibilities would have remained undeveloped. How can you speak of the real without speaking of them? What is the significance of the real life except by virtue of its contrast with the lives not lived? The happy word that you might have spoken remains a regrettable memory of a lost opportunity; but is it merely vain speculation to think of the thing we might have said? The failure to say that also belongs to history. Is not the very significance of what we did determined by its contrast with what we would have done if we had done differently?

When Socrates tells his friends of his situation, he says that as an actual fact he is here awaiting death according to the laws of the State: "If I had done what my desires had suggested, if I had behaved as a frightened man might have behaved, these bones would have long since carried me in safety to Megara."[14] But how could he tell his life and what he did, except by saying that he waited for death because he thought it was a duty under the law to wait for it? In telling the realistically real, he tells the possible.

When we look back on the past, this curious sort of shadowland of possibilities may seem so subjective or capricious that we may attempt to get rid of the possible, never to say "it might have been" but only that it was. The reflective method shows that one cannot deal with the conception of Being in that way.

A friend once said, "It is surprising how little you lose by getting rid of possibilities and confining yourself strictly to facts." But as he spoke, his speech implied what would be the case if he were to use the words "might have been." He contrasted the speech of the man who talks of plain facts with the speech of the man who uses possibilities. His remark therefore inevitably meant, "I might speak otherwise if that were my mind; it is better that I speak as I do than to speak of possibilities; and that possibility I exclude and speak as I do of facts only." Yes, but he is talking about possible speech about possibility. The reflective method gives himself a refutation. He escapes from the possible only by the recognition of possibility.

That being the case, the conception of Being must include the conception of possibility. The question about the Third Conception of Being is one of the range of the concept of possibility. In this view, you assert that the real is to be defined in terms of what is true about it. The being of the mute inglorious Milton consisted in the truth that that villager might have written great poems. Again, while this man never was a Cromwell, he might have been if the conditions in the village had given him the opportunity. That constitutes his being.

When we recommend a man because of his capacities, we recommend him for the being of those possibilities, which consists in the truth of the proposition that he possesses them. The very being of an automobile or a man, of a physical object or a mental object, the very being of any fact has to be defined as consisting in the truth of certain propositions. You have to define everything that you can define at all, at least in terms of the Third Conception of Being.

In what sense is it a fact that this is a book with pages? In some sense that you can test; if you open it, you see the pages. The truth of that proposition is in question before you open the book. Nobody has illustrated the fact that you actually use this account of Being better than Russell, although he tries to escape it.[CA] His whole discussion of the reality of the physical world has consisted in the assertion that the physical world consists of sensible objects, *sensibilia* (vs. present sense–impressions). *Sensibilia* illustrate this third conception.

Possibility in Mill and in His *Examination of Hamiliton*

The eleventh chapter of Mill's *Examination of Sir William Hamilton's Philosophy*, entitled "The Psychological Theory of the Belief in an External World," presents an analysis of the external world as a realm of possible experiences. The being of the external world is made to consist in the truth of certain propositions.

May 13 Idealism is not the assertion that the world is merely inside the mind. The world is itself a world of fact—the question being what the idea of fact turns out to mean.

Professor Perry, in his discussion of the egocentric predicament, criticizes the supposed views of idealists. For Professor Perry the egocentric predicament constitutes a certain situation for anybody who thinks. This situation is one in which one's self must be regarded as an essentially present and inevitable feature of the world whereof he has knowledge. Professor Perry's argument in favor of a realistic view of reality depends upon the doctrine that although indeed the self-conscious activities of the being who thinks about this world are necessary for him, they don't throw any light on the nature of the world. If the world is always known as the world that is known, we don't find out what the world is by that.

What I want to point out at this stage is that one who has occasion to view the world according to the Third Conception of Being is aware that he counts for little in the world which he is talking about.

Sir William Hamilton, a Scottish philosopher, a prominent professor in the University of Edinburgh, after a long and effective experience as a teacher, died leaving the reputation that his philosophy was the most finished expression of the realistic views of the Scottish school. He went back to Reid and Stewart, opposed Hume and the empiricists, insisted on the Scottish category of the first and fundamental convictions as those which throw light on the nature of things. He was a very learned scholar, and it was well thought that his work would prove very important from the scholarly side. At the time when John Stuart Mill wrote the *Examination*, the effort was {in the} making to collect the records of Sir William's scholarship. His lectures in metaphysics, which were also lectures in psychology, were published; so, too, his lectures in logic. Hamilton, though not a mere follower of tradition, was on the whole prevailingly orthodox, and his work remained for a good while the standard for the more conservative philosophers. The former Alford Professor, Professor Francis Bowen, published a book in which he largely set forth the opinions of Hamilton.[15] Another follower of Hamilton's lead was Professor McCosh, afterward president of Princeton, a man somewhat genially amusing to his students, as well as authoritative, quaint, impressive to his community, a leader of Princeton opinion, a man of rugged quality and somewhat stern judgment, but a man of whom President Stanley Hall said his was a very beneficent personality. You can say of all the Scottish school leaders that they were beneficent personalities.

Mill himself was a follower of Berkeley and Hume, a critical empiricist, very fond of a tendency toward a perceptual theory both of knowledge and of Being, the man to whom, by a reminiscent hypothesis, James dedicated his book on pragmatism, as the man "whom my fancy likes to picture as our leader were he alive today."[16] James thus characterized Mill in terms of certain possibilities. Here you have a pragmatist's use of the Third Conception of Being for the purposes of setting forth his own view about the significance of Mill's thinking. For James also unquestionably during the middle period of his life, the Third Conception was prominent, and there is a good deal of that in *Pragmatism*.

Whenever one says that the truth of propositions is tested by their workings, one refers to the actual workings of the proposition as one considers them. In James's case the problem is the connection between the verification of hypotheses that you actually make and your belief about the truths of hypotheses when they are not actually verified. The logical problem is as to how far the truth of hypotheses exists and can be characterized at the times when they are not tested. One would have to say, "Of course, if we declare that we are dealing with true hypotheses when we estimate them in terms of a concrete working, we mean not merely what happens but what would happen if certain things were taken into account." Thus, the Third Conception enters into James's account in a way that leaves the whole matter of truth somewhat ambiguous.

Bergson's business examples about credit well illustrate the same kind of difficulty; for most of the entities of the commercial world are, as usually conceived, entities of the third kind, since it does not require the testing of some of these hypotheses to make sure that these hypotheses are true. The statement on the Treasury note with regard to what one who presents the note at the Treasury can get if he insists is true, but the truth is somehow superior to the truth which you can test by going to the Treasury and asking for your dollar. The truth is "as if" you went there and asked for it.

Now Mill, in the eleventh chapter of his *Examination of Sir William Hamilton's Philosophy,* undertakes to deal with the metaphysical problem which he announces in this way:

> *We have seen Sir W. Hamilton at work on the question of the reality of Matter, by the introspective method, and, as it seems, with little result. Let us now approach the same subject by the psychological.*

[Here Royce read considerable passages of the chapter, and interspersed the reading with the following comments.]

(190:4) {Ch. XI:} *The Psychological Theory of the Belief in an External World.*[17] The theory of our knowledge of the external world is the special problem that Mill attacks, and the sense in which matter is real.

(190:20) {Hamilton's theory postulates, first, that} . . . *after having had actual sensations, we are capable of forming the conception of Possible sensations.* Consider those facts in the light of the psychological views dear to the associationist school in its old form with regard to the association of ideas, and you then have a view which Mill sets forth. What Mill himself accepts is this: Our views about what we may call the possible experiences are dependent on what we may call associations, developed when we form our habits.

(191:13) . . . *no subsequent experience or process of thought can possibly avail to dissolve it {the association}.* Your association of fire with the burning sensation is such an inseparable association.

(191:28) . . . *things which we are unable to conceive apart, appear incapable of existing apart; and the belief we have in their coexistence, though really a product of experience, seems intuitive.* Such beliefs are the product of experience, but may come to seem to us intuitive. Mill goes {on} to lay emphasis upon the theory of vision, on which Berkeley had insisted.

(193:1) *I no longer have the sensations which it* {the paper I left on the table in the other room} gave me; but I believe that when . . . I go again into the room, I shall again have them. I believed I should have these sensations again, because of certain associations of my experience in my memory. That is why Mill calls this a psychological theory of the external world.

(196:24) *We find other people ground their expectations and conduct upon the same permanent possibilities on which we ground ours.* The whole thing tends to complicate itself. One possibility of sensation can be bound up with some other possibility of a very different nature. The social element comes in, though Mill himself doesn't analyze the basis of social consciousness at all.

(197:4) *The world of Possible Sensations succeeding one another according to laws, is as much in other beings as it is in me; it has therefore an existence outside me; it is an External World.* These possibilities have a basis in the laws of the sequence of experience, which remain unvaried even though my experiences change; these laws hold for various people. Mill has found a "psychological reason" for believing that there is an external world. Matter may be defined as "a permanent possibility of sensation" (198:1). Mill doesn't suppose that Berkeley regarded the world as merely in your mind when he said that everything in heaven or earth is an idea.

(198:7) *We are warranted in believing that this is the meaning of Matter in the minds of many of its most esteemed metaphysical champions, though they themselves would not admit as much: for example, of Reid, Steward, and Brown.* Mill tries to point out that the principal members of the Scottish school were always attempting to define matter in terms of permanent possibilities of sensation.

(200:11) *We may infer, therefore, that both philosophers and the world at large, when they think of matter, conceive it really as a Permanent Possibility of Sensation.* Why then should one be a realist and suppose that if you abstracted from knowledge entirely you would define what the world is?

In the subsequent chapter, Mill discusses how this view can form part of the ordinary notion of the material world, without its becoming incomprehensible that we shouldn't notice this to be our actual view.

Mill defines the mind of anybody as "the permanent possibility of feeling."

An Aside on Obscurity in Philosophy

{Here Royce injected the reading of a humorous message.}[18] No such trace of the humor of Heine can be found in the expressions of Germany at the present time. In a way, Heine has been cast out by the modern sentiment, and he has been especially rejected by the official and military party; and, efforts have been made for a generation to keep him out of the life of the people. There is in this something also of the type of a Mephistophelian humor: the flame that plays about everything is negative and destructive, with indications of something deeper. *May 16*

Some of the national influence of philosophers, as representatives of their peoples, has repeatedly been due to their obscurity, the essential depth, and also difficulty of their enterprise, which for them made the perfectly simple self-expression something hoped for rather than attained. Heraclitus, the obscure, is great because of his obscurity. So of Emerson; but here the two qualities went together. James Russell Lowell expressed this by saying of him, "He sits in a mystery calm and intense, and looks all around him with clear common sense.[19] You couldn't take the mysterious quality out of Emerson by asking him to write clearly. His world had to be expressed in ways that were in some respects mystical. Hence Emerson is not merely a puzzling man, but also a constructive and perfectly representative thinker of his nation.[CA]

It is also true that that union of qualities plays its part about what has been most effective about German philosophy, although, of course, you can have a man that stands for the greatness of his nation without having it. The quality about Kant that made him a European influence is not merely due to his technical obscurity but to the fact that the sort of reflection that was central in Kant depended on something that simply could not have been expressed with clearness. This is not {to say} that obscurity is a proof of greatness, but that the process of interpretation—either of one's self or of that with which one is dealing (one's nation)—depends on something that involves sympathetic appreciation. The best expression of Schelling's and Hegel's genius, in the fragments long preserved in the archives of Berlin, stand not merely for the barbarous style but for a genuine depth of appreciation. Your thinking should be an endless fight against whatever it is that keeps you obscure; but the place of obscurity is not ill-stated in these wayward words: "Light the touches but really deep the thought."

To know how to select significant and amusing aspects of things is to bring out an aspect of the world which is a perfectly genuine one. The world isn't merely serious, it isn't merely tragic. It is a world whose very mystery lies in the fact that tragedy is so near to the comic, and the most frightful aspects of the world are those that also are associated with the inspiring and the joyous. Amusement has its metaphysical place, and whatever conception of Being we have, I think it is right to say that whatever else the world also is (and it is a grave and tragic world), it is also a world in which humor has its place as revealing that it is amongst other things a funny world. That is why in the greatest dramatic art Aeschylus and Sophocles are historically so near to Aristophanes, and why the greatest contributions of the Greek mind had that union which is so noticeable in the Shakespearean clown. In Shakespeare the close connection between the humorous and the terrible appears throughout, sometimes explicitly, as in the case of Hamlet.

We so often think of the amusing side as merely the relief; but there is in humor the enlightening element also that suggests something. Heine has been one of the representatives of the deepest in German thinking, simply because of that which he so often expressed in the scornful shape. In his lyrics you have side by side the ridiculous and the romantic in a union which is in his own case fearfully tragic but also very enlightening. Unless you appreciate his scorn, you don't appreciate some of the deepest of the features of the great German poetry.

Goethe had some of that quality. On the whole, however, Goethe's later years were somewhat burdened by his enormous responsibilities. James found him a good deal of a pedant, an intellectualist; he had comparatively little of the genuine mystic about him.

You can't tell that a man is destined to be a great man merely because he can make a good joke; but if he does something that reminds you of Heine or Mephistopheles, he has an insight that a philosopher may well envy. This, like the poetic power, is born, not made.

Glancing at Various Members of the Philosophical Community

We were discussing how in terms of the Third Conception of Being you can deal with the physical world {by relying on possibilities}. [Here Royce began reading and commenting on passages from *The World and the Individual*, 1: 204–206.][20]

(204:28) *But you all know a class of persons whom I may as well call, at once, the Critical Rationalists of our own time.* In the newer realistic movement, this Third Conception has come to much fuller expression. It is perfectly true today that many who speak in terms of this Third Conception do not regard themselves as realists. A good example of that position is to be found in Karl Pearson's *Grammar of Science.*[21] The author has always regarded himself as a subjectivist philosopher. His world consists in sense–impressions. He regards himself as a pure empiricist and is especially anxious to get rid of any realistic statement of the case. But when he goes on to state the characteristics of his world, it turns out that he is using what I here call the Third Conception of Being.

(205:13) *In theology they condemn theoretical construction, and if they are positively disposed, prefer a reasonable and chastened moral faith.* A very good example is Russell's *Scientific Method in Philosophy*, which is through and through an expression of the Third Conception of Being. What is said here of theologians applies especially to those whose theology is mainly an ethical doctrine.

(205:19) *As such a realm of impersonal truth they conceive perhaps the moral law, perhaps the realm of natural law revealed to us by science, . . .* The "moral law" is very easily statable in those terms: its reality consists in the truth of the propositions about it.

(205:21) *. . . perhaps the lawful structure of that social order which is now so favorite a topic of study.* The "social order," from that point of view, would have the being of validity.

(205:22) *Their spiritual father is Kant, . . .* I suppose that that historically is somewhat too overemphasized a statement: but Kant's world in *The Critique of Pure Reason* is a world which he deliberately likes to call the world of Possible Experience. According to Kant, if there are inhabitants on the moon, that means that in the progress of possible experience we could find them. The whole physical world is given that character; light consists of lightwaves, if possible experience would show you that kind of things. So of Kant's hypothesis, in the early thirties of his life, of the origin of the heavens, which related not to any things-in-themselves but to possible experiences. The reality of it was entirely of the third kind; it was what in the progress of possible experience we should find, though here an experience that literally antedates our own. Kant was much interested in the Newtonian *Principia.*

(206:12) Von Hartmann, in his *Philosophy of the Unconscious,*[22] (1860) used the Unconscious, taken as a principle, for explaining mental life. His world is the product of a being called the Unconscious. Fichte, at an important point in his own development, published a paper in which he maintained that by "God" one means solely the moral order of the universe. Ultimately this cost him his professorship at Jena.

(206:17) *One no longer proves that God exists, but only that,* **It is as if he were.** Vaihinger, a man of considerable capacity, whom I had the privilege of seeing at Leipzig in the winter of 1875–6, long a student of Kant and an analytic philosopher, recently published an interesting book, *Die Philosophie des Als Ob* (*The Philosophy of "As If"*),[23] in which he maintains that most of our philosophical constructions are constructions to which you can attribute only that reality, that it is "as if" from a certain point of view something were so.[24] This is a concept of virtual Being, as-if Being. Vaihinger would hold quite deliberately to the Third Conception of Being. He had those ideas in 1875–6, but held them a long time before they were published.

(206:31) . . . *in this age of critical rationalism, and of a cool respect for truths which do everything but take on the form of individual life.* Of all the quite recent thinkers, Russell has, I suppose, most definitely expressed himself in these terms. For polemical reasons and because of his own way of taking the idealists, Russell regards himself as at another extreme. Those who have followed him have thought of his view as essentailly realistic, and so it is in a way; but realism of the sort represented by Herbart or Leibnitz is not the sort of the Third Conception. This view {of Russell's} is intermediate between these two views which[CA] define it wholly in extramental terms, which was the great feature of the realism which regards itself as the characteristic realism.

Historically speaking, there are at least two motives which have played their part in the development of the New Realism: first, this Third Conception, with interesting relations to idealism; secondly, the antiidealistic attitude. At this moment, polemical considerations have exaggerated the tendency to the antiidealistic movement in realism. I wish the whole matter were reviewed in the light of the Third Conception by the new realists.

Santayana's notion of the world of the essences is closely related in some respects to the Third Conception of Being. But these thinkers who speak of the virtual entities are not all of them to be satisfied by Santayana's account. Russell's own realism is intended to involve not an idealistic motive but a motive that isn't completely satisfied by the account that Santayana gives us of the essences. It is hard for Santayana to make clear the difference between the essence when it does exist and when it doesn't exist. The divine ideas in advance of creation—there is little to be said about them, except that there are truths about them. Spinoza's "Virtue is Blessedness" is a concept of this sort.

Credits, prices, rates, and other quasi-social entities are very important for the problem of Being. In what sense is that which is expressed by the credit of a bank a commercial reality?[CA] Is it so in any sense but that the proposition is true that, if you present to the bank certain evidences of value, they will be paid? Is the being of the bank's credit merely a realistic being? The classic remark of the customer of a bank on a day of panic suggests to you a deep metaphysical problem. In General Sherman's memoirs he tells how a terrified customer came to his bank in San Francisco and asked for his money. The bank, confident of its power, handed it out to him. But he wanted a safe place for his money: "If you have got it, I don't want it; but if you haven't got it, I want it very badly." How true it is that the entity called the solvency of the bank is from the point of view of the depositor an entity that he defines in terms of the truth of certain propositions!

[To questions from the class Royce replied]: Relations and the objects related are interrelated; and you very often define relations in terms of their relations to other relations, and also in terms of the laws that govern the things. Equality is a transitive and symmetrical relation of objects; the situation is such that one considers that A = B if A = C and B = C. Equality is a relation such that every object in your world of universal discourse about equality stands in the relation of being equal to itself, while every triad of entities in that world is subject to the law just stated. *May 18*

Russell insists upon it that we have just as definite a knowledge of relations as we have of the things related. Relations are entities peculiarly apt to illustrate to your mind that the characters so often in question are characters that have to be defined in terms of the Third Conception. There is little opposition between any realism that you make at all complete and the Third Conception of Being. Practically, your realism in dealing with things is a realism of the third sort. You express yourself not in terms of real independence of all ideas, but in terms of a certain law to which these are subject when you consider that they are true. On the whole, realism inevitably leads you to the Third Conception, that the Being of these things consists in the truth of these judgments and assertions.

This can be illustrated not merely from the physical and the mathematical world, but from the social world, as in the case of the frightened depositor. Commercial values have come to take the form of a value of confidence; we are dealing in entities that are possibilities of experience—possibilities of payment. In vain you say that the truth of the proposition is its cash value; you don't get the whole truth in that way. The values are defined in virtual or deferred terms; it isn't the cash value of ideas that you want. That, if we could return to it, would be the situation of simple sense; and sense–perception without limit would be mystical fulfillment. We know something about mysticism. The thinking of the sciences, of the various systems of philosophy, is not thinking merely in terms of the virtual. The purely virtual Being is too abstract. You don't want to know the merely "as if": You want to know the facts. Facts, for Bergson and the mystics, are expressed in terms of perception. You want to know the perception that ends the affair. "Give me this water, that I thirst not, neither come hither to draw" (John 4:15). But one doesn't view the fulfillment merely as a virtual entity in that case. One deals with what is essentially a mysterious matter; one has to define that fulfillment of experience in entirely mystical terms. No one intends to utter the unutterable, or to define or express the inexpressible. That cash isn't what we are seeking.

Equally little, however, are we concerned with the merely virtual truth that if we were to drink the living water, then we will not thirst. We are just as little, once more, content with regarding our reality as merely virtual reality. "Leave out your 'as ifs'; tell me what <u>is</u>." {Accordingly, the metaphysical quest leads to an interpretation of Being that is fully determinate.}

Chapter 9

The Fourth Conception of Being: Idealism

The experience that I get if I get it dissatisfies because it is a particular experience; that isn't the whole of what I want. One must go beyond. I have never found Being at any moment. It is the essence of Being that it is always the object of a quest. I never find it; I am always in that position that I am profoundly dissatisfied with the experiments upon what it is to Be that I make. They are all particular and special. What I want is Life, the whole of Life, not defined in terms of virtual entities, not defined in terms of sense–presence in experience, but Wholeness in some other sense. *May 18 cont.*

To put the matter in that way is to give you the very essence of the spirit of idealism. What you seek is the interpretation of life. That is real which deals with just these problems—the life of the spirit, the life of unity, the essentially supertemporal life. You are looking for an experience which no moment of time can contain—the chronosynoptic experience. You define that just so far as you define Being in any sense.

Unquestionably, the concept of virtual entities is a concept through which we must pass on the way to any metaphysical fulfillment. It matters little whether one says that that is a scientific concept due to a reaction of scientifically trained minds against the vagueness of the idealists, or whether one expresses it in terms of the process of interpretation. The polemical side of the discussion throughout *The World and the Individual* is only important so far as it sets forth the inadequacies of the various conceptions in terms of which we approach our idea of what it is to Be. Our polemics merely acquaint us with the situation. The kind of interest is one which, of course, involves an interest in immediate experience. But that is an interest which is never complete, always dissatisfied. You are dissatisfied with the best that experience can give you. So far as it is a temporal experience of a human being—whether you are considering what is delightful or scientifically enlightening about it—considered from the point of view of worth, it leaves you always discontent. [Here Royce quoted Browning]:[1]

Meeting at Night

I.

The gray sea and the long black land;
And the yellow half-moon large and low;
And the startled little waves that leap
In fiery ringlets from their sleep,
As I gain the cove with pushing prow,
And quench its speed i' the slushy sand.

II.

Then a mile of warm sea-scented beach;
three fields to cross till a farm appears;
a tap at the pane, the quick sharp scratch
And blue spurt of a lighted match,
And a voice less loud, through its joys and fears,
Than the two hearts beating each to each!

Parting at Morning

Round the cape of a sudden came the sea,
And the sun looked over the mountain's rim;
And straight was the path of gold for him,
And the need of a world of men for me.

The experience teasingly and fascinatingly calls for something which if you could get it would be the Being, the Reality. That would be the soul, that would be I, that would be the world. Experience gives you this in a form which is both theoretically and practically insufficient, unsatisfying to the desire for Being.

The knowledge of that fact takes numerous forms—religious ascetism, scientific caution. Part of what you learn from experience is the lesson of the insufficiency of experience. The attitude is the theoretical expression of the same sort of thing that Browning's lover expresses on the practical side. "The world of reality is indeed a world of experience, but no general qualifications can be given to it." The classical expression of this position is found in the final form of James's pragmatism.[CA] You must be pluralistic; you never get the whole of experience which you are looking for; there is no solution, nothing to say, no advice to give—go on, search!—a courageous but dissatisfied view. The man who utters it does give advice whenever he undertakes any social enterprise; he is engaged in a quest for somewhat which he cannot define in terms of the mere not finding of it.

One may declare that this world of the realities is best comprehended by saying that this quest is merely the restless search; the "scientific method" is productive but never final. Russell lays stress on the character of the virtual entities, the character which is illustrated everywhere in experience. You are seeking as well as you can inductively, and never with satisfactory results, for principles which guide your science and your art so far as you possess them. You are seeking not what you define as satisfaction but as growing comprehension of the virtual realities of the totality of possible experiences. In terms of this, you can define your somewhat.

Hereupon, your attention[CA] is once more attracted to matters that bring you back from these tentative efforts to regard these problems as insoluble to the positively metaphysical aspect of your undertaking. Despite the fact that you never find the beloved from whom the parting at morning is not the expression of a need for the world of man, your life is determined by its metaphysical effort to define the real quest. The real quest cannot be defined in merely mystical terms as the ineffable satisfaction. Nor can it be defined in terms of the virtual entities. That can't be the true what of things, for that what would never have a determinate character. Your universal laws that would take the place of facts would stand in this endlessly ambiguous position: Are they genuine laws? Then they are based on facts which if stated could be stated not in if propositions merely.

These considerations force us from the Third to the Fourth Consideration of Being. Metaphysics turns not on a perception of the real, nor on a conception of the real, but on an interpretation of the real. This interpretation is ruled by the general thesis that the world contains its own interpreter {and} that while no moment of experience, no deed, is satisfactory, and the final is nowhere faced, and while there never is the final advice to be given, we still can declare that the nature of the complete interpretation is definable in terms which the reflective method can frame. The issue that you are asked to consider is the consideration as to how far the nature of this ultimate interpretation can be defined and defended.[2]

The importance of having stated in some rather inclusive way all the metaphysical problems is to show you that when you can't get your metaphysical solution in perceptual terms, you can tend toward that solution in conceptual terms by viewing the realm of reality as a realm definable in terms of the "as if," in terms of the truth of certain propositions. When you have stated the case in that way, you know where the real puzzle of Being is: you never quite get the whole situation before you. What facts make the true proposition true? Such facts seem to be defined by a vicious circle that leads nowhere.

The commercial and social worlds illustrate the fact that we do so define many aspects of Being. The credit of a commercial firm or the fact which is represented by the standing—social or professional—of a man, are facts of the "as if" character. You can't express it in mystical or pragmatic terms. If you say, as Bergson said, that the concept is true because it can be perceptually cashed, the answer is that the cashing never gives you the cash for all that the concept expresses. The situation always involves something which leads you beyond fact to truth.

That the definition in terms of truth, the definition which makes the Being of things consist in the truth of certain propositions is actually used, is easily illustrated. It is suggested to you strongly when you turn away from the mystical point of view as unsatisfactory. But if you are asked in what consists the truth of a proposition, you can only say that facts show it to be true.

The banking business depends on an opinion about truth. The truth is one that seems to be statable in purely pragmatic terms; but no pragmatic terms are ever sufficient to express it. When the bank is solvent, you have the pragmatic facts that are represented if you look on as the depositors present their evidences of value. But this never adequately expresses the actual situation. The credit of a bank depends on a fact that has to be expressed in terms of an if proposition. Everybody has to admit that an easy hypothetical variation of the normal circumstances would result in making the proposition false. The bank is solvent when it can pay its depositors on demand that which they have deposited with it. But all one's view about the nature of solvency is based on the fact that the bank cannot possibly pay its depositors all that it owes them on demand. The banking business can only be done in case the money put on deposit is used in temporary loans. This temporary use temporarily deprives the depositor of the use that he had of the money. Banking depends on public confidence. Is that confidence a confidence in facts? The independent realistic facts are that the depositors have parted with their money. The paying of it back depends upon conditions which never can be turned wholly into fact.

In 1893[3] everybody knew that if everybody in the United States demanded gold for his notes, the United States couldn't give it to them. The president of the United States tried to borrow from Morgan & Co. large sums of gold which could be used to meet the possible calls. Here was an institution which depended on assuming "facts" that were known not to be facts.

The values upon which the commercial world depends are values which depend upon the truth of certain propositions that under certain conditions are not true, but yet one has to treat them as if they were true. Suppose you find the propositions aren't true: what becomes of the Being of the things under the Third Conception? That is the experience you get in times of panic—valuable for chastening the soul and for throwing a light on certain metaphysical conceptions.

May 20 The fundamental argument for the Fourth Conception of Being rests on the stages of the recent discussion of the Third Conception of Being. The idealist's result may of course be a misinterpretation, but it is then a misinterpretation of a situation which he has been trying to define as a situation not determined merely by anything that belongs to his private person or individual nature. It is a world of fact that he has been trying to tell about. He has been guided by the fact that he wants to find out about the objective nature of things, what he means by fact, and that he is consequently indeed inevitably concerned with a meaning, the expression of that which an idea can express.

The thing that determines his point of view is not the somewhat trivial observation upon which Professor Perry's discussion of the egocentric predicament supposes him to base his opinion, viz., that the I, the entity who thinks these things, is indeed, from his own point of view, at the center of his own world. On the contrary, the idealist's effort is an effort to define the sense in which he is not at the center of his own world, but logically dependent on and engaged in the expression of the facts themselves of that world. The stages of his argument do not depend on saying, "Since I must always think of myself at the center of my own world, perhaps this is objectively true and I am at the center of my own world. Since I must always see my world visually centered about the center of my own nose, perhaps my nose has a unique place in my world."

The point of view of the idealist depends not on that but on the very effort to ignore the decidedly trivial question, "Where is my nose?" It depends on the effort to abstract from the nose and from the process of vision and the idea of the individual from whatever belongs to a person, and to find out what the facts are, not of course in simple independence of one another and the knowing process, for such independence would be meaningless.

The whole discussion depends on the effort to find out the sense in which I am the acknowledger of a world, not only in some wise external to myself but a world whose nature is such that the whole purpose of my undertaking is that I should conform to its ways. I am endeavoring to find out what this world is, which is to be defined as that which doesn't depend on my existence or my senses.[CA]

The negative part of our argument, emphasized by our discussion of Santayana and illustrated by our discussion of the Third Conception of Being, has depended not upon an effort to smuggle in the individual Ego as somewhat without which the world would not be thought of, but has depended upon endeavoring to find out what you are talking about as independent of you.

Without for the moment insisting upon the argument about independence, let us insist that the world of fact is certainly in some sense independent of us, for what we want to know, when we undertake to know, is precisely that which is independent of us. Our arguments, guided by Santayana's discussion of the realm of existence as opposed to the realm of essence, and guided by the Third Conception, have been devoted to finding out the sense in which the world can be independent of us.

The whole intention with which we approach our idealism is the intention <u>to be as realistic as we can</u>. Define the nature of fact in such wise as to take as little account as you can of whatever belongs to your own nature, your own interests, your own reason. Still a feature remains about the world which has to be recognized, and has to be recognized even in order to be realistic. The aspect of the world in question is an extremely instructive one. After all, for a reasonable realist, the real world that is independent of him must be independent of him in some sense in which he has reason to believe that it is independent of him. If the real world is a real world, it must be a real world such that it must be reasonable for him to hold that this world is real.

A Russell or any other realist lays stress on the fact that the unreasonable view is insofar not the view to be accepted, that the requirement of being reasonable is a requirement which throws light on whether or not a given account of the world is the objectively true account.

Everybody recognizes this who uses the principle of contradiction. The absurd and selfcontradictory cannot be real or is not real. Whoever says that says it on the ground of a consideration which surely isn't subjective or private, but on the ground that whoever asserts the presence of the self-contradictory entity, the reality in the real world of the triangle that isn't a triangle, stands explicitly in the position which the reflective method has set before us as a position which cannot be characteristic of reality. It is indeed the case that in acknowledging a real world, I recognize something reasonable in this sense, that in case I declare that something called the principle of contradiction is proper to that world, I make an assertion such that if I deny it I reassert it.

The principle of contradiction cannot be used to discover which of two alternatives is the one that reality requires. The grounds, the "evidence" for existence[4] which indeed will guide one who accepts evidence that somewhat exists, these grounds can't of course be reduced to this, that by mere reason I can prove not only that certain things do not exist, but that certain things do exist. By mere abstract reasonings I cannot find out what <u>is</u>, by using some limited system of ideas and deducing things out of my inner consciousness. That indeed one recognizes. But it still remains true that the world which one calls real is subject to the <u>principle of sufficient reason</u> in this sense, that when one declares that somewhat is, one declares that in case the proposition "This is" is a self-contradictory proposition, that proposition is not true; and in case the proposition "This is not" is self-contradictory, that implies that "This is." In case an existence is contradictory, that of course is a nonexistence. That whose nonexistence is self-contradictory exists. Abstract as this principle is, we use it constantly. In that sense our world always lies in touch with the world of our reason.

You must remember the two distinct ways in which we have come to the Fourth Conception of Being. The world of reality, the world that <u>is</u>, must include or possess as one of its aspects the characters of Santayana's realm of the essences, the characters possessed by the mathematical world, by the moral world, by the world of the Third Conception of Being. You are forced to consider those characters whenever you try to find out in what sense the world is independent of you. When you are trying to define the objective nature of things, you discover that whatever else you mean by fact, you mean an objective essence that has a character that has a curious relation to our thinking process. The universals rather than the individuals, the nature of things rather than the facts of sense—this realm is the real realm. About that there is already a feature which, however much you may insist upon it as realistic, is not exactly the realistic world of which a purely empirical acquaintance with things leads you to suppose the realm of reality composed.

Our idealism depends upon an admission of the considerations that Santayana has insisted upon. The realm of Being must in any case have at least the characters possessed by the realm of Santayana's essences. At the conclusion of the discussion of the Third Conception of Being, I have gradually shown how this conception, when developed, gives us more and more a conception that possesses an idealistic character.

{Secondly}, the reason why the realm of Santayana's essences and the realm of the Third Conception of Being do not wholly satisfy us is that we never can discover the individual nature of Being by considering things in that way. The realm of Santayana's essences leaves us in doubt as to what Being those essences have in advance of creation. What individually are they? What fact lies behind these general natures of things? When we state the nature of a possibility, we are led constantly to ask what lies behind it. That the credit or standing of a bank is something that you can express in general terms, I tried to show you. You can show that without the conception of valid possibilities you cannot get on in the ordinary world of experience.[CA] But it comes out more and more when you find yourself forced by involuntary considerations to define Fact in terms of Santayana's essences and the Third Conception of Being, you get forced upon you the question: What lies at the basis of this possibility? What lies at the basis of the essence which is here in question?

In *The World and the Individual*, at the close of the discussion of the Third Conception of Being, in the transition to the Fourth Conception of Being, I put the metaphysical question in this way:

> *To generalize, then, the problem so far furnished us by our Third Conception of Reality, we find this as our situation. Ask me how I discover, in a concrete case, the validity of my idea, how I make it out for certain that a certain experience is possible; and then I have to answer, "By actual experience alone." When I say then, "A given idea is certainly valid," I primarily mean merely, "A given idea is fulfilled in actual present experience." But if you ask me what I regard as the range of the realm of validity, and what I think to be the extent of possible experience, and of the truth of ideas, then I can only say that the*

> *range of valid possible experience is viewed by me as infinitely more extended than my actual human experience. From the mathematical point of view the realm of truth is in fact explicitly infinite. From the point of view of natural science and of common sense, the world of valid possible experience is not only far wider than our concrete human experience, but is interesting to us precisely because we can select from its wealth of possibilities those that we wish, as we say, to realize. Now what our Third Conception so far fails to explain to us is precisely the difference between the reality that is to be attributed to the valid truths that we do not get concretely verified in our experience, and the reality observed by us when we do verify ideas.*
>
> *In brief,* ***What is a valid or a determinately possible experience at the moment when it is supposed to be only possible?*** *What is a valid truth at the moment when nobody verifies its validity? When we ourselves find the possible experience, it is something living, definite,—yes, individual. When we ourselves verify a valid assertion, it is again something that plays a part in our individual process of living and observing. But when we speak of such truths as barely valid, as merely possible objects of experience, they appear once more as mere universals. Can these universals, not yet verified, consistently be regarded as possessing wholeness of Being?*[5]

When I am endeavoring to tell what one of these possibilities, one of these generals, is, I am obliged to turn to my concrete experience. If one says that, the only way is to test this by handing in one's check at the bank window and finding whether this cash is what one wants or not.

The Paradox of the Frightened Depositor

The problem of Being is determined by this situation, not by the egocentric predicament, but by the problems that determine the paradox of the frightened depositor. I want to test the objective validity of my bank's promise; I want to be sure that my deposit is safe. This is an objective somewhat. The solvency of a bank doesn't depend merely on the private interests of the depositor, but upon something which is determined by what will happen when he presents his call for payment. The real problem arises not when one considers the egocentric predicament that every call for cash is a selfish call but when one considers the paradox of the man who is repaid and then responds in the paradoxical way, "If you have it, I don't want it; it is only in case you have it not that I want it so much." That depositor at that moment faced the genuine metaphysical problem.

This paradox is again the paradox of the difference between the Third and the Fourth Conception of Being; or it is the paradox of the sense in which there is any difference between the nature of things and the existence of things; it is the paradox of the contrast between the essences and the existents, not of the sense in which the world is in my mind. It is the paradox about what it means to Be at all; and it is the paradox of the frightened depositor, not when he laid stress on the desire for his own cash, but when he found out his own difficulty and expressed his own disappointment when his money was returned to him.

The situation which forces our transition from the Third Conception of Being to the Fourth is a situation expressed in pages 258 ff. of the text.

> *And so, in sum, the ordinary world of possible experience has this twofold character. We prove that it is there by testing empirically, from moment to moment, the validity of our ideas about it; but our very belief in its Being means that we recognize its possession of far more validity than, in our private capacity, we shall ever test. It is thus with common sense, much as it was with mathematics. The mathematician finds his way in the eternal world by means of experiments upon the transient facts of the inner and ideal experience of this instant's contents. The student of science or the plain man of everyday life believes himself to be dealing with a realm of validity far transcending his personal experience. But his only means of testing any concrete assertion about that world comes to him through the very fragmentary observations of what happens in his inner life from instant to instant.*[6]

The what of the that, the essence of existence, the reality that is to be the genuinely real, must have the character of the valid possibility and also the character of that which we have at the moment; namely, the present experience. The present experience reveals to me the fleeting {and} hints to me that I am in touch with the reality over and above what is present. The transient shifting and flux of the colors of experience lights up now this, now that aspect of what itself belongs to the eternal realm of the essences.

My question is that without which the metaphysical problem can neither be faced nor solved: What is it that is valid and which can't be tested? One's cash? So he supposes until he gets it. But what one wants is the bank that can pay. All the universal interests of the depositor depend on that. The fact that I cash this check becomes trivial in view of the universal. Of course, I can possess cash in the sense that the bank clerk is patient enough to put up with me when I continually draw it out to see if it is there. Oddly enough, in a way that pragmatists should more carefully notice, it isn't cashing the check or drawing the deposit that is the object of the seeker for dealings with the genuinely solvent bank. Solvency consists not in the paying but in the capacity to pay. That which we talk of when we talk of solvency is not to be stated in merely individual or momentary terms.

We here face a paradox which we find when we approach the whole matter from the mystical side, in the situation that present experience cannot satisfy. So also a realm of merely valid possibilities would never satisfy us. We approach the same consideration when we point out that the truth of propositions doesn't consist merely in their workings, but in the situation that if tested they will work. The merely successful judgment doesn't show its genuine truth; but by its present workings it shows the valid possibility that under certain conditions it will work. That is the possibility in which any rational view of things is interested.

In this way the problem of Being is one that cannot be satisfied in terms of mere presence in experience. That is what the mystic had to test in his own way. He tested it negatively. You don't get the real merely by looking for what has the form of a presence in Being. Presence is always dissatisfying, just as the payment of cash gives the depositor anything but what he wants, dealings with a solvent bank, a desire which can be expressed only in universal terms. The relief of dissatisfaction is not satisfaction. The quenching of the thirst of the moment isn't what one wants: "Give me this water, that I thirst not, neither come hither to draw," just as it is not the mere quenching of thirst that the mystic wanted, but the thirsting nevermore. It isn't the content of experience that you want, as present content, but the nature of things, the law of physical nature, the solvency of the bank, the testing of the character of your friend, the stability of the order of society, the presence of the realm of social unity—that is the sort of thing that we are interested in. We are always defining our reality in terms that mere experience never cashes.

Yet if we try to express it in terms that simply ignore experience and say we are looking for the independently real, we have to express it in terms of the realm of validity, the realm of the credits, standings, laws, energies; we have to use the Third Conception. But as we pass through the world of the Third Conception, we discover that that world is dissatisfying. {Here Royce continued reading}:

> *Or again, we formerly criticized Realism and Mysticism alike because neither of them sufficiently took account of the fact that our ideas of Being and the Being of which we have ideas, must occupy essentially the same ontological position. If, as Realism has said, Being is real independently of ideas, we saw that then ideas are themselves realities independent of Being. And if, as Mysticism had said, ideas are unreal, we saw that the Absolute, which Mysticism undertook to seek, must be unreal in the same sense in which the ideas about it are*

> *unreal. Now the former criticism of Realism and of Mysticism must once more be applied to test the adequacy of our present conception. We must see whether validity means the same in our experience as it means when asserted of Being in general. Validity, so far as it has yet appeared in our account, is an ambiguous term. As applied to the ideas that we actually test, it means that they are concretely expressed in experience whenever we test them. As applied to the whole realm of valid truth in general, to the world of nature as not yet observed by us, or of mathematical truth not now present to us, it means that this realm somehow has a character that we still do* ***not*** *test, and that never gets exhaustively presented in our human experience. But what is this character?*[7]

We then make our whole metaphysical discussion depend, not on the egocentric predicament but on the predicament of the frightened depositor who will not be satisfied if the bank doesn't pay him or if it does pay him. He is dissatisfied with his own dissatisfaction; he comprehends that he was terrified by what he ought not to have been terrified about.

The realm of Being doesn't consist in the realm that is from moment to moment tested, for what we test is the truth of our ideas; but what is the truth of your ideas at the moment when you don't test them? Unless they have a truth which is beyond what you test, they aren't what you want them to be. There is no meaning in finding contents unless you find that meanings are, in universally statable ways, actually exemplified in your experience. Unless there is valid possibility, it isn't a realm of Being. The pragmatist's realm where the roasted pigeons fly into your mouth is the realm where you don't get the reality that you seek; for it is after all the realm of the pigeons that are to be obtained by some other methods than by opening your mouth that is a realm where even significant possibilities of eating can take place. The realm of Being has this character of never being exhausted by the mere present truth of ideas.

So it is well to remember that the whole problem turns, not on the reflection whether the whole world is in or out of my mind in the private sense, but upon the sense in which the world has that Being which gives it validity and secures to it the presence of essences, which gives presence to the realm of ideas.

> *Or, once more, in our concrete experience, the validity of an idea, once seen, tested, presented, gets what we then regard as an individual life and meaning, since it appears in our individual experience. But in the realm of Being in general this same validity appears universal, formal,—a mere general law. Now can this view be final? Can there be two sorts of Being, both known to us as valid, but the one in-*

> *dividual, the other universal, the one empirical, the other merely ideal, the one present, the other barely possible, the one a concrete life, the other a pure form? Is not the world real in the same general sense in which our life in the world is real? Can Critical Rationalism escape the test already applied to its rivals? And if the test is applied, must not all Being prove to be pulsating with the same life of concrete experience?*
>
> *We shall see. History shows that the rigid world of Platonic Ideas, when viewed by later speculation, began erelong to glow, like sunset clouds, with the light of the Divine presence; and Neo-Platonism already called the Ideas the thoughts of God. Shall there be possible experience in the realm of validity, and the Lord hath not known its meaning?*
>
> *This is at present a mere query. Upon the rational answer to this query depends our whole religious philosophy.*[8]

The frightened depositor, who is not disappointed in his own disappointment, discovers the illusion of his own illusory fear; he has learned a lesson, has had an experience. The one who tests nature to find out whether its laws are true, has found out more than the test itself shows.

May 23 I do not myself view the argument of *The World and the Individual* as one that depends on setting up four different conceptions of Being, pointing out that three of them fail, and declaring that the fourth of them alone is left. On the contrary, the whole argument of the book is contained in the seventh lecture,[9] if you presuppose enough of the previous discussion to understand what is at issue.

The Relation of Reality and Truth

Our conception of what it is to be real is inclusive of what it is to be true. It is the case that the Being of the world consists in the truth of certain statements about the world. Neither in terms of immediate experience, nor as the merely perceptual doctrine of reality would have it, nor yet in terms of the essences with some mysterious contrast between existence and non-existence, neither in terms of one nor the other of these ways of stating the case, can we deal fairly with Being.

The question of metaphysics is the question of the sense in which statements are true. These may be statements about past or future time, about possibilities that you don't regard as actually exemplified, statements about Santayana's realm of essences or the realm of existence, but in their truth consists whatever Being the universe possesses. The whole problem of Being is the problem of Truth.

In the case of truth you have, of course, a character that belongs to ideas, ideas that take the form of leadings that can be practically expressed. An idea is a partial expression of a purpose; and it is true or not in case it agrees or not with its object, that of which it pretends to be the portrayal or the expression. {Here Royce began reading and commenting on lecture seven of *The World and the Individual*, starting with p. 318}:

> (381: 2–15)[CA] *Just as truly as the sort of correspondence by which an idea is to be judged is predetermined by the internal meaning of the idea, just so truly is the internal meaning of the idea also to be consulted regarding the intended selection of the object. If I have meant to make an assertion about Caesar, you must not call me to account because my statement does not correspond, in the intended way, with the object called Napoleon. If I have meant to say that space has three dimensions, you cannot refute me by pointing out that time has only one. And nowhere, without a due examination of the internal meaning of my ideas, can you learn whether it was the object Caesar or the object Napoleon, whether it was space or time, that I meant.*

The question is the relation of object and idea, which constitutes the truth of the idea. This study of the matter is not at all subject to the kind of consideration upon which Professor Perry's discussion of the egocentric predicament rests; for here we are dealing with a Being which consists in the truth of certain ideas. We therefore define the ideas that are in question. The ideas that can be true are the ideas that somehow select their object. So now indeed we deal with the mental—not that we say the real is in the mind of somebody, but that if the object is not selected, the idea is neither true nor false.

(319:13–17) *For if it* {the idea} *means to be true, it intends a sort of correspondence with an object. What correspondence it intends is determined, as we saw, soley by the purpose which the idea embodies, i.e. by the internal meaning of the idea.* That is the inevitably idealistic aspect of your view about Being. You may endeavor to abstract from the mind and talk about facts, but you can't abstract from the fact that if your account of Being is that which is intended at all, it is an account that defines itself in terms of the truth of certain ideas. That mental feature belongs to your world. It isn't a question of whether the world consists in ideas in your head. The Being of your world consists in the truth of ideas, and that mental character your world has to keep.

(319:23–25) *Nobody else can determine for me what object I mean by my idea.* Here I rebel against the realist. We may say it is my business to conform to the world as it is, quite apart from me. In vain does he try to say that it is, or should be my intention that my idea should be true of some object of which I do not mean my idea to be true. In that sense your world is your own world; it is the world that you are talking about.

(320:7–8) *Here, then, is the central dilemma as to the nature of truth.* The whole fate of the idealistic doctrine depends on this matter, the central dilemma as to the nature of truth.

(320:22–23) {Concerning the two relations of an idea}: *The one is the relation that constitutes it the object meant by the idea.* This is the aspect of ideas that has been neglected by both realists and idealists—the relation that constitutes an object, the object meant by an idea.

(322:11–12) *The idea is selective. It seeks its own.* That holds whether you are talking about God or man, a fact of experience or the general nature of reality.

(322:28–30) *I ask what reason you can have to say that the object is the object of the idea, unless you observe somehow that the idea chooses for itself this object.* All this I should insist upon expressly in answer to Russell's discussion about Desdemona and Cassio and the deceived Othello. It makes no difference how complex you make the situation; the Desdemona whose love for Cassio counts is Othello's Desdemona, the Desdemona of his own idea.

(323:14–15) *And so much may suffice for our thesis.* The thesis of the dilemma is: All our ideas, so far as they call themselves true, are true.

(326:8–11) *The vaster the world that he* {the apparently submissive observer} *then defines as the overwhelming fate of his intelligence, the larger will be the part that his own consciously constructive will has taken in the definition of the idea.* This is a question of the sense in which the real is real, that is, of the sense in which your ideas are true.

(327:19–21) *When I have an idea of the world, my idea is a will,* ***and the world of my idea is simply my own will itself determinately embodied.*** I am always dealing with what I haven't now in my hands. This is a voluntaristic account of the realm of Being, and it also involves interpretation.

(329:4–7) ***In seeking its object, any idea whatever seeks absolutely nothing but its own explicit, and, in the end, complete, determination as this conscious purpose, embodied in this one way.*** Here you have in miniature the whole metaphysical situation.

(329:31–330:2) . . . *he may attempt to define this Other by a conjectural or hypothetical construction . . .* The hypothesis may itself turn out to be false, i.e., contrary to its own intent.

(331:21–23) ***Whatever the object, it is still the object for a given idea solely because that idea wills it to be such.*** That is the eternally idealistic feature of your world. The more of a realist you are, the more that is true. Whenever I listen to a realist, I say, "Here is a man insisting that the world conform to his attitude."

(333:13–15) *The idea in seeking for its object is seeking for the determination of its own just now consciously indeterminate will.* There is nothing that a realist can insist upon about the fact–character of the world that our conception does not presuppose. You fulfill your will by giving yourself over to a quest, abandoning your self-centered separation.

(335:16–19) *I do not will just now to fly, because my purpose in conceiving nature is now relatively fulfilled in a system of ideas which excludes my possession of the power to fly.* The realistic world, in which we couldn't fly at the time when this text was written, is a world in which it happens that we do fly now—or somebody does; I don't.

(335:19–24) *But were I an inventor trying to perfect flying machines, I should continue the effort to find the determination of my will present in a flying machine, until I became convinced that my purpose as defined stood somehow in conflict with itself, or with the whole idea of nature of which it is a portion.* To view the world in those terms is to view it not in a subjective but in an essentially idealistic way. It is not a world in which the things exist in your ideas. Aviation, with its slowly developing processes, is a good example. "The facts" [p. 335] proved a good deal, and a good deal of that was negative. They never proved that a man couldn't fly. The "try again" maxim stands for a revelation of the unconquerable idealism which in our own case doesn't overcome evil but does make rational life consist not in the abandoning of fact for dream, but in the idealizing of our lives. It is exactly that idealizing which is the practical side of idealism. How far it can take us, aviation has shown us in recent years.

Aviation is an example of what for human beings is a hopeless affair. The world is not what at any moment the then present facts show. It is defined through and through by the truth of judgments, then in consequence by the truth of ideas, then in consequence by processes that are exemplified by the progressive process of interpretation. When you are realistic or mystical, you are dealing with a fragment of that life. I agree that we are a long way from now observing that world, and we do not know in particular how to get the embodiment of our meaning. In that task we succeed only slowly. Under these circumstances we have got to take full account of what other people mean, and of the conflict of various ideas.

Summary

Whether you consider the social approach or the logical approach, the idealistic interpretation of what it is to Be is founded surely not upon merely *May 25* private reflection upon one's personal views of the world. Idealism does not consist in devotion to one's own ideas, in fancying that the world is pretty nearly laid away in one's own head. Nor yet does it seem to me a fair account of the idealistic argument to insist, "Here is a false interpretation of the real world of fact in terms of a very special portion of that world. There is a portion of that world which is mental, exemplified by human beings and their social relations. Idealism tries to declare this comparatively small portion of the world to be the whole of it."

One ground that is given for idealism is, according to Professor Perry, the supposed idealistic ground that we who have minds can define objects only in terms of our minds; and it is supposed that the idealistic doctrine consists in emphasizing this egocentric predicament: we who have minds have to use them precisely as those who happen to wear glasses have to see the world through them, and therefore are likely to take this which is an accidental predicament as something essential, deep, necessary, important. That, as Professor Perry supposes, is the essence of the idealistic argument.

In any case, idealism is not a merely personal doctrine which lays stress on <u>this</u> Ego, this self, nor yet a doctrine that is too personal in its character by laying too much stress on the presence of minds in the world and the importance for them of the instruments that they use, sense organs, modes of making up their minds, etc. That idealism ought to be stated in some of its aspects superpersonally, I have {already} emphasized in the discussion of the Third Conception.

The world of Mill, as stated in the *Examination of Sir William Hamilton's Philosophy*, is not a personal and private world. It is a world that is decidedly a world of which you learn from experience, but so learn that your whole learning consists in the abstracting from your own private point of view. The world of Mill's permanent possibilities of sensation is a world that is as impersonal as the world of Santayana's essences. One may well ask the question as to what Being the essences have, or again as to the Being that the possibilities have; and it is the solution of that question which constitutes the main idealistic argument. To learn to abstract from your own private point of view is, of course, the entire training in which your cultivation—whether practical or theoretical—consists, insofar as you find yourself through contrasting yourself with, but even thereby submitting yourself to, a system of relations which are transcendent of your own personality and individuality.

One can say a thoroughgoing idealism is at least as impersonal or superpersonal in the world that it considers or presupposes, as is Santayana's world of the essences. He leaves mysterious the difference between essence and existence. When you consider his world, you consider something that is to be very matter-of-fact. It is in that sense an impersonal world, a world with which you come into touch insofar as you learn either to overcome and correct or to abstract from your private point of view.

Remember that the world of the Fourth Conception is Santayana's world of the essences and the existents, interpreted and rationalized. Our argument depends on first recognizing all that he recognizes. The world of fact is at least that. It contains at least what he tries to express in terms of the essences and the existents. We don't substitute for them private or romantic views of what it is to Be. We first accept his view of what it is to Be, if only he can make clear to us what that view means. The difficulty was to comprehend the sense in which the essences are, apart from the existents; the sense in which essence is different from existence; the sense in which you cannot determine from the essence of a thing whether it exists or no.

About all these things we found Santayana's account simply incomplete. It is, of course, a trivially obvious refutation of the trivial forms of the ontological argument when one says that out of essence existence cannot be demonstrated. Nevertheless, whoever talks about any reason why he ought to think it true that so and so is there in the world speaks of some essence which has a close connection with existence.

Belonging strictly to the logical approach to metaphysics is the consideration that you simply cannot give any account of the reasons why you accept any opinion about the world of existence without defining a set of considerations relating to the essence of things which has something important to do with the existence of things. If you have any reason for supposing that what is not immediately present exists, your reason is in terms of a whole situation whose essence requires that sort of thing to Be. Whoever has any doctrine whereby he proves the existence of anything not immediately given is using a doctrine which involves essentially the considerations of an ontological proof.

The problem of metaphysics may be defined as the problem, What essences are such that the existence of the corresponding objects is required? That is the problem equally of science and philosophy. You are constantly speaking of that of which you know something concerning its essence, and you are always getting the result that this fact, which you can state with regard to the essence of the thing, throws light on the existence of the thing, so that this is required, rather than that, to fulfill an account of the real world. The world of the existents is throughout a world that is determined by those essences which in their context and their relations to the essentials of experience will be the essences which require certain existents.

Giving the realistic doctrine of Santayana its fullest scope, it forced upon us a problem as to what instances of reality are determined by the nature of the essences which one has in mind who thinks about those essences and their place in the world. It wasn't by retiring from Santayana's clear and cool and objective view of the world into some mystery of romantic consideration of our own inner states of mind that we were led to idealism. It was by endeavoring to find out what evidence there could be for asserting the existence of anything.

If there is any such evidence, there is a what such that in a certain context it demands that a certain somewhat should possess existence. The essential argument for idealism is one that you could reach by simply following Santayana's case by itself.

Another way of approaching our Fourth Conception was the approach through the Third Conception. The world of the Third Conception of Being is surely as impersonal or superpersonal as any world could be. One who finds out how large a part in the realm of facts is taken up by the facts whose Being consists in the truth of certain propositions is surely not laying undue stress on the mental side of things.

The account of idealism that I have defended depends not on the fact that the world is mental in the sense that the realistic critic despises, the sense in which you first pick out the beings that have minds and then try to stow away the world in their minds. It depends on insisting that the Being of the world consists in the truth of propositions about it. That is the point at which you pass over into idealism. The whole issue can be reduced to that. Let anybody say the Being of the world consists in the truth of propositions about it, and he is an idealist. He doesn't need to say anything about an egocentric predicament. Truth is as impersonal a somewhat as he can get. If he defines truth, he defines that aspect of reality which is central for idealism.

Remember that the most significant part of the argument is contained in the transition from other conceptions of Being to the Third Conception, with the consequent inevitable transition to the Fourth Conception.

One who calls himself a realist and thinks of facts may be thinking of facts in terms of the conceptual view which has been called subjectively idealistic. Or one lays emphasis on perception as the mode of knowledge that reveals the real; the Self which they seek is the possessor of the perceptual acquaintance with the real which for them is the goal; and though their idealism is sometimes subjective and they sometimes lay stress on the egocentric predicament, the most important aspect of mysticism is its profoundly impersonal character. If the world is a world of perception, you can hardly call it a world of mind, for all the finite characteristics of mind prove to be illusory, and you dwell upon the world that is the Self precisely so far as you abstract from every personal private human character, turning your eyes in the direction of the remote, the far-off—the difference between the realist and the mystic being rather a difference in the mode of approach than in the doctrines that they can articulate. When a realist tries to tell you what a fact would be apart from knowledge of that fact, he fails to tell you what he could have meant by independence. When a mystic tries to tell you what the ineffable experience of the real is, he deals with an aspect of things so remote from the life he has that he may have to warn you that the human being isn't fit for those things: in fact, nobody can stand at that holy place where the real is directly faced unless he becomes not merely as God but as God was before the creation of the world.

Fantastic that view is, but not a view that depends on mere emphasis upon private or personal considerations.

We found, by a logical consideration of these positions, that indeed pure perception which defines by a presence that nobody has the presence of the real and pure conception which seeks the expression of the essence of things—neither of these would get you into touch with the reality whereof every seeker for reality is speaking when he defines his quest. We thus, of course, came by exhaustion to looking for an idea of reality which is not merely perceptual or merely conceptual. We found it when we reflected upon the sense in which propositions are true. The idealist faces the problem of objectivity, the problem of truth, the problem of that to which one submits his mind whenever one is seeking for fact as fact.

If we try to insist upon what our idealism makes most central, its most important feature, I should venture to put the thing in this way. The realist opponent is continually emphasizing the fact that the idealist is laying too much stress on the states of mind of the individual subject and is distinctly a subjectivist in his whole position. Or, where a realist, endeavoring to be fairer to an idealist than that, brings out the matter that seems to him most suspicious: he is greatly struck by the fact that the idealist selects out the minds and declares that their ideas are especially representative of the stuff out of which all the real is made, so that the minds of the world are taken as if they were the most important realities in it.

Neither of these, I insist, is the position of the idealist. Idealism depends on the considerations which we emphasized in criticizing Santayana's conceptions. It depends on our account of the difference between essence and existence and upon our study of the logic of the ontological proof. It therefore depends on something very different from an egocentric predicament or from laying stress on the minds as peculiarly important portions of the world. The essential portion of our argument is contained on one side in this discussion of Santayana's position. On the other hand, what is essential to our whole development is the study of what is meant by the unquestionable fact that the understanding of the truth of propositions is the understanding of Being.

The idealist lays stress on the fact that meaningless assertions cannot be true accounts of facts. The world, whether you speak of it personally or impersonally, may be regarded as needing no mind in particular to define what goes on in it, and very wild things may go on in the world. But it is good metaphysical sense to say that the real world cannot be what in his black mood Shakespeare makes the King call it; the real world cannot be "a tale told by an idiot, full of sound and fury, signifying nothing." To be is to signify something.*

* {A crucial sentence.}

Santayana uses "evidence" in this sense in his "Some Meanings of the Word Is." (See the earlier section, pp. 105–106). Chaos, irrationality, the presence of that which conflicts with sense, belong to the realm of facts. But it is the essence of idealism to declare the precise negative of the King's proposition. The real world is not a tale told by an idiot. The world signifies; it expresses. That is its business. It expresses a meaning. To be—well, to be is to possess a Being that consists in the truth of propositions. The truth of propositions is the expression of meanings. They may be angels or devils whose meaning is expressed. There isn't the least tendency about idealism to make light of the diversities, the conflicts, or the particular unreasonableness of the world. But on the whole, to be is to signify, to express a meaning.

That is the general proposition that in my seventh lecture of *The World and the Individual* I have expressed in the form of the assertion that the real world in its wholeness, its finality, is the complete expression of the meaning of every significant finite idea, so far as that idea has significance. This world is of course monistic and also pluralistic.* This world of expressed significance is also the world of a community. The process of expressing significance is a temporal process; it involves the gradual expression of meaning, of which the "evolutionary process" gives examples. That is the applied portion of our Theory of Being.

What does one mean by this expression of meaning? I am obliged to say the expression of meaning is present when a purpose is fulfilled. This world has to be essentially purposive, although defeat of purpose plays an unquestionably large part in it. But that too is consistent with the idea itself. Here one has to use mental illustrations. Even so trivial a process as that of the player of any game involves an undertaking to gain victory even through defeat. An opponent whom you can always automatically beat is no genuine opponent. The lover of the game loves the paradox of seeking success through being thwarted. Conflict and tragedy belong to this expression and fulfillment of meaning, both for the individual and for the community, both for the great world of all nature and for our own private lives. This fulfillment of purpose through the thwarting of purpose is not an afterthought of one who has to admit something in the world not wholly ideal. On the contrary, this is one of the deepest features which both the moral and the religious consciousness {as well as} the practical and the logical consciousness of humanity have repeatedly recognized.

Throughout the whole realm of the expression of meaning you will find the same thing holding. An idea is not expressed simply; it is expressed in some sort of tension, conflict, opposition, over against that which hinders or thwarts it. The process of expression is the process of interpretation.

---

* {A crucial sentence.}

How can so abstract an account of the world apply to the realm of experience, where after all we don't always meet what the idea in mind wills? It is utterly impossible to refute the doctrine that the world is the expression of purpose by finding in it purposeless things; for what you find when you discover that which does not fulfill purpose is always expressible as a particular experience. You never prove that nothing of that sort is to be found in the world which you look for. Your situation is illustrated by the lover of aviation and his fortunes. Such a fact as death doesn't prove the loss irrevocable; we can only say that we haven't yet found that what we mean by the survival of mind is a fact of experience; but that doesn't prove that man doesn't survive. You can't prove the universal negative that would be needed to prove that the world is not ideal.

On the contrary, you have that which the whole process of evolution illustrates. The world involves the whole search for the ideals. That is embodied in the whole life of nature. The evolutionary principle is metaphysically of vast significance, not in terms of the Bergsonian vital urge, but in terms of the doctrine of interpretation.

May 27, 1916 Final Meeting

How far has the second half-year's work been a question of what we call the logical approach to metaphysics? I think that our emphasis on Professor Santayana's definition of the meanings of the verb is, and our repeated use of the reflective method in our definitions of our relations to realism, and our analysis of an overtly logical view—such as the Third Conception is—and our definition of the Fourth Conception in terms of the Third, constitute what is substantially a logical approach to the metaphysical problem.

Evil and the Irrevocable Past

Amongst the topics which I should like to discuss would stand very prominently the so-called problem of evil. There is a remark which I may make about that which is worth considering. The historical association of discussions about evil with problems of theology, in particular with the problems of that portion of theology which has been technically called theodicy (the justification of the ways of God), that association has established a certain prejudice against the problems of theodicy which James freely expressed and which has been repeatedly expressed by Professor Perry and by some others of the new realists. From that point of view there is something artificial, theological, unnecessary, in a discussion about the problem of evil. It should not be found in a treatment of philosophical topics. James called it in his own last period an artificial problem, though it was in his own case an insistent problem and one that he always discussed. His skill in polemics apropos of pragmatism, and his fondness for pointing out the inadequacy of particular idealistic arguments, took the form of making him call the whole problem of evil an artificial invention of the intellectualists.

Perry, in his discussion of the feasibility of absolutism, maintained that there is no problem of evil; the only philosophical problem about evil is the problem presented by the existence of evil facts in the world, and that is an empirical problem. The only problem about evil that the philosopher has any reason to emphasize, according to Professor Perry, is the condemnation of evil because it is evil—his problem being the practical problem of how to get rid of evil. So Professor Perry has adopted entirely one of James's later favorite statements: "The problem of evil is the problem how to get rid of it." There is no other problem according to that view.

An effort to explain the world teleologically meets indeed the problem as to how these appearances of evil, or these well-known facts of evil, can be reconciled with the teleological structure of the world. But that is discredited by Professor Perry as being identical with the problem of theodicy. Precisely {insofar} as the abandonment of theology leads to an unwillingness to be guided by the procedure of theodicy, one is indifferent to the effort to give any reason why the world of fact contains as much evil as it does.

With regard to this matter, the practical and theoretical position of Professor Santayana is peculiarly clear and simple. His materialistic world is essentially an unrational, irrational world, in the sense that it has only a chance conformity with the teleological interests of a rational being. From that point of view, it is perfectly vain to inquire why the world is evil, or why the world is as much good as it is. The world is irrational in its essence. It is definable in terms like matter and energy, in terms of whatever account is correct of its natural tendencies. The world is not subject to teleological principles. The question why does this evil thing occur, whether you are dealing with the slightest of ills or with the failure of a social order or of the race or of all rational beings—any such inquiry is excluded by the nature of Being, for Santayana. You have the realm of the essences and then an entirely inexplicable selection of a portion of the essences to exist. As a fact, some of the essences selected for existence have the character of being good and some have the character of being evil. The selection is essentially irrational because nothing about the essence determines whether existence attaches to the given essence at any time or not.

Santayana's position is cold; it is very comprehensible. That belongs to the clearest part of his doctrine and has had a great deal to do with his influence as a philosopher and will have in the future. Of all those who deal with the problem of evil at all, the materialist or naturalist of Santayana's sort remains in the most favorable position for stating his case. If it were not the case that the nature of the distinction between essence and existence becomes more mysterious the more you consider it—unless the difference is viewed as a teleological difference and unless the whole realm of existence as well as the whole realm of essence were such as to force upon you the teleological considerations which have been set forth—then Santayana's position would be peculiarly simple. The problem of evil does indeed vanish for those who, like James in his latest period, declare that the world is whatever the facts show it to be, and who therefore reject any constructive idealistic account of the world in terms of our Fourth Conception of Being.

{Of} the principal positions, there is the position represented by Professor James himself, the position stated by Professor Perry in his discussion of the so-called futility of absolutism, the position stated and very easily, brilliantly, and beautifully summarized by Professor Santayana, and the position that is occupied in passing by Professor Russell. For all these positions there is no problem of evil that deserves to be considered in philosophy. The problem of evil is the inheritance from the older theology, which had a theodicy because it had a God who must be justified if possible; and the Absolute of the idealists is subject to similar conditions.

Now for a general indication of how for us a problem of evil must be considered and, if there were time, would be answered. To say, of course, that there genuinely is a problem of evil, that the comprehension of what it is to Be—the characterization of reality—leads to the facing and the relative clearing up of the problem of evil, {and} that that thesis has its place in philosophy, is dependent first upon whatever considerations there are which lead us to idealism. You know that I hold to an idealistic view of the world first for reasons which we saw in connection with the idea of interpretation. The world is essentially the interpretation of experience. Secondly, the considerations that we have met in passing from the Third to the Fourth Conception: the world is the expression of the idea. That thesis we reach in our second half-year's work when we make the transition from the Third to the Fourth Conception for reasons which may be defended by the reflective method. The world consists in the truth of ideas about it, while this truth has the character of being the fulfillment of ideal purposes.

Such a view about the nature of things, whether from the side of the idea of interpretation or from the side of the notion of Being or reality as the fulfillment of ideal purposes, essentially involves a dealing with the teleology of things. Now the world of fact is disteleological, in the sense that there happens that which from a given point of view does not fulfill our purposes. One has to explain in what <u>sense</u> he holds by that hypothesis. The world is the interpretation of our various assertions about it. It is the interpreter of our problems. But in manifold ways, fragmentary views of this interpretation do not satisfy. Consequently, we have a problem and that problem is the problem of evil. Thus for any idealist there is a definite problem as to the place which is occupied in the whole of reality by the antiteleological or disteleological characters of the real world.

It is that definite problem of evil which in the second volume of *The World and the Individual* I have considered in a decidedly lengthy discussion.[10] You will also find it discussed in the closing lecture of *The Religious Aspect of Philosophy*; in the closing lecture of *The Spirit of Modern Philosophy*; from another mode of approach in one of the lectures of the *Studies of Good and Evil*, where the problem of evil is especially considered; another aspect in *The Problem of Christianity* in the first volume at the close in the discussion of atonement as a function of the community; and in the second volume of *The Problem of Christianity* at the close of the discussion of the World of Interpretation. I have inevitably thought of the matter as a very central philosophical problem.

James also early looked at the matter in a similar fashion. His own most characteristic contribution to the practical solution of the problem you will find in his book *The Will to Believe*, in the essay entitled "Is Life Worth Living?"[11] an essay written in a time of depression by a man who was a pronounced invalid of a certain sort and one might say proud to be so. It was very characteristic of him that he was a constitutional nervous invalid. After a severe fight against a peculiarly difficult situation, the solution in terms of courage is very beautifully stated in this essay. He returns to that in his very last expressions in his latest essays. The problem was prominent in his philosophy when he had not {yet} taken his position with regard to idealism. I once heard him say, "It has long been to me a fact that the principal business of philosophy is to give a man a good reason why he shouldn't commit suicide." That was the word of a vigorous nervous invalid who suffered constant depression and who knew what it was to have the blues in a way that people who talk about having the blues usually do not know. A sense somewhat mystical in character that the world is somewhat worthwhile, a sense that is not mystical that it is man's business to make it worthwhile, these two formed his view. He talked about the "faith ladder" and the "postulate" that the world is worthwhile. He had no question that the problem was one which it was reasonable to consider, though he rejected this and that particular solution.

In Santayana's view it is not rational for a man to despise life, and the suicide is not in the rational position: but since life is dependent upon natural conditions which do not result from teleological principles, it is not part of a rational being's view of things to give himself a ground why the world which is not rational ought to be viewed as rational. Hence the problem of evil has no place in the rational business of the philosopher. Nevertheless, in his *Life of Reason*, Volume III *Religion*,[12] it appears that though we can't show how the world which is irrational should be regarded as rational, it is still possible for a rational being to emphasize those things which by chance make the world seem tolerable. Art, friendship, whatever the Greeks liked to consider, give the world this aspect. To emphasize this aspect, without romanticism or overconfidence, is rational.

James expressed a somewhat equal insistence on postulating that things are better than they seem: then you are dealing with the spirit of true religion; its essence is the laying stress upon the more reasonable aspects of the essentially irrational world in which we live. Though the world isn't rational, the spring mornings are in their own place real. Though what happens is a matter of the cosmic weather, still we have a right to say it is a fine day. If we are considering what holds men together, our emphasis on the good side of things may have a certain religious spirit about it.

Russell expresses a somewhat similar view in his *Philosophical Essays.*[13] There are certain aspects of reality which we can emphasize and which give us a right to a certain religious position of acquiescence—indifferent, stoical, religiously exalted above the power of fortune—when we look to the dignity of those great things which the human mind can grasp. The mathematical objects which you have in mind in the mathematically definite physical sciences have a majesty which is objective and which one can rationally contemplate.

Santayana has somewhat keenly criticized these essays of Russell, insisting on the decidedly subjective character of the grounds which Russell emphasizes: the greatness, wonder, {and} beauty of things is what subjectively interests you.

You cannot declare that the realistic effort to escape facing the problem of evil by these considerations is acceptable, in view of the general consideration that led us to the idealistic point of view.[CA] The world isn't first given to you as a datum and afterward estimated in virtue of the fact that you as a being with certain interests, and standing outside of that whole realm of existence, find some things in it good and some things evil. The very recognition of Being is itself an estimate.[14] The categories of metaphysics are from the first teleological.*

From that point of view you have of course a problem, the problem of clearing up the disteleological aspect of things. The general position of the idealist is that you cannot view the world as real without viewing it teleologically; it is of the essence of the real to be the interpretation of experience, or to interpret experience. The more you know of the real, the more your realm of experience has interpretation, and consequently the more it has the element of reconciliation in it.

Over against the realist, our own position is that we are not first under-

* {These last two crucial statements summarize the course.}

standing what it is to be real, and calling attention to the fact that existence, as that special form or instance of reality, permits all sorts of weather, {and} then observing that today is a fine day. {Rather} what we are engaged in {is} a process in which whenever we ask the sense in which there is any day at all, the sense in which the time–world has its nature, its character, the sense in which there is any difference between existence and essence or between fact and fancy—whenever we consider that, we are considering the teleological. So our answer to the various positions which I have indicated is that the whole process of Being is essentially a teleological problem, and that to have a world is to estimate it either spasmodically or systematically. To stand in presence of the real world is to stand in presence of that which you can rightly define only as the fulfillment of the Self, as therefore one in nature with the Self. You can say of the world with Prajapati that it possesses that which fulfills all desires. Since despite this there are countless antiteleological characters in it, there is a genuine problem.

James sometimes said, and Professor Perry has insisted, that the problem is {as they might put it}, "Can you get rid of evil? I don't want to understand evil; I want to get rid of it. The interest of humanity is to find out how evil can be wiped out; we don't want to understand why Divine Providence makes some men poor; we want to abolish poverty; our question is how to cure evil."

An idealist is influenced in his estimate of these things by the fact that no solution in terms of abolition will ever be a solution of the original problem. That isn't always equally manifest. But the deliberate ignoring of the most important moral aspect of the world, which is involved in the declaration that there is only the problem of how to get rid of evil—that is something to which we must call attention from the point of view of both the first and the second half-year's discussion.

Were all the evils dealt with by the process of abolition, they would have a character which would make it essentially impossible to purge the world from all its real evil, insofar as that evil is real, by any process of abolition. For where we consider not merely a world that we view externally, but the world of the Self and equally the world of our community, then there is a problem which is not to be stated in terms of abolition at all. It is the problem richly emphasized by history, the problem of dealing with the irrevocable past.

I don't get rid of the evil part of me by merely ceasing to do wrong. I can't get rid of evil from my life by saying, "Let's abolish it." The child of a neighbor once uttered a very deep reflection on the problem of conscience. He happened to find in a barn amongst the hay a litter of newborn kittens, queer creatures. Impulsively he killed them with a big club. He was discovered and upbraided by the environment in vigorous fashion. He didn't become especially excited by the storm; he let it pass. He regretted what he had done; it had happened, and he tried to drop the subject. Some time afterward, a too candid and insistent friend said to him in the course of a discussion, "Yes; but you killed those poor little kittens." The boy replied, "I am not killing any kittens now."

In the child's form, that gives you the problem of evil. The moral being can't say that about matters which have most to do with the evils of our lives.[CA] In vain do we endeavor to comfort ourselves for what we have genuine rational grounds to regret, by saying, "But I am not killing any kittens now." For the moral worth of a person is dependent on what he has done as well as what he is doing now. Atonement, if it occurs, is another matter.

If we abolished death, we shouldn't get rid of the evil constituted by those who are remembered and who have died. What we regret is that the evil has Being.

All these things suggest the various metaphysical attitudes which we should consider if we had time.

I will close with a reference to M. S. Gaunt of Methuen, formerly a member of Phil. 9, who died while engaged in ambulance service in France. One of us has seen the vision face to face. The quest of which Tennyson speaks is a metaphysical quest:

> And spake I not too truly, O my knights?
> Was I too dark a prophet when I said
> To those who went upon the Holy Quest,
> That most of them would follow wandering fires,
> Lost in the quagmire?—lost to me and gone,
> And left me gazing at a barren board,
> And a lean Order—scarce return'd a tithe—
> And out of those to whom the vision came
> My greatest hardly will believe he saw.
> Another hath beheld it afar off,
> And, leaving human wrongs to right themselves,
> Cares but to pass into the silent life;
> And one hath had the vision face to face,
> And now his chair desires him here in vain,
> However they may crown him otherwhere.[15]

End of Course.

Midyear Examination, 1915–16
HARVARD UNIVERSITY
Philosophy 9

1. Discuss the nature of Time, and the nature and significance of our knowledge of Time. Use, as the basis of your answer to this question, the lectures of the first half-year in Philosophy 9, and also the passages that bear upon the question, in the book called *The Problem of Christianity*. You need not here say anything about Time except upon the basis of these sources of information. In the course of your discussion, summarize the chapter on "Time and Guilt" (in the first volume of *The Problem of Christianity*), and also summarize so much of the chapter on "Atonement" (in the same volume) as bears upon the metaphysical and epistemological problems about the nature of Time. Summarize also, from the second volume of *The Problem of Christianity,* the discussion of the doctrine which is there set forth regarding the relation between "The Community and the Time–Process."

2. Summarize the argument (set forth at length in the lectures, and contained also in some of the literature to which your attention was called) regarding "The Possibility of Error." Show what the lecturer undertook to prove by this argument, and how the lecturer stated his argument.

3. Having thus stated the lecturer's argument about the "possibility of error," briefly discuss, criticize, and estimate this argument in your own way.

4. Discuss the relations between the general cognitive process called Interpretation, and the reasoning processes commonly called, respectively, Induction and Deduction. Give illustrations of these relations, and state what you think to be the importance of these relations both for the theory of knowledge and for metaphysics.

5. Imagine and briefly describe how in case there are intelligent inhabitants upon the planet Mars, and in case they know what our own powers and limitations are, and in case they also had sufficient control over nature, and, finally, in case they wished to communicate with us, they could arrange a system of signs, or "signals," consisting of series of flashlights such that, if only our attention were attracted to these signals, we could in time get convincing evidence that these Mars people exist and are intelligent. Could we hope to decipher, in time, such a system or signals, and thus learn, in some detail, what ideas the Mars people have?

6. Devote the rest of the time of this examination to a summary of the sense in which, and the degree to which, the "World of Interpretation," as far as it has been defined in the lectures and in *The Problem of Christianity,* is a world that can be known to be good, and not a world whose facts are whatever they happen to be, without regard to what they ought to be, and without regard to the distinction between good and evil.

Midyear, 1916
February 7, 1916.

Final Examination 1915-16
HARVARD UNIVERSITY
Philosophy 9

1. What is the distinction, according to Santayana, between "essence" and "existence"? In what relation does the "existence" of things stand to questions about "where" and "when" the existent objects are?

2. According to Santayana, one of the principal meanings of the word "is" may be expressed by the phrase "is identical with." In each of the following statements, some question about the sense in which some object "is" or "is identical with" a given object is exemplified.

After carefully considering each of the following statements, say what you can about the sort and degree of "identity" which is each time in question, and about the problem concerning the meaning of "identity," and of "difference," and about the true relations between "sameness" and "difference," in each of the cases mentioned in these statements.*

a. "A man's conduct may alter, but his true character never changes. Through all changes of mood and fortune a man is, at heart, whatever he is."

b. "A man, convinced against his will, is of the same opinion still."

c. "No man steps twice into the same stream."

d. "No two observers of rainbows ever see the same rainbow."

---

* {See pp. 143–72.}

e. "The man who presents this draft is the same man as the one to whose order it was drawn."

f. "The new moon is the same moon as the moon of last month."

g. "Oh swear not by the moon—the inconstant moon—that monthly changes in her circled orb" (Juliet to Romeo, in the balcony scene).

h. "The atoms of materialism remain always the same, except for the fact that they move. But when the atoms move, the laws of motion,and the physical processes involved, remain always the same. Hence, in the world of the materialist, there can be no true evolution possible."

3. Have the "essences," as Santayana conceives them, any place in space or in time? If they are neither in space nor in time, what mode or sort of being have they?

4. Devote the rest of this paper to a summary and estimate of the lecturer's own account of the relations between his own present form of Idealism (as expounded in the second half year's work) and the "New Realism" of Russell, and of the other members of the group of the "New Realists." Without endeavoring to make this summary exhaustive, try to show, as well as you can, what have seemed to you to be the most important arguments and criticisms which, in the lectures of the second half-year, the lecturer has made use of in his exposition and defense of what he has called the "Fourth Concept of Being." You are of course at liberty to refer, at your pleasure, to the first-half year's work as far as that may help you to expound the lecturer's present position regarding the "Fourth Concept of Being"; but you are not required to say more of this than you choose.

Final, 1916
June 7, 1916.

Supplementary Essays

Provenance of the Phil. 9 Course and Present Text of Royce's Lectures on Metaphysics, 1915–1916

Frank Oppenheim

How did Josiah Royce's last lectures on metaphysics evolve into the present text?[1] If readers examine this evolution, they can estimate how directly they encounter the metaphysical mind of the mature Royce in the present volume.

The History of "Phil. 9: Metaphysics" from 1894 to 1916

Royce taught metaphysics at Harvard for more than two decades. In fall 1894, he began "Phil 9: Metaphysics," using F. H. Bradley's *Appearance and Reality*. Thereafter, with few exceptions,[2] he taught Phil. 9 regularly until his death in 1916, yet along the way he significantly developed this course. In fall 1897, Royce subtitled his metaphysics course "On the Definition of Reality," thus suggesting a trial run of his theory of the Four Conceptions of Being toward his upcoming Gifford lectures. Once he had delivered these lectures and entered the twentieth century, he replaced Bradley's text with his own *The World and the Individual,* the revised version of his two Gifford series. Soon, during 1904–1906, William James taught the first semester and Royce the second of Phil. 9 Metaphysics. This provided a memorable experience for those taking Phil. 9 at the time. After absenting himself from Phil. 9 during his Walter Channing Cabot Fellowship of 1911–1914, Royce returned to a full year's teaching of metaphysics in fall 1914. By then he had become intellectually rejuvenated because he had come to appreciate C. S. Peirce's thought far more deeply than ever before. So Royce restructured Phil. 9 to disseminate Peirce's theories of semiotic and interpretation by applying them creatively to metaphysics and theory of knowledge, going well beyond Peirce's mainly logical focus. Moreover, in his Phil. 9 course of 1914–1915, Royce unveiled something novel: his "four approaches to metaphysics": the Logical, Physical, Psychological (or Psychical), and the Social approaches.[3]

The "logical (or reflective) approach" continued the effort of Socrates, Plato, and Aristotle to form true opinions and thus overcome ignorance and unclarified meanings by using the principle of contradiction and the process of interpretation to trace out logical and illogical consequences. The "physical approach" compared the results of scientific research, for example, in evolution, and deduced a larger meaning of nature from the current knowledge about it. Royce's "psychological approach" employed self-consciousness as its basis, much as Descartes, Berkeley, and James had done.[4] Royce's metaphysically distinctive "social approach" countered all nominalists who assume that ultimately only individuals exist, while all communities are derivative. By contrast, Royce held that some communities are just as primary and basic as are individuals. Constructing his social approach to metaphysics upon this "doctrine of the two levels," as he called it,[5] he raised such questions as the following: Can any physical object be real for us if it is not observable by two or more human selves? Is the English language a real object? Why does primitive man start by thinking more clearly of his social group than of himself? Why do self-consciousness and individualism arise later? And why does subordination to authority perdure in later stages of consciousness?

In 1915–1916, Royce tried something "both old and new," as our present text illustrates. Wanting both to reinterpret his *World and the Individual* and to muse further upon his more recent *Problem of Christianity*, Royce found that time constraints forced him this year to omit his "physical and psychological approaches." Only thus might he attend adequately in the first semester to the "social approach to metaphysics" with its triadic theory of interpretation and of signs, as suggested both in the *Problem* and in his still more recent *War and Insurance*. Only thus, too, could Royce in the second semester concentrate on the "logical approach to metaphysics" which searched for propositions that reinstated themselves through the process of attempting to deny them.

Since the mature Royce concurred increasingly with Peirce's rejection of nominalism,[6] Royce now portrayed both extreme and abstract realists as holders of different sorts of nominalism. Leibnitz, Herbart, and proponents of the Hindu Sânkhya doctrine are extreme realists because they approach a total independence of knower and object known. Santayana, Mill, Russell, and others are abstract realists because they are not sufficiently teleological to be realistic enough. The abstract realists recognize some idealistic bond between knower and object known, but they rely ultimately on possibilities rather than on actual beings, on the "being of validity" rather than on the "being of individuality." Hence, even the new or critical realists are still caught in a noninterpretational form of nominalism and so lack that needed teleological intent to reach Being as the beloved "object of exclusive interest."[7]

Thus, in spring 1916, Royce focused on the claim of some realists that Being is totally independent of an idea. Revising the ontological argument from its absolute (Anselmian) form into its generalized "relational" form, Royce showed both that existence is not as divorced from essence as Santayana was teaching and that therefore the claim of the extreme realists had to be self-contradictory. Royce then switched to the mystics' claim of an ultimate identification of the conscious subject with Being, and after prolonged study showed such philosophical mysticism to be inadequate. Thereupon, he pointed out that the critical rationalists' abstractly valid propositions failed to reach the unique individuality of the Real. For Reality reveals itself, for instance, in the shock experienced by the "frightened depositor" who during a financial crisis is disappointed by the bank's teller giving him the cash for which he asks. For what he really seeks is that greater social reality of the bank's perduring solvency. That, however, was something that neither present experience nor abstract valid propositions could give him. Accordingly, Royce arrived at his own Fourth Interpretation of Being. Only this interpretation knows the temporal process of reality as it moves ahead teleologically at both levels of the Individual and the Community.

A sketch of just how Royce proceeded in his last lectures on metaphysics can conclude this story of how Phil. 9 developed over two decades. In his final period, Royce had allowed the ideas of Community, Spirit, and Process to grow more vigorously in his mind.[8] These potent seeds, sown by his Peircean insight of 1912 and first revealed in *The Problem of Christianity,* had energized his development of a social approach to metaphysics in 1914–1915.

So, in the first half-year of 1915–1916, Royce further refined his social approach by taking three major steps. Having directed attention to the central contrast between essence and existence, Royce introduced his social approach to metaphysics by focusing on ego and alter, individual and group. These relations immerse human selves unavoidably in a social order which reveals communities to be as real and basic as individuals; (Sept. 30–Nov. 2; pp. 7–32). Since knowledge too is unavoidably social, Royce next showed that interpretation is knowledge in its most basic form—more basic and complete than perception or conception (Nov. 4– Dec. 2; pp. 33–58). Then, concentrating on the problem of truth, Royce reaches the culmination of his social approach to Being. He refuses to let truth be confused with certainty or probability, or a theory of truth to rest merely on coherence or correspondence. For truth to be possible, he requires an interpreter of a knower and object known, a community of interpretation, in which human knowers are caught in a logocentric, not an egocentric, predicament; (Dec. 2– Jan. 24; pp. 59–90).

In the second half-year, Royce generally followed the order of presentation he had used in *WI* 1. For a fresh approach, he selected Santayana's recently published essay, "Some Meanings of the Word Is" because of its clarity and nonpolemical character. Focusing on the First Conception of Being, he laid the groundwork for his critique of the realist and nominalist positions by analyzing judgments of identity and identification and the relational form of the ontological argument; (Feb. 17–March 23; pp. 96–167). On March 23, he subjected this extreme realist view to a careful criticism. Then Royce began exposing and examining the Second Conception of Being, the mystical interpretation; (March 25–April 15, pp. 170–211). After spring recess, Royce offered one lecture introductory to the Third (or Critical Rationalist) Interpretation of Being (pp. 213–17). Then, however, he recurred to his starting point by sharpening his audience's focus upon the logical relation of the unavoidable mutual dependence between object and idea; (April 29–May 9th, pp. 218–32). The extreme realists' denial of such dependence required Royce to start his metaphysics from the First Conception of Being, which some of Royce's opponents had mistaken as a straw man. Then Royce examined the Third Conception of Being in depth, contrasting the positions of Santayana, Russell, and other contemporary thinkers and basing his analysis on the meaning of possibility in contrast to that of individual actuality; (May 9–18; pp. 232–50). Thereupon he was largely concerned with his Fourth and Final Interpretation of Being; (May 18–25; pp. 251–71). Royce closed by exposing the inadequacy of the realists' response to the problem of evil and briefly sketched his own response to it; (May 27; pp. 271–77). The latter achieves a reconciliation of good and the effects of evil through an interpretive process of atonement.

Stages in the Evolution of the Present Text

While Royce was delivering these lectures of 1915–1916, Ralph W. Brown, a special student and stenographer, recorded them in class and shortly thereafter preserved them in a first typewritten version, which the editors call Typescript A.[9] Shortly after Royce's death, when Professor William Ernest Hocking examined Typescript A, he noticed that several gaps in Brown's notes were due to Brown's occasional absences from Phil. 9. Hocking filled in these lacunae by gathering the notes from these lectures that graduate student Byron

E. Underwood, Jr. had taken. Then, by interweaving both sets of student notes into typewritten form, he created a more complete and adequate account of Royce's 1915–1916 Phil. 9 course—a carefully compiled Typescript B. The present editors, Professors Richard Hocking and Frank Oppenheim, have selected this Typescript B as their authoritative source of the present work.

During his 1929–1930 seminars on Royce's philosophy, William Ernest Hocking became the initial editor of Royce's last lectures on metaphysics. Looking toward their publication in book form, he divided the text into nine parts, fashioned their titles and many of their subtitles, and with his seminar members created the needed indices of names and topics. Unfortunately, the Depression prevented publication. As a result, Typescript B lay dormant for sixty years, until the present editors resolved to make Royce's mature metaphysics publicly available.

At first, the present editors preferred a text that would be as faithful as possible to the flavor and style of Royce's classroom rather than one that used contemporary English. They chose to drop the division into nine parts and to present the lectures as literally as possible, including assignments of class reports and supporting bibliographies. In this way they recreated the ambiance of Royce's actually teaching in the classroom. They added endnotes that offered needed references and explanations. In this version they also placed suggested emendations of involved sentences into endnotes. In Typescript A, stenographer Brown had merely indicated by page references certain quotations from Royce's *The World and the Individual* and from John Stuart Mill's *Examination of Sir William Hamilton's Philosophy*. Believing that in 1916 Royce read these passages to his Phil. 9 students before analyzing them, the editors inserted these quotations into the text at the appropriate sites to help the reader grasp Royce's observations on these passages in their original classroom context. At the time, the editorial aim was to present Typescript B as faithfully and unobtrusively as possible. The result was Typescript C.

Challenged by the ideal of what Royce would have done if he had lived to edit these lectures into book form, the editors recognized the value of William E. Hocking's perceptive division of the work into nine parts. They saw the need to handle scholars' concerns about the text by a Critical Apparatus. Where helpful, they created certain linkages between several chapters—indicating them by pointed brackets. They resituated classroom assignments to endnotes and placed lecture dates in margins so that scholars could trace references to these lectures made in earlier researches into Royce's Phil. 9 course of 1915–1916. The editors inserted into the text their revisions of certain poorly worded passages, while preserving Ralph W. Brown's original record of these in the Critical Apparatus. The result was Typescript D, here reproduced in book form.

* * * *

After this initial bird's-eye view, the reader deserves a fuller account of the various developmental stages that led to the present text.

Stage 1: During the fall semester of Royce's final course on metaphysics (his Phil. 9), Ralph W. Brown briefly recorded Royce's lectures merely for his own and his father's eyes.[10] For the second semester, however, Brown was employed (apparently by Richard C. Cabot) as a trained stenographer to record Royce's lectures in Phil. 9.[11] This put stenographer Brown between Royce and the present reader. One may inquire, then, what colored Brown's stenography of these lectures he heard from Royce, who died shortly thereafter.

First, Brown shifted his intent at midyear. As mentioned, during the first semester, he intended his notes only for himself and his father. He neither showed these notes to Professor Royce nor expected any others to read them. During the second semester, however, Brown took notes "for presentation to Professor Royce as well as for my own benefit."[12] Accordingly, Brown described as "greatly condensed" the notes which he took of Royce's lectures during the fall semester of 1915 (on the social approach to metaphysics, using *The Problem of Christianity* as a text). By contrast, his notes are far fuller for Royce's lectures during the spring semester of 1916 (on the logical approach to metaphysics, using *The World and the Individual* as a text). Interestingly, the comments (published after the Critical Apparatus below, pp. 327–8) that Brown interjected into his notes are far more frequent during the first semester than during the second, when he was working full time. His stenographic notes from this second semester sometimes run to a dozen or more typewritten pages per lecture. Accordingly, these second semester lectures constitute Royce's most mature and authoritative commentary on *The World and the Individual.*

Besides Brown's shift in intent, his attitudes toward Royce, the course, and certain topics treated in it also colored his mode of stenography. Brown certainly was no merely passive, note-taking machine. As Brown's comments later make clear, not all his feelings towards Royce were positive.

Moreover, concerning the quality of Royce's 1915–1916 seminar in metaphysics, Brown made a presumption. When expressing his own feelings about it to W. E. Hocking, he presumed that he was reflecting the feelings of the entire class. He wrote, "The course was the despair of those who took it and the lectures fluctuated very greatly."[13] This reaction by Brown fitted an "out of course" legal apprentice confronted with the maturest metaphysical inquiries and subtleties of Royce in 1915–1916. Some of Brown's "despair" with the course becomes understandable, but it contrasts sharply with the sense of "arrest" and gratitude that marked the experience of a fellow student, J. W. Miller, in the same 1915–1916 Phil. 9 course.[14]

Again, in contrast to Royce's keen interest in early Christianity and philosophical mysticism, Brown showed himself hardly interested in such topics. This is evidenced by his unusually brief notes for October 28 and March 28, when Royce lectured on Pauline communities and Hindu mystics. At these times Brown's psychic distance from Royce on these matters impeded empathetic union between note taker and lecturer. Moreover, by his absences during the first semester, Brown also rendered himself less in touch with the immediately preceeding context of some of Royce's presentations.

Finally, Brown was paid for the second semester note taking but not for the first. No surprise then that he absented himself at least six times during the first semester, but only once during the second. This and his shift in intent account for the higher quality of notes for the second semester and the lack of detail on the "social approach" recorded in the first semester. Such then was Brown's mediation.

The second note taker, Byron E. Underwood, Jr., had completed his undergraduate work at Berkeley in 1908 and in 1915–1916 was taking Royce's Phil. 9 in pursuit of a graduate degree at Harvard. His notes for five lectures—indicated by a "U" next to the lecture date—complete the lacunae left by Brown's absences.

Stage 2: Brown transposed his stenographically recorded notes into typewritten form and at the end of the course placed only the text of the second semester of Phil. 9 into Professor Royce's hands.[15] Brown reported that Royce, upon receiving the volume, "expressed his pleasure with it, but did not revise it in any way."[16] Royce also spoke of the "uncommon care" Brown had taken with these notes. Evidently he was comparing them with the less diligent care customary with many other stenographers and reporters.[17] Brown soon united these more detailed notes of the second semester with his "greatly condensed" notes from the first semester to create the earliest typewritten version of Phil. 9 as a complete course. As already indicated, the present editors call this combination "Typescript A."[18]

Stage 3: Soon Brown referred to W. E. Hocking's "plans to print" these Phil. 9 lectures.[19] Brown's occasional absences from class, however, had created omissions in the record of the course, as preserved in Typescript A. Noticing this, Professor William E. Hocking contacted Byron E. Underwood, Jr., who while attending Royce's 1915–1916 course on metaphysics as a graduate student had also taken notes on the course. Hocking sought out Underwood and borrowed his notes for those dates of Royce's lectures on which Brown had been absent. Using these as inserts, Hocking created a more complete version. Then he had three copies of this compilation typed on special India paper. The present editors refer to this fuller version of the Phil. 9 course as "Typescript B"[20] and regard it as the basic text upon which the present edition is founded.

Meanwhile, Mrs. Royce invited Jacob Loewenberg, Royce's former assistant, to help her arrange Professor Royce's papers during the summer of 1917. Loewenberg responded by coming from Berkeley to Cambridge and, during his work of sorting, had Typescript A retyped in a more condensed form.[21] This he took back with him to the philosophy department at the University of California in Berkeley. Eventually, however, Part One of this more compact, Berkeleyan version of Typescript A (the first semester of Phil. 9) somehow disappeared. Its second semester counterpart fared better. For in the early 1920s, at the Johns Hopkins University in Baltimore, Arthur O. Lovejoy began assembling Royceana. In response to his request, Part Two of Loewenberg's more compact Typescript A (the second semester of Royce's last lectures on metaphysics) was shipped in 1923 to the Library at Johns Hopkins.[22]

Stage 4: Sixteen years later, Professor William Ernest Hocking conducted seminars at Harvard on "The Philosophy of Royce."[23] In preparation for these seminars, he began to collect Royceana—texts, letters, articles, and so on—as a library resource for the members of the seminar. One aim of his 1929–1930 seminar on Royce was to prepare a publishable edition of Royce's 1915–1916 lectures on metaphysics. Toward this goal, he invested much care and many hours of labor. He re-examined his earlier combination of the notes of Brown and Underwood (Typescript B). He analyzed this more continuous version of Royce's final Phil. 9 course to identify Royce's arguments and to select his most significant metaphysical ideas. Accordingly and in service of his seminar members' editorial tasks, he sectioned Typescript B into nine "Parts," and created titles and some subheads. He formed a list of *errata* for Transcript B and began creating indices of names and topics. Crediting his student, Miss Elizabeth Wyeth, as chief indexer, he later elaborated these into far more complete indices. Some members in his seminary chose to act as tentative editors of the various sections of Typescript B (as divided into chapters by Hocking), and in their seminar papers offered editorial suggestions.

To sum up the story thus far, there were the original note takings by Brown and Underwood, Brown's unification of his notes from both semesters into Typescript A, Hocking's 1917 compilation of Brown's and Underwood's notes into Typescript B, and in 1929–1930 the endeavors by Hocking and his seminar students to prepare these 1915–1916 lectures for publication.

Stage 5: The Depression of the early 1930s forestalled publication. After World War II, Professor Hocking was preoccupied with more urgent concerns—for example, his Hibbert, Gifford, and William James Lectures, as well as research on Protestant Christian missions. After his death in 1966, Typescript B and Hocking's editorial matrix continued to lie dormant for decades.

Stage 6: In the early 1990s, Royce scholars, Professor Richard Hocking of Emory University, son of William E. Hocking, and Frank Oppenheim, S. J., of Cincinnati's Xavier University, together recognizing the significance of Royce's final lectures on metaphysics, joined forces to make them publicly available. They searched out Royce's references and drafted notes as needed. As an aid to readers, Richard Hocking created an analytical table of chapters.

By breaking up Royce's lengthy sentences, modernizing his punctuation, and repositioning certain paragraphs, Oppenheim produced a tentative version in contemporary English. This failed, however, to present Royce's classroom style as faithfully as possible. So the present editors, aiming instead to be loyal to the style and exact expression of Royce in the classroom, soon were meeting repeatedly and moving toward a more faithful edition. These further revisions and textual decisions often took account of the editorial suggestions, divisions, indices, and *errata* that had arisen from the Royce Seminars of 1929–1930. The result was a penultimate version, arising from still further examination of Transcripts A and B, of critiques by readers, and of yet more careful editorial polishings. All of these efforts aimed at creating as consistently faithful and handy a version of Typescript B as possible. The eventual result was to bring the text into the final shape of Typescript C, which let Royce speak to the reader as directly as possible in the style, pace, and ambiance of his own lecture room in Emerson Hall. Nevertheless, the emphasis on the separate class lectures proved too fragmented for smooth reading.

Stage 7 consisted in producing Typescript D, the manuscript in final book form. The editors recurred to William E. Hocking's division of these lectures into nine parts for our nine chapters, largely adopting his chapter heads and subheads. The reader is thus alerted that, unlike the text itself, these titles and subheads generally derive from the several editors. The inserted linkages of the chapters are marked off with pointed brackets to signal that they are the editors' work, not Royce's. Classroom assignments, editorial aids, fuller references to books that Royce mentions, and other needed bibliographical material were placed in the endnotes. Textual emendations and signs of sentence revisions were assigned to the Critical Apparatus. To aid identification of major thinkers and contemporaries to whom Royce refers, a selected glossary of names was added and placed immediately before the indices.

What results is, the editors trust, an easier yet faithful access to Royce's mature metaphysics. As William E. Hocking discerned more than sixty years ago, "The lectures constitute the clearest and most comprehensive statement of Royce's metaphysical doctrine."[24]

Excerpts from
*"The Ontological Argument in Royce and Others"**

William Ernest Hocking

I

In his last course of lectures on metaphysics, that of the year 1915–16, Josiah Royce brings forward the ontological argument as containing in some form the central doctrine of idealism. In his lecture of February 29, 1916, {see p. 116}, he said:

> Sooner or later, if you are going to take any position about metaphysical questions, you find it necessary to face this matter. There is no more important issue between realism and idealism than this. I don't think you get a fair view of idealism if you think of its issue with realism merely in terms of Professor Perry's egocentric predicament. It is not the most important feature of idealism that it appears to be committed to an insistence . . . that the being of things, whether of God or man or the physical world, is a being in the mind of some thinker. . . . The really most important feature is exactly the issue here concerned: does the existence of anything make any difference to its essence? . . . . is it any part of the essence of a thing that it exists?

During the course of these lectures, he repeatedly recurs to this theme,—the misconception of idealism involved in Professor Perry's exposition with its emphasis on the egocentric predicament; the fact that idealistic metaphysics, like all metaphysics, is concerned with the nature of the objective world, the

* Published in *Contemporary Idealism in America*, ed. Clifford Barrett (New York: Macmillan, 1932), 45–66.

world of reality; that any approach to reality, however completely it moves in the realm of objects, however "realistic" if you like,—if it is capable of reaching the truth at all, will bring the thinker to the result that the world of the reals is a world of spirit. Royce himself stood for no one way of reaching his result: indeed, this last course of lectures was divided into two parts, which were entitled "The social approach" and "The logical approach," in neither of which is there any trace of that subjectivity suggested by the phrase, "The world is my representation." To emphasize this fact, he makes his "logical approach" by way of Santayana

IV

We are now prepared to return to Royce's argument. . . . It is concerned, not primarily with the proof of the existence of God, but with the general argument from essence to existence. For "it is an essential feature of idealism (a difficult thesis, and not the one most commonly made explicit) that there is a connection between essence and reality, such as Santayana doesn't recognize."

Royce appreciates to the full the plausibility of the ordinary refutation of Anselm, and characteristically supplies certain apt illustrations of his own.

> Whoever fills out a check writes out the essence of the thing so far as he can express it. The problem of the contrast between essence and existence is closely analogous to the problem about the relation between the check and the account. . . . If it were possible to define the *greatest possible amount* that one could write out on a check, that would hardly guarantee that the check would be honored. . . . The ontological argument appears to have this fundamental absurdity about it, and has been repeatedly thrown out as utterly insignificant, yet it has a fashion of returning.

He adds an incident which had remained in his memory as further illustrating the absurdity in question. A Maine farmer, having been induced to exchange his greenbacks for counterfeit gold, remarked pathetically "I thought gold was so precious that it couldn't be counterfeited": wherever you had the essence you must, in so precious a metal, have the existence also! But

> Over against these obvious objections, we are using something like the ontological proof all the time. Aren't you using at the moment something like an ontological argument for supposing *that there is a real world*, and answering the question why there isn't rather nothing at all? You reply that something

> has to exist . . . you know there is a world *from the nature of the case*, from the very definition of the world.

Likewise with the time categories, the past, the future,—why not regard them as "all some sort of dream"? Any particular memory may be in error, any particular historical proposition false, any particular expectation misleading. Even the results of scientific induction, as they apply to the future, are merely probable. Nevertheless, past and future must have some reality: we cannot be mistaken in thinking there was a past and will be a future, though we have at hand only their essences. "If the question arises, 'Why anything at all in the place where tomorrow will be if it comes? why not suppose that there is nothing whatever there?' your answer is that somehow the nature of the case seems to forbid this. It is of the essence of the past that it was; it is of the essence of the future that it will be."

The same is to be said of those general principles of the structure of existence which lie at the basis of induction. There is a "coherence of past and present which we verify neither in the past nor in the present, but only by interpreting our relations to a past and a present." Prior to discovering the particular laws of nature we believe in the lawfulness of nature: the conception of a law, its essence as a universal, removes it from the possibility of direct observation; one cannot by the method of "exploration" determine whether a law, or law, exists in the world. It lies in the nature of a universal that it cannot be discovered by inspection, by *Wahrnehmung*; nevertheless the realm of existence cannot be defined without reference to law. It belongs to the essence of law to form an element in existence.

Santayana's method of learning of existence is "only by exploration, through experience or evidence, of the flux of nature." By "evidence" we extend our knowledge beyond the limit of immediate perception: this is Kant's method of tracing outward from present *Wahrnehmungen* along the lines of natural sequence.[1] Royce illustrates:

> You go outdoors in the morning and see in the snow the foot-tracks of a human being, a cat, dog or whatever it is, and thereupon you make an existential judgment: A cat or dog or man has been finding its or his way through the snow. . . . Owing to the laws of nature or to something known about the world, it is the essence of foot-tracks to imply, not the existence of foot-tracks, but the existence of some animal adequate to make them.[2]

It is not the particular meaning of the footprints, but the underlying basis of all such inferences, namely, this *relational form* which we assume; and to say that we assume rather than perceive it is to give it a primary status as essence, but as an essence which we so spontaneously refer to existence that we fail to observe that we are doing so.

> My whole point is this: Whenever one existent is supposed to give you ground for inferring another existent, then the ontological proof is used, insofar as this relational system, of which the evidence and that of which it is the evidence form parts, is a system such that the world cannot but contain it.[3]

Royce designates this a "relational form of the ontological proof."

In this connection Royce makes effective use of his doctrine—that individuals are not objects of direct perception. One is certain, let us say, that his brother is a part of the world of existence, his evidence is that he has seen him this morning. In presence of the skeptical questions regarding the possibility of absolute identification, one is driven to one's conviction of the uniqueness of the personal quality of the brother.

> If common sense is asked, But what evidence have you that this is your brother and not merely somebody who looks like him? you would have to answer, The evidence I have certainly goes beyond experience: this is very like my brother, <u>and there can't be anybody else who looks so like my brother</u>. . . .
>
> Whoever says that, concludes . . . that there is some essence or nature such that the world cannot give it any embodiment unless an individual embodiment, and that the world does give it this individual embodiment.[4]

In brief, there is here, and in all personal relations, a union of observation with belief—a continuous use, in interpreting experience, of a conception of personality which is not derived from existent facts, but contributed to them. "Whoever appeals to *evidence* for existence is using some form of the ontological proof."

There are dogmas about existence which can have no support at all unless by an ontological argument, as that the world of existents consists of individual entities. The realistic tendency to place the realm of essence apart from the realm of existence often goes with a tendency to take it as "inevitably necessary" that all existents shall be individuals. What is the basis of the view of the nominalist, who rejects the existence of universals "as a matter of common sense"? It is certainly not an exhaustive enumeration of particulars! He has not encountered "courage" nor "leoninity" nor "the community" in the flesh: but it is not on account of this merely negative aspect of experience that he issues his denial. It is on account of a preliminary assurance of what the world must be like, an essence which must be existent. Hence

> Nominalism is a doctrine depending on its own form of the ontological proof. The only grounds which you can give for the assertion that this world con-

> sists of individual beings depends on saying it couldn't be otherwise; it is of the essence of existence that the existents should be individual. The world of the Platonic ideas may have its own shadow of reality, but the world of existents must consist of individuals . . . because it is of the essence of an existent to be individual.[5]

Without attributing this sort of nominalism to Santayana, Royce finds that

> Santayana gives you his own carefully shaded version of the ontological proof: "It is idle to say that a thing exists or does not exist if we do not say when or where." That is, you couldn't mean anything unless you were ready to add the time and place. This is to say something about the whatness of the that:—nothing can exist unless its space and time have this determinate character . . . because it is the *nature* of existence to reject existents not determinate by time and space.[6]

Royce has thus given good account of his view that "the ontological proof underlies all your notions of all reality," even to the extent that its severest critics unwittingly employ it. It is the central problem of metaphysics whether reality is such that we can understand it. Those who make a clean break between essence and existence impose a final negative at the outset. Anselm's route is indeed not tenable:

> You cannot get the ontological proof to apply to the divine being in Anselm's way, nor to the counterfeit gold; but unless there is somewhere an ontological proof which holds, then indeed we have no logical proof for any existence, and there need be no real world at all.[7]

Royce regards this result as confirming an idealistic view of the world:

> Giving the realistic doctrine of Santayana its fullest scope, it forced upon us a problem as to what instances of reality are determined by the nature of the essences. . . . It wasn't by retiring from Santayana's clear and cool and objective view of the world into some mystery of romantic consideration of our own inner states of mind that we were led to idealism. It was by endeavoring to find out what evidence there could be for asserting the existence of anything. If there is any such evidence, there is a what such that in a certain context it demands . . . existence.[8]

The direct bearing of this discussion on idealism remains, in these lectures, suggested rather than fully stated; but the purport is clear. The world of existence is a world whose character is ascertained by a process of "interpretation," whose whole concern is with essences: that which distinguishes existence from essence, the actual from the merely ideal, turns out to be itself ideal. The object is shown to be—not subjective, God forbid—but shot through with categorial essences: to those which Kant mentions, Royce adds certain categories from the personal and social order. To be real is to fulfill certain rational purposes.

There are important differences between the positions of Royce and of Kant on this point. For Kant it is only a part of the objectivity of the object that is constituted by the categories: there remains the brute givenness of the material of experience.[9] Royce implies that the entire fabric of the object is derived from the world of the essences. He does not use the word "category" in this connection; nor does he use the freer terms "hypothesis," "postulate." The word "interpretation," which he prefers, suggests a tentative rather than a necessary essence; since it is in general true of an interpretation that it admits a reinterpretation. Nevertheless, it is clear that Royce aims to establish such a relation between certain essences and the existents that one may say, If there is any world at all, it must be of this sort,—an element of invariance in our interpretation of the world for which the term category would be appropriate. And he aims also to eliminate in the end that "if" which distinguishes his ontological arguments from the classical form; for he holds that there can be in the end no "if" about the existence of the world. The essence, world, is such that it must exist.

V

Let us briefly estimate the effect of Royce's discussion.

Royce has established his general thesis that there is a close connection between essence and existence. The central element of logical force in his discussion is the dialectical showing that whoever undertakes to make a rational distinction between essence and existence unites them, precisely in proportion to the vigor and definition of his thought. Existence, for such a thinker, must be thought, and thus taken up into essence.

Royce has also fairly disposed of the assumption that idealism is wrapped up in egocentricity. The ontological argument is the fit weapon for this world, for the ontological argument is precisely *the escape from egocentricity*. It is the demonstration of the essence or essences which cannot be in the mind without being also in the thing. If there is any answer to solipsism on the logical plane, its kernel will be found in what the ontological argument essays to state. It thus deserves the particular attention of the realistic school; for in their characteristic assurance that in knowledge we are dealing with a world "outside of the self," they are either relying dogmatically on natural intuition, or else on a bit of submerged logic which it is greatly to their interest to bring forward. The rifts in the realistic school indicate the pertinence of this comment.

Instead of an egocentric idealism, Royce presents a logocentric idealism. Nothing can escape the net of essence; nothing which can enter into experience or thought can evade the fate of being known as essence.

Royce has no intention of ignoring the value of the actual distinction between essence and existence: he distinguishes throughout between the "conceptual essences" which may be and commonly are *in intellectu* without being *in re* from those essences (which I have called categorial) which must also be *in re*.

Of these categorial essences, Royce does not undertake to demonstrate severally their necessary objectivity. His appeal here is to individual acknowledgement: we are, indeed, "using an ontological argument all the time." Time we regard as such that "in the nature of the case it must be true of existence." If we undertake to defend this habit of reference in any special case, we are reminded that the nominalist is presented as using the same form of objective attribution for his view that the world of existence must consist of individuals, and as using it erroneously. For the completion of the argument there would be required either a separate showing for each of the categories that its essence is such that it cannot not be, or else a deduction of the categories from a single essence which has this demonstrable objectivity. This logical completion lies beyond the scope of Royce's effort in these lectures.[10] He here confines himself to the general thesis, existence has an essence, and to its ample exemplification.

It is perhaps an incident of this fruitful generalization of the ontological argument that the logical keystone of the arch should have been assumed rather than rendered salient.

Notes

Foreword

1. See the close of Peirce's letter to Christine Ladd–Franklin of ca. 1905, published in *The Journal of Philosophy* 13 (1916): 720, and some as yet unpublished Peirce MSS 45 (1904), 284 (*ca.* 1905) and 630 (1909).

2. Letter of Prof. John W. Miller to Frank Oppenheim, February 10, 1976. Miller was a student in this 1915–16 Phil. 9 course and a future professor of philosophy.

3. See p. 255; Royce's emphasis.

Chapter 1

1. From the start, Royce's philosophical method moves through contrasts, interpreting, for example, alternating points of view or counterbalancing ideas and differing contexts. Contrast inserts a striking intrusion, a shock of difference—Peircean "secondness." For Royce's emphasis on contrast, notice this starting list and see pp. 13–14, 16, 18, 57, 93–94, and *passim* via the index, s.v. "contrast."

2. In his metaphysics course of 1914-15, Royce had listed and explained four approaches to metaphysics: the Logical, Physical, Psychological (or Psychical), and the Social. For a fuller description of these, see the first Supplementary Essay ("Provenance"), p. 286, and Walter H. Horton's Notes from Royce's 1914–15 Phil. 9, under date of October 3, 1914, in Harvard University Archives, HUC 8914/ 369.9.

3. Here Royce assigned a report due Saturday, Oct. 9. Topics: Your previous acquaintance with metaphysical studies, books, problems, etc., also with related topics. Opinions, impressions, early childhood interests, etc., bearing on these topics. Royce's

assistant in this course, W. Fergus Kernan, tabulated the statements of Royce's students about their previous acquaintance with metaphysical problems and on October 21 posted on the board the following results, upon which Professor Royce commented quite shrewdly:

A tabulation of the membership of the course:
Graduates 13, undergraduates 9, others 3
Idealists 19, realists 2, others 4
Epistemology:
Scientific methods 3, mystics 3, pragmatists 5, skeptics 2
Others not in any of these classifications (idealists and theologians) 12
Study of metaphysics:
Much previous study 9, little 9
Theological studies prominent 8
Early metaphysical interests:
Metaphysical interests prominent at an early age, 15
Not prominent, 10
Religious interests:
Prominent 14
Not prominent 11

4. Spencer's *Autobiography* comprises vols. 20–21 of *The Works of Herbert Spencer*, 21 Vols., (Osnabrück: Otto Zeller, 1880–1907). The story Royce soon refers to occurs in vol. 20, p. 68.

5. From here to the end of this lecture, Royce seems committed to expound Aristotle's *Metaphysics*, I. 1.

6. *WI* 1: 51–52, n. 1.

7. Royce's "is disposed to contrast . . ." reveals both his starting point in experience and his use of contrast—crucial themes that pervade these lectures of the first half-year.

8. Herbert Austin Aikins, *Principles of Logic* (New York: Henry Holt, 1902); 2d ed., 1907.

9. At this point Royce assigned a report, due Nov. 6: "Some Aspects of Social Reality." [The following was written on the blackhoard.]

> It is a very frequently expressed opinion that "individual human beings are the only real beings in our human social world." The lecturer holds {in PC 82–85, 92–95} that "communities are real" and that their reality may be, and in certain cases is, more important than that of individuals. The main topic of the report is, "What do you think about this doctrine of the lecturer about the reality of communities?"
>
> Topics:
> 1. In what sense is any human being a real being at all?

2. Reality of a man's body, mind, deeds, thoughts, etc.

3. Wundt's sense in which the *Gesamtheit* (totality, collectivity, community) is real.

4. Comparison of individuals to communities as to these senses of reality.

Literature:

Problem of Christianity, Vol. I, lectures 1, 2, 3, 4. Vol. II, first two lectures.
World and the Individual, Vol. 2, lectures 1, 2.
James, *A Pluralistic Universe,* Ch. 5.
Wundt, *Ethics: Principles of Morality,* pp. 20–34.
Paul, *{Principles of the} Science of Language,* xxxi-xl.
Royce, *War and Insurance,* pp. 44–64.

The assignment in Vol. 2, *Problem of Christianity*, is especially important.

10. In 1911, Henri Bergson gave an address to the Fourth International Philosophical Congress in Bologna, which became available in English as "Philosophical Intuition" in his *The Creative Mind,* IV, trans. M. L. Andison, (New York: Philosophical Library, 1945), 26–32.

11. Bertrand Russell, *Our Knowledge of the External World* (Chicago: Open Court, 1914), 24.

12. William James, *Essays in Radical Empiricism* (New York: Longmans, Green & Co., 1912), 77–78.

13. I.e., *WI* 1:19–37.

14. For Royce's far fuller description of mind as a "system of ideas," which "is a will, . . . in essence a mode of self-expression," see his 1916 article, "Mind," in the *Encyclopedia of Religion and Ethics*, Ed. James Hastings (New York: Charles Scribner's Sons, 1916) 8: 649–57, reprinted in *The Basic Writings of Josiah Royce*, Ed. John J. McDermott (University of Chicago Press, 1969) 2: 735–61, esp. pp., 758–61.

15. Hermann Paul, *Principles of the History of Language*, transl. from the 2d German edition (London: Swan & Sonnenschein, 1888).

16. Wilhelm Wundt, *Ethik*, (Stuttgart: F. Enke, 1886); English transl. of the 2d German edit. of 1892: *Ethics: An Investigation of the Facts and Laws of the Moral Life* (London: Swan and Sonnerschein, 1897).

17. Here Royce added for his students, "This will put before you some aspects of the problem to be discussed in your next report."

18. William Graham Sumner, *What Social Classes Owe One Another* (New York: Harper & Brothers, 1883); republished in New York by Arno Press, 1972.

19. Here Royce recited the account in its details, for which see *Dictionary of Culprits and Criminals* (Metuchen, N.J.: Scarecrow Press, 1986), 266–68.

20. Here Royce pointed out, incidentally, the "paradoxical sympathy of the plain

people." The claimant belonged to their class; therefore he must be the true heir, even though that would make him belong to a quite different class.

21. The lecturer dwelt at length on this point.

22. *Principles of Psychology,* 2 vols. (New York: Holt, 1890), Ch. 10, pp. 292 ff.

23. In his Phil. 9 course, Royce here repeated this description.

24. Abbott Lawrence Lowell, *Public Opinion and Popular Government* (New York: Longmans, Green & Co., 1913).

25. These two triads were displayed on the board.

26. For example, see *CPP* 7.97 or 8.228–238.

27. RWB's text here adds, "See Webster, s.v., "generalization": a general inference."

28. Wilhelm Wundt, *Völkerpsychologie*, 2 vols. (Leipzig: W. Englemann, 1900).

29. Here Royce discussed the Pauline Churches as examples of Communities, along the lines of *The Problem of Christianity*, Vol. 1.

30. At this point, Professor Royce read the thirteenth chapter of *I Corinthians.*

31. Mt 5–7; Lc 6:17–49.

32. Here Royce told his class what he neither knows nor can know about Christ.[CA]

33. Masaharu Anesaki, *Nichiren: The Buddhist Prophet* (Cambridge, Mass.: Harvard University Press, 1916).

34. See Josiah Royce, "George Fox as a Mystic," *Harvard Theological Review* 6 (1913): 31–59.

Chapter 2

1. See *PC* 242–71.

2. Royce's elliptical reference to William James's *Some Problems of Philosophy: A Beginning of an Introduction to Philosophy* (New York and London: Longmans, Green & Co., 1911).

3. Here Royce assigned a written report on "The Nature and the Basis of our Knowledge of Social Facts: Interpretation," based on *The Problem of Christianity,* Vol. 2, Lectures 11, 12, 13, and 14, and due November 30.

4. In Kant's introductory statement to the Transcendental Analytic, First Section (on General Logic) in his *Critique of Pure Reason.*

5. Here Royce commented upon the reports dated November 6. There was a general agreement with the lecturer's views; some of the reports fell in with the lecturer's views too readily. What RWB wrote about wiping the slate clean was mentioned as an example of the opposite extreme; this attitude was not necessarily fatal, but it would be unpromising if it were kept up. "In one paper of the course," said Royce, "I found a good deal of difference of opinion expressed. The result was my impression of a dyadic relation, to use the distinctive language of *War and Insurance*. It would appear that the author of this paper and myself constitute a dangerous pair."

6. This paragraph arose in reply to a question from the class.

7. Royce quoting or paraphrasing James.

8. *WI* 1: 19–26, esp., pp. 22–23.

9. See *PC* 273–95.

10. After remarking, "The lecturer had in mind in this lecture the questions which RWB had been asking about inference and belief," RWB cautioned that "these notes are not verbatim."

11. Here RWB records: "Asked after class to account for the prevalence of 'loyalty' under this description of {interpretive} knowledge, the lecturer intimated that lack of confidence is a personal defect not to be approached from the rational side."

12. See *PC* 286–88.

13. After Peirce's death on April 19, 1914, graduate student Victor F. Lenzen, having been urged on by Royce, and instructed and funded by James H. Woods, then chair of Harvard's philosophy department, transferred Peirce's books and manuscripts from Milford, Pennsylvania, to Harvard University, thanks to Mrs. Peirce's gift. The manuscripts were deposited in Royce's office in Emerson Hall, where he and his assistant, W. Fergus Kernan, examined them. They reported their appraisal in "Charles Sanders Peirce," *Journal of Philosophy* 13 (1916): 701–709. For more details, see Victor F. Lenzen, "Reminiscences of a Mission to Milford, Pennsylvania," and W. Fergus Kernan, "The Peirce Manuscripts and Josiah Royce—A Memoir: Harvard 1915–1916," *Transactions of the Charles S. Peirce Society* 1 (1965): 3–11, 90–95.

14. See text, p. 27.

15. Bertrand Russell, *Problems of Philosophy* (Oxford University Press, 1912), Ch. VI, "On Induction"; in the 1973 reprint, pp. 60–69, esp., pp. 67–69. RWB left a blank in his notes where this title was not yet identified.

16. Here Royce assigned the topic for the next report: "The Social Aspects of the Ideas of Truth and of Reality" (to be handed in at the close of the last lecture—around January 27 or 28). The paper was to concern the relation of the ideas of truth and reality to our social approach to metaphysics. Royce added, "Our problems thus far have prepared us for the contrast between realistic and idealistic views. You will see that you will deal not with questions of social psychology but with matters which inevitably in-

volve a view of the universe. Note the value of the community in this report. Centralize this whole social question."

Chapter 3

1. Furthermore, to move from "D^2 is even" to "D is even," mathematician Royce, avoiding an induction from cases of D^2, presupposes instead the following deductive reasoning: D is either even or odd. Supposing D is odd, then $D = 2n + 1$. But then, $D^2 = (2n + 1)^2 = 4n^2 + 4n + 1 = 2 (2n^2 + 2n) + 1$, which means that D^2 is odd. But that contradicts the preceding conclusion that D^2 is even. ∴ D is even. In the second column, Royce's reasoning from "S^2 = even" to "S is even" presupposes an identical intervening reasoning. (For this explanation, the editors are indebted to William J. Larkin, III, Professor of Mathematics of Xavier University, Cincinnati.)

2. In the classroom, Royce here indicated as references:

Royce: *The Religious Aspect of Philosophy,* on "The Possibility of Error."
Harold H. Joachim of Oxford: *The Nature of Truth,* (Oxford: Clarendon, 1906) {Chs. I and III}: "I am on the whole disposed to accept Joachim's criticism of the correspondence theory of truth; but he doesn't lay stress on what I regard to be the most critical matter of all, the essentially social relations involved."
William James published a review of my theory of the problem of truth in the *Atlantic Monthly* 55 (1885): 840–43.

3. Bertrand Russell, *Problems of Philosophy* (New York: Henry Holt & Co., 1910).

4. In the classroom, what follows was portrayed on the blackboard.

5. *Problems*, p. 193, {= pp. 123–24 in the Oxford University Press edition of 1959}.

6. Ibid., p. 194.

7. Ibid., p. 197.

8. The triadic community of past, present, and future is one aspect of Royce's thought that led William E. Hocking to call this chapter "The Social Theory of Truth Applied to the Theory of Idealism."

9. Here Royce echoes a leading theme in C. S. Peirce's article, "A Neglected Argument for the Reality of God," *Hibbert Journal* 7 (1908): 90–112; (see *CPP* 6: 452–93).

10. In RWB's absence this day, Byron E. Underwood took only a few notes. Returning to the "egocentric predicament," Professor Royce insisted that we were really in a logocentric predicament.

11. Here some discussion arose about what Royce called his "chronosynoptic deity."

12. After class, Mr. Kernan recommended RWB to read, on the doctrine that reality rests upon truth, the section on physical and social reality in Royce's *The World and the Individual* {2: 153–204}. This, said Kernan, is about the most wonderful chapter in philosophy.

13. Aware through his diary (now lost) of the "religious insight" gained exactly thirty-three years earlier (January 11–12, 1883), Royce here abruptly breaks his previous line of thought to engage in some revealing intellectual autobiography that fills in and carries further the "Autobiographical Sketch," which he delivered two weeks earlier at his sixtieth anniversary celebration in the Walton Hotel in Philadelphia; (*Hope of the Great Community*, 122–36). Most of the present section describes his intellectual growth from "1875–83 {which} determines my philosophical thinking."

14. J. S. Mill, *An Examination of Sir William Hamilton's Philosophy* (London: Longman, Roberts and Green, 1865), re-edited by J. M. Robson (University of Toronto Press, 1979). Mill's definition of matter as "a Permanent Possibility of Sensation," occurs towards the close of Chapter XI, "The Psychological Theory of the Belief in an External World," which Royce persistently found of great significance. At the start of his lecture of May 13, 1916, Royce recounted how Mill's *An Examination* had exerted an "especial influence" upon his own intellectual development; (see pp. 244–45).

15. Conclusion of James's Dedication of *Pragmatism,* paraphrased.

16. Fred Pamp, a member of William E. Hocking's 1930 Royce Seminar, urged that if two paragraphs from Royce's lecture of January 24, 1916, occurring on p. 89—running, namely, from "Dean Mansel's *Limits* . . . [to] hell I will go."—are relocated to p. 80, following " . . . a large part in the discussion," Royce's intellectual autobiography is better continued.

17. From his first major work onward, Royce referred frequently to this chapter in Mill. See, e.g., *RAP* 363–70, *SMP* 359, and the close of Royce's lecture of May 11, 1916; [p. 242]. This suggests the central influence of this chapter on his thought.

18. See *RAP* 387–88, and 389 ff. for Royce's escape from this position.

19. See *SMP* 101–134, for Royce's "efforts" of 1892, and for those of 1906, his *Lectures on Modern Idealism*, Ed., J. Loewenberg (New Haven: Yale University Press, 1919), pp. 1–63.

20. *Faust*, Part I, Act IV.

21. Note taker B. E. Underwood evaluated Royce's lecture of January 13 and his notes on it as follows: "This was a very interesting lecture because it was so largely personal. He read us Professor Jame's review of his *Religious Aspect of Philosophy*, which occurred in the *Atlantic Monthly* for June, 1885. Professor Royce described himself as young and struggling and stated that he thought Professor James even stretched a point in the way of hospitality to his ideas in order to gain for him the good will of the read-

ing public. On the other hand, he pointed out that James was always singularly open-minded and at this time he was probably closer to Royce than at any subsequent period of his development. Royce read the bulk of the article and commented as he read; consequently, there follow just a few scattered notes of only doubtful value."

22. See *WI* 1: 391–96, where, however, Royce does not yet employ the term "world of interpretation."

23. Two months later, in a letter to Mary Whiton Calkins, Royce acknowledged how these "two ideas, the Community, and the Spirit have been growing {in my mind} ever since" writing *PC;* see *Letters of Josiah Royce,* p. 645.

24. See *PC* 337.

25. The assigned topic for the third report, due one week before the end of the midyear examination period is: "The social aspect of the ideas of truth and reality." In view of the approaching midyear exam, Royce here urged the class, "I am anxious to have you get out of the view of interpretation something more than I have found in your reports of November 30. Your principal difficulty is that you take the contrast between interpretation, conception, and perception too abstractly. For the midyears, consider especially the contrast between our doctrine about truth and the doctrine of pragmatism. Again, what is the essential difference between the situation in which the interpreter interprets in one direction, and when the interpreter interprets in the other direction (A to C, or C to A)? What is the difference between interpreting a fact, a meaning, and forming a conception of a fact, a situation and a meaning? Read especially for the midyears, *Problem of Christianity,* Vol. 2, p. 223 ff., especially section 9, p. 253, {or *PC* 321 ff., esp. 332–33}.

26. Here Royce commenced to comment on some of the students' reports of November 30 on interpretation. He pointed out that Mr. Kernan had written the following significant question on one man's report: "Where do you think the lecturer's doctrine of interpretation would so touch the doctrine of reality that he could speak of interpretation as reality?" Royce then inquired of his class, "How can interpretation be reality?"

27. Pp. 140–145 in the 1883 edition.

28. Here Royce said that the midyear exam will be based on *The Problem of Christianity.* In speaking of his book *The World and the Individual,* which will be used in the second half-year, the lecturer used a typical Roycean phrase: "*The World and the Individual* represents an earlier phase of my own consciousness of what I had in mind." #

29. Royce indicated that in Abraham's[CA] place he would have declined to sacrifice Isaac, though he were to go to hell for it.

30. *PC,* 187–208.

31. Clearly Royce suffers the trauma of World War I. See his "The Hope of the Great Community," *Yale Review*, January 1916, republished in *HGC* 25–70. His mention of " a more or less universal community of hate" occurs in *HGC,* p. 53.

32. For Royce's 1916 midyear examination in Philosophy 9, see pp. 279–80.

Chapter 4

1. From February 15 to May 27, 1916, Ralph W. Brown served as a stenographer hired to create a detailed record of the Phil. 9 course for presentation to Professor Royce. See p. 3, for RWB's characterization of these records of the second half-year.

2. Francis Galton, "Intelligible Signals between Neighboring Stars," *Fortnightly Review* 66, *o.s.* [60, *n.s.*], (November 1896): 657–64.

3. See Question # 5 of the midyear examination, p. 280, above.

4. Camile Flammarion (1842–1925), French astronomer and writer.

5. Here Royce began to read and comment upon some of the answers to the question about the Martians in the midyear examination.

6. At this point in the course, Royce assigned a paper discussing the views of Professor Santayana about "Some Meanings of the Word Is." Students were to give a sketch of the contents of the article and discuss what they thought of the issues raised.

7. *Journal of Philosophy, Psychology and Scientific Methods* 2 (February 4, 1915): 66–68.

8. *Summa Theologiae* I, q. 15; *Basic Writings of St. Thomas Aquinas* (Pegis edition), I: 162–67.

9. See *Summa Theologiae* I, qq. 44–45; *Basic Writings*, I: 446–66.

10. Willilam James, *The Principles of Psychology,* 2 vols., (New York: Henry Holt & Co., 1890) 1: 391–92.

11. Here Royce discussed with his class the planning and writing of a report in Phil. 9.

12. Here Royce and the class discussed the relation of the electoral college to the essence of a president.

13. Here was discussed the proposal made by Godkin of the New York *Nation* that one of the Hayes electors should vote contrary to his pledges as Republican elector and cast his ballot for Tilden, since in his opinion Tilden had been substantially the choice of the country.

14. George Santayana, *The Life of Reason or the Phases of Human Progress*, 5 vols. [Reason in common sense, in society, in religion, in art, and in science] (New York: Charles Scribner's Sons, 1905–1906).

Chapter 5

1. Ps 14: v. 1.

2. Robert Browning, "The Last Ride Together," second stanza.

3. Excerpted from paragraph # 3 of Santayana's article; see above, pp. 105–106.

4. Bertrand Russell, *Scientific Method in Philosophy* (Chicago: Open Court, 1915).

5. See pp. 132–33.

6. For bodily things, Aquinas' principle of individuation is literally *materia quantitate signata.* Royce, in his 1897 *Conception of God* (pp. 223–30), had accurately translated this phrase both as "matter quantitatively determined" and as "matter of determinate dimensions" when, with references to *Summa Theologiae* I, QQ. 29–30, 50, and 76, he carefully described St. Thomas's "skillful and vulnerable" principle of corporeal individuation. In the same pages Royce pointed out Aquinas' different relation-based principles of noncorporeal individuation which function in God, angels, and human souls.

Chapter 6

1. Here Royce's excerpt is from the start of Santayana's section 1; see above p. 98. Royce's two subsequent excerpts from Santayana (on p. 145) are from the same section 1.

2. A. N. Whitehead, *A Treatise on Universal Algebra* (Cambridge University Press, 1898). RWB reports Royce referring especially to Whitehead's section on Equivalence, pp. 6–7; (see note 3).

3. RWB gets a somewhat different impression of Whitehead's attitude on consulting his *Universal Algebra*, where Whitehead says (p. 6):

> *No investigations which proceed by the aid of propositions merely asserting identities, such as A is A, can ever result in anything but barren identities. Equivalence on the other hand implies non-identity as its general case. Identity may be conceived as a special limiting case of equivalence.*

There follows below the paragraph to which the lecturer had special reference:

> *It is to be observed that the proposition asserted by the equation, b=b', consists of two elements, which for the sake of distinctness we will name, and will call respectively the 'truism' and the 'paradox.' The truism is the partial*

identity of both b and b', their common B-ness. The paradox is the distinction between b and b', so that b is one thing and b' is another thing; and these things, as being different, must have in some relation diverse properties. In assertions of equivalence as contained in a calculus the truism is passed over with the slightest possible attention, the main stress being laid on the paradox. Thus in the equation 2 + 3 = 3 + 2, the fact that both sides represent a common five-ness of number is not ever mentioned explicitly. The sole direct statement is that the two <u>*different*</u> *things, 3 + 2 and 2 + 3, are in point of number equivalent. (Op. cit., pp. 6–7, section on Equivalence.)*

4. This case is sketched in *Dictionary of Culprits and Criminals* (Metuchen, N.J.: Scarecrow Press, 1986), 266–68.

5. The phrase, "an individual reality . . . from the world," offers a 1916 version of Royce's earlier " 'American' definition of an individual" as "the object of exclusive interest"; see his *The Conception of God*, 2d ed. (1897), 258–65.

6. *The Ethics*, in the *Works of Spinoza*, 2 vols., (New York, Dover, 1951), 2: 282–83;

7. See *Warner's Library of the World's Best Literature*, Vol. XXIII, pp. 13785–93, "Benedict Spinoza" by Josiah Royce; also pp. 13793–13804, Spinoza's own essays: "The Improvement of the Understanding," "Mental Freedom," "Superstition and Fear."

8. Probably Russell's "Mysticism and Logic," *Hibbert Journal* 12 (July 1914): 780–803, republished in Vol. 12 of *The Collected Papers of Bertrand Russell*, "Contemplation and Action, 1902–1914," (London: George Allen & Unwin, 1985), 155–80.

9. *Independent Review* I (December 1903): 415–24.

10. B. Spinoza, *Ethics*, Bk. 5, Prop. 42.

11. At the session on March 21, Royce distributed to the class copies of his address, "The Duties of Americans in the Present War," delivered at Tremont Temple, January 30, 1916, and later published in *HGC* 1–13. He discussed the war and various matters of history and legend from the standpoint of "principles" and of "moral issues," on a level far removed from concrete happenings and difficulties. He said, "That {concrete data} would throw no light upon the merits of the issue. One's posture toward the Teutons and toward one's own government in its acts is to be determined by reference to Principles alone."

12. Here Royce assigned reading in *WI* 1, Lectures 2, 4, and parts of 5.

Chapter 7

1. *La perception du changement* (London: Henry Froude, 1911). Royce refers to these Oxford Lectures in *PC* 277–78.

2. William James, *Some Problems of Philosophy: A Beginning of an Introduction to Philosophy* (New York: Longmans, Green & Co., 1911).

3. John 4: 7ff.

4. Here Royce gave a general account of the way in which the Hindu sages lived and taught. His comments on examples of mysticism from the Hindu Upanishads are not recorded in the present and later sections of this chapter. He read and commented upon two passages from *The World and the Individual*, Vol. I, p. 158 ff., and another on p. 164 ff.

5. Paul Deussen, *Sechzig Upanishads des Veda aus dem Sanskrit Übersetzt mit Einleitung und Anmerkungen Versehen* (Leipzig: Brockhaus, 1905). Translated into English by V. M. Bedeker as *Sixty Upanishads of the Veda* (Delhi: Mitilal Bernarsidass, 1980).

6. James Haughton Woods, translator with C. B. Runkle, of Paul Deussen's *Outline of the Vedanta System of Philosophy According to Shânkara* (New York: Grafton, 1906).

7. Here Royce read and commented upon a passage in Max Müller, *Sacred Books of the East,* Vol. XV, pt. 2, p. 181, in reference to the *Atman*, the Self.

8. From *The Poetical Works of William Blake*, Ed. John Sampson (Oxford, Clarendon Press, 1905), 279–280. Written about 1800.

9. *WI* 1: 169.

10. Here Royce continued the reading and discussion of the passage in which Prajapati instructs Indra about the Self, found in Max Müller, *Sacred Books of the East* (Oxford: Clarendon, 1904), I : 134, 140 ff.

11. Royce read this poem to the class.

12. Royce's essay, "Meister Eckhart," published later in *SGE* 261–297, from which Royce soon read and commented on large portions, beginning at p. 261.

13. For the next twelve pages, parenthesized references in the text are to "Meister Eckhart," *SGE* 261–297.

14. Following his text at this point, Royce amplified the contrast between Eckhart and Herbert Spencer.

15. Before this class, Royce asked RWB to record the first part of this lecture.

16. *WI* 1: 170.

17. Here Royce resumed the reading of his essay, "Meister Eckhart," with comments interspersed, beginning at the bottom of its p. 278.

18. *WI* 1 169.

19. Ibid., 158–59.

20. Ibid., 169–70.

21. Ibid., 165.

22. *SGE* 293.

23. In his class Royce recited several stanzas of this poem (the third, eighth, and then the sixth and seventh), saying, "The rest of the poem I can leave you to bring to your own memory as you choose."

24. John 4: 15.

25. Evelyn Underhill, *Mysticism* (London: Methuen, 1911); and *Practical Mysticism* (London: J. M. Dent, 1914).

26. Kuno Francke was born in Germany, but in 1916 was an American citizen, serving as Professor of the History of German Culture at Harvard (1905–1917) and Curator of its Germanic Museum.

27. William Scherer, *A History of German Literature*, translated from the third German edition by Mrs. F. C. Conybeare, 2 vols. (New York: Charles Schribner's Sons, 1906).

28. Royce's paraphrase of Scherer 1: 92–94?

29. Royce's paraphrase of Scherer 1: 96?

30. Mary Whiton Calkins, *The Persistent Problems of Philosophy* (New York: Macmillan, 1907).

31. George Santayana, *Three Philosophical Poets: Lucretius, Dante, Goethe* (Cambridge, Mass.: Harvard University Press, 1910).

32. World War I.

33. According to John Clendenning's *Life and Thought of Josiah Royce* (Madison: University of Wisconsin Press, 1985), 336, Royce attended the Wagner Festival in Bayreuth in August 1909 with his son Edward, where *Parsifal*, *Lohengrin*, and the *Ring des Nibelungen* were performed.

34. For Royce on this entire thirteenth chapter of Paul, see *PC* 92–94.

Chapter 8

1. *WI* 2: 111–51, 155–204.

2. See George Santayana, "The Ethical Doctrine of Spinoza," *The Harvard Monthly* 2 (June 1886): 144–52.

3. *Winds of Doctrine: Studies in Contemporary Opinions* (New York: Charles Scribner's Sons, 1913), 124–25, 102–103.

4. On April 27, Royce treated of "the nature of the noetic relation according to realism," but since RWB was absent that day in New York City and BEU left no notes, Typescripts A and B provide nothing beyond the theme of Royce's lecture of April 27.

5. Here Royce, following the polemic in *The World and the Individual*, criticized a realism that would assert a total independence, since "a necessary and mutual independence is a derived independence, ergo nonindependent"—William E. Hocking, initial editor of Typescript B.

6. Here the Sânkhya system was discussed, which made the independence absolute in both directions.

7. Here Royce alluded to the Sânkhya psycho-physical theory described in *WI* 1: 102–103.

8. In *WI* 1, Ch. 3, pp. 102–103.

9. Ralph Barton Perry, *Present Philosophical Tendencies* (New York: Longmans, Green; 1912).

10. At the May 6 session, Royce read to the class his address, which was delivered at Tremont Temple, Boston, on the following day, on the anniversary of the sinking of the Lusitania. This address was printed in full in the *Boston Evening Transcript*, May 8, 1916.

11. Lecture VI is entitled, "Validity and Experience"; *WI* 1: 225–62.

12. William E. Hocking summarizes this section: "Much illustration of possibility. As 'capacity,' it cannot be unreal. As ' freedom,' it is valid of human beings: they are their possibilities. (Long in advance of Whitehead, Royce emphasizes the importance of the category of possibility, whose puzzles had been brought out by Aristotle.)"

13. The recital of these lines was interspersed with the preceding comments and those that follow.

14. "Crito," 53b.

15. Francis Bowen, *Treatise on Logic* (Cambridge, Mass.: Sever and Francis, 1864).

16. Dedication, p. 3 of *Pragmatism* (Harvard University Press, 1974).

17. References are to page and line of the *Examination* as, published by Longman, Roberts & Green, London, 1865. This edition is accessible at the Boston Athenaeum. In the next three pages, the italicized statement at the start of a paragraph is from Mill's *Examination,* which the editors presume is the beginning of the passage that Royce read before commenting. Without writing out these statements, RWB recorded only the page references.

18. Here Royce read a communication entitled "Give Us Philosophers!" written by Marvin M. Lowenthal, which appeared in *The New Republic*, May 13, 1916, p. 43.

19. In his poem, "A Fable for Critics," *The Complete Poetical Works of James Russell Lowell* (Boston: Houghton Mifflin, 1897), 127.

20. Throughout the next eighteen pp., (i.e., down to p. 265), the italicized statement at the start of a paragraph or the italicized paragraph is presumed by the editors to be the beginning of the passage read by Royce from *WI* 1. It was not written out in RWB's text. Royce's emphases are given in boldface type.

21. Karl Pearson, *The Grammar of Science* (London: W. Scott, 1892).

22. Edward von Hartmann, *Philosophy of the Unconscious*, trans. W. D. Coupland (London: Routledge & Kegan Paul, 1931).

23. Hans Vaihinger, *The Philosophy of "As If": A System of the Theoretical, Practical, and Religious Fictions of Mankind*, trans. C. K. Ogden (New York: Harcourt Brace & Co., 1924).

24. Cf. *PC* 348–49.

Chapter 9

1. Robert Browning, *Dramatic Lyrics*, 1887.

2. See *PC* 341–43.

3. 1893 was a year of financial panic.

4. Santayana uses "evidence" in this sense in his "Some Meanings of the Word Is." See above, pp. 105–106.

5. *WI* 1: 259–60.

6. *WI* 1: 258–59.

7. *WI* 1: 260–61.

8. *WI* 1: 261–62. Here Royce completed the reading of *WI* 1, Lecture 6.

9. "The Internal and External Meaning of Ideas," *WI* 1: 265–342.

10. See *WI* 2: 379–411 and the references Royce next makes: *RAP* 449–459, *SMP* 435–71, *SGE* 1–28, and *PC* 165–86, 201–206, 381–84.

11. William James, "Is Life Worth Living," in *The Will to Believe and Other Essays in Popular Philosophy* (Harvard University Press, 1979), 34–56.

12. *Life of Reason*, Vol. 3: *Religion*, 143–47.

13. Bertrand Russell, *Collected Papers of Bertrand Russell,* 12 vols. projected (London: Allen & Unwin, 1983), 1: 88–99; 2: 96–99.

14. By stating, "The very recognition of Being is itself an estimate," Royce unites the categorizing, discerning, and evaluating functions of human intelligence.

15. Alfred, Lord Tennyson, *Idylls of the King*: "The Holy Grail."

First Supplementary Essay: "Provenance"

1. During his "Phil. 9 course" of 1915–16 at Harvard University, Royce delivered what proved to be his last lectures on metaphysics, since he died on September 14, 1916.

2. In 1898–1899, when Royce headed to Aberdeen for his Gifford lectures, William James handled Phil. 9 and in 1903–4 George Santayana taught Phil. 9, using Royce's *The World and the Individual* as a text. During Royce's Walter Channing Cabot Fellowship of 1911–14, when he centered largely on the philosophy of religion, Royce did not teach Phil. 9, except for a half-year in 1913–14.

3. The description of Royce's "four approaches to metaphysics" that follows derives from Walter H. Horton's "Notes from Royce's 1914–15 Phil. 9," under the date of October 3, 1914; (Harvard University Archives, HUC, 8914/369.9).

4. According to W. H. Horton's notes, under the date of Oct. 3, 1914, Royce thought that James's disgust for "barren intellectualism" had channeled his thought into a brand of pragmatism which, by using this approach, tended to turn all philosophical problems into psychological ones.

5. *PC* 218.

6. For example, *CPP* 5. 61–63. from Peirce's 1903 "Lectures on Pragmatism" at Harvard.

7. See Chapter 8 in Royce's text, esp., pp. 213–50.

8. *The Letters of Josiah Royce*, Ed. John Clendenning (University of Chicago Press, 1970), pp. 645–46.

9. Ralph W. Brown was one of Royce's twenty-five students in the latter's 1915–16 course in metaphysics at Harvard. Receiving a bachelor's of law degree from Harvard in 1920, Ralph W. Brown entered a successful career in admirality law and later in corporation law.

10. See Brown's Prefatory Note (p. 3). Royce delivered this first half-year of forty-three lectures from September 30, 1915, to January 24, 1916, lecturing usually on

Tuesday, Thursday, and Saturday. None of stenographer Brown's shorthand notes from either the first or second semesters seem extant.

Although the class list for this 1915–16 Phil. 9 course designates most of Royce's students in this metaphysics class as graduates, divinity students, or undergraduates scheduled for graduation in 1916 or 1917, only Ralph W. Brown is designated as "ooc," meaning "out of course"—shorthand for "candidate for degree out of course." Thus, in 1915–16, Ralph W. Brown was aiming for his degree at some date later than that achieved by students maintaining their regular course.

In 1915–1916, the address of Ralph W. Brown was 710 Barristers Hall, Boston, where legal affairs could call upon his stenographic skills and provide apprenticeship in legal matters. Meanwhile, Brown pursued a bachelor of law degree part time at Harvard. (*The Quinquennial Catalogue of Harvard University 1636–1930* lists a "Ralph Wolcott Brown" as receiving a bachelors of law degree in 1920, on p. 1240.)

11. On February 2, 1917, four and one-half months after Royce's death, R. W. Brown wrote to W. E. Hocking, "Of course, I had to produce what I had of Phil. 9 at Mrs. Royce's request." By this acknowledgment, Brown did not mean that Mrs. Royce had hired him to take stenographic notes of Royce's Phil. 9 lectures—to "produce" them in that sense. For on October 2, 1916, scarcely a month after Royce's death, Brown had already informed Hocking that Mrs. Royce had urgently tried "to secure from me the notes of the first half of last year's Phil. 9 with a view of submitting them to Macmillan."

Hence, I interpret Brown's "produce" to mean "hand over" his first semester notes to Mrs. Royce. She had requested the notes which he, without being hired to do so, had spontaneously recorded. Nonetheless, they contained the intellectual property of her deceased husband, and through Macmillan she wished to publish the entirety of his final course in metaphysics. As for Brown's notes from the spring semester of Royce's Phil. 9 in 1916, not Mrs. Royce but R. C. Cabot seems to have hired Brown to create a stenographic record.

12. See Brown's Prefatory Note (p. 3).

13. Ralph W. Brown to William Ernest Hocking, October 28, 1916; Houghton Library, Hocking Papers, Box c-6–3–m.

14. See Foreword, p. x.

15. About fifteen years later, Brown wrote that a Professor Dykhuizen wished to borrow the "typewritten notes which I made of Royce's lectures in Phil. 9." (R. W. Brown to W. E. Hocking, December 27, 1933; Houghton Library, Hocking Papers, Box c-6–3–m.)

16. Brown's Prefatory Note; (see p. 3).

17. See R. W. Brown to W. E. Hocking, October 30, 1916; (Houghton Library, Hocking Papers, Box c-6–3–m).

18. A copy of Transcript A is preserved among the Richard Clarke Cabot Papers in the Harvard University Archives in Pusey Library.

19. R. W. Brown to W. E. Hocking, February 2, 1917; W. E. Hocking papers, Houghton Library of Harvard University.

20. A copy of Transcript B is preserved in the W. E. Hocking Papers in the Houghton. That a copy of Transcript B can also be found in the Department of Special Collections in the library of the University of California at Los Angeles seems due to the influence and efforts of UCLA Chancellor Ernest C. Moore and Dean Charles Rieber, former chair of UCLA's philosophy department. Both men sought to draw attention to Royce as "California's gift to philosophy" and promoted various Royceana on the UCLA campus.

21. In this way, Cabot's Typescript of 467 pp. was reduced in size to 330 pp.; (1–108 for first semester; 109–330 for the second).

22. This compact copy of Typescript A for the second semester of this course is preserved among the "Josiah Royce Papers" within the MSS Room of the Milton S. Eisenhower Library at the Johns Hopkins University.

23. A half-year seminar in spring 1929 and a full-year seminar (Phil 20g) in the 1929–30 school year.

24. William E. Hocking to Harvard University Press, April 18, 1935; Houghton Library, Hocking Papers, Box "Royce."

Second Supplementary Essay: "Ontological Argument"

1. K. d. r. V., *Postulate des empirischen Denkens überhaupt*, 2 *Aufl.*, 273.

2. Lecture of March 7, 1916; {see p. 130}.

3. *Ibid.*, {see p. 133}.

4. Lecture of March 2, 1916; {see pp. 124–5}.

5. Lecture of March 9, 1916; {see p. 139}.

6. *Ibid.* {see p. 140}.

7. Lecture of March 7, 1916; {see p. 132}.

8. Lecture of May 25, 1916; {see pp. 267–8}.

9. "*Die Wahrnehmung aber, die den Stoff zum Begriff hergiebt, ist der enizige Character der Wirklichkeit.*" *K.d.r.V.* 2 *Aufl.*, 272.

10. His essay on "Principles of Logic" in *Encyclopedia of Philosophical Sciences* indicates that his thought would take the latter direction; perhaps appealing to the conception of "order" as the essence which most fundamentally must characterize existence.

Critical Apparatus

Chapter 1

p. 3: Into this description R. W. Brown also inserted the following paragraph excerpted from an earlier précis of Philosophy 9, which does not fit the course as Royce gave it in 1915–16; namely

> The course will begin with a study of Professor James's recent volume on Pragmatism, and with a discussion of the present state of philosophical inquiry regarding the definition of truth. After this introduction, Royce's Gifford Lectures, entitled *The World and the Individual*, and James's *Pluralistic Universe*, will be used as the principal textbooks. The main questions of metaphysics will be studied, including the problem of the nature of individual selves, and the problems of evil, of immortality, and of theism.

p. 8: Correction of "Augustine" found here in Typescript A and B, because Augustine wrote no work entitled *Compendium* (*Theologiae* or *Fidei*). Royce seems to have used "compendium" here to refer quite accurately to Aquinas' *Summa Theologiae* (*Pars Ia, q.2, a.2, ad 2um*). It is unknown whether Royce or stenographer Brown slipped here.

p. 16–1: This opening clause is an editorial reconstruction from the context.

p. 16–2: Inversion of RWB's sentence.

p. 21: Relocation of "there is a passage."

p. 22: Emendation of Typescript B's introductory phrase.

p. 27: Omitting "which I have put on the board."

p. 28: "by naming" emends "namely" of Typescript B.

p. 29: "the group's deed" replaces "that thing" of RWB's text.

p. 30–1: Addition of "the concern for."

p. 30–2: "unlike, for instance" corrects "E.g., cf." of Typescript B.

Chapter 2

p. 36: Addition of "Recall the" to RWB's "(Banknote analogy)."

p. 37: Correction of RWB's "1877," since Royce heard James lecturing at the Hopkins in spring 1878.

p. 45: Here Typescript A adds after "interpreters," "i.e., says that they dispense with revealed truth."

p. 47: Emendation of "the following examples (later in lecture)."

p. 49: "deductive" corrects RWB's "inductive."

p. 52: "falls" corrects RWB's "follows."

p. 56: "as" substituted for ": these signs are"

p. 57: Emphasis added.

p. 58: Inversion of BEU's last two sentences.

Chapter 3

p. 60: Revision of RWB's text: "This is a fundamental reason why the doctrine that no rational being has ever held as a philosophy but which has often been played with—the doctrine of solipsism (that I am the only real being)—has never been expressed as a rational coherent sort of philosophy; for one would refute it by expressing it."

p. 61–1: "about" corrects BEU's "between."

p. 61–2: Emendation of BEU's incompleted record that reads: "It is expressed in the text that the statement that my belief of truth is an appeal to a standard view about the matter about which I am making an assertion."

p. 64–1: "S^2" corrrects "n^2" of Typescript B.

p. 64–2: "or" replaces "and" of RWB's record.

p. 64–3: "if one" replaces "whichever" of Typescript B.

p. 67: "on Othello's part" transposed.

p. 73: "Berkeley's" replaces "the Berkeleyan" of Typescript B.

p. 77: "intended" replaces "defined" of Typescript B?

p. 78: "his students" replaces "us."

p. 80: "especially obnoxious" repositioned.

p. 81: inversion of "1875 to 1883 determined my philosophical thinking."

p. 85: "doesn't apply" repositioned.

p. 87: "imply" repositioned.

p. 90: "irrevocable" replaces "inevitable" in Typescript B.

Chapter 4

p. 93: Correction for RWB's *Contemporary Review.*

p. 95: Omitting "says Royce,"

p. 101: Inversion of sentence.

p. 103: Emendation of "[In reply to a question:] From Santayana's point of view, I suppose we should have to call multiple personality . . . "

p. 104: Uncertain of the spelling of Bourne, RWB here adds "(?)."

p. 107–1: Inversion of Typescript B's order of the two preceding sentences.

p. 107–2: Emendation of "[Here "2" was re-read with comments interspersed:]"

p. 113: Repositioning "eternally."

p. 114–1: Relocation of the remainder of this paragraph, which in Typescript B follows the next two paragraphs.

p. 114–2: "paragraph" emends "section" of Typescript B.

Chapter 5

p. 128: Revision of Typescript B's sentence: "In what we commonly call our experiences of individuals, how little it is that we experience of the individuality of a door, or a blackboard, how little we experience of the identity of a friend from day to day, the legend of Solomon by the very wildness of the story illustrates."

p. 134: "just" replaces "in the last lecture."

p. 140: Royce inverts the order of these two excerpts from the close of Santayana's #3; see above, pp. 105–106.

Chapter 6

p. 147: Inversion of sentence.

p. 148: Omitted in Typescript B, bracketed material derives from Typescript A.

p. 149: Omitted in Typescript B, bracketed material derives from Typescript A.

p. 151: The plaintiff's true name, "Arthur Orton," corrects the name "Robert Otten," which was recorded mistakenly in Typescript A and repeated in Typescript B.

p. 159: Revision of RWB's text: "The result was that instead of regarding virtue as through some process leading to good, and thinking of life in that way as virtuous action pointing towards a good result, because of gods or men or one's own conscience, Spinoza, who is very clear that you don't know what a day will bring forth, and is willing enough to try the device of escape from entanglements in a solitary way since the faiths of the various churches do not appeal to him, seeks for the good of life by viewing from above, looking down on the whole situation."

p. 160: "defy" corrects "decline" of Typescript B.

p. 161: The "B" shown in the following diagram corrects the "G" that RWB recorded, apparently by mistake.

p. 165: "the arch" replaces "that" of Typescript B.

p. 166: Emendation of RWB's recording: "but the foam meanwhile is in somewhat like the relation to the eyes which gives you the spray relations of Niagara . . . "

p. 169: Correction for "of."

p. 170: Correction for "the Hector" in RWB's text.

Chapter 7

p. 176: Emendation of RWB's sentence: "The mystical view comes to one as a significant view so far as there comes to his mind that the approach to the real when we deal with the relations of things is not the view that gives us what we want while there is a hope that if we could get more into touch with a perceptual view of the world, we should reach what we want."

p. 177: "for important" repositioned.

p. 180: Elimination of Typescript B's reduplicative "of the nature of the evidence."

p. 185: Revision of RWB's text: "He found the tendency an evil tendency, where it approached something, so what Kant has . . ."

p. 193–1: Instead of giving Royce's complete sentence from "Meister Eckhart," as done in the present text, RWB here recorded only fragments, which included "if I don't use concepts" for "if I form no image" of Royce's own text.

p. 193–2: Here RWB records, "P. 286—God = Godhead." On p. 286 of *SGE*, however, instead of such an identification the editors find rather an insistence on the mystic's not resting with the explicit God but returning to the depth of the implicit Godhead.

p. 193–3: Because of Royce's own text in *SGE* 286, adopted by the editors, they have revised RWB's draft here: "Only direct experience can really touch the higher truth."

p. 197: "one" emends "other" of Typescript B.

p. 209: "you" replacing "members of this class" of Typescript B.

Chapter 8

p. 214: Revision of RWB's text: "The mystics of what was at the beginning his own Church, the mediaeval mystics, he treated with respect, precisely insofar as, from the point of view of their Orders, they were contributing to a life that, from the social point of view and the point of view of the values that men can attain and enjoy together, Santayana has regarded as important."

p. 219–1: Omitting for clarity RWB's reduplicative phrase, here italicized: "to see *what it is of such a nature* that the nature of things itself conform to that view."

p. 219–2: Emphasis added.

p. 225: In the classroom, Royce here wrote "interrelation" on the board, and had the following chart of <u>The Problem of "External Relations"</u> portrayed on the board.

p. 228–1: For clarity's sake, these two sentences of Typescript B are revised by inserting "found that" and a period, omitting "by" and repositioning "slaves."

p. 228–2: On the board.

p. 230: Or, as in Typescript B, "realm of universal discourse,"

p. 233: Revision of RWB's text: "The Real consists of what Russell has skillfully called, speaking in terms of sense–impressions and when he is discussing physical reality—the Real consists of *sensibilia,* not the sense data that are present at a given time, but the data that <u>would be</u> there under given conditions."

p. 235: From "The realistic movement . . . {to} . . . human beings" the editors revise into three sentences what RWB recorded as the following single sentence: "The realistic movement in its revived form has tried to emphasize the fact that one feature which the world must contain may be expressed by saying that the world is to be defined in terms of whatever <u>would be</u> if we weren't there, in terms which are realistic in this sense, that while it does make a difference to what things are, what you believe about them, since all independence is relative and limited, we must try so far as possible to abstract from the subjective, the limited and the accidental in the way of experiencing that is characteristic of human beings."

p. 238: Inversion of sentence order.

p. 242: Inversion of sentence order.

p. 246: Inversion of adjectives.

p. 248: Emendation of "the views that."

p. 249: "is expressed by" replaces "expresses" of Typescript B.

Chapter 9

p. 252: "in the final form of" repositioned.

p. 253: "attention" inserted for Typescript B's "intention."

p. 255: Deletion of reduplicative phrase, "what this world is."

p. 257: Inversion of sentence order.

p. 263: Both here and in the following quotations RWB's references to lines in *WI* have been made more accurate.

p. 275: Inversion of "acceptable."

p. 277: "about" for "over" in RWB's text.

Endnotes

p. 306: Revision of RWB's "does not know or care about Christ."

p. 310: "Abraham" revises RWB's "Jacob."

Comments Interjected by the Stenographer, Ralph W. Brown

p. 9: Here Uncle Royce recited from Wordsworth: "My heart leaps up when I behold a rainbow in the sky," etc.

p. 22: This statement would be equally true, and less misleading, if the lecturer had said, "express what you feel" instead of "express the thing." Admitting that you sometimes have a feeling of "we," it still remains your feeling. At the same time, somebody else also may be having a feeling of "we" and your feeling may include a notion that this is the case. That covers the situation.

p. 26: Not illustrated.

p. 35–1: Royce stands for this.

p. 35–2: In connection with (1) above, RWB is interested in what Royce calls our familiar inner perceptions; see *Problem of Christianity* 2: 137; {or *PC* 285}.

p. 44–1: After class, Royce made much of this last point, the bearing of which is incomprehensible to RWB.

p. 44–2: Notice how Royce shifts the issue from the finality of validity to the finality of completeness. Nobody has called the latter into question.

p. 45–1: Notice that the element of subjective confidence is rigidly barred in this presentation.

p. 45–2: RWB persists in asking, "How then do you account for the prevalence of "loyalty" or belief?

p. 46–1: Not specified here.

p. 46–2: RWB would like to find in philosophy an analysis of certitude from the side of epistemology. Certitude is a phenomena easily seen to exist.

p. 46–3: How about ethical life going on at all?

p. 50: H. Gordon Johnson did.

p. 65: RWB has been asking whether knowledge is ever divorced from certainty.

p. 71: Good night!

p. 88: Royce seemed to think this forces us into the admission of a triadic layout in knowledge.

p. 89: Royce this day was impossible to follow.

p. 131: Here RWB is reminded of Professor Perry's written comment on a thesis in Phil. 18: "Do you mean by mean a thing's systematic relations? If so, then an isolated term could never mean anything. But what of that?" The matter remains a mystery to RWB.

p. 168: Not in the case of any one "essence" or "principle."

p. 214: RWB says when his interest finds sustenance, it seeks to act absorbently, and that's a sufficient occupation.

p. 220: RWB says you ask your teachers first to state explicitly an intelligible alternative to that view.

p. 310: Good night!

Selected Glossary of Persons to Whom Royce Refers in His Phil. 9 of 1915–1916

Bergson, Henri, (1859–1941), French philosopher, friend of William James, both of whom stressed the intuition of life as flowing in time and considered concepts derivative.

Berkeley, George, (1685–1753), idealist philosopher and Anglican bishop, whose starting principle "to be is to be perceived" influenced James and Royce.

Eckhart, Meister, (1260? –1327?), German philosopher and Dominican mystic, distinguished between God as explicit and the Godhead as mysterious ultimate ground of being.

Herbart, Johann Friedrich, (1776–1841), German philosopher and psychologist, who elaborated a pluralistic realism.

James, William, (1842–1910), Royce's closest philosophical friend and colleague, pragmatist and pluralist, author of *The Principles of Psychology* and *The Varieties of Religious Experience.*

Mill, John Stuart, (1806–1873), inductive logician, empirical philosopher, utilitarian moralist, liberal economist.

Peirce, Charles Sanders, (1839–1914), American logician and philosopher, father of pragmatism, and creative source of three basic categories, semiotics, and a theory of interpretation.

Perry, Ralph Barton, (1876–1957), biographer of William James, proponent of the "egocentric predicament" criticized by Royce, and principal founder of the New Realism.

Russell, Bertrand, (1872–1970), British philosopher, logician, mathematician, and pacifist, co-author with Whitehead of *Principia Mathematica.*

Santayana, George, (1863–1952), Spanish-born American philosopher, student and later colleague of Royce, who by animal faith sought to reconcile the skeptic, the materialist, and the Platonist in his thought.

Schopenhauer, Arthur, (1788–1860), German philosopher, voluntarist, and romantic pessimist, author of *The World as Will and Idea.*

Spinoza, Baruch, (1632–1677), Dutch philosopher and theologian of Sephardic-Jewish descent, author of "blessedness is virtue itself" in his *Ethics*, and the theological identity of God and "nature naturing."

Tennyson, Alfred, (1809–1892), English poet and poet laureate, author of *In Memoriam.*

Whitehead, Alfred North, (1861–1947), British mathematician and process philosopher, who spent his latter years at Harvard and acknowledged intellectual kinship with William James.

Wundt, Wilhelm, (1832–1900), German philosopher and experimental psychologist.

Index of Persons

By Wm. E. Hocking, Elizabeth S. Wyeth, Richard Hocking, and Frank Oppenheim
[Underlined references indicate a principal treatment of the person. Hyphenated references, (e.g., 22–45), include both pp. indicated.]

Index of Topics

By Wm. E. Hocking, Elizabeth S. Wyeth, Richard Hocking, and Frank Oppenheim
[Underlined references indicate a principal treatment of the topic. Only substantive treatments are indexed. Hyphenated references, (e.g., 22–45), include both indicated pages.]